HC
106.8
L665
1990

Losman, Donald L.

The promise of
American industry.

DATE			

THE PROMISE
OF AMERICAN
INDUSTRY

Recent Titles from Quorum Books

THE PROMISE OF AMERICAN INDUSTRY

AN ALTERNATIVE ASSESSMENT OF PROBLEMS AND PROSPECTS

Donald L. Losman
and Shu-Jan Liang

Q

QUORUM BOOKS
NEW YORK • WESTPORT, CONNECTICUT • LONDON

Library of Congress Cataloging-in-Publication Data

Losman, Donald L.
  The promise of American industry : an alternative assessment of
problems and prospects / Donald L. Losman and Shu-Jan Liang.
    p.   cm.
  Includes bibliographical references.
  ISBN 0-89930-508-3 (lib. bdg. : alk. paper)
    1. United States—Industries—Case studies. 2. Steel industry and
trade—United States. 3. Machine-tool industry—United States.
I. Liang, Shu-Jan. II. Title.
  HC106.8.L665   1990
  338.0973—dc20   89-24329

British Library Cataloguing in Publication Data is available.

Library of Congress Catalog Card Number: 89-24329
ISBN: 0-89930-508-3

First published in 1990 by Quorum Books

Greenwood Press, Inc.
88 Post Road West, Westport, Connecticut 06881

Printed in the United States of America

The paper used in this book complies with the
Permanent Paper Standard issued by the National
Information Standards Organization (Z39.48-1984).

10 9 8 7 6 5 4 3 2

To
my mother
Isabell S. Losman
and
my children
Vickie, Ari, and Catherine

To
the memory of my parents
We-nan and Kao-hsiung Liang

Contents

Part III

Tables and Figures

TABLES

FIGURES

Preface

The once unchallenged preeminence of the U.S. economy and its industrial capabilities is today clearly a "thing of the past." The world as it enters the 1990s is a dynamic and formidable environment, a shrinking planet in terms of transportation, communications, and technology flows. Foreign competition—from advanced industrial countries such as Japan and those in Europe, from the newly industrializing nations, and from more traditional Third World producers—has greatly increased, while at the same time it appears that U.S. vibrance has waned. It is also frequently suggested that the American work ethic has become anemic, that the educational system is faulty, and that industrial capabilities are shrinking. American managements are roundly criticized; U.S. corporations have been labeled "hollow," and American labor is deemed intransigent and careless. Further, the evolving American social structure—breakdown of the traditional family, drug and alcohol abuse, ethnic tensions—seems to exacerbate industrial problems and magnify the perceived economic malaise.

The nation is awash with statistics on our large trade deficit, on foreign purchases of U.S. corporations and land, and with information from the ubiquitous six o'clock news programs, which highlight and emphasize budget deficits, plant closings, and events in regionally distressed areas. "D-word" expressions—debt, decline, deficit, and dependency—abound, permeating not only all discussions, but becoming a mind-set and filter through which all contemporary data are interpreted. These support and reinforce the self-doubt and gloom that seem to characterize the U.S. self-image concerning its economic and industrial capabilities. They point to a questionable, if not downright dismal, future.

Yet the picture, by any objective assessment, is hardly so one-sided or negative. Americans are most familiar with what is (or seems to be) happening here, and in this self-conscious sense, our warts and blemishes do appear large and offensive. Yet there is much in the United States that is unseen or unreported, but very important, and it presents a different picture. Alternatively, while the Japanese and Germans may have lost the war, they appear to many of us to be "winning the peace." However, Americans as a group are unfamiliar with the problems and challenges these economies face. They too have problems—bigger than life for them—but relatively invisible to us, hence the perception that they hold all the winning cards and we are destined to walk away losers.

The facts demand a more balanced perspective. Policy deliberations must be based on realities, not on distorted fantasies or nightmares. The world is far more complex, yet the future far less troubled than public discussions imply. U.S. industry does have many problems; it faces serious challenges. On the other hand, there are major strengths, capabilities, and positive changes taking place. Accordingly, the prime function of this book is to "clear the air" by providing a framework for analysis as well as the relevant data. We believe the readers are likely to be surprised at the results.

Acknowledgments

Since all useful human activities are truly the products of a wide assortment of inputs, any undertaking such as this reflects far more than the efforts of the authors alone. In this study we were greatly assisted by untold numbers of individuals at a variety of organizations who provided data, guidance, and interpretation. Hence it is not possible to thank individually all those who had a hand in shaping this work. Accordingly, to those not mentioned we still wish to express our sincerest appreciation. There are others whose inputs and assistance have been so important that we would be remiss not to recognize their contribution.

Dr. David Tarr, Senior Trade Economist at the World Bank, wrote chapter 8. His thoughts and expertise are also reflected throughout this work. Dr. William J. Corcoran, Associate Professor, University of Nebraska-Omaha, authored chapter 9. He too contributed elsewhere via numerous discussions and suggestions. Colonel Herbert R. Haar, Jr. (U.S. Army, retired) was of great assistance on an earlier version. Brad Kyle helped with chapter 3. The librarians at Loyola University (New Orleans) and Tulane University and the National Defense University rendered great service. Mike Ellis, Crafton Hayes, Johana de Onis, and Mary Quintero were particularly helpful in bringing this book to completion. A very special thanks is due Brenda Rideau Floyd, without whose word processing excellence as well as constant, cheerful encouragement, this book could not have been completed. Very professional editing by Katie Chase made the book far more presentable and consistent. Lastly, a work such as this requires a major time commitment. To our families we give special thanks for their patience and help.

Despite assistance, the authors alone are solely responsible for the contents. The views expressed do not reflect the official policies or position of the Department of Defense, the United States government, the National Defense University, or Loyola University, New Orleans.

Introduction

This book examines America's industrial structure and its role in the United States and in world economies. The contemporary U.S. economy is examined in considerable detail, but particular emphasis is placed on manufacturing, a sector of great importance, yet much misunderstood. As with similar industrial studies, the structure, conduct, and performance of U.S. manufacturing is analyzed in depth. Typical contemporary analyses, however, suffer from several seemingly generic oversights that this book attempts to remedy.

First, the international economy, in earlier analyses barely mentioned, is now described by glittering generalities and oversimplifications. Its omission was perhaps acceptable in a previous age when the United States totally dominated the world's economic stage. The world danced to our tune and impinged on us only slightly. Today, however, oversight ignores a major force and important players in the U.S. business environment. Yet current analyses, while now recognizing international factors, have been unbalanced and unappreciative of the true complexities.

Second, while performance measures are both discussed and conceptualized in many books, empirical data and evidence are conspicuously lacking. The absence of this dimension not only obscures the performance and contribution of industry, but lends a disappointing air of unreality to all such undertakings. Third, the productivity dilemma, perhaps the greatest economic challenge facing the contemporary United States, is rarely discussed. These gaps are deliberately addressed.

Additionally, the justification and economic rationale explaining the existence of firms is generally not addressed. In this work the principal-agent paradigm is introduced. It is used to explain the existence of firms, business integration, financing choices, and general relations between economic entities, be they businesses, individuals, stockholders, or whatever.

Finally, a minor but continuing theme involves national defense. Defense is very big business ($290 billion in 1989) and any study of U.S. industry that omits a sector larger than motor vehicles and almost six times bigger than steel is presenting a distorted and incomplete picture. In point of fact, however, defense is almost nowhere to be found in industrial structure studies, even in the indices. This absence is readily explainable, although much to be lamented. First, ever since the Vietnam War, national security endeavors have been somewhat tainted in both academia and in the minds of the American people. Second, defense spending covers many industries, so it is more difficult to isolate and trace. Third, most academics have traditionally had an unfamiliarity with matters military.

Yet despite this lack of "fit," the size and impact of defense expenditures demand that they be included in any study of the U.S. economy. Further, in today's political and budget climate, defense spending is a topic that needs to be understood. As will be shown, the defense industrial base is an integral aspect of U.S. national security, and the ability to surge production and mobilize industry for defense purposes is a critical element both in national power and world influence. Further, as the U.S. economy proceeds through the globalization process, defense needs raise serious questions concerning offshore procurement.

Part I of this volume, chapters 1 through 7, focuses on the industrial sector in general, "The Big Picture," while Part II, which could be titled "Troubled Waters," analyzes two specific industries—steel and machine tools. Part III describes a new dawn. It contains a summation and points to areas where policy must be directed. It concludes that while there are future battles we must win, the war has been going quite well and there is no cause for despair.

Abbreviations

AFC	average fixed cost
AFL	American Federation of Labor
ATC	average total cost
AVC	average variable cost
BLS	Bureau of Labor Statistics
CAD/CAM	computer aided design/computer aided manufacture
CEO	chief executive officer
CIO	Congress of Industrial Organizations
CNC	computer numerically controlled
COCOM	Coordinating Committee
COMECON	Council of Mutual Economic Assistance
CPI	Consumer Price Index
DARPA	Defense Advanced Research Projects Agency
DM	deutsche mark
DOD	Department of Defense
EC	European Community
FEMA	Federal Emergency Management Agency
FMS	flexible manufacturing system
FTC	Federal Trade Commission
GATT	General Agreement on Tariffs and Trade
GDP	gross domestic product
GNP	gross national product
IISI	International Iron and Steel Institute

ITC	International Trade Commission
MC	marginal cost
MITI	Ministry of International Trade and Industry
MNC	multinational corporation
NATO	North Atlantic Treaty Organization
NIC	newly industrializing country
NIP	national industrial policy
NTB	nontariff trade barrier
OECD	Organization for Economic Cooperation and Development
OPEC	Organization of Petroleum Exporting Countries
P&E	plant and equipment
PEP	Production Equipment Package
R&D	research and development
RSI	rationalization, standardization, and interoperability
SDI	Strategic Defense Initiative
SIC	Standard Industrial Classification
TPM	trigger price mechanism
VRA	Voluntary Restraint Agreement

PART I

1

An Introduction to American Industry

The United States has been the premier and dominant national economy throughout the post-World War II period. Anchoring this economic colossus is a strong industrial sector, which has been a crucial factor in generating economic growth, providing job opportunities, and ensuring national security. This sector consists of two types of industries: (1) goods-producing industries, such as manufacturing, construction, mining, and agriculture; and (2) service-producing industries, such as trade, finance, transportation, and services. Historically, agriculture was the most important economic activity in the early stages of economic development. However, as the economy evolved, manufacturing activities rather than agricultural came to dominate and function as the real economic pacemaker. In this book, when the term "industry" is used it will generally refer to these goods-producing activities.

Yet the continued evolution of the U.S. economy has witnessed substantial relative growth in the service-producing sectors. Signs of this evolution coupled with increased international competition have called into question the capabilities and vibrance of the industrial sector in particular and the American economy in general. Scholarly articles often refer to the "postindustrial society" while expressions such as "nation of hamburger stands" abound in the popular press. What is the exact nature of this economic evolution? Has the industrial sector lost its dynamism and become an ailing, cancerous growth on the U.S. economic landscape? Will it fade to insignificance, and if so, whither the general economy? These and similar questions are the topic of this book. They are important and relevant areas of inquiry and merit a close and dispassionate examination.

INDUSTRIALIZATION AND GROWTH

At the outset of the nineteenth century, the United States was still overwhelmingly rural in character and agriculture predominated the economy. While the

3

industrial revolution continued to advance in Great Britain, the United States remained dependent on the farm sector for income and employment. However, the construction boom for canals in the 1830s and railroads in the 1840s created arteries of commerce that knitted the nation's producers and consumers together into an economic whole. The creation of infrastructure also stimulated the development of such crucial industries as iron, steel, locomotive manufacture, and metalworking in general. By 1870 there were over 50,000 miles of railroads, and one-quarter of the U.S. population lived in urban areas. This transportation network tremendously widened the market area, thereby encouraging mass production, mass marketing, and mass consumption. The industrial revolution in the United States increased its momentum and entered the stage of take-off, resulting in an acceleration of national economic growth.

In the nineteenth century the United States gained recognition in the development of standardized interchangeable parts. Under this concept, components of a finished good are so much alike that one can be substituted for another, almost at random, to make the final products. It is interesting to note that the first serious moves toward standardization and interchangeable parts were made in government armories and arms factories. This technology later spread into other areas (to include clocks, watches, agricultural machinery, and machine tools), resulting in immense gains in productivity. As the industrialization process continued, the United States made numerous technological improvements in many different fields of production. For example, between 1840 and 1860, the number of patents increased by 1,000 percent.[1] A series of improvements in basic metals, power production, and machinery made mechanized mass-production facilities possible in manufacturing. As a result, a great number of mass-production consumer goods industries were created, turning out a variety of products that changed the U.S. life-style. The dynamics of industrialization thus set into motion a chain effect, a widening and deepening of the apparatus of industrial production, exerting profound and lasting impacts on the entire structure of the U.S. economy.

At the turn of the twentieth century, the first billion-dollar company—United States Steel—was born. Other industrial giants, such as Standard Oil, DuPont, General Motors, also entered the scene with an enormous productive capacity. Manufacturing momentum was acquiring a life of its own.

Industrialization continued to transform the U.S. economy, elevating the nation to an economic power with a high level of industrial production capability. During World War II, U.S. military power went hand in hand with its economic power. Productive capacity was a major factor in the war. The demand for tremendous quantities of weapons and materiel led to the application of the methods developed by the automobile industry and others. Perhaps the most notable of these applications was the manufacture and assembly of B-24 bombers by the Ford Motor Company at Willow Run, Michigan, where the continuous production of one bomber per hour was achieved. It was primarily due to industrialization that the United States emerged as a leading economic power in the post-World War II era. In recent decades, other economically strong countries, such as

Japan and West Germany, have also derived their economic strength from industrialization.

The role played by technology in the industrialization of the United States is pivotal. Technological innovation has enabled U.S. industries to introduce a constant stream of new and improved products and services, to create new jobs, and to improve the productivity of both labor and capital. Manufacturing has been in the forefront of utilizing new technology to enhance productivity. Of equal importance is the evolution of productive technology, which has been matched and facilitated by an evolution in business organization. This is exemplified in modern multiunit corporations with several centralized offices, subsidiaries, and diversified plants. Indeed, the technology of management—the coordination of financial and human resources, markets, and distribution—has been pushed no less vigorously than the technology of physical production.

TRANSITION FROM AGRICULTURE TO INDUSTRY

In the process of industrialization, significant structural changes occurred. By the end of World War II, the U.S. economy had long since been transformed into an advanced industrial system, with its agricultural sector reduced to a minor proportion of the overall economy. In 1849, the share of national income from agriculture was 32 percent, as compared to 13 percent for manufacturing. By 1987 manufacturing accounted for 19 percent of national income, while agriculture had fallen to only 2 percent. Many of those who left the agricultural sector eventually moved into the service industries, such as trade, transportation, and finance.

The agricultural share always tends to fall as per capita incomes rise because income elasticity of demand for foodstuffs is typically low (i.e., consumption of basic farm food products is limited largely by the rate of growth of total population),[2] while the share of manufacturing output (and service as well) tends to increase because the income elasticity of manufactured goods is typically high. As a result, with higher levels of income the proportion of funds spent for food shrinks, reducing the relative importance of the agricultural sector.

Another factor stimulating the transition from agriculture to industry is rapid technological change in farming. The introduction of new seeds, fertilizers, and pesticides; the improvements in breeds and feeds for livestock and poultry; and the mechanization and electrification of farming have all contributed to the striking progress in farming productivity since 1930. Indeed, the productivity gains of the last few decades are greater than those achieved in the previous two centuries. These significantly reduced labor input requirements in farming. Accordingly, rising agricultural productivity together with inelastic demand for farm products forced many people to leave farming to seek employment in the nonfarm sector. In short, people go where the jobs are.

According to an estimate by Lester Thurow, using U.S. Department of Commerce data, 9.1 billion man-hours of work (some 8 percent of the total number of hours in the private economy) left agriculture to enter industrial employment between 1948 and 1965.[3] By the early 1970s this transition was almost complete; there were only 0.2 billion man-hours of work released from agriculture from 1977 to 1983, less than one-tenth of the 1948–65 annual average. In 1948 agriculture's productivity in terms of output per hour was just 40 percent of the national average. A worker released from agriculture who found a job in other industries represented, on the average, a 60 percentage point gain in the output per hour of work. Such transition meaningfully contributed to the productivity growth of the nation. Accordingly, the United States seems to have passed through another stage in the evolution of industrial structure.

FACTORS OF PRODUCTION

The growth of the U.S. economy relies on various economic resources that are called inputs or factors of production. These resources consist of the following broad types:

1. *Natural resources,* such as land, minerals, timber. These are often lumped together under the rubric *land.*

2. *Human resources,* which consist of the productive physical and mental abilities of the people. These may take the form of direct labor, management, and human skills. Some authors list entrepreneurship as a separate factor of production. Entrepreneurs found and operate new businesses. They bear risk, manage uncertainty, and inject dynamism into the system. Entrepreneurs reap the gains of success or suffer the losses of failure. For our purposes, anything involving the human factor, including entrepreneurship, will be included under the rubric *labor* or *human resources.*

3. *Capital,* which is a produced means of furthering production. Capital or investment (producer) goods must be created via an economic process. Buildings, machinery, and tools are all examples of physical capital. In common parlance, money is often deemed capital, but in the economic sense it is not. Rather, it is a medium of exchange that can be used to acquire real producer goods. Although money itself is not directly productive, it is crucial to the smooth functioning of any modern economic system because it provides the financing that facilitates business operations and expansion.

As will be explained in chapter 5, capital is a key factor affecting productivity growth. The concept of capital can be divided into physical and human components. Just as inputs can be mixed together to create capital goods (physical capital), which speed and augment the production process, so too can human resources be developed via training and education to form *human capital.* Thus, basically, natural and human inputs represent the resource base for the economy. Let us examine them now. Technology, which affects the efficiency with which these resources are used, will be discussed in chapter 4.

Natural Resources

Natural resources (and access to them) are vital to a nation's survival, welfare, and security. Land and its products, water, mineral fuels, and nonfuel minerals are indispensable physical inputs that provide the material basis of modern civilization. The United States is by far the world's largest user of raw materials. The absolute volume of resource production and consumption has been steadily increasing to reflect rising demands from a growing industrial sector. As the American population grows, the need to produce more consumer and capital goods as well as to maintain a strong defense establishment requires increasing natural resource inputs.

Can the United States rely on sufficient supplies to meet current and future domestic demand for natural resources? In the wake of unprecedented increases in world petroleum prices in 1973 and 1978, this basic question catapulted to center stage in public discussions. In the eighteenth century, it was predicted that there would not be enough primary resources to meet the ever-increasing demands of an expanding population in the long run.[4] For a static economy, such doomsday predictions could become a reality.

Modern economies, however, are dynamic; they move and grow with changing technology and resource availabilities. This modifies the dimensions of the resource supply concept. Mineral resources, for example, are usually considered to be nonrenewable. Increases in current production or increased government regulations reduce mineable reserves of these resources. On the other hand, resource products may be increased by new discoveries and by new technological and economic developments that make it possible to produce them from deposits that could not previously be mined economically. Therefore, the degree of the relative economic scarcity of natural resources varies not only with the intensity of demand for products, but also with the technology of exploiting them or developing substitutes. For example, there is abundant oil in the shales and tar sands of the North American continent and there is abundant manganese and other metals in the nodules that cover much of the the ocean floor. But at the present time, the cost to extract and put them to use is too high to develop such resource products because alternative sources of supply are available at substantially lower costs. In the future, however, changes in market demand, price, technology, or government policies can make these resources economically attractive and feasible to bring to the market. Economic theory predicts that as a product becomes scarcer (or more plentiful), changes in relative costs and prices will take place. While high prices will lead to lower demands, often through encouraging the use of substitute products, lower relative prices will usually stimulate demand. Supply will also respond to price changes, but in the opposite direction of demand responses.

Accordingly, supply and demand tend to move closer together and may achieve an equilibrium condition, given sufficient time and resource mobility. Of course, radical movements in either supply or demand could cause temporary shortages, shock the system, and disrupt both the industrial sector and the whole economy.

In 1972 a group of social scientists wrote a report for the Club of Rome's project. The book, which received great notoriety, was entitled *The Limits to Growth*.[5] The authors used a computer model to demonstrate that the world as a whole was outstripping resource limits in fossil fuels and other resources. A collapse of the world's food and industrial production was projected sometime in the twenty-first century. Many economists, however, feel that this view represents extreme and unwarranted pessimism.[6] The resource and commodity markets usually have a set of adaptive mechanisms—technological change and price movements—that will automatically set into motion when shifting patterns of resource scarcity occur. Almost any projections into the next century are hazardous, and uncertainties multiply with each decade into the future. However, if past history serves as a guide to the present and future use of natural resources, technological change will help avoid catastrophic outcomes. Accordingly, the resource scarcity problem is more likely to be a short-run rather than a long-run phenomenon. When one views the broad range of U.S. natural resource inputs—which often come from great distances and unstable suppliers—short-run vulnerabilities are immediately suggested. The 1973 oil embargo/price shock is a classic case in point.

To place the U.S. natural resource base in perspective, according to several empirical studies, this country would not face any general depletion of resources during the remainder of this century;[7] the United States can obtain the natural resources and resource products that it needs from domestic and foreign sources. However, this does not exclude problems of shortage from time to time in particular segments of the economy for particular raw materials. Further, the likelihood of such shortages is greatly increased if domestic policies are inappropriate or foolish. The importance and relevance of imports will be further discussed in chapter 6.

Since World War II, the federal government has developed some important policies to help address the resource question and ensure an adequate supply of industrial materials for peace or war. For example, the National Commission of Materials Policy, established in 1971 (through provisions in Title II of the Resource Recovery Act of 1970), issued a 1973 report which stressed that the United States should "rely on market forces as a prime determinant of the mix of imports and domestic production in the field of materials, but at the same time decrease and prevent whenever necessary a dangerous or costly dependence on imports." It also urged conservation of "our natural resources and environment by treating waste materials as resources and returning them either to use or in a harmless condition to the ecosystem." In 1980, facing the mounting concerns about import dependence of such strategic mineral resources as cobalt, manganese, chromium, platinum, and bauxite, Congress passed the National Materials and Minerals Policy, Research and Development Act. Since this act calls for replenishing strategic materials, it has significant implications for national security as well as U.S industry. The establishment of the Strategic Petroleum Reserve is yet another example of policy efforts to reduce industrial and national security resource vulnerabilities.

Human Resources

The size of the U.S work force is directly related to a demographic category called "noninstitutional population." Counted in this category are all persons 16 years of age and older, including members of the resident armed services, but excluding persons in institutions and the armed forces overseas. In October 1988, the U.S. noninstitutional population reached 187 million. Of this population, 124 million were in the labor force, which is defined as those in the noninstitutional population who are working or actively seeking employment. Thus it includes the unemployed as well as the employed. If we subtract the number of persons in the resident armed forces from the total labor force, the remainder is known as the civilian labor force.

Roughly three-fourths of the nation's gross national product (GNP) derives from labor inputs. This value depends not only upon the quantity of labor, but also its quality. High labor productivity is achieved by a trained and skilled labor force, which in turn reflects human capital investment, incentive systems, management, and cultural factors.

In recent decades, the U.S. population has experienced some significant changes that have exerted profound impacts on economic activities. Fertility and the rate of population growth surged upward after World War II and then, in about 1960, turned around and plummeted.[8] Today's 1.8 births per woman of childbearing age is just above the 1.7 low of 1978. In the last decade, mortality rates, after a period of leveling off, have unexpectedly started to fall sharply, with especially surprising declines occurring at older ages. There has also been a dramatic increase in illegal immigration in the post-World War II period. "Interestingly, the highest rates of job creation in America have been in those areas with the heaviest immigration."[9] In addition, the historical trend toward growing urbanization appears to be reversing and a number of rural areas not adjacent to cities have shown renewed population growth. These developments in fertility, mortality, and migration have had important effects on the labor markets of all ages and skill levels and have aggravated problems of economic stabilization in the 1980s.

Types of Unemployment

The participants in the U.S. labor force fall into two categories: the employed and the unemployed. According to the Bureau of Labor Statistics, which compiles the official labor data, a person in the labor force is considered unemployed if he or she is not working and is either actively seeking employment or waiting to begin or return to a job. Unemployment may reflect demand conditions for labor, policy changes, or imperfection in the labor market. It can also be a sign of economic inefficiency in the allocation of human resources. Economists usually divide unemployment into the following four categories.

1. *Seasonal unemployment:* This comes at regular intervals and is fairly easily anticipated. Demands and/or supplies, for example, often vary with the onset of winter or summer. This form of unemployment presents no policy problems and it is not addressed by policy makers. The basis for this inattention is the fact that the unemployment is temporary and can be easily anticipated by business participants and workers who have time to make other arrangements.

2. *Frictional Unemployment:* This condition characterizes almost all labor markets. It derives from a lack of perfect information on the part of both job seekers and employers and results in job search (unemployed) time spent by job seekers in locating openings. Workers in the labor market are constantly being hired, fired, quitting, and relocating from one job to another. According to Herbert Stein, a former chairman of the Council of Economic Advisers, during "an ordinary year when unemployment is constant and employment is rising, probably about 10 percent of the work force will lose jobs . . . an equal number . . . will also find jobs."[10] This type of unemployment is usually short-term.

3. *Cyclical unemployment:* This results from recessionary business conditions and inadequate aggregate demand for labor. Much of the high rate of unemployment associated with recent recessions of 1974–75, 1980, and 1982 was cyclical in nature. Since this type of unemployment is due to insufficient aggregate demand, measures to strengthen demand by raising consumption, investment, government expenditures, and exports can improve business conditions and reduce cyclical unemployment.

4. *Structural unemployment:* This is caused by an imbalance between the skills possessed by workers and those demanded in the labor market. Changes in the basic characteristics of the economy can impede the matching of available jobs with available workers. Some skills may become obsolete, whereas others may be in short supply relative to demand. For example, in the industrial sector, workers are often displaced because of technological developments and automation. Sometimes, changes in consumer spending patterns and government policies may also affect unemployment in this fashion. For example, dramatic shifts in defense and other government expenditures in recent years have often promoted excess demand and job vacancies in one area while generating excess supply and unemployment in another. Other factors, such as minimum wage laws and demographic changes, can similarly affect structural unemployment.

Mandated by lesislation in 1946 and 1978, the federal government has the obligation to pursue a policy of full employment. The concept of full employment, however, is somewhat ambiguous. Economists generally consider this to be the level of employment that results when the rate of unemployment is normal (a minimum consistent with a stable price level), considering both frictional and structural factors. Most economists think that the 5–6 percent range is now the normal or natural rate of unemployment. Legislators, by contrast, apparently believe that 4 percent is consistent with full employment (the Humphrey-Hawkins Act of 1978 mandates the 4 percent measure).

Important Demographic Changes

Recent demographic changes associated with trends in fertility and mortality have influenced both the nation's unemployment rate and its saving rate. There is reason to believe that changes in the age composition of the U.S. population were partially responsible for high unemployment and low saving rates in the 1970s and 1980s. The age structure of the work force was altered by the post-World War II "baby boom." During the 1970s, there was a tremendous increase in the 18-to-34 age grouping, one in which new job seekers are concentrated and job switching in search of a career path is most common. This group normally has a high rate of unemployment. The unemployment rate was thus pushed upward during that decade when these youthful workers comprised an increasing proportion of the total work force. On the other hand, in the same period there was also a high rate of increase for those who were 65 years and over in the population. The changes in these two age groups—the young and the old—also contributed to the depressed saving rates, since both are traditionally low savers and they accounted for a larger proportion of the population. In contrast, the 35-to-54 age grouping, which generally has a stable employment pattern and saves a high proportion of current income, grew very slowly in the 1970s, resulting in a decrease in their proportion of the labor market.

Bureau of the Census data indicate that fewer people are now turning 18 and thus entering the work force. By the end of the 1980s, there will be a decline in the number of people in the 15-to-24 age group and only a moderate increase in the 25-to-34 age group. But the number of people in the 35-to-44 age group will increase dramatically. This is a natural result of the recent fertility trends. Such demographic changes have important economic implications. Individuals in the 35-to-44 age category generally have stable employment patterns and a higher saving rate because they generally (1) desire home ownership, (2) seek to establish education funds for their children, and (3) begin retirement planning. The relative increase in this age group will reduce unemployment rates and should also raise the saving rate. Concurrently, because of the expected decline in the number of people under age 25, the economy is likely to experience a relative shortage of unskilled workers. Industries will have to make adjustments to accommodate such changing demographic patterns. One such adjustment is likely to be an increase in demand for labor-saving capital equipment as producers seek to substitute capital for the increasingly scarce unskilled labor inputs.

The significance of demographic trends cannot be overemphasized; they will have major economic and policy implications. During 1988 the United States generated almost twice as many new jobs as new working-age Americans. Indeed, "the 16-to-19 age work force fell by 150,000" during that year.[11] This will translate into a nearly 4 percent fall in the 18-to-24 new worker category in the 1990s. Accordingly, after 30 years of 1.7 percent annual increases in working age Americans, the rate in the 1990s will be a mere 0.8 percent.

There are numerous implications deriving from these changing demographic trends. First, with the exception of possible business cycle downturns, the decade of the 1990s will not witness the relatively high unemployment rates that characterized much of the economic expansion of the 1980s. As previously mentioned, shortages of relatively low-skilled, entry-level workers will be common. Such a condition should be a boon to minority and unskilled workers, whose unemployment rates have traditionally been higher than the U.S. average. Second, as Warren Brookes has effectively argued, the combination of lower growth in the labor force and a national educational system with significant deficiencies suggests a second shortage in the coming decade—a major skills gap for relatively higher paid workers.[12]

Two policy implications immediately come to mind. First, the educational system must be upgraded and geared to the skill demands of the twenty-first century. Yet this progress takes significant time. A quicker and more traditional fix is to allow meaningful and tailored increases in immigration. But in the past several years, partly because of the crackdown on illegal aliens, much of this source has dissipated. Additionally, since the late 1970s an increasing share of legal immigration has shifted from a skills criterion to one of kinship. "In 1986, for example, out of 601,708 immigrant visas issued, only 23,162 or 3.8 percent, were admitted based on the skills they would bring. . . ."[13]

Labor Force Participation

If normal growth in labor force numbers has substantially declined, perhaps labor force participation rates, which have been increasing over the past few decades, can make up the difference. At the beginning of this century, only about 31 percent of the entire population was in the labor force. By mid-century, this ratio had risen to 42 percent, and by 1986 was 65 percent, with a still higher ratio predicted for the year 2000. The labor force participation rate jumped noticeably in the 1970s due to the entry of large numbers of women and youthful workers. For example, in 1958 youthful workers (age 16 to 24) constituted only 16 percent of the labor force. In contrast, as a result of the entry of the baby boom generation into the labor market, one out of every four workers was in the 16-to-24 age group by 1980. Reflecting such age composition movements, the share of prime-age workers, those 25 or over, shrank from 84 to 75 percent.

On the other hand, the representation of females has been continuously growing. In 1930, 22 percent of all labor force participants were females and less than 15 percent of all wives living with their husbands participated in the work force. By 1980, more than one-half of all wives were in the labor force, and women constituted 42 percent of the labor force total. This is likely to continue to increase, albeit more slowly, as successive generations of younger women move into their adult years in a society in which it has become more socially acceptable and more economically necessary for women to devote themselves to careers.

According to economic theory, supply decisions in the labor market reflect economic incentives. Increases in market wages relative to the value of time spent working at home will naturally raise female labor participation. In addition, improvements in household technology (refrigerators, washing machines, microwave ovens, etc.) also play an important role in inducing women to join the labor market. This increase in the number of females, especially married, at work for pay has been considered the single most important development in the U.S. labor market over the past 40 years.[14]

This trend coincides with several major socioeconomic changes in U.S. society. For example, the divorce rate has increased substantially, as has the proportion of unmarried adults. Today one out of five babies is born to single women.[15] These and related developments have and are exerting profound impacts on marital patterns, family formation, the demand for child care, the division of labor within households, and even the nature of household work itself.[16]

These changes in age and sex composition of the labor force also exert important impacts on employment and productivity. For example, the growing number of two-career families tends to generate new consumption patterns and demands for more flexible working hours. Many of those women and youths entering the labor force over the last two decades joined the lower paid service sector because they generally were unskilled and were unable to find jobs in the goods-producing industries. Labor productivity rates may have been adversely affected by the entry of inexperienced youthful and female workers. If so, such adverse effects should be offset by the maturing of the labor force as the baby boomers enter prime productive years. Looking ahead toward the year 2000, the labor force is projected to have about 29 million more people than in 1980. It will be older, the average age increasing from 35 to 38 years, and will have a higher proportion of women and ethnic minorities.

Returning to the question posed earlier, can increased labor participation maintain traditional labor force growth in the face of recent demographic changes? The answer is no. These increases are now moving at a much slower pace; the 1989 participation rate was almost 65 percent, the same rate that prevailed during World War II. The statistics speak clearly. Since 1980, when the 16–24 age grouping peaked at 28.4 million persons, there has been a decline every year. The mid-1989 figure was 24.6 million, with a further drop of 2.5 million expected by the year 2000. Small businesses will be the most affected by this decrease because they hire two-thirds of all entry-level workers. At the other end of the employment spectrum, it is likely that efforts will be made to bring retired skilled workers and managers back into the labor force, probably on a part-time or flexible hours basis.

Demand, Technological Changes, and Job Opportunities

In any dynamic economy there will be declining sectors as well as expanding ones. The economy must generate sufficient additional jobs to absorb both a growing labor force and the workers whose jobs are displaced by technology and other advances in productivity. Economic theory suggests that the industries likely to provide employment growth will be those favorably affected by future expenditure patterns related to demand and by shifts in technology. During the past decade the industries associated with the production of defense goods grew faster because of higher government expenditures on national defense due to changing national priorities. In the 1990s, however, a new set of priorities is likely to yield lower real defense outlays. Conversely, industries for consumer durables and recreation will do well because of rising incomes. Similarly, the health care industries should fare well because of the aging of the population.

Census data indicate that the fraction of workers employed in white-collar occupations, in government, and in the service industries has increased, while the proportions working as factory operatives or laborers, and in agriculture, have declined. The trend is expected to continue for the remainder of this century. Dynamic shifts in demand for labor in association with changes in expenditure patterns (which alter employment along a relatively elastic labor supply schedule[17]) appear to be the major factor for the structural change in employment among occupations and industries.

Another important shift in job opportunities in recent decades is the relative employment decline in the Eastern and Midwestern industrial belt. The fastest growing regions in the United States have been the South, Southwest, and West Coast. Many industries have relocated to these regions, building new plants in states such as Texas, Florida, Arizona, and California. Industrialization of these areas has absorbed large numbers of workers in recent decades.

How do technological changes affect the level of employment in industry? Contrary to popular notions, empirical evidence indicates that rapid increases in productivity associated with improvements in technology do not cause massive dislocations and widespread unemployment. Technological change affects the distribution of employment among industries and occupations, but does not generally have the feared effect of creating significant loss of jobs in the industries that experience rapid productivity growth. Lower production costs and lower product prices due to technological progress generally stimulate demand and expand market shares for those in the forefront of change. Thus, rapid productivity growth can produce more rather than fewer employment opportunities. For example, during Great Britain's industrial revolution, textiles was a leading industry. Between 1700 and 1800, employment in the British textile industry increased by 350 percent even though the industry was mechanized. When Henry Ford adopted assemby line production techniques for automobiles, employment in the automotive industry increased by 450 percent. More recently, according to the Machinery and Allied Products Association, between 1955 and 1976 employment rose three times as fast in five high-technology industries as it did in all other industries.[18]

Some economists believe that computer-based technologies and microelectronically controlled equipment such as robots and word processors will bring forth another industrial revolution in the next 30 years. If so, employment patterns in the industrial sector will experience some fundamental changes. While some workers will be displaced, the new technologies will also create new job opportunities. Assembly line workers and low-level clerical employees will be the ones most likely to be negatively affected.

Influence of Labor Unions

Unions have played an important role in the industrial sector. Currently, about 17 million nonfarm workers belong to nearly 200 national unions in the United States. The objective of unions is to improve the status of workers by bargaining collectively with management. The major issues usually involve wages, fringe benefits, industrial relations, multiunit bargaining, working conditions, and the settlement of labor-management disputes. In the United States, unions are generally found in the heavy industries in the North, while unorganized workers are in the traditional industries in the South.

Unions are in a monopoly position; that is, labor is often organized as a single seller of labor services on the supply side of the labor market. Unions may resist technological innovation, obstruct the adoption of new methods, or refuse to work with new tools. They may also engage in restrictive practices in order to achieve wages above the free-market equilibrium levels that would exist without unions. Empirical studies indicate that some unions, in such industries as construction, trucking, steel, and automobiles, have made extraordinary gains in wages; but for unions in general, the measurable monetary gains have been rather small.[19]

At the end of World War II, about 35 percent of the nonfarm labor force was unionized; but this share has since fallen to 14.5 percent. The two major labor organizations—the American Federation of Labor (AFL), founded in 1886, and the Congress of Industrial Organizations (CIO), founded in 1933—were merged in 1955 to form one huge labor organization (AFL-CIO) for the purpose of strengthening worker solidarity and the political voice of the labor movement.

The two largest unions—Teamsters and United Auto Workers—have since left the AFL-CIO. Despite organized labor's lower percentage today than several decades ago, industry-wide bargaining in certain major industries has important impacts on almost every aspect of the industrial operation.

It is worth noting that the declining share of the work force that is organized would be much more devastating were it not for increases in unionized federal, state, and local government workers. Whereas in 1960 only one in 20 union members was a government employee, today one in three is. The manufacturing sector, still 25 percent unionized, reflects a greater union presence than the economy as a whole, but substantially less than the government sector. Some manufacturing unions, such as the United Steel Workers and the United Automobile Workers, have lost over 40 percent of their members since 1973. In the service-producing sector slightly less than 10 percent belong to unions, although one category, transportation and public utilities, has a very large (37 percent) union presence.

Important factors accounting for the erosion of union influence are the demographic and employment changes previously discussed. The workers who have historically tended to be less organized—women, the young, and white-collar workers—have grown more than proportionately, while the percentages in the traditionally organized categories have fallen. Furthermore, in the aftermath of World War II, union corruption, public distaste for cost-push inflation, and many disruptive strikes shifted public opinion against unions. These feelings led to the passing of the Taft-Hartley Act of 1947. It outlawed closed shop arrangements and prohibited labor unions from coercing employees to join them. In ensuing years, many states passed right-to-work legislation that further eroded union economic and political influence. More recently, the inability of unions to maintain jobs and wages in the face of changing technological and market conditions in several industries has greatly reduced their attraction to potential members. Finally, the Reagan position in the air traffic controllers' strike and the damage to unions as a result of takeovers have further weakened their posture. Nonetheless, organized labor remains a major element in the U.S. economy. Many of the nation's important industries, such as automobiles, construction, and steel, today still have more than 80 percent of their wage earners unionized.

THE PRICE SYSTEM

In the industrial sector, the factors of production—human resources, natural resources, and capital—are combined in different industries to produce goods and services for the American people and for export. U.S. industries are operating in a framework of the so-called mixed capitalistic economy. Basically, the system is characterized as one of free private enterprise, a system giving high priority to freedom of opportunity for the individual, who may be either a producer or a consumer (and frequently is both). Such a system leaves the fulfillment of economic wants largely to the private action of individuals and organizations competing in the production and exchange of goods and services in open markets.

In such a market-oriented system, the important questions facing all industries—what to produce, how to produce, and for whom to produce—are decided largely through the interaction of supply and demand. Markets collect and register information reflecting the choices of consumers, producers, and resource suppliers. This vast amount of information is tabulated into a summary statistic—the market price—which provides market participants with current information on relative scarcity and desirability of products. Movements in supply and/or demand alter market prices, which in turn serve to eliminate or minimize shortages or surpluses. In deciding which input combinations are most appropriate to produce a given product, the guidance of relative market prices is crucially important.

The distribution of output also depends on prices, for they determine the income of the owners of productive resources as well as the actual quantities that can be purchased from that income. Additionally, market prices direct entrepreneurs to take the production of products that are demanded most intensely (relative to their cost) by consumers. Price is also the decisive factor in determining whether or not a project is profitable. Accordingly, prices are the main guiding mechanism in the United States for determining what shall be produced, how it shall be produced, and how that output shall be distributed.

The price system also serves an important motivation function. It establishes a reward-penalty system that provides strong incentives for the efficient production of intensely desired goods. Rewards include profits for the market participants who succeed. Penalties include losses for those who fail. Pursuit of personal gain is clearly a powerful and primary motivator in the U.S. economic system.

It should be obvious that the U.S. economy has never relied exclusively on private enterprise and the price system to solve its economic problems. The U.S. economic system is hardly free of nonmarket influences. Government has played an increasingly important role in the operation of the economy in recent years. The economy is thus called a mixed economy because of meaningful government participation, legislation, regulation, and influence. Impacts of government on the operation of U.S. industries will be further discussed in chapter 3.

PROFIT MAXIMIZATION

Clearly, the desire for pecuniary gain is the major motivational force in the U.S. business system. Economists generally presume that the objective of firms is to maximize profits. While this seems to be a very reasonable assumption for businesses run by their owners, when separation of ownership and management occurs, as in most large U.S. corporations, this assumption is more questionable.

Profit maximization is probably best defined as the attempt to maximize the present value of the profits expected from the firm's productive activities over some particular time frame. Business assets are deployed to yield revenues over a number of years. These revenues, some of which will be forthcoming many years hence, must be adjusted (discounted) due to the time value of money. One dollar received today is worth one dollar, but a dollar a year from now is today worth less than a dollar. If interest rates are 10 percent, it is only worth 91 cents today. If one has to wait two years, the present value is even lower. An appropriate interest rate must be applied to find out exactly how much future net receipts need to be discounted.[20] Profit maximization thus constitutes activities that maximize the present value of the firm's assets.

There are, however, a number of nonvalue maximizing goals that can be and probably are pursued. Corporate managements may choose to maximize sales revenues, either because management remuneration is often more closely associated with sales rather than profits or because various individual corporate leaders may simply "feel" better heading a bigger company rather than a more profitable one. Alternatively, managements may choose to maximize the growth of some other particular variable, such as the value of corporate assets, the number of employees, or the number of countries in which the product is sold or produced. Most deviations from profit maximization reflect the personal goals and ambitions of top managements. In an extreme form, one can readily imagine a condition in which a business has been quite profitable, but is in a clearly declining activity. The present value of stockholder resources may well be maximized if a decision is made to cease business, liquidate corporate assets, and distribute the proceeds to stockholders rather than remain in a sector with little future. This value-maximizing activity, however, would put top management out of work. It would thus require a particularly courageous management team to make such a recommendation. More than likely, management would instead confidently urge that the firm apply its talents in new directions or remain in the field as the likely sole survivor. Here, then, is a situation in which value maximization clearly conflicts with managerial desires.

Deviations from profit maximization, however, cannot be too radical, at least not for long. When a nonvalue-maximizing goal is paramount, there are generally minimal levels of profits that still must be achieved. Stockholders do have expectations from managements, with profits and perhaps dividends a part of these expectations. While it is often difficult for stockholders of very large corporations to dislodge incumbent managements, if owner expectations are not met, they will make their unhappiness known. Top executives are aware of this and their freedom of action is thus somewhat circumscribed. Accordingly, economists often describe such management pursuits with the term "constrained maximization." If sales revenues are chosen as the prime goal, this effort will still be subject to a minimal profit level necessary to satisfy stockholder expectations. This is revenue maximization subject to a minimal profit constraint. Most other nonvalue-maximizing goals may also be described as constrained maximization endeavors.

Business objectives are very important since they—in conjunction with a number of other factors—will determine the firm's behavior. Organizations that seek to maximize profits will carry production to the point where marginal cost equals marginal revenue, whereas revenue maximizers will produce more, carrying production to the point where marginal revenue approximates zero.[21] The latter will clearly produce larger outputs since they are willing to sell any product that adds to the firm's revenues (so as to maximize revenues), whereas the former cease production when additional outputs no longer yield revenues in excess of the additional costs they entail. Extra production, then, comes at the cost of greater profits.

Both the time frame of corporate managers and general economic conditions are additional factors influencing corporate behavior. If profit maximizers have only a three-year time horizon, activity A may be the best choice. However, if the time horizon is extended to seven years, activity B may be more suitable to maximize the firm's present value. General economic conditions also have an influence. During boom periods a number of nonvalue-maximizing goals, most constrained maximizations, may be pursued. The profit levels of boom economies may well satisfy equity holders, thus allowing management to concentrate on other goals. However, there may be periods in which profits are unobtainable. Here the profit-maximization goal means loss-minimization and the same operational rule (marginal revenue should equal marginal cost) prevails. Interestingly, nonvalue-maximizing activities tend to dissipate during hard times because weak economic conditions mandate that losses be kept to a minimum. Managements, then, are likely to abandon other goals when the ship appears to be sinking and instead work toward profit maximization (or its corollary, loss minimization). Lean years, then, tend to homogenize the business objectives of corporate America.

RELATIVE IMPORTANCE OF INDUSTRIES

The U.S. economy produced a GNP of approximately $4.4 trillion in 1987, leading all nations. The 1988 level was $4.9 trillion. Among all major industrialized countries, the United States also had in 1987 the highest per capita GNP ($18,200), as compared to Japan ($13,180) and the European Community ($11,690).[22] The most important single contributor to our GNP is manufacturing. As pointed out earlier, it was industrialization that propelled the U.S. manufacturing industry to such a prominent position, making it the pillar of the industrial sector. Table 1.1 reveals the relative importance of manufacturing and other major industries in the nation's economy. The 19 percent manufacturing share is followed by service (18 percent), finance (17 percent) and trade (16 percent).

A relatively small number of firms in manufacturing account for roughly one-fifth of the nation's GNP and total employment. These figures imply that our economy is highly industrialized, characterized by giant business firms in its manufacturing industry. A more detailed discussion of the structure of this industry will be given in chapter 2. However, it should be noted that the manufacturing

Table 1.1
Income, Employment, and Number of Firms by Industry, 1987*

Industry	Contribution to national income ($ billon)	%	Full-time workers employed (thousands)	%	Number of firms (thousands)	%
Agriculture	94.9	2	1,790	2	560	3
Mining	85.4	2	715	1	251	2
Construction	218.5	5	5,078	5	1,758	11
Manufacturing	853.6	19	19,126	17	622	4
Transportation	408.2	9	5,430	5	721	4
Trade	740.4	16	24,916	22	3,463	22
Finance	775.4	17	6,757	6	2,272	14
Service	793.5	18	26,067	24	6,220	37
Government	535.3	12	20,938	19		
Rest of world	29.5	1				
Total	4,526.7	100···	110,817	100···	16,077	**

*Income and employment are for 1987; the number of firms is for 1984.
**Does not add up to 100 percent because the total includes business not allocable to individual industries.
***Does not add up to 100 percent due to rounding.
Sources: Computed from U.S. Department of Commerce: *Survey of Current Business*, July 1988; and *Statistical Abstract of the United States, 1988*, p. 496.

share of total nonagricultural employment in the United States has declined steadily over the postwar period from roughly 35 percent in the late 1940s to 17 percent by 1987. Increases in manufacturing productivity have facilitated production growth without requiring commensurate additional labor inputs. Those working in the nonfarm sector have been increasingly absorbed by the service industries where many new jobs have been created.

Not all the nation's income and employment are orginated in private domestic enterprises. Government and foreign enterprises also make important contributions to our income and employment (foreign trade will be discussed in chapter 6).

Agriculture is now relatively insignificant as a source of income and employment. Formerly, there were a large number of small firms in the agriculture industry. As recently as 1977, about 2.3 percent of the U.S. private businesses were in the farm sector. In the past few years, however, increasing numbers of farmers, caught in the price-cost squeeze of lower commodity prices and high interest costs, have been leaving farming. By 1984 only 3 percent of private businesses were engaged in agriculture production. The even lower present number will fall further if financial stress continues to bring forth more foreclosures on farms. The remaining firms in the farm sector will be larger and likely to be more efficient.[23]

In the traditional classification of industrial groups the service sector has by far the largest number of firms.[24] This sector has become an important source of income and employment, as Americans have spent increasing proportions of their incomes on services. As income has risen, spending has shifted from consumer products that are basic necessities, such as food, housing, and clothing, to outputs that enhance life-styles, such as recreation and travel. Furthermore, the broadening of the consumer market has resulted in more diversified and varied consumer products. Some are combinations of goods and services complementary to each other and all in one package, such as automobiles with financing and maintenance warranties. Thus, as demand for automobiles increases, demand for related finance and maintenance also rises. As a consequence, the service sector has increased its share of income and employment throughout the post-World War II period. In the most recent decade, service industries created most of the new jobs. The gain in employment in the 1970s—almost 19 million jobs—was also mainly in services (some two-thirds of new employment opportunities created in that decade).

INDUSTRY, ECONOMIC POWER, AND NATIONAL SECURITY

Manufacturing occupies a strategic position in the industrial base of the U.S. economy; it is a major engine for economic growth, pulling all other industries in the nation. In the first 40 years of the twentieth century, the growth of the manufacturing industry made the United States one of the world's economic leaders, although the United States did not stand alone. World War II witnessed significant changes. Equipped with the only surviving advanced industrial base, the United States for the first time became a political and military superpower. Its economy stood alone, with a huge technological gap between it and the world's next best economies.

In the early 1960s, however, technologically competitive nations were beginning to make their appearance in Europe and Asia. In the most recent decade, the United States has been losing its industrial preeminence and, consequently, its ability to compete so successfully in many world markets. The big technological edge enjoyed by U.S. industries in the 1950s and 1960s has disappeared.

Weak productivity growth has been a major factor for the relative decline in U.S. economic power (chapter 5 will provide a detailed discussion on productivity). There is also evidence suggesting that the U.S. business sector has been sluggish in introducing new outputs and technologies necessary for U.S. competitiveness in world markets. To revive what was once a stand-alone U.S. economy, some economists think that remedial measures need to be taken to improve the performance of manufacturing and service productivity. Related to this is the issue of the so-called national industrial policy (NIP), which involves interferences in the operation of industries by the public sector. Chapter 3 will provide a discussion concerning the possibilities in this area.

In the manufacturing sector, industries engaging in the production of steel (chapter 8) and machine tools (chapter 9) occupy a pivotal position in the industrial base. Their performance is directly linked to the growth of the overall economy, and the level of their activities generates a ripple or multiplier effect on income and employment throughout the industrial base. They are thus vital to the nation's prosperity and security. They are also problem areas, sectors that have had many disappointments, but also have lessons for public policy and public understanding. In the long run, it is also clear that a strong, vibrant industrial base is a critical ingredient for a democratic nation's defense posture.

NOTES

1. Robert L. Heilbroner, *The Economic Transformation of America* (New York: Harcourt Brace Jovanovich, 1977), p. 47.

2. Income elasticity of demand refers to the sensitivity of changes in quantity purchased to changes in income. Increases in income do not evoke proportionate increases in the quantity of food demanded.

3. Lester C. Thurow, *The Zero-Sum Solution* (New York: Simon and Schuster, 1985), ch. 3.

4. Thomas Malthus predicted in the eighteenth century that the unchecked growth of population inevitably would press upon the earth's limited supply of natural resources.

5. D. H. Meadows, D. L. Meadows, Jorgen Randers, and W. Behrens III, *The Limits to Growth: A Report for the Club of Rome's Project on the Predicament of Mankind* (New York: University Books, 1972).

6. See, for example, Nathan Rosenberg, "Innovative Response to Materials Shortage," *American Economic Review*, May 1973; Robert M. Solow, "Is the End of the World at Hand?" *Challenge*, March–April, 1973; and Wassily Leontief, James Koo, Sylvia Nasar, and Ira Sohn, *The Future of Nonfuel Minerals in the U.S. and World Economy—Input-Output Projections, 1980-2030* (Lexington, Mass.: Lexington Books, 1983).

7. For example, see Edward S. Mason, "Natural Resources and Environmental Restrictions to Growth," *Challenge*, January–February, 1978; and Hans H. Landsberg, *Natural Resources for U.S. Growth—A Look Ahead to the Year 2000* (Baltimore: The Johns Hopkins University Press, 1964).

8. See Richard A. Easterlin, "American Population Since 1940," in Martin Feldstein, ed., *The American Economy in Transition* (Chicago: University of Chicago Press, 1980).

9. Denis P. Doyle, "Capital Formation and Movement: The Human Dimension," AEI *Foreign Policy and Defense Review*, 5, no. 4 (1985), p. 41.

10. Herbert Stein, "Best-Selling Fiction: Three Million Lost Jobs," *Wall Street Journal*, July 29, 1985, p. 14.

11. Warren Brookes, "Immigration and the Skills Gap," *Washington Times*, March 20, 1989, p. C1.

12. Ibid.

13. Ibid.

14. Morley Gunderson, "Male-Female Wage Differentials and Policy Responses," *Journal of Economic Literature* 27 (March 1989), pp. 46–72.

15. Victor R. Fuchs, "Women's Quest for Economic Equality," *Journal of Economic Perspectives* 3, no. 1 (Winter 1989), p. 25.

16. Gunderson, p. 46.

17. Elasticity in this instance refers to the responsiveness of quantities (hours) of labor to changes in wage rates. A relatively elastic schedule means that hours of labor supplied are very responsive to wage changes—that is, a higher wage attracts much more labor, while a lower wage attracts much less.

18. Cited in Isabel V. Sawhill, "Human Resources," in G. William Miller, ed., *Regrowing the American Economy* (Englewood Cliffs, N.J.: Prentice-Hall, 1983), p. 109.

19. Clair Wilcox and William G. Shepherd, *Public Policies toward Business*, 5th ed. (Homewood, Ill.: Irwin, 1975), p. 631.

20. The basic present value (PV) formula is $PV = \dfrac{v}{(1 + r)^n}$ where V is the net revenue to accrue after n time periods and r represents the discount (interest) rate deemed applicable. Clearly, value today depends upon the amount of future revenues, how long one must wait to receive them, and how high the discount rate is. Calculation in practice is far more complicated than this simple formula suggests. Choosing the appropriate discount rate is often difficult. Further, both the anticipated number of time periods and expected future profits are estimates that must often be adjusted by probabilities.

21. For the uninitiated, any microeconomics text can explain these concepts. The section entitled "Costs" in Chapter 7 of this book provides some elaboration.

22. See Karen Elliott House, "The '90s & Beyond: For All Its Difficulties, U.S. Stands to Retain Its Global Leadership," *Wall Street Journal*, January 23, 1989, p. 1.

23. Average farm size increased from 175 acres in 1940 to 437 acres in 1984. See Hilary H. Smith and Eric J. Weigel, "Financial Stress Begins to Idle Acres," *Dallasfed*, Federal Reserve Bank of Dallas, February 1986.

24. The service sector provides the following: (1) distributive service—transportation, communications, and utilities; wholesale and retail trade; (2) intermediate service—includes establishments whose output is used as input for production in other industries—for example, accounting, engineering, and business services; (3) consumer services—services for final consumption such as auto repair, barbers, and motion pictures; and (4) government and nonprofit services—include nonprofit health and education, charity, and government activities among others. See U.S. Department of Commerce, *1985 U.S. Industrial Outlook* (Washington, D.C.: U.S. Government Printing Office, 1985).

2

Profile of American Industry

Efficient input utilization of human and natural resources is a major goal of any economic system. How much output the economy can produce from these resources depends on the performance of its business entities and the macroeconomic environment. Performance, in turn, is affected by the market structure within which a firm operates. Technology, input prices, and government policies fundamentally shape and influence that structure. This chapter provides a profile of U.S. industry and markets, with manufacturing at the center of the stage. Market structures, industrial organizational patterns, financial conditions, and important operational characteristics will be discussed.

INDUSTRIAL CLASSIFICATION

Data on U.S. industry are gathered, developed, and published as part of the Standard Industrial Classification (SIC) system. SIC categories describe industrial groups much like the Dewey Decimal library classification system—the fewer the digits, the broader the category. Table 2.1 lists the 20 major two-digit manufacturing industry groupings.

Each two-digit category is subdivided into more focused industry groupings. Major industry group 27, for example, is printing, publishing, and allied industries. Within this two-digit category are three-digit industry numbers, such as 271, newspapers: publishing and printing; or 273, books. Three-digit classifications are further subdivided, with at least one four-digit category in each. SIC 273 (books) is broken down into 2731, books: publishing, or publishing and printing, and 2732, book printing. These four-digit industries are further divided into five-digit product categories. Data are gathered on the basis of business establishments, which are defined as economic units, generally at a single physical location, such as a factory, mill, or airline terminal. Establishments are thus distinguished from

Table 2.1
Two-Digit Manufacturing SIC Industry Groups

SIC	INDUSTRY GROUP	SIC	INDUSTRY GROUP
20	Food & kindred products	30	Rubber/plastic products
21	Tobacco manufactures	31	Leather & products
22	Textiles	32	Stone, clay, & glass
23	Apparel	33	Primary metals
24	Timber & wood products	34	Fabricated metal
25	Furniture & fixtures	35	Nonelectric machinery
26	Paper & allied products	36	Elect/Electronic equipment
27	Printing & publishing	37	Transportation equipment
28	Chemicals/chem products	38	Instruments
29	Petroleum/coal products	39	Misc. mfg. industries

enterprises or companies, which generally consist of multiple establishments. Each establishment is assigned an industrial code based on its primary activity.

While this system and the enormous efforts that go into data collection and processing provide a wealth of information and statistics, there are many problems involved in basing analyses on these data. First, many categories include several distinct economic markets. Conversely, products that economists would consider economically identical—such as beet and cane sugar—are classified as different products in different industries. Third, most establishments produce more than one kind of output, but they are classified into only one industry. A plant producing three items, A, B, and C, in the proportions 40:30:30, would be classified into industry A, despite this product being only 40 percent of total production. Further, the total output of products A, B, and C would be added to industry A, thus "puffing" that industry's production figures while at the same time understating corresponding figures for the industries of B and C. Finally, when making comparisons over time it is important to note that industry definitions change, particularly for those fields experiencing the greatest dynamism. Accordingly, these data must be used with great care. Nonetheless, a tremendous volume of information is available and, if used correctly, can greatly aid in the understanding and analysis of the U.S. economic structure.

TYPES OF MARKETS

A market generally consists of a group of buyers and sellers of a particular product engaged in setting the terms of sales of that product. The sellers participating in a given market are called collectively the industry.[1] However, the products and services generated by the firms in various industries are not sold identically. Rather, different market conditions exist. While we may find one single producer in some industries that completely dominates, we also discover a large number of firms in other industries, each of which supplies a small fraction of the market output. In between there are many other possibilities.

What causes market situations to vary? According to economic theory, there are three basic structural factors affecting the market: (1) the number of firms, (2) the degree of product differentiation, and (3) the ease of difficulty encountered by new firms entering the market. Based essentially on these factors, market conditions can be classified into the following four categories:

1. *Monopoly:* This is a market in which there is only one seller of a rather unique product for which there usually exists no close substitute. The single seller must address and cater to market demand, but possesses the power to set price because of monopoly control over the quantity supplied. Substantial obstacles exist to keep new competitors from entering this market. These include legal obstacles, as in the case of public utilities, and financial barriers.

2. *Oligopoly:* This type of market has a few sellers who are supplying either a standardized product (e.g., homogeneous steel) or differentiated products (e.g., automobiles). Because there are few sellers, there is a high degree of interdependence among the firms in this market. Action taken by one firm with respect to pricing, output, or promotion will be watched closely by its rivals. Few actions are initiated without careful consideration of competitors' potential responses. Price wars are most likely to take place under such conditions. They tend to result from a misreading of expected responses by rival producers or from small producers attempting to expand sales in order to spread fixed costs. Most cases of collusion are also found in this market structure because fewness of sellers makes such collusion easier.

A classic example of possible oligopoly behavior, one reflecting both the threat and actuality of price war and the ease of collusion when there are relatively few sellers, is the following telephone conversation. The call had been taped and was reported by the *New York Times*. It is between Robert Crandall, president and chief operating officer of American Airlines, and Howard Putnam, president and chief executive of Braniff Airways. Fierce competition between the two airlines had been taking place for several years and a fare war had broken out as each tried to undercut the other in order to gain market share. On February 21, 1982, Mr. Crandall called Mr. Putnam.[2]

Mr. Crandall: I think it's dumb as hell for Christ's sake, all right, to sit here and pound the @!#%&! out of each other and neither one of us making a @!#%&! dime.

Mr. Putnam: Well . . .

Mr. Crandall: I mean, you know, goddamn, what the hell is the point of it?

Mr. Putnam: But if you're going to overlay every route of American's on top of every route that Braniff has—I just can't sit here and allow you to bury us without giving our best effort.

Mr. Crandall: Oh sure, but Eastern and Delta do the same thing in Atlanta and have for years.

Mr. Putnam: Do you have a suggestion for me?

Mr. Crandall: Yes, I have a suggestion for you. Raise your goddamn fares 20 percent. I'll raise mine the next morning.

Mr. Putnam: Robert, we . . .

Mr. Crandall: You'll make more money and I will, too.

Mr. Putnam: We can't talk about pricing!

Mr. Crandall: Oh @!#$%&!*, Howard. We can talk about any goddamn thing we want to talk about.

3. *Monopolistic Competition:* Many sellers of similar, yet differentiated products, are found in this market. The number of sellers make the market competitive, yet each is a monopolist for their own particular output. Price differences exist and producers compete on the basis of service, quality, and advertising. This structure is commonly found in retail and service industries, but it also exists in some branches of manufacturing, where there are many producers, each selling under its own brand name.

4. *Pure Competition:* There are many sellers (each being small relative to total volumes) of a standardized product (e.g., wheat or steel) in this type of market. There is relative ease of exit and entry and information about current prices and transactions is relatively easy to obtain. Because sellers each provide an insignificantly small fraction of total market supply, they are said to be "price-takers." The market establishes a product price to which they must conform. Their decisions are restricted to choosing the right input mix and appropriate quantities to offer. In the real world purely competitive markets are hard to find, although there are some approximations. American agricultural markets, in the absence of government intervention, are often an example, as is the stock market without large institutional investors or the foreign exchange market without central bank intervention.

Purely competitive markets would tend to bring about optimal resource allocations and maximum efficiency. If consumers desire more of a particular item, the associated increase in demand raises the market price. Existing suppliers respond by increasing output, while the higher profits induced by the increased price tend to attract new suppliers. Increased market supplies in turn tend to reduce existing price. Because the market is so competitive and sellers cannot influence price by their own actions, businesses strive for larger profits via cost reduction efforts.

With relative ease of information, those firms that succeed in gaining profits through cost reduction find that their actions are emulated by their competitors. By increasing total market supply, this process lowers prices. If equilibrium is achieved market price will not exceed unit cost of production—for example, no excess profits. Not only would consumers pay a price equal to cost, but costs would be at a minimum as firms adjust their plant sizes and input combinations to reduce expenses. Finally, the social efficiency condition that price equals marginal cost will also prevail.[3] In short, profit maximizing sellers will be forced by competition and information availability to offer products at the lowest possible price for the appropriate volume demanded by consumers.

To the degree that less competitive market structures prevail, these three optimality conditions (price equals average total cost, average total cost is a minimum, and price equals marginal cost) will fail to be achieved. As the pressure of competition is reduced, the profit-seeking activities of private parties will yield results that increasingly depart from these optimality conditions. For this reason, then, monopolies tend to be frowned upon and there are many legislative enactments that attempt to restrain, prevent, or regulate monopoly situations.

In the U.S. economy, the market structures for industries range from nearly pure competition to nearly complete monopoly. For example, a small potato farmer in Idaho operates in a competitive market condition, while the United Shoe Machinery Company occupied a monopoly position in manufacturing prior to 1954 because it was then the sole supplier of certain important kinds of shoemaking equipment. Today, the DeBeers syndicate has a virtual monopoly on global diamond mining. There is also a spatial dimension to market structures. Monopolies, for example, are commonly found in local neighborhoods—the only dry cleaner or immediate neighborhood theater. But if a wider geographic area is considered, other supplies can be found. Over larger areas, then, monopolies tend to give way to oligopoly and perhaps to monopolistic competition. As will be explained later, major U.S. industries in the industrial sector are primarily oligopolistic. What is important to recognize is that market structure tends to shape the operational conduct and economic performance of an industry. Accordingly, behavioral patterns, prices, and profit levels will vary depending upon market circumstances.

UNCERTAINTY, PROFIT MOTIVE, AND THE ENTREPRENEUR

In any dynamic market, particularly where technological changes occur, uncertainty plays an important role. Associated with uncertainty is not only the risk of failure, but the potential for profit making. It is the prospect of profit that motivates entrepreneurs to take risks, to innovate, and to break new ground. In *The Spirit of Enterprise,* a book about entrepreneurial behavior, author George Gilder writes:

The capitalist is not merely a dependent of capital, labor, and land; he defines and creates capital, lends value to land, and offers his own labor. . . . He is not chiefly a tool of markets but a maker of markets; not a scout of opportunity, but a developer of opportunity; not an optimizer of resources, but an inventor of them; not a respondent to existing demands but an innovator who evokes demand; not chiefly a user of technology but a producer of it.[4]

By their willingness to take risks, their inner drive to succeed, and their ability to identify new products and markets, entrepreneurs often spark sudden breakthroughs in technology, reaping large fortunes as a result. For instance, Silicon Valley, as the business enclave south of San Francisco is called, is the cradle of the world's high technology industries, the birthplace of innovative products that are changing the globe. It is a place of vast wealth and overnight success, a model for America's industrial future. It is also a shining example of how profits drive entrepreneurs to do their best in an uncertain business world. A great strength in the U.S. economy is the blossoming of our inherent entrepreneurial spirit—a spirit that responds to economic incentives and thrives in a basically free and dynamic economic system. This spirit has spawned numerous technological breakthroughs in a long tradition of Yankee ingenuity. It also underlies the energetic high tech environment of Silicon Valley.

In the development of the nation's economy, no one authority planned the industrialization of the United States. This enormous process was largely left to the operation of the market mechanism, with government providing basic infrastructure. Profit-seeking entrepreneurs have played the key roles in coordinating the bulk of the nation's production. Because of the drive for profit, entrepreneurs are induced to engage in the pioneering of new fields and the development of new products (as well as the expansion of existing product lines). The profit motive not only injects dynamism into the system, but allocates resources as well. There are a large number of new firms entering various industries each year in the hope of making a profit, while many existing firms leave because of losses.[5] Thus the composition of our business population changes all the time.

EXPLAINING THE FIRM: TRANSACTION COSTS AND THE PRINCIPAL-AGENT PARADIGM

Traditional economic analysis has centered on markets and their associated price/output results. The existence of firms is taken as given and they are studied mainly to analyze their response to market signals. Firms, however, are an important locus of economic activity in and of themselves. They come in a wide variety of sizes, shapes, and organizational modes, with differing operational characteristics and decision-making apparatuses. Importantly, it must be recognized that markets and firms are alternative means of organizing economic activities—both serve to allocate resources and direct economic endeavors. Indeed, markets and firms are substitutes for one another, with some transactions occurring in external markets and others occurring within the firm. Such choices—internal production or external procurement—are a frequently addressed challenge. In fact, the existence of the firm can largely be explained in terms of the avoidance or minimization of costs associated with dealings in the marketplace.

In theory, at least, one could envision an economy without firms as we know them, a system relying strictly upon markets to allocate resources and exchange goods and services. For example, rather than hiring a home builder to construct your dream house, you might decide to be the general contractor yourself. You could procure plans in the marketplace (from architects) and commence construction via a number of contracts with carpenters, plumbers, electricians, and others. In this sense, there is no traditional firm, just an individual contracting out and coordinating each phase of production. Nor is this example extremely farfetched. Americans do build homes this way. Further, rather than maintain an in-house capability, builders themselves often contract for plumbing and electrical services, thus relying on the marketplace rather than their own firm to supply vital functions.

Although production can take place without firms, the latter do exist and are established because it is often too costly to use the price system to coordinate transactions. Somewhat ironically, economists have often treated the firm as if it were a black box—its functions are described, where it fits into the system is depicted, and the results of its interactions with other firms are examined. However, what goes on inside the firm, aside from some mechanical rules, is too often ignored or taken as given. Firms exist essentially because the transaction costs of negotiating and implementing the many contracts that would otherwise be required for the conduct of business are just too great. These transaction costs come in a variety of forms, going far beyond the legal and administrative expenses related to the writing of contracts themselves.

The social function of business organizations is to minimize both transaction and production costs. The major demands placed on any organization are threefold: (1) assessing and promoting input productivity, (2) metering rewards, and (3) coordinating activities. While it is sometimes thought that firms have the power to settle issues by fiat within a hierarchical organization, the fact of the matter is that firms must to some degree negotiate and bargain with the economic agents they employ, just as they generally do with those from the outside whom they temporarily hire through the marketplace. Just as the terms of contracts with outside agents must be acceptable to both parties, the same is true within the firm. If not, employees will leave. Indeed, a major challenge is to bring about needed changes without employees leaving. Doing so often requires innovative contracts and work relationships, including features such as profit-sharing, job flexibility, and so on. Accordingly, what distinguishes allocations by firms from ordinary market transactions is not the degree of authority, but the fact that the firm is a centralized contractual mechanism working in a team production process. This team effort and the resulting internal exchanges, monitoring of productivity, and metering of rewards always take place within a particular organizational structure. Some such structures are more conducive to success and profits than others and businesses from time to time restructure in an effort to find the optimal combination. Business profits, then, are not only related to technical and production efficiencies, but to organizational form as well.

The principal-agent paradigm is a handy device for illustrating transaction costs and the major management problem that firms continually address. In principal-agent relationships, the agent carries out or caters to the wishes of the principal. Recognizing that the firm constitutes a team production effort among the various inputs, the firm generally acts as a principal that employs agents (factors of production either within the firm or external to it) to achieve desired outputs efficiently. However, the firm can also be an agent, as when it acts as a supplier to another firm. Indeed, in dealing with any customers, the seller assumes the posture of an agent. Economic agents—the owners of land, labor, capital, and materials— are almost constantly involved in a system of exchange relationships that are essentially contractual in nature. Sometimes the contracts are implicit, as when ordering a beer for a certain price at a local tavern. Dollars are exchanged for beverage at a particular ratio. Alternatively, contracts may be formal and written, such as the purchase of an automobile or house. In either event, contractual relations and complex economic exchanges generally involve information asymmetries, which in turn create three possible conditions: (1) adverse selection, (2) moral hazard (shirking), and (3) bounded rationality.

These attributes are often likely to generate opportunistic behavior—that is, actions engaged in by one partner to exploit some advantage to the detriment of the other partner. In its crudest form, opportunistic behavior would include lying or cheating. For example, someone interviewing for a job might claim to have far greater skills and capabilities (which may not be easily verified) than is actually the case. Accordingly, he or she can bargain for higher remuneration on the basis of employer ignorance. This is the problem of adverse selection. Due to information asymmetries, one party can misrepresent what it has to offer. In insurance markets those with the highest risks attempt to minimize their potential costs to insurers so as to obtain lower rates. This has the effect of raising average rates, thus penalizing true low-risk insureds to the benefit of high-risk cases. Similarly, in the used car market the seller's ability to offer a "lemon" for the same price as a good car tends to increase the proportion of lemons in the market. Seller informational advantages are so strong that buyers tend to discount all cars offered because they cannot distinguish between good cars and lemons. Similarly, where it is difficult or very expensive to monitor quantities (or quality) of supplies exactly, sellers might deliver lower quality or smaller amounts than promised. In such a case, where trust weighs heavily, rather than procuring in the market it may be wiser for a firm to develop in-house production capabilities.

Information asymmetries are the most common cause of opportunism. They exist when the parties to a contract are not equally informed. While economists often assume perfect or near perfect knowledge by all market participants, in the real world information asymmetries are more likely to be the rule. It is important to recognize that the establishment of a team production effort requires the coordinating authority to locate the appropriate individuals and resources. These should be the skills and assets relevant to produce the desired output efficiently. Often, however, it is not perfectly clear exactly what these should be. For new and unique products, like a space shuttle to Mars, this is an obvious challenge; for mundane projects, however, it is also often true. Indeed, many agents hired have better knowledge of what needs to be done or how much is required than the coordinating authority. As a simple example, consider a malfunctioning automobile taken to a garage by its confused and unhappy owner. Under most circumstances the mechanic has greater knowledge of the problem and the appropriate adjustments than the owner. More generally, throughout the business world individuals hired for many positions often have more job-specific knowledge than those hiring them. This gives rise to all sorts of opportunistic possibilities. Further, such information asymmetries are increasingly the case as society becomes more complex.

Firms must face the challenge of asymmetric information whether they deal with outside suppliers or with their own employees. Transaction or agency costs are involved either way, but one approach may entail far fewer than the other. If, for example, one can simply make a number of phone calls and get prices from market suppliers, then a fixed-price contract for a standardized item or job may be appropriate, for it tends to insure that possible opportunism by the provider will be minimized. On the other hand, the more unique the problem and the fewer the potential suppliers, the more the contracting authority is vulnerable. In such a situation, where trust is an important necessary ingredient (or monitoring costs are high), it is often best for the firm to bring the work in-house and attempt mainly to utilize long-term members of its own production team. Similarly, opportunism (or potential opportunism) may raise transaction costs to the point where no market exists at all. In such cases, to obtain a product or service a firm will be forced to produce it by itself.

Other significant transaction costs relate to the two remaining attributes, moral hazard and bounded rationality. The latter expression refers to the fact that in an uncertain world we do not know all the possible options and contingencies we are likely to face. Energy shocks, strikes, wars, and Bhopal-type disasters are generally unanticipated. Our decisions today are bounded in their selection by the narrow range we currently see. In a world filled with surprising and unanticipated events, it is important to embody some flexibility into relationships. As suggested earlier, firms can be viewed as a system of bilateral contracts, ones that often cannot be highly specified due to bounded rationality. Ordinarily, the employee joining a firm agrees to do, within limits, what the firm asks, without demanding details concerning every work requirement. In short, within the firm many obligations are implicit and flexible, whereas in the marketplace they are more rigid and explicit.

The limitations of bounded rationality often leave firms unprepared to deal with unanticipated contingencies; as the latter arise, the scope for successful opportunistic behavior against the firm is enlarged. As the new circumstances appear, contracts with external agents must be renegotiated, a costly process consuming time and entailing administrative and other expenses in addition to possible agent opportunism. Bounded rationality, then, evokes another group of transaction costs that can be reduced by the formation of a firm. Within a firm the factors of production are more adaptable and the trust bred of continuing association tends to reduce opportunistic efforts.

Moral hazard (shirking) is the final characteristic of transactions that lead to greater costs. It is a form of opportunism arising from the conjunction of team production and the inability to monitor input effort and contribution perfectly. When detailed information is hard to obtain and rewards are not fully tied to productivity, there is a tendency toward shirking or untruthful reporting. In a joint productive effort all individual contributions are shared with every member of the group, whereas the benefits of shirking are enjoyed exclusively by the shirker. Accordingly, there is an asymmetry in incentives that tends to raise costs by reducing relative efforts. Similarly, buyers are subject to moral hazard when it is not easy to determine if a contract has been completely fulfilled. Were problems allegedly encountered by the provider and paid for by the buyer real or merely an excuse to pad bills? Both the Department of Defense and many private businesses have encountered this kind of problem. Whereas adverse selection may be deemed precontractual opportunism, which exploits information asymmetries about future performance, moral hazard represents postcontractual opportunism, which exploits asymmetric information about project implementation.

Like bounded rationality and adverse selection, moral hazard biases the participants and may harm either party in a transaction. Ordinarily one thinks of the principal as the one attempting to repress shirking by an agent, such as the firm's coordinating authority monitoring its employees or sending a quality control expert to sample vendor supplies. However, shirking by the coordinating authority is also possible and perhaps common. In the modern corporation, with the legal owners separated from actual management and with the bulk of managerial rewards not tied to profit maximization, managements may choose a style and modus operandi less demanding than a profit maximization goal would dictate. A corporate "good life," then, may derive from managerial shirking and is likely to result in higher prices to consumers, reduced returns to equity, and lower earnings to the resources employed in the business. This may also be deemed the agency cost of having a particular management team represent stock and bondholders.

A final form of opportunism has been labeled "holdup" and presents itself most frequently when one party must undertake investments somewhat unique to a particular transaction. Specific investments are deemed those that have a much greater value in one use than in any other. If, for example, a supplier has made heavy investments that can really only be employed to produce the special component being demanded, the firm is subject to buyer opportunism. The buyer can pressure the seller to reduce prices or threaten to stop purchasing altogether, leaving the seller with heavy capital outlays that reap no returns. Suppliers are clearly reluctant to make such investments for fear of exploitation. Inducements to do so include charging higher prices (to compensate for the risk) and writing long-term contracts with stiff penalty clauses for buyer withdrawal. Interestingly, defense production often requires such specific investments, but defense transactions have an implicit third party. Not only are a producer and a military buyer involved, but the U.S. Congress as well, with the latter intermittently withholding funding or forcing changes in the procurement. Not surprisingly, with Congress reluctant to permit multiyear contracts, recourse to higher selling prices is a main inducement for firms to remain as defense contractors.

Alternatively, a buyer relying on a sole supplier may be subject to holdup if the supplier believes he or she can justify price increases without losing the customer. Similarly, if a firm makes investments in an employee that are specific to that firm, the employee may attempt to exploit such investment by threatening to leave the organization. If the firm instead requires the employee to make such specific investments, the incentive for opportunism moves the employer. Here again asymmetries in a transaction provide fruitful ground for opportunistic behavior.

To summarize, internal production and markets are alternate modes of organizing transactions. In a world of perfect information there would be little need for firms. Firms, however, are established and broaden their scopes when transacting costs associated with external suppliers become significant. The firm may be viewed as a system of contracts with a coordinating authority that attempts to provide strategic direction as well as promote productivity and meter rewards. The latter two activities may be subsumed under the rubric *monitoring* which combines output (productivity) assessments with an appropriate incentive system. Finally, entrepreneurial functions are involved in strategic direction, and in coordination, and in the continuous adaption by the firm to changing conditions.

LEGAL FORMS OF ENTERPRISES

The U.S. business population is extremely diverse, ranging from big companies, like General Motors, with billions of dollars of sales and hundreds of thousands of employees, to some small business concerns with only one or two workers and very low sales. In addition to size, one measure of classification is legal structure. There are three basic legal forms: proprietorship, partnership, and corporation. Under the first two, owners bear unlimited personal responsibility for any debts that the business concern may incur. Both are relatively easy to form and generally relatively small in size. Corporations, by contrast, are legal entities, distinct and separate from the individuals who own them. The owners are limited in their liability for the corporation's debts to the capital they initially subscribed— that is, the cost of the stock they purchased.

Because of limited liability and a business life independent of the owner, the corporation is by far the most effective form of business organization for raising financial capital. It also generally has the ability to obtain more specialized and more efficient management than can the other two types of enterprises, although operationally it may have less flexibility than partnerships or proprietorships. With such important advantages, corporations occupy the most conspicuous position in modern U.S. capitalism. Many of our major industries are dominated by corporate giants that enjoy assets and annual sales ranging in billions of dollars. Ownership in such corporations is widespread, but owners have little to do with actual operations.

Although proprietorships are the numerically dominant (about 75 percent) legal form of business organization, corporations, which represented only 20 percent of the business population (1982), accounted for more than 90 percent of total business sales. In the early 1980s the average corporation size (measured by constant dollar receipts) was more than ten times that of partnerships, which in turn were four times larger than proprietorships. Corporations also employ far more workers than proprietorships and partnerships. Further, in the last decade the corporation as a legal form has gained in its relative position. Clearly, in terms of economic importance corporations are the dominant form of business organization.

Some additional clarification is warranted. Corporations differ widely in their sizes. One common measure is value of corporate assets, which ranges in categories from under $1 million to over $250 million. The most recent data indicate that small companies (under $1 million in assets) increased by 1.3 million over the 1970–83 period, while all other categories increased by only 9,000. "In 1970, 2.7 percent of all corporations had assets exceeding $10 million (constant 1983 dollars), compared with only 1.4 percent in 1983."[6] Clearly, then, small companies are proliferating and the trend within the overall corporate community has not been for the largest corporations to increasingly dominate. Of course, corporate assets are only one measure of size, but other data are supportive.

In addition to profit-seeking proprietorships, partnerships, and corporations, there are many not-for-profit organizations, such as churches, colleges, charities, labor unions, and so on. They participate in markets producing goods and services and providing job opportunities. Some not-for-profit firms depend on donations for their income, but many receive income from fees and from sales of goods and services. Most of these nonprofit firms are incorporated. However, they have no stockholders and are run by independent boards of trustees whose members are chosen based on the organization's bylaws.

MANUFACTURING TECHNIQUES AND OPERATIONAL CHARACTERISTICS

Because manufacturing is at the center of the industrial sector, it is important to understand its production techniques and operational characteristics. In manufacturing, unit and small batch production are common where the market is limited in size, styling is important, and technical change is very rapid. According to Robert Averitt, the unit and small batch approach includes:

1. production of units to customer's requirements (large electrical generating equipment)
2. production of prototypes (experimental aircraft and automobiles)
3. fabrication of large equipment in stages (major missile systems)
4. production of small batches to customer's orders (dies from the machine tool industry).[7]

This type of production relies on skilled craftspeople who critically affect product quality and set the work pace. Operations tend to be flexible, but costly, while schedules are based on orders received. Prices too are flexible, reflecting market conditions. Once rather pervasive, this type of production has given way to other forms. Nonetheless, given the nature of the demands served, it is unlikely ever to completely pass from the industrial landscape.

Expanding markets evoked a new mode of operation: large batch and mass production techniques. Large numbers of relatively unskilled workers replaced craftspeople, while high-volume production generated standardized outputs. The automobile assembly line is a classic example. In this setting, production efficiencies tend to displace product development as the main managerial concern. Cost minimization is critical for the mass markets necessary for high-volume output. Oligopoly is the typical market structure, with prices often fairly inflexible.

A further development in large batch techniques may be called process production. "When the product is liquid or has liquid properties, as, for example, petroleum, most chemicals, steel, aluminum, and most plastics,"[8] production can be carried out in a continuous flow. "Absolute capital costs soar in process production, making barriers to new firm entry substantial."[9] High plant capacity utilization is essential to spread large fixed costs, and the marketing function becomes critical due to required production volumes and the difficulty and expense involved with storage. Process production greatly reduces the need for unskilled labor, while formal management, previously highly involved in supervision, gives way to more informal procedures involving committees representing various technical capabilities.

Contemporary production generally combines two or more of the aforementioned techniques. Further, automation has blurred some of the practical distinctions between mass and process production, both of which also share a dependence on product flow, large markets, and considerable overhead expense. What is clear, however, is that U.S. manufacturing trends are away from unit and batch efforts, and that managerial systems and emphases differ in mass versus process production operations.

CORPORATE FINANCE

Sources of Capital

Activities of industrial firms both directly affect and are affected by the nation's financial markets. A study of the structure of the industrial sector must involve analysis of the sources and uses of corporate funds. Corporate financing of long-term capital projects normally draws upon external as well as internal sources. Internal sources are composed of retained profits and depreciation allowances. Externally, corporations finance their production activities through the so-called capital markets, which largely deal in corporate and noncorporate bonds, stocks, mortgages, long-term federal obligations, and customers' loans. Bonds, debentures, and notes together with preferred and common stocks make up the external source of the long-term corporate funds.

Table 2.2 reveals that the chief source of funds by far for long-term investment in plant and equipment for the corporate sector has been internal. In only three of the 18 years listed did retained earnings plus depreciation allowances account for less than 80 percent of capital expenditures (column 9). Clearly, U.S. corporate financial policy evidences a dominant preference for internal financing of long-term investment. These data underscore the criticality of tax laws with regard to corporate finance and investment efforts. Capital consumption allowances—depreciation and amortization—provide the lion's share of internal funds. These deductible, noncash expenses shelter revenue from taxes and generally finance well over 60 percent of capital expenditures. Clearly, any government policies that alter depreciation and amortization schedules will impact upon corporate capital spending decisions.

With regard to external financing, the corporate sector has another clear preference. Debt instruments (as opposed to new equity funding) have accounted for the vast bulk of external funds. Traditionally, this has mainly been due to legislation that allows for the tax deductibility of interest paid on borrowing. In contrast, dividends from stockholdings are taxable. Furthermore, the attraction of additional equity capital (by issuing more stocks) will dilute existing stockholder interests, so corporate managements use this tool sparingly. The data, however, reveal an interesting new development. New equity issues have historically been an external source of fresh capital, albeit far smaller than borrowed funds. But beginning in 1978 the figure turned negative. The value of stock bought back by nonfinancial corporations exceeded by a small amount the new stock issued. In the eleven years following 1977, nine witnessed negative values for net new equity funding, including a record $130.5 billion for 1988. This new phenomenon is associated with the leveraged buyout and merger/acquisition activities of recent years. Accordingly, borrowed funds, which have been the predominant source of outside capital prior to 1977, have since become virtually the only source. It should be stressed, however, that this corporate cash drain does not mean an equivalent loss of investment funds from the economy. Instead, such funds will appear in other investment vehicles and locations as the recipients reallocate and redeploy their investment portfolios.

Thus, in addition to being producing entities, firms both generate and allocate capital. While internal funds are responsible for the major portion of business investment, outside sources are employed as well. Here is another situation in which the firm must again decide whether to produce in-house (utilize its own funds) or tap external suppliers. Allocation of such funds by the coordinating authority is done on the basis of its own strategic vision and the information at its disposal. Interestingly, transaction and information costs are an important cause of businesses employing internal funds so extensively despite the "borrowing bias" of U.S. tax laws. Firms have a fuller knowledge of the details, probabilities, and risks of their own investments than do outside lenders. The latter, understanding adverse selection, moral hazard, and bounded rationality, are wary of opportunistic borrowers and thus act conservatively when committing their monies.

Table 2.2
Sources and Uses of Nonfinancial Corporate Funds, 1970–87

YEAR	INTERNAL SOURCES			EXTERNAL SOURCES			Ext. & Int. ($ BILL) (3)+(6)	Capital Expenditures** ($BILL)	Ratio (3) to (8)	Ratio (2) to (8)	Ratio (4) to (8)
	Adjusted Retained Earnings ($ BILL)	CCA* ($ BILL)	Total ($ BILL)	New Borrowing ($ BILL)	Net New Equity ($ BILL)	Total ($ BILL)					
	(1)	(2)	(3)	(4)	(5)	(6)	(7)	(8)	(9)	(10)	(11)
1970	14.5	49.9	62.8	28.4	5.7	34.1	96.9	79.2	0.79	0.63	0.36
1971	20.3	54.8	74.7	25.9	11.4	37.3	112.0	85.1	0.88	0.64	0.30
1972	27.4	60.1	86.4	31.5	10.9	42.4	128.8	95.0	0.91	0.63	0.33
1973	43.3	65.2	93.9	68.4	7.9	76.3	170.2	119.0	0.79	0.55	0.57
1974	51.1	76.3	89.3	50.8	4.1	54.9	144.2	138.6	0.64	0.55	0.37
1975	50.8	91.9	124.8	13.2	9.9	23.1	147.9	112.3	1.11	0.82	0.12
1976	65.1	102.3	142.0	40.1	10.5	50.6	192.6	156.9	0.91	0.65	0.26
1977	76.7	114.3	165.1	66.7	2.7	68.8	233.9	179.6	0.92	0.64	0.37
1978	89.1	129.8	182.3	71.0	.1	70.9	253.2	217.0	0.84	0.60	0.33
1979	105.2	149.6	197.6	69.0	-7.8	61.2	258.8	238.3	0.83	0.63	0.29
1980	88.1	171.3	200.1	57.8	-12.9	44.9	245.0	243.7	0.82	0.70	0.24
1981	78.7	198.8	239.5	102.1	-11.5	90.6	228.0	286.5	0.84	0.69	0.45
1982	39.7	221.4	242.3	43.4	6.4	49.8	248.7	256.5	0.94	0.86	0.17
1983	52.4	228.2	285.7	54.4	23.5	77.9	363.6	270.7	1.06	0.84	0.20
1984	72.7	238.4	336.3	170.3	-74.5	95.8	432.1	370.6	0.91	0.64	0.46
1985	47.8	251.0	352.3	132.4	-81.5	50.9	403.2	342.3	1.03	0.73	0.39
1986	38.2	262.6	357.5	202.1	-80.8	121.3	478.8	331.5	1.08	0.79	0.61
1987	52.4	274.7	352.8	145.0	-76.5	68.5	421.3	361.0	0.98	0.76	0.40

* Capital consumption allowances (depreciation and amortization).
** Plant and equipment, residential structures, inventory investment, and mineral rights from U.S. Government.
Sources: Council of Economic Advisors, *Economic Report of the President* (Washington, D.C.: U.S. Government Printing Office, January 1989), p. 414; Federal Reserve Bank Statistical Release, *Nonfinancial Corporate Business* (Washington, D.C.: Federal Reserve Bank, June 21, 1989).

Accordingly, in some instances few or no funds may be provided, making business investment impossible unless internal capital is employed. In other instances, capital may be obtained, but the risk premium built into the lenders' interest charges may make the use of outside funds unappealing, if not prohibitive.

The financial function and activities of U.S. corporations have greatly changed, becoming far more complex over the past 20 years. The structure of corporate finance has become more debt-oriented, with total corporate bond issues almost quadrupling from 1970 to 1985. In 1986 nonfinancial corporations raised a record of $121.3 billion via credit of some form. In 1987 and 1988 the figure dropped into the $60+ billion range, numbers very much akin to the late 1970s.[10] When measured in book value terms, corporate debt-equity ratios have risen steadily in recent years. Figure 2.1, however, shows this ratio measured at market values and depicts a different perspective. The 1970s witnessed explosive growth because of the substantial increase in debt coupled with the relatively depressed value of the stock market. Despite continuing growth in debt, however, the market valued ratio has declined in the 1980s, in large measure due to a rising stock market. Accordingly, Federal Reserve Chairman Alan Greenspan was able to note in his February 21, 1989, report to the Congress that "the overall corporate debt-to-equity ratio is not out of line with observations since the early 1970s. . . ."[11] If one further adjusts for inflation and changes in the ability of assets to generate cash, the debt-equity ratio has fallen substantially. "In 1985, for example, the estimated market value debt-equity ratio for U.S. corporations was .37, compared with .61 in 1974 and an average of .46 for the period 1975–84."[12] Therefore, while the use of debt instruments has grown steadily, appropriate adjustment casts this trend in a far less worrisome light.

A potential factor making for instability, however, is the percentage of business cash flow absorbed by interest payments. This figure averaged roughly 21 percent from 1980 to 1987, but rose to 25 percent in 1988.[13] In the event of a recession, with its concomitant reduced cash flows, the likelihood of business insolvencies increases with higher fixed interest payments. However, it is unclear as to whether or not this new, higher proportion is temporary or a new plateau. Further, if stock prices remain relatively strong, the ability to offer new issues can be an important source of liquidity, as can asset sales or various arrangements with the banking community. Corporate financial assets, for example, increased by $200 billion over the 1986–87 period.[14]

More troubling to many, however, is the quality of corporate debt. In recent years high-yield debentures, those paying relatively high rates due to the market's assessment of the risks involved—the so-called junk bonds—have gained great notoriety. Dispassionate analysis, however, suggests that public concerns have been greatly exaggerated. Although experiencing great growth, these issues, which do not qualify for investment grade ratings, are still not a significant portion of total corporate debt, rising from 4 percent in 1979 to 9 percent by 1985. "Since only 6 percent of the roughly 11,000 public corporations in the United States qualify for investment grade ratios,"[15] these issues have made available new,

Figure 2.1
Debt to Equity Ratios of Nonfinancial Corporations*

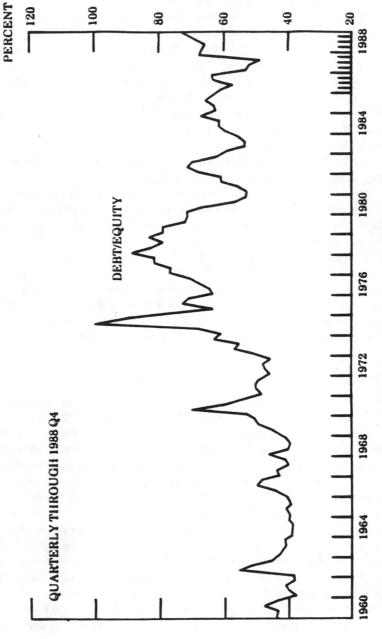

* Debt and equity are at market value. In computing net worth, tangible assets are valued at replacement cost or market value while financial assets are valued at cost.

Source: Alan Greenspan, ''Monetary Report to Congress,'' Board of Governors of the Federal Reserve System, February 21, 1989, p. 13.

albeit expensive, financing sources. Whether or not the typical cost of funds is commensurate with the risk (whether they have been "worth it") is an empirical question. Thus far, the studies suggest that they have. Between 1980 and 1986 "employment, productivity, sales, and capital spending at companies that issued junk bonds all improved at rates substantially higher than those of U.S. industry in general."[16] Capital outlays in these firms ran at a rate more than twice the national average. Apparently, the investment funds made available by junk bonds have thus far been channeled into high-yielding projects, ones sufficient to pay for themselves and the associated interest costs.

In short, junk bonds are still a relatively small portion of total corporate borrowing. Only minor portions have been used to finance acquisitions. Most finance ongoing business activities. They have opened up a new avenue of funding, have performed relatively well, and have thus far created little harm or vulnerability, despite public perceptions to the contrary.[17]

Lastly some elaboration of tax influences is warranted. Already mentioned is the bias toward debt because corporations can deduct interest payments from their tax liabilities. U.S. law also includes tax "shields," which allow other deductions from taxable income. This list is long and has included items such as tax loss carry-forwards, investment tax credits, and accelerated depreciation. The greater a firm's tax shields are, the less likely it is to finance via debt because tax shields reduce the value of interest deductibility. Interestingly, recent U.S. tax legislation has reduced corporate income tax rates, thus lessening the bias toward debt, but at the same time it also reduced or eliminated many tax shields, which favor equity financing. At this juncture the net impact is unclear.

Capital Expenditures

Outlays on plant and equipment represent business investment that directly contributes to capital formation. They are vital to the growth of the economy. Such expenditures not only improve productivity and stimulate employment opportunities, but also encourage investment in inventive and innovative undertakings.

Capital expenditures for new plant and equipment by manufacturing industries amounted to $74.6 billion in 1982, about 30 percent of the U.S. total in this category. This amount was distributed almost evenly among durable and nondurable goods industries. The combined new capital expenditure of industries producing chemicals, machinery, and transportation equipment represented almost 44 percent of total industrial investment. The chemicals industry led the manufacturing sector, with more than $9 billion of investment. The preliminary data for 1987 show manufacturing capital outlays increasing to almost $80.5 billion. Transportation equipment led the way with almost $11 billion, followed by chemicals, electrical machinery, and food products, the latter two investing more than $7 billion.[18] Since the late 1970s capital expenditures in high tech industries have become a major source of the nation's capital formation.

INDUSTRIAL DISTRIBUTION AND CONCENTRATION

In 1984 there were some 12.9 million nonfarm proprietorships and partnerships in the United States, along with 3.2 million incorporated enterprises. Yet these small numbers of corporations, as mentioned previously, are large producers of both goods and services. According to data from the Internal Revenue Service, in manufacturing, communications, transportation, and banking industries, more than half of all corporate assets are controlled by enterprises with assets of $250 million or more.[19] On the other hand, firms in agriculture, real estate, construction, and services are relatively small in size.

The 1977 Census of Manufacturers revealed that those big manufacturers with 1,000 employees or more accounted for less than 1 percent of business establishments, but provided 28 percent of total manufacturing employment, with a total payroll of $86 billion, or 35 percent of total wage and salary compensation in the manufacturing industry. More than one-third of value-added and shipments originated from these large manufacturing enterprises. According to *Fortune* magazine, the 800 largest firms from manufacturing, banking, finance, insurance, retailing, transportation, and public utilities comprise only 0.01 percent of the American business population, but they have total assets of $3 trillion, or about one-half the nation's total wealth, and employ approximately one-fourth of the entire labor force.[20]

What are the trends? In terms of manufacturing assets held by the 100 and 200 largest corporations, there was a steady increase in their share over the years from 1929 to 1960. In 1960 the largest 100 firms held 45.5 percent of manufacturing assets. This proportion edged upward during subsequent years, peaking at 50 percent in 1987 and dropping to 49 percent in 1988. The 200 largest firms have evidenced more annual variation, but no particular trend since 1968 when they held 60.4 percent of all manufacturing assets. In 1988 the figure was 61.1.[21] A different measure of aggregate concentration is the percentage of manufacturing value-added by the top 100 firms. This figure, which rose from 23 percent in 1947 to 30 percent in 1958, has remained at roughly 33 percent from 1963 through the 1980s.[22] In short, in terms of asset concentration there has been little change in the aggregate manufacturing sector over the past 25 years. Value-added, which is far less concentrated, has also been relatively stable.

Employment is even less concentrated in the hands of the largest manufacturing corporations than value-added. In 1986, more than 55 percent of those working in the industrial sector found their jobs in the smaller firms with less than 100 employees. Almost half of these small firms have no more than 20 workers. The less than proportionate employment in the leading producers in the manufacturing industries reflects their extensive use of capital-intensive production processes that turn out high value-added products.

What about concentration of assets in all of U.S. industry (excluding financial institutions), not just manufacturing? The latest data show a clear reduction trend. While the 50 largest firms held roughly 23 percent of all assets over the 1958-77 period, a downward trend set in during the late 1970s. By 1985 the figure had fallen to 19.1 percent. The top 100 firms held around 30 percent for years, but by 1985 were down to 25.5 percent. The top 200 firms fell from 40 percent of assets in 1958 to 32.3 percent in 1985.[23]

Three points of significance should be drawn from these data. First, the manufacturing sector is clearly more concentrated than the U.S. economy in general. Second, aggregate concentration of assets measures, for whatever they tell us, do not point to an increasing concentration trend. Rather, the figures have been relatively stable in the manufacturing sector and clearly declining in the overall economy. Finally, it remains to be stressed that aggregate concentration measures (those encompassing all industries), while often quoted in the press and used in political rhetoric, are of little value in explaining or predicting economic actions or events. On the other hand, concentration data and trends in particular markets may well have explanatory usefulness.

Some manufacturing firms have attained positions approaching monopoly for a considerable length of time. IBM, for example, accounted for 72–82 percent of market share of general-purpose digital computer systems during the 1960s and early 1970s; Dow Chemical produced 90 percent of U.S. magnesium until 1969; General Motors produced 77 percent of diesel locomotives between 1956 and 1971. There are many other big manufacturing companies that control a significant percent of the total market. According to the Bureau of the Census, in half of the manufacturing industries, the leading four firms control more than 40 percent of the market in their individual industries. This half of U.S. manufacturing industries can be considered to be oligopolistic.

It should be noted that the big corporations in the top ranks have experienced turnover and changed relative positions. Movement up and down on the list of the largest corporation is related to broad shifts in the pattern of national demands. As the U.S. economy transited from a period when food and basic clothing represented principal items in the average consumer's budget into an era of automobiles, aircraft, and electronics, relative demands changed accordingly. Those industries and firms enjoying higher consumers' demand tend to gain in relative importance. Further, from the perspective of comparatively long periods, say 50 years, the industrial structure appears remarkably fluid, with new names rising to the list of giant firms while others fall in importance.

INDUSTRIAL LOCATION

Industries are distributed unevenly in the U.S. economy. Historically, regional features such as terrain, geology, access to navigable waterways, and climate have been important factors affecting the growth of an industry in a region or state. Over time, the relative importance of these features has changed. Access to waterways, for example, became less important as railroad and highway transportation became available and economical. In recent years, other economic factors also came into play to effect a firm's location decision. U.S. manufacturing activities were once concentrated in the Northeast region, which consists of New England and the Middle Atlantic states. At the turn of this century, this area accounted for half of the nation's manufacturing employment and value-added. Since that time, the Northeast has continuously lost its employment share, while the North Central region—Ohio, Indiana, Illinois, Michigan, and Wisconsin—stengthened its position and became a leading industrial arena. By the late 1940s it surpassed the Northeast in the share of manufacturing value-added. But these older urban centers in the Northeast and Midwest became less attractive places in which to invest in the late 1960s and 1970s due to relatively older factories, high wages, high taxes, and high energy cost. By the early 1980s, however, a number of this region's important industries, to include steel, autos, and machine tools, were experiencing major problems and decline, the "rust belt" phenomena. Capital flowed elsewhere—first to the suburbs, but more recently to the Sunbelt, the West Coast, and overseas. Finally, as industrialization spread into the South and the West, these latter two regions have gained substantially in relative importance, with the rise in the Sun Belt coming mainly at the expense of the North Central region.

While there are many reasons why some regions grow more rapidly than others, one important source of differential development is dependence upon growing or shrinking industries. As the Federal Reserve of San Francisco has reported,

states with defense-oriented economies performed quite well through most of the 1980s, as federal spending for weapons systems and military supplies rose. For example, California received 23 percent of the nation's defense contract awards in 1984. Thus, it is not surprising that California's employment growth averaged 2.5 percent per year between 1980 and 1987, compared with average growth of 1.8 percent nationally.[24]

Conversely, concentration on industries suffering shrinkage can be highly detrimental. Alaska, Texas, and Louisiana, for example, have been quite depressed. "In the two years following the oil price plunge of early 1986 employment fell 7.6 percent in Alaska and 2.3 percent in Texas."[25] Property values have also declined and financial institutions in these regions have been placed in precarious positions.

BUSINESS SIZE, SCOPE, AND ENTRY BARRIERS

As already noted, there is a concentration of economic power in the major industries of the U.S. industrial sector. In a market with concentration, there generally exist entry barriers. One well known barrier is patent rights, which grant a legal basis to be the sole producer for a period of time. Such rights facilitate dominance of a market by one or a few firms and make entry by newcomers difficult or impossible. Examples can be found in such industries as shoe machinery, copying machines, telephone equipment, photographic materials, synthetic fibers, and some pharmaceuticals.

Another factor that could lead to concentrated market structures is the existence of substantial scale economies.[26] Scale refers to size. Both economic theory and empirical observation suggest that operating costs in some industries may vary with business size. Scale economies occur when larger-sized firms have lower per unit production costs than smaller ones. If, however, the optimal size firm is big relative to the potential market, there is insufficient business volume to accommodate a great number of producers. Accordingly, market supply will be concentrated in a small number of firms that can manufacture and market their products at lower average cost per unit than smaller ones. In the manufacturing sector, scale economies have led to various oligopolistic markets in such industries as refrigerators, passenger automobiles, tractors, typewriters, diesel engines, and so forth.

Ownership of essential raw materials can create monopoly in the product market if the raw materials source restricts its sales. For example, the Aluminum Company of America at one time had a virtual monopoly position in that industry because it owned almost all the basic sources of bauxite. International Nickel Company of Canada once controlled roughly 90 percent of the world's known nickel reserves. Accordingly, control of essential raw materials can constitute a significant entry barrier.

Perhaps the most significant barriers are legal, most commonly found in fields such as public utilities. Local governments will often allow only one local telephone company or one electricity supplier. In the airline industry during the period of regulation, the Civil Aeronautics Board frequently granted monopoly status to various carriers servicing particular (generally low traffic) routes.

Financial demands may also represent an entry barrier. When start-up costs are relatively low, it may be fairly easy to commence production. On the other hand, if minimally efficient size and technical demands require enormous dollar outlays, it is clearly more risky (difficult) to enter the industry. For example, a new computer chip factory may today cost more than $250 million, a capital commitment of substantial magnitude.

Finally, control over the distribution systems may serve as a significant impediment for new entrants. Indeed, this is a common complaint leveled by foreign companies attempting to gain a foothold in the Japanese market today. With the exception of legal restrictions, however, barriers to entry are rarely complete. Instead, they are a matter of degree. The greater the barriers, the more likely the market will approach oligopoly or monopoly conditions.

Business size is also a function of information hurdles, specifically the gathering and processing of relevant data. Because information is costly to obtain, it is an obstacle to efficient exchange and the growth of firm size. To the degree that communications gains have made information more readily available (telephone costs, for example, are roughly 5 percent of what they were 35 years ago), they have facilitated increases in business size. Interestingly, the tremendous growth of information flows in the past 20 years has today often made processing the greater challenge and there are many situations in which available data far outweigh the firm's ability to effectively digest and process. Additionally, as businesses grow larger and the information chain lengthens, there is increased likelihood of information distortion, a condition complicating decisions at the top and serving as a limiting factor on enterprise growth.

In terms of the organizational characteristics of production, business growth may occur horizontally, vertically, or in conglomerate fashion. "Generally speaking the production process can be divided into three stages: the assembly stage, the subassembly stage, and the component stage; at each there is a separate tier of factories and businesses."[27] These separate tiers may or may not be a part of the firm. This is the challenge of deciding whether to procure in the marketplace or to produce within the firm. If the choice is external procurement, decisions as to the kinds of suppliers and relationships—close, long-term ties to one or two suppliers, short-term arrangements with many sources, and such—must be made. Alternately, firms may opt for internal production and do so by some form of business integration.

Horizontal integration may take the form of a merger between directly competing firms. It consists of the replication of the same stage of the same production process. A manufacturer building an additional plant to produce the same products is one example. Another is the merger of airline companies. Horizontal integration enables a successful business to expand and continue specializing in what it has done well. It also allows the spreading of many administrative or advertising overheads.

Vertical integration, on the other hand, combines different stages of the production process. A corporation can integrate backward by acquiring firms producing its raw materials and semifinished inputs. This is also known as upstream integration. Conversely, it can integrate forward by moving toward further processing and/or wholesaling and retailing operations. This is also referred to as downstream integration, a move that brings the business closer to the ultimate customer. The petroleum industry is a classic example of a field integrated in both backward and forward directions. Major refiners own oil reserves (upstream) as well as service station outlets (downstream). Some degree of vertical integration is present in almost all firms, although the expression "vertically integrated producers" is generally reserved for those with several, clear stages of production under a common ownership.

Vertical integration has several aims. It minimizes transaction costs associated with purchasing and marketing functions and it promotes the pooling of R & D (research and development) and design efforts. It can also reduce the uncertainties that firms face in both input and output markets. Finally, there are a number of possible synergisms and other benefits that may be engendered.

Conglomerate integration takes the form of combining activities from entirely different markets; it tends to be diversification oriented. In 1968, the peak year of one massive merger movement, mergers were mainly conglomerate. Gulf + Western, for example, which began the 1960s as an automotive bumper manufacturer, acquired some 80 firms by 1968, to include businesses as disparate as

Madison Square Garden, New Jersey Zinc, and Paramount Pictures. Other examples abound. DuPont moved from its original specialty (explosives) into synthetic fibers, plastics, and paints; Procter & Gamble, besides producing soap, has taken up food and paper products. In recent decades, cigarette companies have diversified into chewing gum, snack foods, wine, distilled liquid, and pet food. The major incentive for a corporation to diversify is to spread risk and make use of its established capabilities in new lines of business. In general, the big industrial corporations at the top of the rankings tend to be more diversified than smaller firms.

VERTICAL INTEGRATION, INFORMATION, AND MONITORING

The decision to procure externally or internally turns on several factors. If (1) monitoring costs are low, (2) the product is standardized, (3) relations with suppliers have been long-term and close, and (4) suppliers value a "good reputation," then one can rely on inputs from external vendors without undue risk of adverse selection or moral hazard. But these conditions require both the existence of quality suppliers and knowledge concerning the composition and quality of the items involved. If there is only one, or perhaps two, suppliers, as is often the case in defense and high tech work, the risks become greater and there is a much stronger incentive for backward integration. Similarly, firms may backward integrate in order to gain knowledge of the product they are buying so that information asymmetries associated with external procurement can be reduced. Then they utilize both the outside suppliers and their own production, having a much greater knowledge of how to monitor and assess external procurements. This is common in the electronics industry. Alternatively, the buyer may send inspectors and technical personnel to the suppliers' production operations. Such monitoring efforts are very prevalent in defense procurement, but are also found in many civilian fields as well.

The use of markets will also be cumbersome where bounded rationality looms large. If, for example, a firm attempted to purchase research and development services from another organization, the inherent uncertainties of this type of service coupled with the "distance" outsiders have from the purchasing entity make it difficult to design, execute, and enforce such contracts.

Regarding forward integration, such as manufacturers going into retailing, the more homogeneous the outputs, the less likely it is that such moves will take place. With standardized products the traditional producer-wholesaler-retailer chain works well and transaction costs are minimal. However, if a manufacturer cares where or how his goods are retailed (perhaps because faulty handling can damage them or a particular image is supposed to be associated with the product), transaction costs rise. Such cases can be addressed either by the manufacturer sending monitors to or training the retailers (a practice common to franchising operations), or by forward integration, where the producer can more easily control handling and image-creating activities at the retail level. In short, integration tends to result when the costs of monitoring market exchanges exceed those of internal supply.

Vertical integration can occur for other reasons as well. A prime one is to manage environmental uncertainty. Many resource-dependent producers, for example, have backward integrated in order to reduce supply uncertainties arising from economic fragility of sources, political risks deriving from foreign procurement, and so on. Owning one's own supply base is also a defensive maneuver to offset opportunistic recontracting due to transaction-specific investments (holdup) and asymmetric information. Additionally, it reduces pre- and post-contractual bargaining costs. This also applies to forward integration. Finally, forward integration is a means of getting closer to the ultimate customer and thereby gaining valuable information concerning market desires, trends, and product receptiveness.

It has been argued that vertical integration may deprive a company of the benefits of having several suppliers who compete on the basis of price, quality, and R&D as they strive for additional sales.[28] It may also distract management from strategic decision making and from areas of its greatest expertise. Despite these possible limitations, vertical integration is a central feature of the U.S. industrial landscape, although measurement problems prevent us from knowing its frequency with any great precision. Michael Gort, in a classic study of 111 large firms, estimated vertical integration to range from a low of 10 percent in the transportation industry to a high of 67 percent in petroleum.[29] Other research has found vertical integration to be unrelated either to the business cycle,[30] market concentration,[31] or firm size.[32] This suggests that the potential advantages discussed earlier seem to be the main motivating impulses.

It has recently been suggested that the major sources of productivity advance today are now coming from the subassembly and components stages of the manufacturing process.[33] These gains have taken two main forms: (1) a tremendous reduction in the number of components and parts, and (2) subassemblies that have a better "fit" with each other. There are important synergisms between component producers and subassemblers and between subassemblers and assemblers. Close working relationships between tiers of production are very important and can be achieved either through stable long-term relationships between firms or via vertical integration. Unfortunately, the costs involved in introducing advanced technology at the components stage are soaring and many independent producers are likely to be unable to continue in business if present trends remain. This will leave fewer, although probably larger, components producers in the market. Even these, however, are likely to be squeezed financially. "Since most of the technology content of end products is in components, where earnings are shallow, major producers of technologically sophisticated goods will have to compete more aggressively for world leadership in component development and production—something the Japanese companies have been doing all along."[34] This tends to mandate an integrated business in which there are assured cash flows to component production to assure a stream of advanced components to end product manufacturers. With acute financial pressures on lower tier businesses, the alternatives for end product producers may well be either the procurement of components from their vertically integrated competitors or queuing to await supplies from relatively distant (in business relationship sense) sources.

Government revenue policies may also play a role in integration endeavors. If market transactions are taxed, such as a sales tax, the desire to minimize such levies biases firms toward vertical integration. Further, as long as the business losses of an acquired firm can reduce the income taxes of an acquiring entity, such tax laws will also promote integration. It is of interest to note that the Tax Reform Act of 1986 contained provisions that reduced the income tax benefits of merger activities.

Finally, firms might vertically integrate to avoid the effects of price controls. If a government ceiling price were imposed on an item in relatively short supply, the integrated firm is more likely not to have its source dry up as it continues to supply the parent company but rations output to others. This motive is really a subset of the environmental uncertainty problem discussed earlier.

CONGLOMERATES

Conglomerates are formed for a variety of reasons. In large measure they may be explained as one means of facing bounded rationality. Such integration is primarily a diversification procedure in a world of uncertainty and structural and cyclical change. If a business is wholly rooted in one industry, a slowdown in that field can be very damaging. On the other hand, if it operates in a variety of fields, weakness in one may be offset by growth in another.

Firms also become conglomerate when their strategic direction changes. Management may sense that the company's traditional area will no longer be a growth field, perhaps due to changing demographics, shifting comparative advantage, new technologies, or evolving consumer tastes. Accordingly, it branches out to new areas while still maintaining production in its historic arena as well. The United States Steel Corporation (now USX) is a prime example.

Additionally, technological and marketing skills are quite important today and many such capabilities can be transferred or applied across a broad spectrum of industries. Consequently, it may be feasible to move into other fields in which the organization believes it can successfully transfer and deploy the expertise it already possesses.

Financial considerations may also be a stimulus. Conglomerate mergers may take place to avoid the transaction costs involved in going into the capital market. Thus, firms may "raid" a "cash cow" and attempt to "milk" its funds and deploy them elsewhere. Further, as previously mentioned, tax laws that enable an acquiring firm to reduce or eliminate its own tax liabilities will also encourage conglomerate integration.

Finally, the motivation for conglomerate integration may derive from the ambitions of strong corporate leaders and managements. A part of the ethos of corporate America seems to be that greater status is accorded those who manage larger entities—for example, the greater the number of employees or sales volume, the more esteemed the associated managerial status seems to be. Aggressive corporate leaders tend to be optimistic in their assessments of the problems and prospects for new acquisitions. Conglomerate mergers offer a fertile outlet for such energies, one that runs a far lower risk of antitrust complications than would similar efforts at horizontal or even vertical integration.

Two important social functions are associated with conglomerates. First they can serve to monitor or restrain the misuse of managerial discretion. In today's large corporations, with management generally well insulated from ownership control, the investors' capital may be misallocated or hoarded by opportunistic managements. The ability of the principals (owners) to monitor the agents (management) has become quite muted in today's megacorporations. Such managements, however, if absorbed by a conglomerate, must then justify their capital allocations and corporate strategy to the acquiring company, which can far more easily supervise and assess the acquired company's activities. As William Dugger observes, "the central office can do better than stockholders, because the stockholders are treated as outsiders when they seek sensitive performance information while the central office cannot be so treated."[35] Interestingly, it is not only the occurrence of conglomerate merger, but the threat of such takeover as well that may serve to keep managements on their toes. On the other hand there is no guarantee that positive social benefits will ensue. Dugger continues:

This does not mean that the benefits of doing so will be passed on to consumers and/or stockholders. Quite the contrary is often the case: Consumers find that the prices they pay actually rise and stockholders find that the returns they receive actually decline. . . . The central office managers of a conglomerate can raid the treasury of the acquired corporation to feather their own personal nests. . . .[36]

It is therefore not perfectly clear whether the potential for greater efficiency will be realized or whether the new overseers will also be equally guilty of wasteful opportunism.

Second, large conglomerates often serve as self-contained (or partially so) capital markets. The central management allocates capital among the many corporate subsidiaries. Having access to inside information, conglomerate managers should be more efficient in allocations than individual investors or the capital markets, both of which are more distant and must rely on far more limited (and probably biased) information, which they are naturally inclined to discount. Thus, conglomerate capital transfers will tend to be both more rapid and at lower cost than those from outside investors.

To the degree that business integration becomes relatively more important, decisions will increasingly be removed from the marketplace and undertaken within the firm by an administrative hierarchy. In short, the scope of the market will tend to diminish as the purview of the firm expands. Conglomerate capital allocations are a prime example of transactions previously accomplished almost wholly in the financial markets but that now are substantially done within business enterprises.

MERGERS, ACQUISITIONS, AND THE MARKET FOR CORPORATE CONTROL

During the twentieth century the U.S. economy has experienced four distinct periods of heightened merger activity. The first wave, spanning roughly 1895–1905, primarily involved horizontal combinations and resulted in the formation of many very large firms and concentrated markets. For example, AT&T, U.S. Steel, and American Tobacco were created during this period. The second wave took place during the decade of the 1920s and early 1930s. Although primarily horizontal in nature, there were many vertical combinations as well. This cluster involved a larger number of mergers, both at its peak and over the whole period, than did the first wave. By the early 1930s, national oligopoly markets were firmly entrenched.

The third wave began in the mid-1960s and continued through the very early 1970s, peaking about 1968. The horizontal mergers of this period generally encompassed relatively smaller firms rather than the combinations of more dominant businesses that characterized earlier activities. More important during this period were conglomerate combinations, which rose from just under 20 percent of mergers in the second half of the 1920s to roughly 80 percent over the 1966–75 period. Most major U.S. conglomerates were established during this wave. Significant vertical integration also occurred in the oil industry.

The 1980s have witnessed yet another intensification of merger and acquisition activities. The very large number of firms involved coupled with enormous capital outlays, publicity, and visibility in the financial markets have given this wave considerable public attention. Interestingly, although the actual number of mergers increased very substantially over earlier periods (a condition characterizing each preceding wave), when placed in the perspective of the substantially larger economy, recent activities are really quite subdued. If one adjusts the number of mergers by billion dollars of real GNP, the period at the turn of the century was by far the most significant, with the succeeding wave (particularly during the second half of the 1920s) in second place. Peak merger activities during the third and fourth waves are far smaller and relatively similar by this measure. If another standard—value of assets acquired as a share of GNP—is employed, the first wave is again far away the largest, while all others (except for the late 1960s) appear roughly equal and relatively small. Accordingly, despite the fanfare and megadollars involved in current merger and acquisition undertakings, it was at the beginning of this century that such activities had their greatest relative economic impact.[37] The dollars involved during the past several years have nonetheless been mindboggling. Table 2.3 shows major activities during 1985. The largest acquisition that year turned out to be relatively small compared to the five times larger RJR Nabisco deal of 1988.

Interestingly, despite the large number of combinations in the 1980s, "there has been no noticeable impact on industrial or overall corporate concentration."[38] This can be explained in large part by the associated divestiture activities—a record of 1,200 divestitures in 1986 valued at almost $60 billion—which are also part of the merger and acquisition process. Since one company's acquisition is frequently another company's divestiture, it is somewhat anomalous that public outcries seem to focus only on acquisition and not the other side of the coin. This does not, however, prove that mergers have been a net benefit to society. The issue of social costs and benefits is a very complex one and is the subject of significant debate among scholars.

The activities and nature of the market for corporate control—as well as the new jargon that has accompanied its rise—merit brief attention. Essentially, a corporate raider makes a public tender offer to the shareholders of the target company, offering a price in excess of the current stock market value. If enough shares are tendered, the raider will purchase them and acquire controlling interest in the target organization. The latter's management is likely to negotiate with the raider. If mutually satisfactory arrangements are forthcoming, management will endorse the tender offer (perhaps trying to "sweeten" it during negotiations) and it will be deemed a friendly takeover. Alternatively, if negotiations fail, target managements can utilize company funds and the weight of their authority and offices to oppose what is then deemed a hostile takeover.

Defensive activities include legal actions, newspaper advertising, and a variety of financial manipulations. Managements may ask for "golden parachutes," provisions that grant incumbent managers lavish payments if they are terminated by the new owners. Presumably, such protection will eliminate management bias and fear of personal economic loss, thereby freeing it to negotiate the best deal possible for the shareholders. Target managements may seek out a "white knight," an organization that aids the target company either through loans or as a preferred merger partner. Managements may sell attractive corporate assets, distribute cash to current shareholders, or take on additional debt. Such actions have been labeled "poison pills" because they are taken to make the target company less desirable. The previously discussed junk bonds are below-investment-grade obligations issued by corporate raiders in order to raise sufficient money to accomplish the tender offer. Target management may decide to pay "greenmail," which is the repurchase of its own shares at premium prices from the potential raider. "Super poison puts" are the newest wrinkle,[39] but it is to be expected that this market and its participants will continue to produce financial innovations and techniques until virtually all opportunities are exhausted or until the government decides to reduce the pace and scope of activities.

The interpretation and enforcement of antitrust laws clearly influence the size and nature of merger activities. Interpretations have varied over time, depending

Table 2.3
Billion-Dollar Deals Closed in 1985

BUYER	SELLER	TRANSACTION TYPE	VALUE (In billions)
Phillip Morris	General Foods	Acquisition	$5.75
Royal Dutch/Shell Group	Shell Oil	Acquisition	5.67
General Motors	Hughes Aircraft	Acquisition	5.20
Allied	Signal	Acquisition	5.00
R.J. Reynolds Industries	Nabisco Brands	Acquisition	4.90
Baxter Travenol Laboratories	American Hospital Supply	Acquisition	3.80
Capital Cities Communications	American Broadcasting	Acquisition	3.50
Nestle SA	Carnation	Acquisition	3.00
Monsanto	G.D. Searle	Acquisition	2.80
Coastal	American Natural Resources	Acquisition	2.46
InterNorth	Houston Natural Gas	Acquisition	2.26
Kohlberg, Kravis, Roberts	Storer Communications	Leveraged Buyout	1.90
HHF	Levi Strauss	Leveraged Buyout	1.85
Pantry Pride	Revlon	Acquisition	1.80
Olympia & York, Developments	Chevron (Gulf Canada unit)	Divestiture	1.80
Kohlberg, Kravis, Roberts	Allied (50% interest in Union Texas Petroleum)	Leveraged Buyout/ Divestiture	1.80
Rockwell International	Allen-Bradley	Acquisition	1.65
Cooper Industries	McGraw-Edison	Acquisition	1.50
Farley Metals	Northwest Industries	Leveraged Buyout	1.40
Textron	Avco	Acquisition	1.40
Chesebrough-Ponds	Stauffer Chemical	Acquisition	1.30
Cox Enterprises	Cox Communications	Acquisition	1.26
Procter & Gamble	Richardson-Vicks	Acquisition	1.24
MidCon	United Energy Resources	Acquisition	1.14
BASF AG	United Technologies (Inmont unit)	Divestiture	1.00
Wickes	Gulf & Western (consumer and industrial products group)	Divestiture	1.00

Source: *Wall Street Journal*, January 2, 1986, p. 6B.

upon economic conditions, public sentiments, and the political philosophies of various administrations. Since 1950, however, intraindustry acquisitions by firms with substantial market shares have been frowned upon by the antitrust authorities. This has tended to channel mergers into vertical and conglomerate directions. The Reagan administration took a rather benign posture concerning business combinations, undoubtedly a contributing factor in the spurt of the 1980s.

Mere acquiescence by the antitrust authorities, however, is insufficient to explain such heightened activities in the market for corporate control. Clearly, a major motivating force in the late 1970s and early 1980s was the depressed stock market, which created a situation in which it was sometimes cheaper to obtain production capabilities by buying existing companies rather than building new facilities. The process has sometimes been described as "digging for oil on Wall Street instead of Texas." This explanation, of course, suggests that the stock market has erred, either due to inflation distortions or other reasons, in its valuation of the prospective takeover's assets. Hence, the stock purchase is a "deal." Alternatively, a recently popular theory suggests that the market has correctly assessed as low value those companies whose managements are inefficient—who are not effectively deploying the capital at their disposal to the highest and best uses. If these inefficient managements can be replaced, the stock market would then reflect the true value of the underlying assets.

Several other factors have contributed. For example, recognition of structural change in the economy has hastened the transfer of resources from low growth industries to more productive areas, with mergers being one transfer vehicle. Takeovers have clearly been concentrated in particular sectors—oil and gas, banking, insurance, transportation—rather than being spread evenly throughout the corporate landscape. Further, deregulation in several industries, such as financial services, transportation, and broadcasting, has also created new opportunities. Finally, innovations in financing and greater experience in takeover techniques have been important contributors to the recent wave. At one time huge size itself represented a significant corporate takeover defense, but with new financing tools and Wall Street brokerage houses gaining experience and new expertise, even the very largest businesses today cannot feel immune from takeover possibilities.

The management inefficiency theory merits elaboration. Managements are essentially agents of the stockholders. They presumably act to maximize the value of the firm's assets. However, as discussed in chapter 1, they may seek other objectives and thus engage in nonvalue-maximizing activities. In their attempt to monitor management, equity holders experience agency costs, which may take the form of audited financial statements, incentive management compensation schemes, and so on, but the conflict of interests cannot be perfectly resolved. Because it is always present, it is likely that nonvalue-maximizing activities, to varying degrees, almost always take place and that their influence will generally increase during periods of substantial economic expansion.

The free cash flow theory helps explain agency costs and managerial behavior in the context of current corporate control controversies. Free cash is that amount of cash flow in excess of the funds required to finance all a firm's projects that yield a positive net present value. These funds should be distributed to stockholders rather than being invested in activities with negative present values. However, because such payments would reduce the discretion and control of managements, the latter do not tend to fully distribute all free cash flow. The greater the value of free cash flow, the greater this conflict between owners and management.

The U.S. petroleum industry stands as a prime example of free cash flow theory. The energy market in the middle to late 1970s experienced radical change. Conservation efforts mandated reductions in capacity by the 1980s, yet profits were still quite high:

1984 cash flows of the ten largest oil companies were $48.5 billion, 28 percent of the total cash flows of the top 200 firms in *Duns Business Month* (July 1985) survey. . . . However, management did not pay out the excess resources to shareholders. Instead, the industry continued to spend heavily on exploration and development even though the returns on these expenditures were below the cost of capital.[40]

Additional evidence of the lack of profitable projects within this industry were the efforts to invest outside the oil field, efforts that generally failed. "Ultimately the capital markets, through the takeover market, forced managers to respond to the new market conditions."[41] That such acquisition activities facilitate resource reallocations is quite clear. When Socal purchased Gulf for $13.2 billion in cash, the industry shrank by an equivalent amount as the Gulf stockholders took their cash and transferred it to other investment arenas. Food companies, drug companies, and the broadcasting industry are other current examples of fields generating large cash flows without commensurate investment opportunities.

Interestingly, the growth of debt in corporate America is likely to serve a control function, particularly in the kinds of industries described above. If debt is issued, but the proceeds are distributed to stockholders (a common takeover defense), the agency cost of free cash flow is reduced because the discretion of management has been circumscribed. Management can no longer be tempted to undertake questionable investments by easy availability of funds. Further, the obligation to pay the interest associated with debt issuance provides additional motivation for management to allocate the firm's resources to the highest and best uses. In short, there is greater pressure to keep nonvalue maximizing activities to a minimum.

Acquisitions outside the buying company's industry have on average not been as successful either as anticipated or as compared to acquisitions within the industry. In part this reflects the unfamiliarity of the acquiring management team with the demands and complexities of an industry new to them. "Thus, some acquisitions are a solution to the agency problem of free cash flow while others, such as diversification programs, are symptoms of those problems."[42]

The debate as to the utility of mergers and acquisitions is quite heated and competent professionals are divided. Some hotly condemn the merger/acquisition movement, maintaining that there are great costs involved, both in terms of diverting management attention from basic issues, preempting financial capital, accentuating short-term time horizons, and applying industry-specific expertise to unfamiliar areas.[43] They believe a "casino" mentality has developed that is socially dysfunctional. Others maintain that the facilitation of resource transfers and the monitoring or eviction of nonvalue-maximizing managements are well worth the costs. Further, the activities of the 1980s have usefully served to undo the foolish management diversification efforts of the 1970s. As George Gilder has written, "The misbegotten conglomerate binge of the 1970s created a huge opportunity in the 1980s. Raiders could achieve massive gains merely by liberating thousands of companies then caught up in the gummy webs of large corporate bureaucracies."[44] In this view, "good" merger/acquisition activity in the 1980s undid the "bad" or foolish undertakings of the 1970s. But what if such activities had been severely limited in the first place? Would society not have been spared both the "doing" and "undoing" costs? The question is a difficult one.

Accordingly, the market for corporate control is not simply a competition over ownership, but also a regulating mechanism for owners over management, and a competition among alternate management teams for the opportunity to control and deploy corporate resources. A major difficulty is the imperfect capability of outsiders to determine whether or not a firm is being run efficiently. Even if financial results are poor, it is never clear whether this is due to uncontrollable outside forces, inefficient management, or simply to the assets of the firm not being what they seem.

As this market has developed, the various financial firms that have brokered mergers have earned many millions of dollars. Table 2.4 lists the activities of the leading Wall Street buyout broker. Such firms thus have a vested interest in a vigorous market and will undertake numerous efforts to clarify the ambiguities discussed in the preceding paragraph.

MULTINATIONAL CORPORATIONS

When a corporation expands its market size and operates production facilities across national boundaries, it becomes the so-called multinational corporation (MNC). While some U.S. multinationals horizontally diversify by producing and selling lines of products abroad, others invest abroad vertically to produce raw materials or manufactured components that are inputs to their principal products in the United States.

It was estimated that as early as 1919 there were 180 U.S. multinational companies.[45] The number is now much greater. Today almost every major corporation has some foreign subsidiaries. Their influence on the nation's economy is impressive. In 1977, for example, U.S. MNCs produced a total of $651.7 billion of goods and services. Manufacturing activities accounted for almost 60 percent. Of this total, $490.5 billion, or 75 percent, was contributed by the U.S. parent operations and the rest ($161.1 billion) by their majority-owned foreign affiliates.[46]

Table 2.4
Kohlberg Kravis Roberts' Biggest Deals

- RJR Nabisco Inc., $25.07 billion, 1988.

- Beatrice Cos., $6.1 billiun, 1986.

- Safeway Stores Inc., $4.2 billion, 1986.

- Owens-Illinois Inc., $3.7 billion, 1987.

- Storer Communications Inc., $2.5 billion, 1985.

- Jim Walter Corp., $2.43 billion, 1987.

- Macmillan Inc., $2.36 billion, held up by court fight.

- Duracell, $1.8 billion, 1988.

- 50 percent of Union Texas Petroleum unit, $1.7 billion, 1985.

- Rheem, World Color, Uarco (with Merrill Lynch), $1.25 billion, 1984.

- Stop & Shop Cos., $ 1.23 billion, 1988.

Source: *Washington Post*, October 25, 1988, p. D5.

This latter amount exceeded the value of U.S. exports that year. From a different perspective, MNC output accounted for almost 26 percent of U.S. domestic output in 1977. By 1986 total sales of U.S. MNC parent companies reached $2.5 trillion, providing more than 17 million jobs and a payroll of $562 billion.[47] The value of the output produced by their foreign subsidiaries, of course, represented contributions to income of the respective countries. Because of their gigantic size, the worldwide operations of MNCs are now a major factor in shaping trade patterns, international investment, and technology flows among nations. MNCs play a very important role in the international diffusion of innovations by carrying technology overseas. They generally exploit their technology in foreign markets through wholly owned subsidiaries rather than through licensing. In addition to diffusing technology, MNCs have linked the capital markets of many countries and promoted international transfer of important managerial labor services. MNCs also pose a new challenge to national jurisdictions in taxation, antitrust, and other policy areas. Nations constantly try to monitor and control economic activities within their boundaries, while MNCs regularly deploy funds and operations overseas at least in part to avoid such controls. However, because MNCs have tended to break down some of the barriers between nations, they have exerted an important impact toward integrating the economies of the world into a worldwide system.

Based on how activities are structured, MNCs may generally take the following three forms:[48]

1. Resource-oriented MNC—The corporation seeks natural or human resources with a view to obtaining lower cost inputs and components. An MNC may establish an affiliate to produce components (or undertake an assembly function) in, say, Hong Kong or South Korea. Materials or components are received and processed or assembled for shipment back to the home country.
2. Market-oriented MNC—This type of investment abroad serves the host-country market from production within that country. Examples include the automobile companies in some newly industrialized countries such as Brazil, Mexico, and Argentina, especially during the 1960s and 1970s. The product line of the affiliate is often similar, though not identical, to that of the parent. Adaptions are made for the host-country market that make it unlikely to sell easily outside of the host country. Alternatively, production is located overseas to get "under" host-country tariffs and other trade barriers.
3. Efficiency-oriented—This type of MNC makes foreign investment to create the most efficient network of worldwide production to serve multiple markets. These are also called multinational enterprises and have come to the fore in the past 20 years. The parent headquarters adopt a centralized policy covering a wide range, from financing and pricing to technologies and R&D. These multinational enterprises are found in most of the major industrial sectors, except basic steel, cement, shipbuilding, and textile mill products.

Any given MNC may have all three orientations. Indeed, few are purely or completely only one of these three types. Most operate some divisions with market orientation, some with resource and efficiency orientation. The choice depends on the market conditions, government policies, technologies, and company experiences.

The MNC is hardly an American phenomenon. Other countries (Canada, Great Britain, Japan, the Netherlands, Switzerland) are also homes for important MNCs. In recent years, the United States has attracted many such organizations. In 1982 there were about 2.4 million people in the United States working for 1,744 foreign-owned U.S. firms. Their payroll amounted to $49 billion. Most of these firms engaged in manufacturing and wholesale trade. More than two-thirds have 100 percent foreign ownership. Foreign direct investment reached $220.4 billion in 1986, playing an increasingly important role in the U.S. economy. Further, the existence of such foreign corporate power has policy implications to decision makers in the public sector when they consider problems of capital and technology flows, the balance of payments, and national security.

DEFENSE INDUSTRIAL BASE

In 1983 the federal government spent $210 billion for national defense; the 1989 estimate is $290 billion, a little under 6 percent of the GNP. Charles Schultze estimates that defense absorbs over 30 percent of our technical manpower and almost 40 percent of our durable goods production.[49] Such expenditures have very special and profound impacts on manufacturing industries. Defense projects are responsible for the development and production of advanced weapon systems, space vehicles, and other technically sophisticated military and civilian equipment. Such projects involve almost all key manufacturing industries, but most particularly transportation equipment (principally aircraft and aircraft engines, shipbuilding, guided missiles, and space vehicles) and electrical and electronic equipment (primarily communications items). Indeed, the nation's defense industrial base includes the 25,000–30,000 prime firms and also more numerous subcontractors concentrated in missiles and space vehicles, electronic components, shipbuilding and repair, aircraft engines, aircraft equipment, semiconductors, and ammunition as well as a web of suppliers that pervades the entire U.S. industrial structure.

Table 2.5 ranks U.S. industries in terms of output shares going to defense. The military is obviously the dominant customer for those defense (or defense-oriented) products near the top as well as a significant purchaser from other sectors. For example, over 20 percent of optical instruments (and lenses) and electron tubes are purchased by the Department of Defense. About 13 percent of machine tools and metal-cutting tools as well as 12 percent of iron and steel forgings go to national security uses. The table clearly demonstrates that defense needs span a very broad range of industries and that the military is an important customer for a wide assortment of producers not normally associated with defense production, yet nonetheless a vital part of the U.S. defense industrial base.

Importantly, these are the prime sectors that will be called upon to surge production in the event of a military conflict. Generally speaking, those industries in which defense absorbs a relatively low share will be able to more easily shift out of civilian items and into greater defense production. The speed of this shift will depend upon many factors, to include advance planning procedures by both government and industry, flexibility on the part of management and the labor force, and general public support for the war effort. On the other hand, unless excess capacity and labor are available, those sectors toward the top of the listing in Table 2.5, which already have in excess of 60 percent of their output going toward defense, will have much greater difficulty in contributing further to a war effort. For example, when the high attrition rates of the 1973 Yom Kippur War left the Israelis in a very weakened posture, the United States supplied the Israeli forces with over 1,000 M60 tanks, which were taken primarily from war reserve stocks in Europe and from the active inventory of regular Army forces. When the Department of Defense decided to accelerate tank production from 30 to over 100 per month in order to replenish the void so created in U.S. capabilities, officials were surprised to learn that Chrysler Corporation, the primary contractor, could produce no more than 40 such tanks per month due to a limited supply of tank hull and turret castings from commercial foundries. In an appropriately functioning defense industrial base, such a bottleneck needs to be anticipated so

Table 2.5
Major Industrial Suppliers to Department of Defense Ranked by Defense Share of Production, 1985 (millions of 1983 dollars)

Rank	Industry	Defense Share (%)		Defense Production			Nondefense production % growth
		1984	1989	1984	1989	% growth 84 to 89	84 to 89
1	New military fac.	89.9	90.7	864	1,048	3.9	2.1
2	Other ordnance & accessories	85.7	90.1	2,160	2,825	5.5	-2.9
3	Ammunition, ex. small arms, nec	81.8	90.5	2,864	5,312	13.2	-2.7
4	Tanks & tank component	81.2	85.4	1,404	1,697	3.9	-2.3
5	Complete guided missiles	65.8	73.6	6,847	10,716	9.4	1.6
6	Small arms ammunition	61.1	76.3	1,107	2,655	19.1	3.1
7	Shipbuilding & repairing	63.1	66.7	8,881	12,520	7.1	3.7
8	Aircraft	54.5	49.2	13,669	16,682	4.1	8.5
9	Aircraft parts & equip, nec	51.1	51.7	6,523	8,547	5.6	5.1
10	Aircraft engines & engine parts	50.3	52.8	7,228	9,726	6.1	4.1
11	Radio & TV communication equip.	51.0	54.2	22,915	35,952	9.4	6.6
12	Engineering & scientific instr.	47.5	48.6	1,645	2,235	6.3	5.4
13	Electric measuring instr.	43.5	42.0	4,962	6,737	6.3	7.6
14	Explosives	40.9	49.3	488	872	12.3	5.0
15	Nonfer forgings	32.1	34.0	382	524	6.6	4.8
16	Electronic components, nec	25.4	28.2	5,858	9,891	11.0	7.9
17	Measuring & control instr.	24.7	25.2	2,185	2,927	6.0	5.4
18	Semiconductors	19.6	21.5	2,526	4,289	11.2	8.6
19	Plating & polishing	19.0	21.9	660	1,060	9.9	6.0
20	Nonfer castings, nec	18.0	20.2	187	257	6.6	3.6
21	Steam engines & turbines	18.4	18.1	798	891	2.2	2.6
22	Primary metal products, nec	15.9	19.8	299	482	10.0	4.4
23	Optical instr. & lenses	15.4	22.7	619	1,316	16.4	5.8
24	Electron tubes	14.7	20.9	268	435	10.2	1.2
25	Elec. ind. apparatus, nec	14.8	15.5	191	252	5.7	4.6
26	Nonfer rolling & drawing, nec	14.0	16.4	458	736	10.0	5.9
27	Copper ore mining	13.6	17.2	304	439	7.6	2.0
28	Nonmetallic mineral products, nec	13.7	16.0	75	118	9.5	5.6
29	Cold finishing, steel shapes	13.6	15.6	21	27	5.5	2.2
30	Industrial trucks & tractors	13.7	17.4	397	667	10.9	5.0
31	Aluminum castings	13.2	15.2	499	740	8.2	4.7
32	Footwear cut stock	12.8	15.9	62	83	6.0	0.7
-33	Secondary nonfer metals	12.4	15.5	47	73	9.2	3.5
34	Metal heat treating	12.3	14.2	134	192	7.5	4.1
35	Misc. machinery	12.1	13.5	2,093	2,857	6.4	3.8
36	Machine tools, metal cutting	14.2	13.3	515	690	6.0	7.8
37	Primary copper	11.1	13.5	580	851	8.0	3.1
38	Electronic computing equip.	11.1	12.9	5,266	10,081	13.9	10.2
39	Iron & steel forgings	10.9	12.3	615	841	6.5	3.7

Source: DRI/McGraw-Hill, *Defense Economic Impact Modeling System*, July 19, 1984, p. 1

it does not occur in the first place. It is essential that the economy be capable of producing a sufficient quantity of bullets and beans to allow the United States to bring a conflict to a politically acceptable termination with a minimum of casualties and loss of human life.

The firms dealing with defense contracts are in an area noted for rapid technological change and a high rate of obsolescence. It is often difficult to find a way to balance costs against the risk of technically inferior weaponry. The larger firms do not wholly replicate the typical industrial concern and mode of operation. Instead, administrative supervision and controls from the outside are used as a partial directing mechanism. Because of the technological uncertainties, complexity, and unique applications associated with defense projects, a relatively small number of quite large corporations are the recipients of the majority of defense contracts (see Table 2.6). As a result, this market often lacks substantial competition. Being the sole buyer of defense goods, the government is in a monopoly position on the demand side and can exert a great degree of influence. In the early stage of the acquisition process, government generally initiates the competitive bidding for the development of a new weapon system. But in many cases there are only two or three large firms competing for a program that will eventually be worth billions of dollars during its development and production stages.[50] Once the full-scale development contract is awarded, the recipient is very likely also to gain at least a portion of the production contract, which will be carried out over many years. In the 1980s substantial efforts have been undertaken to promote greater competition among defense suppliers.

Firms in the defense industry are generally vertically integrated. To carry out production the prime contractor will often supply its own inputs through acquisition of competing parts suppliers or construction of its own factory to produce for itself instead of buying externally. Such conduct of defense firms makes this market highly concentrated. Data for the 1960s and 1970s reveal that the largest 100 U.S. corporations were awarded 70 percent of the value of total contracts, while the top 25 corporations received 50 percent and the top five controlled 20 percent.[51] Table 2.6 provides rankings of the top 20 defense contractors for a selected year in the 1960s, 1970s, and 1980s. The big firms in the defense sector— Lockheed, Boeing, Martin Marietta, General Electric, McDonnell Douglas, Rockwell, IBM, Westinghouse, General Dynamics, and Hughes Aircraft—have generally maintained positions in the top ten for almost two decades.

The cost structure of the firms working on defense projects is quite different from that for an ordinary commercial project. Monitoring activities are pervasive, the buyer imposing far more administrative controls and supervision than is characteristic of civilian production. In addition to price, performance criteria, technical dimensions, and delivery schedule also play very important roles. When contracts are finalized, cost increases come primarily from negotiated changes to the contract or from overruns on contracts that may have been bid very low intentionally (in order to get the initial contract with the hope of future renegotiation). As a result, according to Jacques Gansler, the average cost for defense

Table 2.6
The Twenty Top Defense Contractors in 1985 with Their Respective Rankings in 1967, 1977, and 1985

DEFENSE CONTRACTORS *	1967	1977	1985
Lockheed	3	2	1
Boeing	6	4	2
Martin Marietta	**	**	3
General Electric	4	5	4
McDonnell Douglas	1	1	5
Rockwell International	7	6	6
IBM	**	17	7
Westinghouse Electric	15	12	8
General Dynamics	2	8	9
Hughes Aircraft	17	9	10
Grumman	12	7	11
Sperry Rand	13	14	12
TRW	**	**	13
Raytheon	19	11	14
United Technologies	5	3	15
RCA	**	**	16
Honeywell	20	20	17
Ford Aerospace Communications	**	**	18
ITT	**	**	19
Texas Instruments	**	**	20

* Ranked in terms of dollars awarded.
** Rank below the twentieth.
Source: From Jacques S. Gansler, *The Defense Industry* (Cambridge, Mass.: MIT Press, 1980), p. 40; and Department of Defense, *500 Contractors Receiving the Largest Dollar Volume of Prime Contract Awards for RDT&E in Fiscal Year 1985* (Washington, D.C.: U.S. Government Printing Office, 1986), pp. 13–15.

equipment generally has risen over 5 percent per year.[52] This raises concerns about the economic inefficiencies and incentives in the defense acquisition process.

Questions have also been raised as to the capability of the defense industry to respond rapidly to increased demand for military goods in times of national emergency. This is a question of surge capabilities and mobilization potential. Evidence seems to indicate that the United States has been able to mobilize troops far faster than it has been able to arm them in the early months of its wars.[53] Lead times are even longer today than in past decades because modern military equipment is more complex and sophisticated. Low production rates and a limited number of suppliers further lengthen the time span. Given the uncertain nature of the world and the high attrition rates characteristic of modern warfare, it has been cogently argued that it is of vital importance that the United States develop an efficient program to enhance industrial preparedness.[54] Strategic stockpiling of completed military equipment, components, and raw materials must be carefully considered and evaluated.

EVOLVING STRUCTURE OF MANUFACTURING

In the Census of Manufactures, taken every five years, the manufacturing statistics are fully updated. In 1977 the 20 manufacturing industry groups had almost 19.7 million employees, with 60 percent working in the durable goods sectors. This figure peaked in 1979 at 21 million. By 1982 total manufacturing employment had fallen to 18.8 million, with the preliminary 1987 census data indicating 19.1 million. Thus, some recouping of manufacturing employment since the severe 1982 downturn has occurred, but the number of employees still remains roughly 2 million below the 1979 peak. These data are further broken down into operating manufacturing establishments and auxiliary operations. The latter include services in support of manufacturing such as storage, repair, research, and promotion. Interestingly, the actual number of production workers over the 1982–87 period evidenced a slight decline, but was offset by growth in the increasingly important auxiliary operations. Hours worked by production employees, however, rose 4 percent nonetheless.

Table 2.7 provides details concerning various manufacturing sectors (excluding auxiliary operations) from the 1982 census and preliminary 1987 census. For all manufacturing, the cost of materials was by far the largest expense category, with payrolls being only 19 percent of material costs for nondurables, but almost 45 percent for durables. The transportation equipment industry had the largest payroll, followed by nonelectrical machinery, electrical machinery, fabricated metal products, printing and publishing, and food products. The latter had the highest value of shipments ($280 billion) in 1982, followed by petroleum (one of the lowest payroll sectors), and motor vehicles. Of the 20 industries listed, only petroleum and leather failed to witness increases in value added, the former clearly reflecting the relatively low oil prices that characterized most of the 1980s. For all manufacturing industries

Table 2.7
Manufacturing Industries, by Number of Employees, Payroll, Value-Added, Cost of Materials, and Value of Shipments, 1982 and 1987

Industry*	Year	All Employees (Thousand)	Payroll ($ Bill)	Value Added ($ Bill)	Cost of Material ($ Bill)	Value of Shipments ($ Bill)
All industries	1987	17 852	431 179	1 176 472	1 329 566	2 494 997
	1982	17 818	341 406	824 118	1 130 143	1 960 206
Food and kindred products	1987	1 450	30 248	124 187	210 116	333 666
	1982	1 488	26 088	88 419	192 217	280 529
Tobacco products	1987	45	1 489	14 738	6 432	21 173
	1982	58	1 324	8 965	7 100	16 061
Textile mill products	1987	690	11 544	26 592	37 110	63 390
	1982	717	9 046	18 550	28 713	47 515
Apparel and other products	1987	1 077	13 916	33 127	33 183	65 827
	1982	1 189	12 129	26 061	27 088	53 388
Lumber and wood products	1987	696	12 637	28 392	40 918	69 160
	1982	576	8 445	15 377	27 126	42 935
Furniture and fixtures	1987	511	9 105	20 265	17 151	37 232
	1982	436	6 084	12 829	11 229	24 129
Paper and allied products	1987	617	16 984	49 725	59 248	108 734
	1982	606	12 948	33 376	46 620	79 895
Printing and publishing	1987	1 500	33 595	90 204	46 015	135 810
	1982	1 292	22 707	54 423	31 377	85 797
Chemicals and allied products	1987	818	24 978	120 867	108 670	228 875
	1982	873	20 836	77 315	92 557	170 737
Petroleum and coal products	1987	120	4 129	19 095	115 489	133 677
	1982	152	4 339	22 069	185 191	208 919
Rubber and misc plastics products	1987	858	18 060	45 562	43 214	88 462
	1982	682	11 597	27 219	27 950	55 416
Leather and leather products	1987	128	1 804	4 246	4 633	8 821
	1982	200	2 219	4 773	4 917	9 719
Stone, clay, and glass products	1987	520	12 254	32 553	28 089	60 615
	1982	532	10 097	22 986	22 149	45 181
Primary metal industries	1987	702	19 888	47 137	73 760	120 404
	1982	854	20 603	33 291	68 791	104 667
Fabricated metal products	1987	1 474	35 435	76 055	73 355	149 141
	1982	1 460	28 283	58 928	59 394	119 444
Machinery, except electrical	1987	1 871	51 156	117 538	101 720	219 924
	1982	2 189	46 911	102 270	83 788	187 896
Electric and electronic equipment	1987	1 600	39 295	98 332	77 002	175 162
	1982	(NA)	(NA)	(NA)	(NA)	(NA)
Transporation equipment	1987	1 835	59 558	139 091	201 711	335 534
	1982	1 596	40 812	84 932	120 011	201 346

*Operating establishments only are included; auxiliary operations (and employees) are excluded.

Source: Derived from U.S. Bureau of Census, Advance Press Release, December 23, 1988, p. 2.

the value of 1987 shipments approximated $2.5 trillion, up 27 percent from the 1982 level and more than four times the 1977 figure. Accordingly, while employment levels are below peak years, most other aggregate production and value figures show solid advances rather than the generally anemic performance so commonly depicted in the press and in political circles. Finally, it merits note that capital spending by U.S. manufacturing industries in 1987 was almost $80.5 billion.[55]

INDUSTRIAL TRANSFORMATION

In recent years the nation's economy has derived much of its momentum from the vigorous growth of new manufacturing industries, which embody sophisticated technology in both their production processes and their final products. These are the so-called high tech industries—those producing office and computing machines, copiers and related equipment, electronic communications, electronic components, and medical instruments. They have accounted for most of the growth in total industrial production since the 1970s. Interestingly, the manufacture of high tech equipment tends to be relatively labor intensive. Its rapid growth has created many new job opportunities for people working in the manufacturing sector. Between 1977 and 1983, for example, growth in high technology employment exceeded 30 percent, more than triple the national average. Accordingly, high technology industry, representing less than 3 percent of total employment, accounted for 7 percent of the new jobs created in this period.[56] This momentum continued throughout the 1980s.

On the other hand, some older industries have matured and slowed in their rate of growth. Some even experienced declines. This group of low-performance industries included farm equipment, construction and mining equipment, railroad equipment, commercial shipbuilding, and primary metals. Many nondurable manufacturing industries, such as those producing refined petroleum products, agricultural chemicals, textile mill products and apparel, have also been somewhat stagnant. A major factor for slow growth in these industries has been the low rate of growth of real income in the United States, which restrained the demand for industrial goods. Additionally, international factors have also contributed. The high-valued dollar of 1980–85 (see chapter 6) made export sales more difficult, while at the same time providing foreign supplies of chemicals, textiles, metals, and the like at very attractive prices. Thus, both domestic and international factors have combined to slow growth in manufacturing demand.

In terms of market aggregates, the growth rate of business equipment production has exceeded that of consumer goods. This fast growth in the 1980s has been due to the generally strong demand for computing equipment. Rapid innovation has reduced costs, while lower prices and increased knowledge (as well as familiarity) have increased their usage. Another growth area in the 1980s, reflecting changes in national priority, was the output of defense and space equipment, which increased considerably over the decade.

TECHNOLOGICAL ADVANCE, COSTS, AND AUTOMATION

As noted earlier, technology is a key factor raising industrial productivity. Technological progress brings efficiency and economies of scale. Industrial firms use new product technology, new organizational techniques, or new process technology to produce better and larger quantities of output at lower per unit production costs. For example, in the early stage of U.S. industrialization when Connecticut manufacturers began to mass-produce clocks with machinery and interchangeable parts, the cost of a clock dropped from $50 per unit in 1820 to $6 in 1840 and to 75 cents by 1860.[57] Technology has likewise affected production costs and prices for such products as the pocket radio, portable calculator, microcomputer, and VCR, each of which was introduced into the market in recent years.

In industrial production, technological changes have led to automation. In manufacturing there has been an upsurge in the established trend toward substitution of mechanical direction of operations for direct human supervision. The worker who formerly tended a machine or operation is now to a greater extent tending a control, feeder, or handling mechanism based on a feedback principle and integration of process. Automation helped U.S. manufacturing industries to attain a significant technological edge in the 1950s and 1960s. In recent decades, however, other countries, especially Japan, have caught up with the United States with respect to technological changes in automation. Japanese industry is now ahead in the so-called robotics revolution (the impact of robotics is examined in chapter 4; Japanese machine tool progress is discussed in chapter 9). Those who lag in this technological race will not be the most efficient producers and they will not fare well in international competition. Robots in factory automation and word processors in office automation will greatly affect the way the American people work. These innovations have accelerated the automation trends already in motion and they penetrate areas of the economy, such as white-collar occupations, that previously had been lightly touched. Even more profound will be the impacts upon the heavy and durable manufacturing industries.

To summarize, U.S. industry is active, dynamic, and undergoing a metamorphosis. New forms of financing have been enlisted to help fund an extensive capital investment program. While the manufacturing sector is more concentrated than the rest of the U.S. economy, in recent years it has become less so. This same move toward more competitive conditions is even more pronounced in the general economy, and these trends have been reenforced by the substantial increases in foreign competition that have occurred over the past two decades. Both economic and corporate restructuring have been important and continuing phenomena. Each reflects adjustments by U.S. industry to changing world realities and forces. Industrial restructuring has clearly been in the direction of high tech production and away from the old line, heavy industries. While there are many indicators of this industrial transformation, one of the most visible has been the loss over the 1972–86 period of 487,000 jobs in five industries that can be labeled metal-bashing. The less-publicized gain (of 653,000 jobs) occurred in five other industries, which could be called electron-bashing.[58] Unfortunately, necessary changes such as these do not take place without friction and adjustment pains. To fail to make the right adjustments, however, will in the long run entail far greater costs. Accordingly, U.S. manufacturing industries are doing the right thing. They are deploying their assets so as to be appropriately positioned for the challenges of the twenty-first century.

NOTES

1. In practice, it is often difficult to specify industries exactly because many produce heterogeneous products and most enterprises are multiproduct firms.

2. From the *New York Times*, February 24, 1983.

3. Price (*P*) represents the value society places on the item, while marginal cost (*MC*) is the additional expense society incurs in producing that good. For any quantity at which *MC* exceeds *P*, society has produced too much, for the extra cost exceeds the value created. As less is produced the value of each of the fewer units is greater (*P* tends to rise) and eventually the socially correct quantity, where $P = MC$, is attained.

4. George Gilder, *The Spirit of Enterprise* (New York: Simon and Schuster, 1984), pp. 16–17.

5. In 1986 there were some 702,100 new business incorporations and roughly 61,200 failed businesses. Forty percent of the failures were in the services, 19 percent in retail trade, 11 percent in construction, and 7 percent each in manufacturing and wholesale trade. U.S. Department of Commerce, *Statistical Abstract of the United States, 1988*, pp. 500–501.

6. Dale Jahr, "Corporate Wealth: More for the Little Guys," *Wall Street Journal*, January 21, 1987, p. 21.

7. Robert T. Averitt, *The Dual Economy* (New York: W. W. Norton, 1968), pp. 23–24.

8. Ibid., p. 33.

9. Ibid., p. 27.

10. Federal Reserve Bank Statistical Release, *Nonfinancial Corporate Business* (Washington, D.C.: Federal Reserve System, June 21, 1989).

11. Alan Greenspan, *Monetary Report to Congress,* Board of Governors of the Federal Reserve System, February 21, 1989, p. 12.

12. Robert A. Taggart, Jr. " 'Junk' Bond Market's Role in Financing Takeovers," in Alan J. Auerbach, ed., *Mergers and Acquisitions* (Chicago: University of Chicago Press, 1988), p. 16.

13. U.S. Department of Commerce, *Survey of Current Business*, July 1988, p. 47 and July 1984, p. 31.

14. *Nonfinancial Corporate Business*, June, 1989.

15. Taggart, p. 9.

16. Glenn Yago, "Junk Bonds Are Food for Growth," *Wall Street Journal*, July 28, 1988, p. 24.

17. No doubt the name—"junk" bonds—evokes skepticism and negativity, which is one reason for the vehicle's low esteem in public perception. And professional controversy is also alive on this topic. See Mathew Winkler, "Junk Bonds are Taking Their Lumps," *Wall Street Journal*, April 14, 1989. Skeptics claim that because the economy has

experienced a prolonged economic advance, the weight of debt in general and the quality of these bonds in particular have not yet been tested. No doubt, a heavier debt burden will indeed witness a higher bankruptcy rate. However, as Harvard's Lawrence Summers has noted, "Our goal is not to minimize bankruptcy. In a well-functioning economy, bankruptcies will take place. It would be easy to ban bankruptcy by banning debt, but it wouldn't be very efficient." See Hugh Vickery, "Junk Bonds Here to Stay," *Harrisburg Patriot-News*, April 16, 1989, p. F6. See also George Gilder, "The Victim of His Virtues," *Wall Street Journal*, April 18, 1989, p. A24.

18. U.S. Bureau of the Census, Advance Press Release, December 23, 1988, p. 2.

19. See F. M. Scherer, *Industrial Market Structure and Economic Performance*, 2nd ed. (Chicago: Rand McNally, 1980), p. 46.

20. Wallace C. Peterson, *Our Overloaded Economy* (New York: M. E. Sharpe, 1982), p. 104.

21. Bureau of Economics, Federal Trade Commission, "Concentration in Assets for Manufacturing Corporations, 1974–1988," Table 3, Revised, June 15, 1989, p. 40. Drawn from *Quarterly Financial Report*, Department of Commerce.

22. John S. McGee, *Industrial Organization* (Englewood Cliffs, N.J.: Prentice-Hall, 1988), p. 246.

23. Bureau of Economics, Federal Trade Commission, "Concentration in Assets for the Nonfinancial Sector, 1958–1985," Table 4, Revised, June 15, 1989, p. 42. Drawn from *Quarterly Financial Report*, Department of Commerce.

24. Carolyn Sherwood-Call, "Why Do Regions Grow?" *Weekly Letter*, Federal Reserve Bank of San Francisco, November 25, 1988, p. 1.

25. Ibid.

26. See Figure 7.2 and the accompanying elaboration in chapter 7.

27. Ted Kumpe and Piet T. Bolwijn, "Manufacturing: The New Case for Vertical Integration," *Harvard Business Review*, March-April 1988, p. 76.

28. Robert A. Hayes and William J. Abernathy, "Managing Our Way to Economic Decline," *Harvard Business Review*, July–August 1980.

29. Michael Gort, *Diversification and Integration in American Industry* (Princeton, N.J.: Princeton University Press, 1962).

30. Arthur B. Laffer, "Vertical Integration by Corporations, 1929–1965," *Review of Economics and Statistics* 51 (February 1969), pp. 91–93.

31. Ralph L. Nelson, *Merger Movements in American Industry, 1895–1956* (Princeton, N.J.: Princeton University Press, 1959).

32. Gort.

33. Kumpe and Bolwijn.

34. Ibid., p. 80.

35. William M. Dugger, "Transaction Cost Analysis," *Journal of Economic Issues*, March 1983, pp. 104–5.

36. Ibid., p. 109.

37. Devra L. Golbe and Lawrence J. White, "Mergers and Acquisitions in the U.S. Economy," in Auerbach, pp. 36–39.

38. Auerbach, p. 2.

39. These are bonds with greater investor safeguards. See Mathew Winkler, "Harris, Williams Cos. Unit Are First to Offer Super 'Poison Puts,'" *Wall Street Journal*, November 16, 1988, p. C1.

40. Michael C. Jensen, "Takeovers: Their Causes and Consequences," *Journal of Economic Perspectives*, Winter 1988, pp. 33.

41. Ibid., p. 34.

42. Ibid.

43. See Walter Adams and James Brock, *The Bigness Complex* (New York: Pantheon Books, 1986), for a superbly documented critique.

44. See Gilder.

45. Ralph L. Andreano, *Superconcentration/Supercorporation* (Andover, Mass.: Warner Modular Publications, 1973), Part III.

46. U.S. Department of Commerce, *Survey of Current Business*, February, 1983.

47. U.S. Department of Commerce, *Survey of Current Business*, June 1988, p. 89.

48. Jack N. Berhrman, *Industrial Policies: International Restructuring and Transnationals* (Lexington, Mass.: D.C. Heath, 1984), chapter 5.

49. Charles L. Schultze, "Economic Effects of the Defense Budget," *Brookings Bulletin*, Fall 1981.

50. Jacques S. Gansler, *The Defense Industry* (Cambridge, Mass.: The MIT Press, 1980), p. 68.

51. Ibid., pp. 36–37.

52. Ibid., p. 94.

53. Ibid., p. 109.

54. Ibid., chapter 5.

55. U.S. Bureau of the Census, Advance Press Release, December 23, 1988, p. 2.

56. Robert T. Clair, "The Labor-Intensive Nature of Manufacturing High-Technology Capital Goods," *Economic Review*, Federal Reserve Bank of Dallas, March 1986.

57. Herman E. Krooss, *American Economic Development*, 2nd ed. (Englewood Cliffs, N.J.: Prentice-Hall, 1966), p. 364.

58. James P. Moore, Jr., "Highlights of the 1989 U.S. Industrial Outlook," in U.S. Department of Commerce, *U.S. Industrial Outlook 1989* (Washington, D.C.: U.S. Government Printing Office, January, 1989), p. 21.

3

Government and Industry

Government influence on private industry, indeed on the entire economy, is pervasive. Government has the authority to tax, the ability to spend the proceeds of that taxation, and the capability of issuing rules and regulations determining, influencing, or prohibiting private behavior. It also affects the environment in which firms operate by shaping and altering macroeconomic policies. In addition to setting the economic stage (monetary and fiscal policies), government can serve as a seller, such as postal services, a buyer (defense products), a subsidizer (agriculture, education, transportation), a guarantor (unemployment compensation, social security), a provider of collective goods (defense and education), or a regulator (minimum wages and food, health, and safety regulations). Private economic behavior is also influenced by governmental loans, tax preferences, contracts, and subsidies, which are implemented by various government agencies. Finally, the flow of products into the United States and to other countries is also highly influenced by federal law and administrative practice. Thus, through numerous policies and programs—selected subsidies, tariffs, quotas, investment credits, price supports, and taxes—government provides diverse forms of assistance to newly developed or mature industries. Further, government plays a pivotal role in building the nation's infrastructure (social overhead capital), which is essential for industrial development.

As both the economic environment and political philosophies have evolved, government has grown steadily larger over the last several decades and its scope and impact on the economy have considerably broadened. The one important exception to this trend has been the Reagan administration's significant steps toward deregulating specific sectors of the economy. Nonetheless, in recent years, over one-fifth of the nation's total output (GNP) has been purchased by government and about one-third of total income is collected in taxes. Indeed, government (federal, state, and local) today is the nation's largest landowner, insurer, employer, educator, and producer of electricity.

Generally, the major functions performed by government include the following: (1) producing public goods,[1] such as national defense; (2) improving resource allocation in the areas where externalities exist;[2] (3) promoting competitive markets; and (4) providing economic stability. Government performs the first function as a contributor, the remaining three as a regulator. Among the three levels of government, the federal government is present in all four of these government functions. While state and local government spending and related influences are indeed important, the discussions in this chapter will concentrate on the effects of the federal government's activities. Clearly, federal programs and laws have very significant impacts on industries in the U.S. economy.

EFFECTS OF GOVERNMENT EXPENDITURES

The federal government has been a large buyer in a variety of markets in recent decades. The purchase of goods and services by federal authorities surged during World War II and has expanded considerably since then. This upward trend in federal expenditures on goods and services reflects several influences. First is the fact that the United States, as leader of the free world, has had to maintain a strong defense posture, which in turn requires an active defense procurement program. In addition, in the post-World War II period, the federal government has moved into such areas as the exploration of space, interstate highway building, railroad operations, and the encouragement of energy technology development. The federal government's purchases of goods and services produced by private business enterprises reached $386 billion in 1987. This enormous amount of expenditures affects the structure of U.S. industry in a number of ways.

Such outlays are often called exhaustive expenditures because government receives an immediate command over an economic agent. It can use (exhaust) this economic agent. Procurement of tanks, for example, gives the government command over that resource. Tank production, in turn, diverts steel away from automobiles. Exhaustive government expenditures, then, have a role in shaping the composition of the economic pie (GNP)—guns or butter, to put it very simplistically. Not all governmental outlays, however, are exhaustive. Transfer payments, such as unemployment compensation or social security outlays, yield no equivalent control. They merely transfer purchasing power from the government to a recipient. They do, however, greatly influence resource allocation throughout the economy since recipients spend those funds in different ways than the government or taxpayers in general would have spent them. The dollar value of such indirect influences upon resource allocations has traditionally been smaller than government's direct purchases of goods and services. Beginning in 1973, however, the rapidly growing volume of transfer payments started to exceed exhaustive expenditures and this condition prevails today. The influence of these transfer payments is extremely complex and has been the subject of thousands of studies. For example, national rates of consumption are undoubtedly higher and rates of saving lower due to the tax/transfer system. Such a result, however, cannot be judged by itself as either good or bad, but must be assessed in a larger context, hence the proliferation of analyses on this subject.[3] For this chapter, however, transfer payments will be ignored and discussion will be limited to the impact of government's exhaustive outlays.

Impacts on Industry

Expenditures on defense have been a major item in the federal budget. Since the awarding of defense contracts tends to be quite concentrated in the largest corporations, this practice has probably contributed to U.S. industrial concentration. The 100 largest defense prime contractors received about two-thirds of all military prime contract awards in the post-World War II period.[4] Indeed, some government defense contracts have enabled several defense-oriented firms to join the club of multibillion-dollar sales organizations. However, while such defense expenditures are stimulative, they do not affect all industries equally. They confer benefits and place demands in a highly concentrated fashion.[5]

The Reagan administration's increased outlays on defense procurement and on R&D gave defense-oriented industries a tremendous stimulus. This in turn has resulted in significant programs in both physical (plant and equipment) and human (skilled labor) capital in order to meet growing demands.[6] Table 2.5 ranked the major defense supplying industries according to SIC. The defense share of sales for the top 14 industries exceeded 40 percent. Those with the fastest projected rates of increase in defense production over the 1984–89 period were small arms ammunition (19 percent), optical instruments (16 percent), electronic computing equipment (14 percent), and other ammunition (13 percent). Given the Reagan administration's emphasis on defense, it is hardly surprising that growth in defense production exceeds nondefense output growth in 35 of the 39 industries listed. Finally, the defense share of industry output was projected to grow most rapidly in optical instruments and lenses (from 15 to 23 percent) and electron tubes (from 15 to 21 percent). Accordingly, defense outlays in the 1980s have greatly stimulated the recipient industries and have significant implications concerning industrial capabilities both within the defense industrial base and in the general economy.

The federal government is the biggest buyer in the U.S. economy. Its military and civilian installations purchase a wide assortment of goods and services. In the case of government procurement related to national security, such as aircraft carriers, nuclear submarines, supersonic bombers, ICBMs, space exploration systems, and equipment associated with SDI (Strategic Defense Initiative, or Star Wars), government is in a monopsonistic position in the market—it is the sole buyer.[7] Therefore, where such government contracts are involved, government dictates to potential suppliers; contractors in various supplying industries must do business the government's way.

Through its selection of contractors, the government can influence the growth patterns of the recipient firms. When military buyers search for newer and more sophisticated weaponry, they are usually not looking for an on-the-shelf product, because such products do not exist at the time of purchase. They actually buy the contractor's R&D capacity and its ability to transform the result into fully developed weapon systems. By awarding contracts for R&D, government strongly influences which new products its contractors will design and produce.[8] It shares much of the risk of new product development as well. However, there are many military procurement regulations that give government contracting and surveillance officers great influence over the internal operations of the firms doing business with the Pentagon.

In his famous farewell address in 1961, President Eisenhower warned the nation that "we have been compelled to create a permanent armaments industry of vast proportions . . . we must guide against the acquisition of unwarranted influence, whether sought or unsought, by the *military-industrial complex.*" President Eisenhower did not clearly define the military-industrial complex. However, it would seem to include military officers, government officials, political representatives of regions in which defense spending is concentrated, and defense-oriented firms, all of whom would seemingly favor maintaining and expanding U.S. military power (presumably in excess of legitimate need). According to Seymour Melman, a critic of the military establishment, our condition may have moved beyond the military-industrial complex suggested by Eisenhower.[9] The Pentagon, he argues, has become a central management office, with producers of military goods serving as subsidiary enterprises or branches. In terms of principal/agent relationships discussed in chapter 2, rather than the Pentagon being a principal (buyer) obtaining outputs from independently operating agents (supplying companies), the entire military industrial complex is so interwoven and connected that notions of independent and competing suppliers are not credible. The logic behind this claim derives from the great dependence of the firms upon military contracts and the fact that elaborate military procurement procedures and practices have resulted in deep penetration of the managerial decision making of military suppliers by the Pentagon. Thus the conduct and structure of these defense-oriented industries are significantly altered and they are inextricably interwoven with and controlled by a military industrial oligarchy. This thesis, of course, is not universally embraced either as a complete explanation for levels of military spending or for the composition of defense outputs. Nonetheless, the closeness of relationships between the Pentagon and military suppliers as well as the interest and influence of bureaucratic and political individuals can hardly be questioned.

Clearly, defense outlays have differential regional impacts. Because such spending is concentrated in a relatively small number of products that in turn are produced unevenly geographically, industrial growth and development is given tremendous impetus in just a few areas, although subcontracting does tend to diffuse the benefits. Measuring wages and salaries paid by defense industries and agencies as a percentage of state personal income, the greatest benefits have gone to Alaska, Hawaii, Virginia, California, Maryland, Utah, and Washington. Using an alternate standard, total dollar outlays, in recent years California, New York, and Texas have received more than one-third of all military contracts. Obviously, the growth of industries in these states is considerably influenced by defense procurement. Within these states there is further regional concentration, which can be highly destabilizing if the pattern of defense outlays should change. Seattle, for example, experienced double-digit unemployment rates in the early 1970s (when national rates were below 6 percent) after defense spending was cut.

The structure of the work force and the composition of R&D outlays are also affected. The defense labor force, for example, is somewhat more skilled than the overall labor force. It also contains a very large proportion of engineering capabilities (particularly aeronautical and electrical) and physicists. Finally, roughly half of all federal spending on research and development is funded by the Department of Defense.

A final word addressing government spending in general and defense outlays in particular is in order. This concerns seemingly notorious charges, such as a $7,000 coffeepot found on military aircraft or the cost growth associated with weapon systems. Several factors are at work in this regard. First, large bureaucracies are fertile fields for procurement inefficiencies, with governments at most levels, defense agencies, and other large organizations particularly vulnerable. Second, it should be recognized that if outlays are not for standardized products, but instead for relatively unique procurements on the technological frontier, such as new airplanes or nuclear power plants, errors in cost estimation are very likely. Projects that span long time periods involve greater cost estimation risks. If one further factors in disturbing external macroeconomic factors, such as the rapacious inflation of the 1970s, cost overruns become even more understandable. None of this reasoning, of course, should be interpreted as a denial of illegal, corrupt, or inept actions on the part of some government and private individuals. Such regrettable activities clearly occur and play a role in cost escalation.

Nonetheless, there is often far less than meets the eye in our newspaper headlines and reports. For example, the seemingly outrageous $7,000 military aircraft coffeepot is less disturbing when one realizes that commercial airlines spend about $6,000 on theirs. And the pervasiveness of cost growth problems was made abundantly clear by two careful studies in the mid-1980s. The Rand Corporation found significant cost growth in six major catgories of outlays.[10] Forty-nine highway projects in 1972, with cost growth about 30 percent, were lowest. Fifty-nine public buildings that year more than doubled highway cost growth. Twelve very large construction projects in 1977 were well over 100 percent. In the 1980s, 19 pioneering processing plants reached almost 200 percent. Rand found that cost growth on major weapon systems in the 1970s was relatively low, just a little above highway projects. Further, in the 1970s it was below the corresponding figure for the 1960s, a somewhat surprising finding in view of the relatively stable price levels of the earlier period.

Another study found comparable results.[11] COMSAT satellites, highway projects, and the Bay Area Rapid Transit system were at the very low end of the overrun array. Major weapon systems and water projects had virtually identical cost growth and were in the lower middle of the survey range, both well below 50 percent. At the high end were energy processing plants (180 percent), the New Orleans Superdome (225 percent), the Concorde (580 percent), and the Trans-Alaska pipeline (593 percent). Two conclusions are inescapable. First, cost growth seems to be an inevitable fact of life with major projects of this kind. Second, average cost growth in Department of Defense acquisitions is generally lower, and often far lower, than corresponding activities elsewhere in government or in private undertakings.

Federal Credit Programs and the Financial Market

The federal government can influence financial markets and the allocation of credit by providing credit to individuals and organizations. A classic example of a credit instrument is the Reconstruction Finance Corporation of the 1930s. Existing examples include the credit programs offered by the Federal Mortgage Association, various farm credit agencies, and the Export-Import Bank. The Chrysler Corporation debt guarantee is another well-known example. Federal credit program subsidies are now provided to various sectors of the U.S. economy, ranging from housing to small business.

Such federal government credit programs can be classified into the following three categories:

1. *Direct loans by federal departments and agencies*: Such loans are generally made at an interest rate below those available in the private financial market. Direct loans have become less important in the era of sizable budget deficits because they require use of federal funds. Included in the $37.5 billion estimate for 1986 were federal financing bank loans ($15.3 billion) and agricultural loans (which exceed $6 billion).

2. *Loans guaranteed and insured by federal departments and agencies*: These loans are made by private lenders. The government merely assumes a contingent liability to pay the private lender if the private borrower defaults. Since there is little collateral in connection with the guarantee, the risk is relatively high. Loans guaranteed and insured by the federal government represent a big chunk of the recent expansion in federal credit subsidies. Importantly, the allocation of private capital can be significantly influenced by such government guarantees. At any given interest rate, government-backed Chrysler bonds attract more funds than private bonds without such guarantees. Accordingly, firms that in the absence of guarantees for Chrysler might have attracted capital find that financing for their projects is more expensive and less available.

Similarly, government deposit insurance also influences the allocation of capital. In the savings and loan crisis of the late 1980s, for example, it now seems clear that some institutions, recognizing that deposits were protected (or partially so) by government insurance, were willing to invest in high-risk projects, many of which failed to achieve expectations. In the absence of such federal insurance and facing the prospect of ruining friends, neighbors, and local businesses, lending officials are likely to have been far more conservative in their assessments and allocations.

3. *Loans by federally sponsored and privately owned agencies*: Little direct federal subsidy is involved in this type of loans. Federally sponsored agencies, such as Federal Home Loan Banks and National Mortgage Association, receive various tax advantages and can borrow at low interest rates in the market because of government backing. Loans by these agencies have become the dominant form of federal credit assistance today. They too influence that nation's allocation of credit by diverting funds from other arenas to favored ones (such as housing).

In the financial market, the interest rate is the price private businesses pay for the use of borrowed funds. It is affected by the total flow of saving and investment. According to empirical studies, federal credit programs do little to increase the total flow of saving and investment.[12] However, they do affect the allocation of investment funds. When they direct more investment funds to a specific industry, they correspondingly reduce the supply to other sectors, which may have received the funds had market forces alone been allowed to operate. This lowers total economic efficiency and tends to raise interest rates. Higher interest rates in turn will exert negative impacts on both private investment and Treasury borrowings from the public.

Influence of Antitrust Laws

Economic theory suggests that firms in monopoly positions make inefficient use of society's scarce resources. Such firms may reap monopoly profits by restricting their output and the flow of resources. Antitrust laws were passed by Congress specifically to promote more competitive market conditions. Historically, these laws reflected problems of an early stage of industrialization. In the latter half of the nineteenth century, as pointed in chapter 1, the network of railroads and canals drew the nation together economically; transportation costs fell, reducing the physical distribution constraint on plant size. At the same time, technology changed rapidly, encouraging capital-intensive production on a large scale. Local markets were widened into national markets. Business monopolies in the form of trusts appeared in the 1870s and 1880s in almost all major industries including the petroleum, meat-packing, railroad, sugar, lead, whiskey, coal, and tobacco industries. Associated with the development of trusts were a wave of horizontal mergers, resulting in a higher level of market concentration. Engaging in predatory pricing and price discrimination, these organizations made enormous profits.

Widespread resentment from small business and farmers led Congress to pass the Sherman Antitrust Act in 1890. The act made monopoly, attempts to monopolize, and "restraints of trade" illegal. Either the Justice Department or parties injured by monopolies could file suits under the Sherman Act. Other cornerstones in the antitrust arena are the Clayton Act and the Federal Trade Commission Act, both passed in 1914. The former made price discrimination, tying contracts, intercorporate stockholdings, and interlocking directorates illegal, while the latter created the Federal Trade Commission, which has the authority to investigate antitrust violations and to prevent the use of unfair methods of competition. In 1950 the Celler-Kefauver Antimerger Act was passed; it prohibits vertical mergers and conglomerate mergers if such mergers significantly lessen competition. This law was enacted to plug the loopholes associated with Section 7 of the Clayton Act, which prohibits potentially anticompetitive mergers. It outlaws mergers "where in any line of commerce in any section of the country, the effect of such acquisition may be substantially to lessen competition, or tend to create monopoly." Thus a firm is not permitted to acquire the assets of another firm when such acquisition would lessen competition. However, this law is far from problem-free; it also has some loopholes of its own. Nevertheless, hundreds of cases involving various types of industry have been decided under this act.[13] It is important to recognize that the courts and enforcing agencies have been placed in the position of having to assess difficult empirical issues, particularly the degree to which competition is reduced. Even if an uncontested numerical measure could be calculated, an assessment would have to be made as to whether or not such decline in competition is substantial or significant. Obviously, a large number of factors, including philosophic and political orientations, will influence such assessments.

Enforcement of the Sherman Act and subsequent competition legislation has exerted important impacts on anticompetitive behavior. However, anticompetitive activities have not ceased. Managers continue to seek market power through a variety of channels, many of which are quite legal. It should also be pointed out that the institutionalization of antitrust may mislead the public into a belief that entrenched economic power is being policed successfully, thereby legitimizing such power and abetting its escape from effective social control.[14]   There are some important exceptions to antitrust laws. Exports, unions, and agricultural cooperatives are excluded. Such exclusions promote concentration of economic power. Other legislations, such as patent laws and protective tariffs on imports, also encourage the development of business monopolies. Recent public discussions have also witnessed voices suggesting the abridgement or modification of antitrust enforcement as an aid to making U.S. business more internationally competitive.

How have the antitrust laws been applied to the business sector? Empirical evidence seems to indicate that the enforcement of antitrust is rather strict with respect to cooperation and mergers, but lenient toward existing concentrations.[15] The existing big firms are generally not subject to antitrust prosecution. But if smaller firms in the same industry attempt to merge, they may have problems with the antitrust laws. In recent years, there have been a few antitrust cases involving large, well-known corporations that resulted in a partial opening of Xerox patents to competing firms (1972 decision), and an out-of-court settlement (in 1982) requiring AT&T to divest itself of some 22 locally operating phone companies. It is important to note that both the existence of antitrust laws and their anticipated application may significantly influence business behavior. Corporate executives will often think twice when considering attempts to merge or cooperate to fix prices. Each administration, of course, has a different emphasis and vigor in applying antitrust and other laws. The Reagan administration, for example, permitted many mergers of competing firms, as in the airline industry, in the belief that the competitive environment would not be substantially harmed or that efficiency would be enhanced.

Facing fierce competition in the world markets, U.S. manufacturing firms have increasingly asked for import protection and for relaxation of the antitrust laws in order to help U.S. producers to compete more effectively in the international market against aggressive, low-wage, overseas competitors and/or alleged foreign monopolizing.[16] Such adjustments, however, would generally weaken the competitive environment both by reducing foreign competition and by softening the Clayton Act's prohibition of mergers that tend to lessen competition. Clear and significant benefits should be demonstrated before such actions are initiated.

Macro Policies and Aggregate Economic Activities

Stable economic conditions are important to the efficient functioning of a firm. Severe fluctuations in the form of inflation, recession, or depression will adversely affect the firm's output, employment, and profit as well as distort its planning horizons and strategic behavior. The Great Depression of the 1930s, for example, seriously harmed the business sector. Many businesses failed, and many workers lost their jobs. The unemployment rate was pushed to an incredible 25 percent, clearly an enormous economic loss to the nation. Although such a major depression is rare, economic fluctuations are a fact of life in the U.S. mixed capitalistic economy. They are commonly called business cycle swings, characterized by uneven, alternating upswing and downswing movements. In the post-World War II period, the United States has experienced eight business cycles. British economist John Maynard Keynes suggested that government policies can be used to alleviate these cyclical fluctuations, by reducing their duration and amplitude.[17] His theory is accepted by a majority of contemporary U.S. economists and has served as the basis for changes in the direction and use of fiscal policy.

Indeed, a federal enactment now commonly referred to as the Full Employment Act of 1946 officially marked the end of laissez-faire by mandating that it is government's responsibility to promote a maximum of employment, growth, and purchasing power. Rather than "hands off," it became formal governmental responsibility to intervene in the economy when the stated goals were not being met. These responsibilities were further reenforced by the Humphrey-Hawkins Act of 1978. Some believe that it was not until the Kennedy administration that the government made any serious efforts to uphold this mandate. Today, however, there are few, if any, who question these responsibilities, although opinions widely differ as to which policies and actions best meet the goals.

According to Keynesian theory, economic instability is caused by erratic fluctuations in aggregate demand—that is, total demand from consumers, businesses, government, and foreigners. When the economy is already operating at capacity, increased aggregate demand causes prices to rise—that is, inflation. On the other hand, when aggregate demand is deficient, abnormally high unemployment and lost production result. Government can influence aggregate demand through tax and expenditure policies (which are the major ingredients of fiscal policy) so as to promote economic stability and help industry produce maximum attainable output. Because government spending is a major component of aggregate demand, it can directly influence its level. Similarly, since taxes affect the disposable income of consumers and profitability of business firms, tax policy has an important indirect impact on the consumption and business investment components of aggregate demand. The federal budget, therefore, can be a powerful weapon to combat instability, unemployment, and inflation. Alternately, these potent tools, if misapplied, can aggravate economic stability.

Another public policy that may be utilized to influence the economy is monetary policy. Money plays an important role in our economy, serving three basic functions: medium of exchange, standard of value, and store of value. The quantity of money can affect the nation's output and price levels. If "too much money chases too few goods," the price level will increase. On the other hand, inadequate supply of money has a restrictive effect on economic activities. According to monetarists, a group of economists whose best known spokesman is Nobel Prize-winner Milton Friedman, there is a direct link between money supply, price levels, and aggregate demand. In the United States the Federal Reserve System (the Fed) is the custodian of the money supply, manipulating it via a variety of techniques to attain the goals of stable prices, full employment, and adequate growth. The Fed is a quasi-autonomous agency that acts as the central bank; it implements monetary policy. Its activities also influence interest rates, the price of loanable funds (a rate that is deemed by many to be particularly important in business investment decisions). In recent years the Fed has come under great criticism because of the sustained high level of real interest rates that has characterized all of the 1980s. Clearly, both monetary and fiscal policy have important contributions to make to economic stability. In the opinion of most economists, to be successful these policies need coordination rather than running at cross currents.

Policies for Promoting Growth

In a capitalistic economy, the major source of instability, according to Keynes, is the instability in the level of private capital investment. A change in investment will generate a multiple change in income because the increased investment leads to higher production and income, which in turn stimulate higher consumption. Higher consumer demand evokes even more capital investment. A chain reaction is thus set into motion by investment, the well-known "multiplier effect." When business conditions are sluggish, government can either increase its spending to make up the slack or reduce taxes to encourage business investment. Keynesians traditionally stress the effect of tax cuts in raising levels of aggregate demand. Tax cuts, however, may also have favorable impacts on the supply side of the market; they stimulate incentives to work, save, and invest, and to undertake entrepreneurial risks. Tax incentives are emphasized by supply-side economists. The tax cuts embodied in the Economic Recovery Act of 1981 were touted as supply-side economic policies. The tax reform bill of 1986 also embraces some supply-side concepts.[18] A major objective of such policies is to stimulate aggregate supply. According to proponents, these policies will cause employment, production, and real income to increase, thus expanding the tax base. At the higher level of real income, they believe that the loss of tax revenue would be relatively small. However, it takes considerable time for this kind of policy to be fully effective; it is a long-run strategy.

In the 1970s and early 1980s when the U.S. economy experienced stagflation—an economic condition in which stagnation of real production coincides with rapidly rising price levels—government's attempt to correct the inflation aspect of stagflation with Keynesian demand management policies may well have depressed the national output and worsened unemployment. Attention was thus directed to the supply side, in the hope that tax incentives would be strong enough to raise aggregate supply substantially. However, the supply-side incentives require time and may depress government revenues in the near term. In the meantime, the federal budget deficit will increase if government expenditure programs are not cut sufficiently. In 1985 the federal budget deficit reached an unprecedented level exceeding $200 billion. It increased in 1986, then declined and should be about $152 billion in 1989. Continuing huge budget deficits, it is feared, may affect the stability of the economy. If so, it will be an example of fiscal policy gone awry and powerful tools inappropriately applied. The Gramm-Rudman-Hollings Act was specifically passed by Congress with the aim of getting the federal government to balance the budget by 1991.[19] The objective of this act is to control government spending, balance federal revenues and expenditures, and thereby reduce pressures upon the Fed for a highly restrictive monetary policy.

Supplying and Maintaining Basic Infrastructure

Within the category of exhaustive government expenditures (government as contributor) are outlays that merit special treatment when studying the U.S. industrial structure. In order for the private sector to perform properly, there must be adequate investment in basic infrastructure, or what economists call social overhead capital. This grouping includes transportation systems such as interstate highways and local roads, water systems, and ports. Some would also include jails, hospitals, and education in this category. The nature of such investments is such that the private sector will undertake only limited efforts in these areas. Accordingly, if these investments, critical to the successful functioning of our industrial system, are to be made, the responsibility falls upon various levels of government.

The current condition of U.S. infrastructure raises many questions and suggests future problems. The nation's interstate highway system, for example, which handles over 20 percent of all highway traffic, is "deteriorating at a rate requiring reconstruction of 2,000 miles of road per year."[20] The Department of Transportation estimates that in 1989 it would cost $50 billion just to "repair the nation's 240,000 deficient bridges and another $315 billion to maintain highways" in their 1983 condition through the year 2000.[21] Port facilities are spotty and a water resource crisis looms on the horizon.[22] While depreciation of basic infrastructure continues to grow, budgetary outlays have been restricted. In 1977, for example, depreciation accounted for over 76 percent of government (all levels) gross investment, leaving net investment a mere $7 billion (1972 dollars). This stands in contrast with data of a decade earlier. In 1967 net investment was $24 billion; depreciation claimed only 41 percent of gross outlays.[23]

This is a very serious indictment of government priorities in the allocation of public funds. The implications of an ineffective infrastructure are pervasive (and will be further discussed in chapter 5). According to W. W. Rostow, "estimates of the total investment outlays to rehabilitate and maintain the nation's physical infrastructure over the next decade or fifteen years range from about $650 to $2,500 billion."[24] Whereas in 1965 some 4.1 percent of GNP was allocated to public works, in 1977 the figure was only 2.3 percent. Accordingly, an extra 2 percent of GNP must be directed to basic infrastructure simply to attain the 1965 percentage, and this effort would still encounter depreciation levels more than 50 percent larger than in the 1960s.

These sums are staggering. If met, this spending would provide a great stimulus to the construction industry and its suppliers. Further, it would raise productivity throughout the economy by reducing transportation and other impediments. However, in an era of Gramm-Rudman budgetary stringency, it is open to question as to how seriously infrastructure needs will be addressed. It may well turn out to be the Achilles' heel of future U.S. economic progress.

Direct Government Regulation of Business

In addition to relying on taxation and expenditure programs to achieve national objectives, the federal government can influence economic activity through regulatory processes. Entrepreneurial decisions fundamental to the functioning of private enterprise are now subject to widespread governmental regulation. The following is a partial list of the many important regulatory agencies existing in the U.S. economy:

- Interstate Commerce Commission (ICC): regulates the operation of railroads and the transportation industry.
- Federal Communications Commission (FCC): regulates the management of radio and television stations.
- Food & Drug Administration: oversees the manufacturing of ethical drugs.
- Nuclear Regulatory Commission: controls the production of nuclear materials.

These are examples of federal agencies that directly implement regulations related to pricing, output, and overall economic performance of particular industries. State and local government regulation also abounds. Accordingly, the presence of government in the functioning of many private businesses is an important feature of the U.S. mixed economy.

Additionally, the federal government has moved into the area of social regulation in the last two decades.[25] Here, the regulations are related to product safety, working conditions, opportunity to work, or environmental impact of products. The following listing enumerates four better known agencies that were created to implement such goals:

- The Occupational Safety and Health Administration
- The Consumer Products Safety Commission
- The Environmental Protection Agency
- The Equal Employment Opportunity Commission

Social regulations cover virtually all industries. Their objective is to help achieve improvements in the quality of life, including safer and better products, less pollution, and better working conditions.

The implementation of all these regulations has been costly. In addition to the government's spending substantial public funds to operate these agencies, businesses also bear heavy costs to comply with the regulations.[26] It is estimated by the U.S. Office of Management and Budget that businesses spend over 143 million hours each year to fill out government forms. Reporting alone obviously entails enormous costs, as do (would) compliance actions such as pollution controls or airbags. Additionally, there are indirect costs in the form of production delays, inconsistent regulations, delays for regulatory approval, and greatly increased managerial uncertainty. Total costs clearly involve many billions of dollars, although this heavy expense does not prove that regulation is not worth the cost (we must compare this to the value of regulatory benefits, a figure extremely difficult to derive). It is nonetheless a heavy burden and gives rise to the claim that U.S. business is overregulated and that this condition has contributed to its difficulties in competing internationally (against the goods of countries that do not impose similar requirements).

In addition to being costly to implement, regulatory activity tends to confer benefits on certain groups or firms at the expense of others, thus exerting an important influence on organized (or potentially organized) interest groups. Further, it is alleged that regulation has contributed to inefficiency and that the regulatory commissions have tended to be captured by the industries they were supposed to regulate. Such public sentiments have led to regulatory reforms. These efforts have been directed to relax or eliminate regulations in some industries and place greater reliance on market forces to serve consumers. During the late 1970s and early 1980s there has been a notable movement toward deregulation. The industry first affected was the airlines, but deregulation later spread to railroads, trucking, petroleum, and elsewhere.[27] The federal government continues to review and revise existing and proposed regulations in the hope of finding better ways to attain the social and economic goals that regulations are to achieve.

INDUSTRIAL POLICY DEBATE

As pointed out in chapter 1, the U.S. economy shed its preeminence in the last decade. Some economists claim that U.S. industries have lost their competitive edge in the world markets because the free-market idea is not working. As a result, the United States is deindustrializing. These economists argue for more government involvement in the operation of the industrial sector. According to this view, if the Japanese economy is prospering by the guidance of the Ministry of International Trade and Industry (MITI), the United States also can target specific industries for special government assistance, thereby revitalizing our economy. Thus, the notion of a national industrial policy (NIP) was born. Major advocates of NIP include Robert Reich (Harvard) and Lester Thurow (MIT).[28] Others suggest that if the United States has indeed lost competitiveness and vitality, it is largely due to too much government intervention. They maintain that activist government policies have been misguided.

Historically, NIP originated in the period of mercantilism (fifteenth to eighteenth centuries). But NIP has become popular in the post-World War II decades by its perceived success in France and Japan. Generally speaking, NIP directs attention to specific industries rather than to industrialization as a whole. It proposes a series of sector-specific, and even company-specific, supports. NIP is designed to promote the sectors that seem to be advancing, to maintain the mature sector, and either to protect or ease the adjustments in the declining sectors. In other words, the major objective of NIP is to strengthen industry for the future and to ensure that domestic manufacturing and service industries can compete effectively in the world market. Policy instruments for NIP include tax incentives, subsidies, public investment, and other government regulations.

Those who argue for NIP for the U.S. economy point out that this country actually has a form of NIP as illustrated by the federal government's industrial support for agriculture, the Department of Defense's industrial initiatives, general tax incentives for business investment, and ad hoc bailouts for such well-known companies as the Chrysler Corporation and Continental Illinois National Bank. But, they claim, these are piecemeal policies and are ineffective in increasing the U.S. competitive edge. Thus they advocate a coherent NIP.

Adoption of such an NIP would represent a major move toward industrial planning. While appealing on paper, such industrial planning may be fraught with flaws. For example, why should industrial planning help declining industries after the market has transmitted a signal that the demand for their products has diminished? Since NIP is supposed to provide support for "winners," is government in a better position than bankers and investors to pick those winners? Further, information is costly to obtain and process. The policy makers may not have sufficient information, expertise, or time to help them make the correct choice. And even with perfect information, would the decisions reflect only economic realities, or would they be seriously tainted by political pressures? Thus the opponents have attacked the NIP proposals as being based on a belief in the ability of government direction to enhance the economy's performance.[29] NIP remains a controversial concept. No consensus has been reached. The NIP debate, however, has triggered discussion on such important questions as industry aging, economic maturity, and market-generated renewal.

During the 1984 presidential campaign, Democratic candidates Walter Mondale, Gary Hart, and Jesse Jackson tried to use the NIP issue to challenge Reagan. Among their proposals were the revitalization of basic industries through a mixture of protectionist trade policy and government aid to firms and industries, stimulation of the high tech sector, which would produce new jobs, and an industrial policy with overtones of an expanded welfare state, which would mandate government aid to industries and private firms in relation to specific trade-offs for job development, affirmative action, and urban revitalization. They addressed the issues with different stress to different constituencies—industrial unions, high tech industry, and black voters. Yet it was the diversity of constituencies that made it impossible to unite these special interest groups during the primaries to form a generally accepted NIP, revealing deep social and economic fault lines that the industrial policy debate has often been unable to overcome. As Richard McGahey put it, "industrial policy's only hope of success would be a broad political coalition with a credible vision of a future that combined economic growth with increased social equity and programs to ease the pain of economic transition."[30] Evidence seems to indicate that, given the diverse and often conflicting interests of heterogeneous social groupings, it is difficult, if not impossible, to unite such disparate constituencies.

NOTES

1. An essential feature of public goods is that they cannot be provided to one person without others also receiving the benefits. Public goods, then, are jointly consumed goods.

2. Externalities (spillover effects) represent the side effects of an action (consumption or production) that influences the well-being of those not directly related to the transaction or undertaking. Smoking, for example, involves negative externalities (costs imposed on others).

3. Taxation, of course, is used to at least partially finance government's exhaustive spending and transfer payments. Interestingly, in 1989 the average American had to wait 124 days—until May 4—to satisfy all state, local, and federal taxes. See Tax Foundation, *Tax Features*, April 1989.

4. F. M. Scherer, *Industrial Market Structure and Economic Performance*, 2nd ed. (Chicago: Rand-McNally, 1980), p. 142.

5. U.S. Department of Commerce, Bureau of Industrial Economics, *Sectoral Implications of Defense Expenditures* (Washington, D.C.: U.S. Government Printing Office, 1982), p. 4.

6. See Data Resources Incorporated, *Defense Economic Impact Modeling System* (Washington, D.C.: July 19, 1984), p. 1.

7. Foreign purchases of military equipment are generally channeled through the Department of Defense.

8. For a detailed discussion of government influence on private business via government procurement, see Murray L. Weidenbaum, *Business, Government, and the Public*, 2nd ed. (Englewood Cliffs, N.J.: Prentice-Hall, 1981), Ch. 9.

9. Seymour Melman, *Pentagon Capitalism* (New York: McGraw-Hill, 1970).

10. Michael Rich and Ed Dews, "Improving the Military Acquisition Process—Lessons from Rand Research" (R-373-AF/RC) (Santa Monica, Calif.: The Rand Corporation, 1986).

11. F. Biery, "Cost Growth and the Use of Competitive Acquisition Strategies," *The National Estimator* 6, no. 3 (Fall 1985).

12. See Weidenbaum, p. 189.

13. For a detailed discussion of some well-known cases, see Douglas F. Greer, *Industrial Organization and Public Policy* (New York: Macmillan, 1980), pp. 158–67.

14. See Willard F. Mueller, "Antitrust as a Planning Economy: An Anachronism or an Essential Complement," *Journal of Economic Issues* 9 (1975), pp. 159–79.

15. William G. Shepherd, *The Economics of Industrial Organization* (Englewood Cliffs, N.J.: Prentice-Hall, 1979), p. 434.

16. *Newsweek*, January 27, 1986, p. 46.

17. Keynes published a book entitled *The General Theory of Employment, Interest, and Money* (New York: Harcourt, Brace, 1936). He became the most influential economist of the twentieth century.

18. The tax reform bill approved by Congress cut high marginal tax rates—the rates on the last dollar of income—from 50 percent to 28 percent. According to the Council of Economic Advisers to the president, the new tax system may raise economic growth 0.25 percent a year and add $100 billion to the economy's annual output. See *Newsweek*, August 25, 1986, p. 30. From a supply-side perspective, however, the bill did contain negative features as well. One such feature was the repeal of the investment tax credit, an action of much consternation to supply-side adherents.

19. The Supreme Court, by a 7–2 vote, struck down a key portion of the Gramm-Rudman Act on July 7, 1986. The justices said the central provision of the act—ordering automatic deficit reduction—violates the constitutionally required separation of powers between the executive and legislative branches. Congress has since passed legislation amending the act to conform with the court's objections.

20. Pat Choate and Susan Walter, *America in Ruins: Beyond the Public Works Pork Barrel* (Washington, D.C.: Council of State Planning Agencies, 1981), p. 2.

21. Bob Rast, "Infrastructure Crisis Grips U.S.," *Times-Picayune* (New Orleans), April 9, 1989, p. A3.

22. Choate and Walter, pp. 1–5.

23. J. C. Musgrave, Bureau of Economic Analysis, special tabulation; U.S. Department of Commerce, *A Study of Public Works Investment in the United States* (Washington, D.C., U.S. Government Printing Office, 1980), p. I-63.

24. W. W. Rostow, *The Barbaric Counter-Revolution* (Austin: University of Texas Press, 1983), p. 121.

25. William Lilley III and James C. Miller, "The New Social Regulation," *The Public Interest*, Spring 1977.

26. Murray L. Weidenbaum, *The Cost of Government Regulation of Business* (Washington, D.C.: U.S. Government Printing Office, 1978).

27. For elaboration of major deregulatory initiatives in the period 1971–82, see Roger G. Noll and Bruce M. Owen, *The Political Economy of Deregulation* (Washington, D.C.: American Enterprise Institute for Public Policy Research, 1983), p. 4.

28. Robert Reich, *The Next American Frontier* (New York: Times Books, 1983); Lester C. Thurow, *The Zero-Sum Solution* (New York: Simon and Schuster, 1985).

29. For an argument against the NIP, see Richard B. McKenzie, *Competing Visions: The Political Conflict over America's Economic Future* (Washington, D.C.: CATO Institute, 1985). For a careful review of the NIP concept and a survey of the literature, see R. D. Norton, "Industrial Policy and American Renewal," *Journal of Economic Literature*, March 1986.

30. Richard McGahey, "Industrial Policy's Problem," *New York Times*, July 6, 1984.

4

Technology

The growth of the industrial base of the U.S. economy is directly related to technological progress. Thirty years ago, the United States was the world's undisputed technological leader, and until the 1970s the U.S. economy was characterized by a rapid rate of innovation. Such technological progress enabled the industrial sector to produce new or improved goods and services. These advances, of course, derive from a combination of resources and efforts. The human factor is a primary input and reflects human capital development, management, and incentive systems. Most technical progress also requires capital investment, either in plant or equipment or both. Finally, raw materials may also play a role. U.S. economic growth in terms of the change in output per worker has come predominantly from the application of new and better production techniques by an increasingly well-trained work force. Technological progress has not only raised standards of living, but also provided greater national security. Since World War II, the United States has relied on a lead in military technology supported by a technically advanced industrial base to maintain its military posture and a creditable deterrence.

TECHNOLOGICAL DEVELOPMENT

Technological progress stems from learning-by-doing, from fortuitous accidents, and from research and development. R&D include three kinds of activities: basic research, applied research, and development. According to the National Science Foundation, *basic research* is the original investigation for the advancement of scientific knowledge that does not have immediate commercial objectives, while *applied research* involves using the results of basic research to prove an applicable idea in a laboratory setting and to aim at a specific practical payoff.[1] Both in the United States and in Japan some 12–13 percent of total R&D outlays in the mid-1980s went to basic research. *Development* tries to direct research findings for commercial practicality; it includes the construction of pilot models and demonstration plants, as well as any related feasibility studies that management may require. Research is oriented toward the pursuit of new knowledge whereas development is oriented toward the capacity to produce a particular product.

Commercial application of invention resulting from R&D activities is called *innovation*. To activate innovation requires capital investment, access to raw materials, labor, marketing facilities, and consumer demand for the output. Development and commercialization (marketing) of a new or improved product are usually marked by uncertainty about the extent of the market and planned introduction dates of rivals. Research may or may not produce a useful idea; it may lead to new technology that can be patented, or lead to new technology that can be exploited by the institution that undertook the research. Therefore, inventive activity is economically very risky. To make risk-bearing palatable, society relies primarily on the potential of economic gain. The market system rewards innovative activities by awarding payments to holders of the ownership or property rights. Applied research can yield ownership rights if the resulting new technology can be embodied in a patentable production process. If such rights to new technology are not protected, there would be little incentive for people to undertake costly and highly uncertain R&D. We will discuss further the impact of patents in a later section.

The fact that almost all large industrial producers have dedicated R&D departments attests to the importance these firms place upon such activities. It is, of course, difficult to assign an exact value to such efforts, either at the firm, industry, or national level. Indeed, the "growth accounting framework yields no satisfactory measure of value of R&D in stimulating economic growth."[2] Nonetheless, estimates from some econometric studies suggest significant effects on aggregate output and productivity. It has been found that R&D has its biggest effect on productivity in those businesses where major technical changes have occurred within the recent past.[3] On an industry level, there have been some spectacular results. The marginal rate of return from R&D was estimated about 50 percent for the chemicals industry[4] and 57 percent for agriculture.[5]

R&D EXPENDITURES

Total R&D spending in the United States has shown a general upward trend. However, R&D expenditures as a percentage of the GNP declined in the 1970s and did not reachieve 1960s comparability until the late 1980s. In 1987, 2.87 percent of the GNP was devoted to R&D, whereas in 1978 it was only 2.1 percent. The 1964 high was 2.9 percent. In terms of international comparisons, the 1985 U.S. ratio (2.7 percent) was slightly below Japan's 2.9 percent, equal to West Germany's ratio and higher than France's 2.3 percent. All these proportions, however, fell substantially below the 3.8 percent estimate for the Soviet Union.[6] Further, the United States, along with France, allocates a relatively high share of its R&D resources to defense-related projects, while West Germany and Japan perform relatively far more civilian R&D. On the other hand, the Soviet Union's R&D effort, which was the highest percentage, may not necessarily lead to a stronger relative overall science and technology system. If the vast bulk is concentrated in defense and there is little diffusion to the rest of the economy, total economic and technical gains may be small. Additionally, such percentage measures are merely indicators of relative R&D efforts, not actual amounts or results. Indeed, in 1987 the United States, despite a lower ratio of R&D to GNP and its high proportion allocated to defense, still spent almost twice the dollars on civilian R&D as did Japan, whose defense proportion of total R&D was negligible. Finally, outlays do not guarantee results, and nations may differ in the amount of technical progress that each garners from a given dollar investment. The efficiency of R&D efforts, diffusion of ideas, and ability to implement innovation are all important factors that are likely to vary greatly among nations.

The federal government finances about half of the R&D in the United States with private industry funding roughly 47 percent, and the remainder coming mainly from universities. In terms of who actually performs the R&D, industry's share is close to 75 percent, universities and others do about 15 percent, and the federal government itself performs only 12 percent. Military and space projects have traditionally taken the lion's share of federal support. Defense alone in 1989 is expected to account for about 66 percent of federal R&D funding. As a share of total U.S. R&D outlays, military and space projects were once as high as 56 percent (1961 and 1964), but declined virtually every year through 1980 when they hit a low of 29 percent. The space share dropped very significantly during the second half of the 1960s and has remained at roughly 7 percent since 1978, while a steady decline in the defense share began around 1973. In the 1980s, however, the defense proportion rose from 22 percent of total R&D outlays to 32 percent in 1987. Health now absorbs about 12 percent of federal R&D, while energy takes 4 percent.[7]

Because of uncertainties that often are entailed in R&D seeking major technological advance, financial constraints are likely to prohibit many firms from undertaking such projects, especially in the area of basic scientific research. Additionally, it is difficult for any one firm to retain exclusively for itself all the derivative benefits. Other firms that did not undertake such outlays are likely nonetheless to enjoy some of the results. Therefore, both high risk and the existence of externalities (positive spillovers) suggest that the federal government should subsidize or supplement private R&D (which would otherwise be conducted at less than socially optimal levels). This is done in several ways.

Government provides R&D incentives by sharing the risks. It does this via tax credits and loss writeoffs. Further, in some major industries with strong national security linkages, like aviation, semiconductor, and computer, there is federally funded R&D. R&D outlays in these industries have significantly influenced their structures and progress. During the 1920s and 1930s, for example, the National Advisory Commission on Aeronautics (which later gave rise to NASA) undertook research and testing, resulting in the development of the modern passenger airliner. Additionally, the semiconductor industry benefited greatly from the support of research in basic physics and materials research sponsored by agencies ranging from the National Science Foundation to the Defense Department. The first operational computers were developed on a government contract.[8]

Total expenditures on R&D (including government, industries, and universities), after adjustment for inflation, more than doubled in the United States between 1960 and 1984. While the federal share of R&D outlays declined in the past two decades, private-sector spending has grown considerably. The National Science Foundation reports that private industry steadily increased funding of R&D activities between 1980 and 1984 at an average annual constant dollar rate of 6 percent.[9] It is significant that such a high rate of growth persisted even during the recession period of the early 1980s. This reflects the importance industry places on this type of activity. However, because the potential for innovation is not evenly spread across all industries, expenditures on R&D vary greatly. In 1982, the industries that were the leading performers of R&D were those producing aircraft and missiles ($14 billion), electrical equipment ($12 billion), machinery ($8 billion), chemicals ($7 billion), motor vehicles ($5 billion), and professional and scientific instruments ($4 billion). These proportions did not change materially as the decade progressed. This group accounted for about 85 percent of all R&D performed by industry. Generally speaking, R&D outlays in high technology manufacturing have increased much faster than in other manufacturing and non-manufacturing industries. It is worth repeating that much of the R&D they performed was actually financed by the federal government.

INNOVATION AND MANAGEMENT'S ROLE

Innovation involves putting invention gained from R&D into commercial application. Management plays a vital role in this phase. It is responsible to coordinate factors of production and to acquire fixed investment in plants and equipment that use the new technology. According to Joseph Schumpeter, innovation involves the entrepreneurial functions required to bring a new technical possibility into commercial utilization for the first time—identifying the market, raising the necessary funds, building a new organization, cultivating the market, and so forth.[10] Of course the entrepreneur and manager may not be the same person. Regardless, implementation of new technology through commercialization requires risk taking as well as organizing the effort and obtaining financial support.

In the process of technological change, innovative management puts together a team of scientists and engineers. The development of complex systems requires large multidisciplinary groupings, thus complicating the decision-making process. The R&D manager, who may be an engineer or a scientist, must make decisions that may be outside his or her own area of expertise. Cooperation and planning are thus important for efficient operation. It is critical that R&D managers recognize the dynamics of the planning-execution matrix of decisions in which they are ultimately involved. A primary role of management is regulating the boundaries between the several subsystems and many sub-subsystems. In addition, because government is often the principal customer in the R&D market, the securing of government contracts has become a major preoccupation of R&D management. Successful R&D managers must not only have technical knowledge, but negotiating skill as well. They are dealing not simply with government, but also with competitors (since subcontracting is an important part of the effort). All these require diversity in management skills and creativeness in managerial techniques.

Table 4.1 lists the top 10 U.S. corporations in terms of R&D spending in 1987. R&D effort as a percent of sales shows considerable variation, as do outlays per employee. While these were generally the leading firms in their respective industries, it is not necessarily the case that it was R&D effort that gave them top positions. All are very large organizations and can afford to spend more generously (and bear the greater risks) than many smaller firms.

Table 4.1
R&D Measures for the Top Ten U.S. Corporations, 1987

Company	Sales		R&D Outlays		R&D as percent of sales	R&D per employee ($)
	Amount (mil$)	Rank in Industry	Amount (mil $)	Rank in Industry		
General Motors	101,781	1	4,361	1	4.3	5,362
IBM	54,217	1	3,998	1	7.4	10,269
Ford Motor	71,643	2	2,514	2	3.5	7,176
AT&T	33,598	1	2,453	1	7.3	8,096
Du Pont	30,468	1	1,223	1	4.0	8,727
General Elec.	39,315	1	1,194	1	3.0	3,954
Digital Equip.	9,389	3	1,010	2	10.8	9,114
Eastman Kodak	13,305	1	922	1	7.5	7,974
Hewlett-Packard	8,090	4	901	3	11.1	10,988
United Tech.	17,170	1	879	1	5.1	4,626

Source: Derived from *Business Week*, June 20, 1988.

Gerhard Rosegger studied U.S. innovations from 1953 to 1973.[11] His figures, which should be taken only as rough indicators (due to classification problems and subjective assessments), suggest three industries as most dynamic over that period: electrical equipment and communications, chemicals and allied products, and machinery.

This discussion also raises a question concerning the source of invention underlying such innovations. Have well-financed, corporate laboratories replaced the individual inventor? Do greater outlays generally yield more patents? Are large firms better innovators? Appropriate replies to these questions are not totally clear, but there appears to be more public belief in positive answers than the facts and data warrant. Empirical evidence, for example, finds "no obvious relationship between either expenditures or labor input on the one hand, and the production of patentable, and patented, inventions on the other."[12] It seems that individual inventors and small organizations still have great advantages in flexibility and incentives. And, while the great majority of the inventions underlying the innovations listed were generated inside the innovating organization, as Rosegger points out,

it is a reflection on the importance of inventive activity outside corporate R&D laboratories that approximately one-third of the innovations covered can be attributed to various "outside" inventors. Of these, the independent's role is perhaps most remarkable. . . . Surely, it would be premature to announce his demise under the onslaught of organized inventive activity.[13]

TECHNOLOGY'S ROLE IN THE RESOURCE MARKET

As noted in chapter 1, technology is a critical factor for growth and efficient utilization of resources. In the previous century and in episodes of the more recent past, there has been a widespread belief that mineral resources would become increasingly scarce during economic growth because the physical endowments of such resources are fixed, yet they must serve continuously increasing demands. Further, societies tend to use the best economic resources first, thereby leaving lower quality as well as reduced quantities to face burgeoning needs. Thus many economists, including Smith, Malthus, Ricardo, and Mill, conceived that mineral resources, like agriculture, was a decreasing returns or increasing cost industry. Despite the recurring popularity of such themes, empirical evidence compiled by economists has shed new light on the concept of scarcity of mineral supplies. The principle of diminishing returns is not necessarily applicable to long-run trends. In the long run a variety of factors affect the scarcity of mineral resources, including increases in knowledge and technological improvements in production, transportation, and use of resources. Furthermore, discovery of new resources and substitutes, growth in international trade, recycling, conservation, and other socioeconomic-technical changes all affect the supply of minerals.

Empirical studies indicate that in the United States over a period of almost a century, minerals production has not been subject to increasing costs.[14] To the contrary, the opportunity cost of minerals in terms of man-days of labor to produce them has declined persistently. Therefore, the long-run trend for nonfuel minerals is toward less scarcity and lower prices. Further, the cost trends of almost every natural resource have also been downward.[15] For example, in the United States an hour's work has bought increasingly more copper, wheat, and oil from 1800 to the present. Figure 4.1 graphically illustrates the substantial secular decline in the relative price of copper as measured by the ratio of copper prices to wages over a 185-year period. Clearly, the facts demonstrate an increasing relative availability of raw materials and a reduced (rather than greater) scarcity relative to human work effort. Not surprisingly, the prices of raw materials have been falling relative to the Consumer Price Index (CPI). These trends, not widely recognized by the American public, are made possible mainly through the progress of technology. Clearly, the consequences of technological change are pervasive, leaving a strong imprint upon economic growth, quality of life, and the ways Americans work, play, and defend the nation.

Figure 4.1
Scarcity of Copper as Indicated by Its Price Relative to Wages, 1800–1984

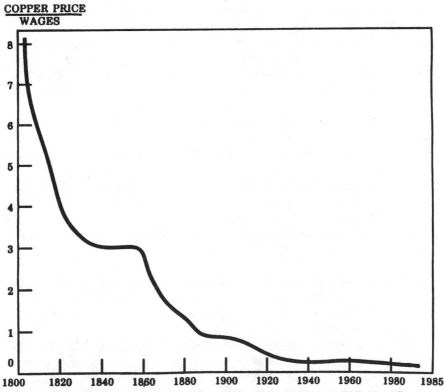

Source: Adapted from Julian L. Simon and Herman Kahn, eds., *The Resourceful Earth—A Response to Global 2000* (New York: Basil Blackwell, 1984), p. 15.

THE PATENT SYSTEM

Since R&D is a costly and risky undertaking that often has widespread beneficial results, the federal government has contributed heavily to the nation's R&D efforts in order to stimulate technological progress. Because private firms are frequently unable to capture all of the benefits of their R&D in terms of company revenues (some benefits "spill over" to others), there is less research than is socially optimal. Accordingly, government subsidies are warranted. In addition to much financial support, patent laws, the first of which was passed in 1790, provide protection and monetary incentives for innovators by granting them a right to exclude others from making, using, or selling the patented invention for a period of 17 years. These laws derive from the Constitution of the United States. Article 1, Sec. 8, Par. 8 empowers Congress "to promote the progress of science and useful arts, by securing for limited times to authors and inventors the exclusive right to their respective writings and discoveries." According to current patent laws, a patent can be issued to cover any invention that is new, useful, and unobvious to one of ordinary skill in that art at the time the invention was made.

Patent grants are intended to promote innovation, to stimulate the development and commercial utilization of inventions, and to encourage inventors to disclose their discoveries to the public. The incentives generated by patents include the ability to earn royalties through licensing, the enjoyment of an exclusive market position, and the ability to accumulate a patent portfolio that facilitates the exchange of technology with other companies. Patent laws make technology a controllable personal property. Without such protection, competitors in the market could imitate at relatively low expense the results produced by one innovator's major R&D effort, thus sharing in the profits but not the costs. This protection also has an international dimension that has now reached center stage. The *Economic Report of the President, 1986* indicated the global aspects of the problem.

When foreign producers can copy these innovations with impunity, the rewards to innovation decline and the pace of technical change slackens. A priority for the U.S. Government is to establish wider international agreements protecting intellectual property. . . . Basic ground rules tend to be lacking in these areas, especially in countries that feel little need to protect domestic innovation.[16]

Note also that the granting of a patent frequently amounts to the granting of monopoly power in the production of the patented item. Accordingly, patents, because they are monopoly rights, may be employed as a means of controlling output and dividing markets.

One use of patents is licensing, whereby others are permitted to utilize the invention in return for royalty payments. Patents can be licensed to competitors via (1) *restrictive licensing*, in which the patented firm has the right to specify the price, output and marketing area of the patented product; and (2) *cross-licensing*, which is a sharing device for related patents; several firms in an industry pool the patents they own and exclude potential rivals from their use (*patent pooling*). In addition, firms owning a patented product have used *tying agreements* to require the buyer to purchase one or more additional products as a condition for purchasing the patented item.[17] For example, prior to 1954, Eastman Kodak sold amateur color film at a price that included the charge for finishing. Licensing and tying agreements have the effect of making a business that owns the patent the dominant firm in the industry. Patent laws have been an important factor for the growth of such big corporations as AT&T, Eastman Kodak, G.E., DuPont, and others.

The U.S. Patent and Trademark Office issues patents to both American and foreign inventors. The number of patents held by foreign inventors reveals a slow but steady upward trend, while successful patent applications by American inventors declined sharply in the 1970s, then began to increase in the early 1980s. By 1987 roughly half the patents granted went to foreigners, with Japan being the largest single source. Exactly what such trends mean, however, is difficult to discern. They do not necessarily indicate that Americans are less inventive than in the past. What is clear is that in "purely numerical terms, the role of patents as a device for protecting technological advancements has declined in importance."[18] The reasons are several, including "a shift of invention from purely empirical to more science-based work, a less favorable political and judicial treatment of corporate patent activity, and the development of other means for the protection of technological ideas."[19]

With the advent of the Reagan administration a U.S. Court of Appeals for the Federal Circuit was established in 1981 and given exclusive jurisdiction in connection with the appeal of patent-related matters. Judge Markey articulated ten areas of the Federal District Court system where the patent law was unsuitably and improperly applied. He stated that the Court of Appeals of the Federal District Court intended to remedy this. By reversing poorly reasoned district court precedent, this unitary court of appeals sent a message throughout the judicial system that has resulted in more evenhanded and favorable patent treatment, thereby providing a degree of predictability and optimism heretofore unknown. Accordingly, during the 1980s the position and importance of patents clearly increased.

Few question the desirable encouragement provided by the patent system to innovation and its beneficial impact on resources allocated to inventive activities. However, the inventor's monopoly position can have drawbacks for society as a whole. Once a process or knowledge has been discovered, there are no additional costs to society for that information. Yet a patent gives the inventor the right to charge a price for its use. Because of this charge the product is used less widely than is socially optimal. Reform of the patent system is a much discussed, yet difficult topic. There have been many proposals put forward, including a reduction in years of protection, stricter examination processes, and compulsory licensing to reduce monopoly restrictions. Currently, however, most proposed reforms are in the direction of strengthening patents. Nonetheless, major legislative changes appear unlikely.

Administrative changes, on the other hand, particularly concerning the speed of patent processing, are clearly warranted. Yet they too are unlikely in the near future. With a backlog that might reach 8,000 in 1990, there are numerous industry complaints concerning the time consumed in patent application/processing procedures. In the biotechnology field, for example, industry spokespersons claim it is taking from 30 to 48 months, far too long for start-up companies or for quick investment in production facilities. More examiners are the main means of speeding the process, but Washington's budgetary stringency strongly militates against this for the near term.

The patent system has differing impacts on various industries. Patents are very important to an industry like pharmaceuticals. The ability to patent a new drug is virtually essential if that drug is to be profitable for the company that creates it. Patents also played an important role in the evolution of mechanical machinery in agriculture and in producing new chemical compounds such as fertilizers and pesticides. In the semiconductor industry, however, patents are less important because the speed of innovation outpaces the ability of the system to define and provide patent rights. Patents also appear not to have particularly important impacts on the automobile and aircraft industries, where there has been a tradition of relatively easy patent licensing or even patent pooling.[20]

AUTOMATION AND ROBOTICS

The spectacular growth of the U.S. economy in the past one and a half centuries was due, in significant part, to advances in automation technology. The development of this technology began with the industrial revolution of the eighteenth century. Mechanization first led to the creation of the factory system and separation of labor and management in production. Mass production techniques introduced in the late nineteenth and early twentieth centuries brought forth the assembly line and the divorce of business ownership from management. Since World War II, automation technology has added the element of automatic control, turning the production process into an integrated system. Automation today is the integrated operation of a production system using electronic or other equipment to regulate and coordinate the quantity and quality of production.

Automation did not become practical on a large scale until World War II, when some significant theoretical breakthroughs led to the development of high-speed electronic computers. Generally, widespread growth in automation got under way in the mid-1950s. It is the computer that has helped launch the U.S. economy into a new age of automation. Automation enabled U.S. manufacturers to gain a competitive edge in the world markets in the 1950s and the 1960s. Since the late 1960s, other countries, including Japan and Germany, have caught up with the United States.

Automation has raised productivity enormously. For example, in the late 1950s, only one man was needed to operate a transfer machine, performing over 500 operations in a Cleveland engine plant of the Ford Motor Company. Prior to automation the job required 35 to 70 men. In a Chicago radio plant, 1,000 radios a day were assembled by only two men, whereas 200 had been required prior to automation. Even at its early stage of development, computers made miracles. It was reported that the DuPont Company, using a computer at MIT, solved in 30 hours a chemical problem that would have required one man working 40 hours a week for 20 years for the arithmetic alone.[21] It appears that with the awesome capacity created by rapidly developing computer technology in the past two decades, the future is limitless. Clearly, computers have become a key component and major source of change for modern factory production.

Computers also brought automation to military technology. Automatic control of guided missiles (ICBM, MX) is a vital part of the U.S. defense program. Computers handle hundreds of thousands of instructions and perform millions of calculations with lighting speed. Modern sophisticated weaponry cannot function without these automatic control systems.

Additionally, computers have brought precision control to numerous industrial operations. Accordingly, quality of products and greater homogeneity of output have been greatly enhanced in fields such as metal cutting and shaping and in service operations such as loading and unloading ships or obtaining items from inventory.

In recent years, office automation through the use of computers has revolutionized the operation of office work, including scheduling, inventory control, billing, payroll, cost accounting, and so forth. Word processors nowadays can handle large volumes of information highly efficiently.

In the United States there is already a high degree of automation. But the trend and recent developments indicate that we are heading toward even higher levels of automation, both in the office and in the factory. This will pose many challenges. In the area of factory automation, this trend will have an even greater impact due to the advent of robots.

Only a few years ago, robots began replacing automation machines that were designed to carry out a specific task. Robots are automated industrial equipment. They bring industrial production to a higher level of automation. In the United States, the bulk of all robots are found in manufacturing industries located in the Great Lakes states, New York, and California. Their primary applications include welding, painting, and various pick-and-place operations in automobile production. They are also used in other durable goods industries producing fabricated metals, machinery, and electrical equipment. The economic incentive in using robots in production is rather attractive. In the production of automobiles in 1981, for example, the cost of using a robot was about $6 per hour, as compared to the labor cost of $17 per hour. Further, quality improves. No wonder General Motors alone planned to install at least 14,000 robots during the 1980s.[22]

According to the official definition developed by the Robot Institute of America, "a robot is a reprogrammable multifunctional manipulator designed to move material, parts, tools, or other specialized devices through variable programmed motions for the performance of variety of tasks."[23] By this definition, a robot (which is a computerized device) can perform the same task on identical work-pieces repetitively or different tasks on the same workpiece. It can also be repro-grammed so as to perform entirely new tasks. However, at the present stage of development, robots are generally stationary machines with a manipulator arm that can perform motions repetitively and tirelessly. Furthermore, relatively few robots today are truly reprogrammed. Most repeat the same program. It is the dull, repetitive, hazardous task that is ideally suited to today's robots. The im-pacts on product quality are obvious.

According to the U.S. International Trade Commission, there were about 50,000 robots installed worldwide in 1982.[24] Almost two-thirds of them were located in Japan. The United States had about 7,400, or roughly 15 percent of the world robot population and about 22 percent of Japan's robot total. In 1983, U.S. domestic shipments for robots were 2,666. More than one-third were used as assemblers and material handlers, and 631 (valued at $33.7 million) were ex-ported to other countries. As 1987 began, industrial robots in the United States numbered 25,000, twice that of the Federal Republic of Germany, but still only 22 percent of Japan's 116,000.[25]

Robots usually lack visual or tactile sensory perception. However, recent developments indicate that vision-guided assembly and machining operations are growing in importance. At the Robots IX Exposition held in Detroit in June 1985, virtually every major robot manufacturer demonstrated some type of vision-guided application. Vision-guided autonomous mobile robots for materials transport, com-mercial cleaning, construction, agriculture, remote and hazardous site operations, and military applications have been under commercial development and are now entering the marketplace. According to Robert T. Savely, NASA engineers are developing talking, thinking robots that eventually may work as astronaut assistants aboard a U.S. space station.[26] The development of such robots depends on the technology of *artificial intelligence*, or machines that think, see, and do. Through a technique called *parallel processing*, clustered computer functions are put together to perform complex tasks. This is an important breakthrough in automa-tion. Indeed, as Savely puts it, "the evolution of parallel processing technology may well be the most important technology in the history of mankind. It will make possible the intelligent robot which will be able to perform complicated tasks without human supervision."[27] New frontiers are repeatedly being em-braced. Interestingly, robots are currently employed in a Pasadena, California, restaurant, serving food and waiting on customers. Larger fast-food chains are studying use of robots for food preparation.[28] Thus the service industry as well as goods production will be affected by the inroad of robotics.

The accompanying social and economic impacts of this new generation of robots will be significant. Since robots with computer-based vision systems are typical-ly faster than people and work with greater consistency and accuracy, the new robotics technology is expected eventually to shift unskilled and semiskilled workers from their present jobs to others or even to displace them altogether. According to one empirical study, job displacement due to robots will not be a general problem until after 1990.[29] The jobs that will be most affected are painting and welding, for which today's robots are so well adapted. Others, such as metalworking machine operatives and assemblers, will feel the impacts when vision-guided robots are placed into commercial applications, something already happening. It has been forecasted that robots will take 18 percent of jobs in the automobile industry and 15 percent in the electronics industry by 1995.[30] Geographically, states such as Michigan, with its heavy dependence on the automobile industry, will suffer greater displacement than other areas. Two points, however, merit emphasis. First, associated with the development of robotic technology will be new and different jobs. These employment opportunities will be found in the sectors related to robot manufacturing, direct suppliers to robot manufacturers, such as robot system engineering, and corporate robot users. While manual semiskilled jobs will continue to decline, the new jobs created will be increasingly technical and scientific. Second, in an era of labor shortage, robots will be increasingly useful and welcomed.

As noted, Japan is considerably ahead of the United States in applying robotics. Since robots not only raise productivity and lower production costs, but also enhance product quality, they have greatly assisted Japanese goods in selling competitively in world markets. Their lead in robotics technology is a major factor that has made their automobile industry so successful. U.S. manufacturing industries, including labor unions and management, must meet the challenge of robotics; many accommodations and adjustments must be made because robotics will definitely continue to grow in usage and applications. The robotics revolution is here; it must now be successfully employed.

Although robots are simply sophisticated machine tools, when reinforced with such technological innovations as computer-aided design and manufacturing, artificial intelligence, and machine vision, they are very powerful and may generate an entirely new industrial revolution. Just as the transition of the U.S. economy earlier in this century from a farm-based system to an industrial society benefited workers, so can this transition to robotized factories—if it is handled properly.

TECHNOLOGY AND INDUSTRIAL STRUCTURE

Technology plays a critical and often overlooked role in the evolution of industrial structure. A technological trajectory composed of three stages—initial (or emerging design), consolidation/stabilization, and maturity—can be clearly depicted. When a new product is discovered or invented, a rather chaotic, competitive market generally forms. Many firms attempt to capitalize on the innovation, with visions of megabucks attracting entrepreneurs and venture capital. Uncertainties abound, both with product development and the manufacturing process. As a dominant design emerges, the previous technical and financial uncertainties tend to decrease. Focus shifts more to manufacturing process innovations that will provide low-cost high-volume output of the dominant design item.

Development of the manufacturing process in turn requires new and expensive equipment. Workers must be retrained. There is an explosion of capital demands due to this "lumpiness" in investment, and this tends to flush out firms with insufficient financial resources. Even assuming that the total market is growing (a fair assumption since it is in the initial product design stage that the market as well as the product are being developed), the need to recoup fixed cost outlays drives firms to seek such high volumes that the market frequently may not be able to accommodate many firms. So a consolidation/stabilization phase begins.

Yet as time passes and the industry further evolves, both product and process technologies become more appropriable. New firms, including foreign ones, will find it relatively easy to purchase capital equipment that embodies the developed process technology. Manufacturing difficulties will have generally been eliminated, so that a relatively standardized manufacturing process can be fairly easily duplicated. Accordingly, in this maturity stage, even if the total market continues to grow, new entrants will reduce the market share of existing producers and the field will become more competitive.

At some critical point during this final stage, the dominant product design changes, thus greatly diminishing the edge of the leading firms. Their investments will no longer be exactly on target and the benefits of entrenched position in the old technology will become dissipated. Here again is an opportunity for new entrants, with the market share of existing sellers tending to diminish. A new technological trajectory is established. It is thus clear that technology and technological innovation play an important role in the structure of industries and markets.

The early electronics industry illustrates the influence of technological factors. In the initial phase of experimentation and development there were many firms, with overall profitability low due to large development costs and a relatively small market. Lee de Forest's triode tube ultimately became the dominant design; later, process (and product) changes became incremental. Investment demands surged, while patents and proprietary knowledge tended to block entry. A consolidation phase ensued, ending in dominance by a tight-knit oligopoly. Profitability increased, not simply due to lessened competition, but also because of reduced costs emanating from high production volumes and greater experience.

The history of the U.S. auto industry provides another illustration. Since 1894 over 100 firms have participated for five years or more. Entry accelerated rapidly after 1900 in the initial or emerging technology stage. It declined substantially prior to World War I, then reached a peak of 75 firms by 1923. By 1930, 35 firms had exited or merged and during the Great Depression another 20 left. There was a flurry of entrants and exits following World War II with relative stability in the number of participating firms through the early 1960s. These movements strongly correlate with technological innovation. Prior to World War I, the introduction of the Model T and its associated production systems reduced the number of producers by roughly 70 percent. Dodge introduced the closed steel body in 1923, and by 1925 half of all U.S. autos were closed steel body; by 1926 the figure rose to 80 percent. This change in dominant design correlates with more than 30 producers exiting by 1930. The adoption of automated transfer lines between 1948 and 1954 represented another lumpy investment based on technical change that raised levels of industrial concentration. "The post-World War II stability in market shares and number of firms reflects the fact that approximately three-quarters of the major product innovations occurred before the start of the war."[31] Interestingly, just as periods of technical ferment have had the effect of raising auto industry concentration, growth in market size and international trade have served to reduce concentration. Clearly, the more appropriable the new technology, the more easily new entrants can find market niches.

To summarize, as a dominant design emerges, a technological trajectory is established. There will of course be subsequent modifications, both in product and manufacturing process, all based upon the dominant design. At some point in time, however, perhaps years or even decades, a new design will take hold and a new technological trajectory begins. The initial dominant design is then in the maturity stage and will eventually be supplanted. Those firms specializing in it will attempt to take it as far as they can, but at the same time will switch to the new technical trajectory. While it may be comfortable for an organization to retain the old product and production processes, falling profits and competitive factors will create pressures for important changes to take place. Nonetheless, change generally tends to be resisted in various aspects of the organization; discomfort levels rise and an important challenge must be surmounted.

R&D outlays play an important role in shaping the nature and pace of technical change. Although measurement and assessment problems are extremely significant and always make results somewhat tenuous, the many empirical studies undertaken have been almost uniform in two conclusions. First, industrial R&D generates relatively high private rates of return. Second, because of spillover benefits to other parties, the social rates of return, both average and marginal, are very high, ordinarily double the private rates. For example, a study by Mansfield and others found the median social rate of return to be 56 percent, while the corresponding private figure was 25 percent.[32] Another analysis reported the social rate of return at 70 percent, while the median private rate was 36 percent.[33] Clearly, the returns to R&D are very significant and not restricted to the organization undertaking the expenditures. Such empirical findings lend support to the argument that government assistance is warranted in encouraging such innovative endeavors.

Both product and process innovation are undertaken because of sufficiently positive expected returns. One factor in this very difficult estimating process is the likelihood of successful imitation. Estimates suggest that imitation costs are only 65 percent of innovating costs. Further, the time frame is 30 percent less.[34] Clearly, if imitation expenses for product or process innovations are relatively low, the sector is likely to have lower levels of industrial concentration.

While patents have often been imitated in relatively short periods, they do raise copying costs and thus serve to discourage duplication and increase rewards to the innovating parties. One survey found that 50 percent of the patented innovations examined would not have been introduced in the absence of such protection.[35] That analysis included the ethical drug industry, which evidenced great sensitivity to patents. Excluding drugs, the lack of patent protection would have affected less than one-fourth of the innovating firms. Accordingly, the data still clearly indicate that patents have an impact.[36] Far less clear, however, is their net social value due to the ambiguity of assessing all social costs and benefits.

One important factor for society and often a critical factor for firms is the time period from invention to innovation. Clearly, the shorter this span, the more competitive is the firm and the larger the likely financial return. There is no rule of thumb in this regard, as every invention faces unique conditions and obstacles. Some require significant adjustments in user tastes, technology, or factor prices; some need to overcome major psychosocial barriers. Time intervals between invention and innovation can be incredibly long, as was the case with the fluorescent lamp (79 years), the gyrocompass (56 years), the cotton picker (53 years), and, surprisingly, the zipper (27 years). The jet engine required 14 years; radar and xerography, 13 years each, while the safety razor (9 years), the wireless telephone and telegraph (8 years each), titanium reduction (7 years), the spinning jenny (5 years), and DDT (3 years) were all under a decade.[37]

Interestingly, external sources have been a very important reservoir of innovation. Firms in other industries, independent inventors, and universities have all played important roles. For example, numerical control (see chapter 8 for elaboration) "was not developed by the machine tool industry, but the Massachusetts Institute of Technology, which carried out the work for the U.S. Air Force."[38] In some fields, of course, resistance to change is inherently weak, such as those operating on the technological frontier in dynamic and technically sophisticated industries. Here, change is the name of the game, so organizational resistance is low. Accordingly, the proportion of really major innovations developed and introduced in industries such as electronics, chemicals, or aerospace has been far greater than in older, less dynamic fields.

In terms of financial returns the initial, emerging technology phase generally produces only small gains in value-added per worker or income growth, whereas much more sizable gains tend to accrue in the consolidation and stabilization phase. Nonetheless, it has been the emerging stage—which is technically stimulating, novel, and creative—on which the United States tended to put great emphasis, whereas the Japanese have concentrated on the more profitable incremental improvement features of the stabilization phase. Clearly, in a world in which innovations are becoming increasingly appropriable, the gains to those specializing in the emerging technology phase are relatively smaller and more fragile. Accordingly, it is clear that the ability to generate technological advances does not by itself guarantee an enhanced international competitive position.

Of course, since the Japanese are now in the technical forefront in many arenas, they too will be forced to put more emphasis in this relatively low return stage. Nonetheless, the Japanese will remain significant competitors because they do so many things right. They concentrate on incremental improvements during the stabilization phase and regularly gain cost and qualitative advances. It certainly behooves U.S. industry to more carefully manage the evolution of product and process technology as well as recognize that dominant designs do not last forever. Indeed, the innovating company itself—the one most likely to absorb the greatest potential losses from a successful challenge or substitute—should be attempting to provide the new technological trajectory. For example, "when nylon came out 50 years ago, DuPont immediately put chemists to work to invent new synthetic fibers to compete with nylon. It also began to cut nylon's price—thus making it less attractive for would-be competitors."[39]

Finally, diffusion of new techniques is a critical ingredient in the ability to benefit from innovations. Diffusion itself is essentially a learning process that encompasses both producers and users. During the initial phase improvements and adjustments to the innovation may well be as important as the breakthrough itself. These are generated in the diffusion process. Upon what factors does diffusion turn? What are the key ingredients?

Diffusion may be broken down into two categories—intrafirm and interfirm/interindustry. The importance of external sources has already been mentioned in discussing the spread of new products and processes throughout an economic system. Diffusion has historically been a relatively slow process, impeded by lack of information and familiarity, and by institutional, organizational, and financial barriers. The risks and costs inherent in new ventures are very substantial and thus act not only as a financial constraint, but serve to make personnel cautious. Few ambitious corporate managers want to be associated with losers, although the most aggressive and least risk-averse do indeed take bold moves. Yet losers are the rule, at least initially. In a study drawn from the top 200 companies on the Fortune 500, Ralph Biggadike's sample of 68 reported only 12 with profits during the first two years. The average loss of return on investment was 40 percent in the first two years and 14 in the next two; Biggadike concludes that new ventures require roughly eight years before they become profitable.[40]

Imitation, it should be noted, varies widely among industries and firms. Despite this diversity, a number of factors seem certain. First, the greater the pecuniary advantages associated with the innovation, the more likely (and sooner) its adoption. Second, the greater the uncertainty associated with the undertaking, the slower its adoption. And third, the greater the amounts of specific capital, human and nonhuman, devoted to the old product or process, the greater the resistance to adoption.

It is also of interest to examine the rate at which firms, having once introduced a new technique, proceed in-house in substituting it for older ones. What is clear is that there exists enormous variation in this intrafirm diffusion pattern. Small firms, having once adopted an innovation, seem to be quicker in substituting out of the old and fully embracing the new.

There seems little question that the greater the expected return from innovation, the quicker its adoption by the business community. Here government tax policy can clearly have an influence. To the degree that there are tax breaks of various kinds for investment and innovative undertakings, the increased rewards will serve to speed both the generation and adoption of innovation.

According to empirical evidence, in the United States it takes about five to ten years, on the average, before one-half of the major firms in an industry begin using an important technology.[41] Clearly, the more rapid the diffusion, the greater the social benefits, but the lower the returns to the innovating firm. Herein we find the dilemma mentioned earlier. Patents, by granting monopoly status, tend to stimulate inventive activity, but at the same time serve to slow its diffusion. Public policy, then, faces some difficult trade-offs.

As to which size firms might be optimal in innovative undertakings (both initiation and adoption), the empirical data again are not perfectly clear.[42] No doubt, the analyses are complicated by the diversity of industries, time frames, and conditions unique to each field. However, the Galbraithian and Schumpeterian view that large firms possess inherent advantages for innovation and technological progress seems very questionable, their vast financial capabilities notwithstanding. Smaller firms appear to exert greater R&D efforts and innovate at relatively lower cost. They tend to be less bureaucratic and information disseminates more easily. And, while large organizations have certainly been associated with some important innovations, they seem to have just as frequently missed the boat.

Examples include telephone, cable, and electrical manufacturing companies that greeted the invention of radio with enthusiastic indifference; aircraft engine producers who accorded a similar reception to the jet engine; chemical companies that resisted penicillin . . . the nation's largest industrial concerns rejected xerography, while Eastman Kodak dismissed the newly invented instant camera as a toy with no commercial appeal.[43]

U.S. technology policy is perhaps best described as mission-oriented. It serves objectives of national goals, such as space and defense. Concentration occurs in decision making, implementation, and evaluation. "Concentration also extends to the range of technologies covered."[44] In Germany, Switzerland, and Sweden, on the other hand, technology policy is diffusion-oriented. Rather than specializing in relatively few, big problems, the goal is to diffuse technical capabilities through the economy so as to incrementally raise productivity and adapt to change. Japan's policy seems to be a unique blend of mission-oriented and diffusion-oriented.

It should be stressed, however, that national technological policies are more facilitating and guiding than prime moving forces. These instead reside in the economic system and technical ethos of the particular society. "The critical variables lie in how industry responds to the results and signals of efforts to upgrade national technological capabilities."[45] Technology policies are grafted to a national technological infrastructure—education, training, and research facilities— and an ongoing economic system. They can help shape the infrastructure and within this context they can guide and direct. They can often provide jump-starts, but they are always acting within the larger context of the socioeconomic system.

The U.S. technological base and infrastructure can perhaps be best described as huge, if not awesome. In 1986 the United States had twice the number of nonacademic scientists and engineers as Japan. In that year the United States also had a higher ratio (300 per 10,000 in the labor force) of scientists and engineers than any other leading industrial nation, including Japan and Germany.[46] In 1986 the United States granted twice as many science and engineering first university degrees as Japan and ten times as many as Germany. Although over one-half of the U.S. engineering doctoral degrees are going to foreigners, the total number is more than double the corresponding Japanese figure.[47] Finally, the United States has over 1,500 firms with R&D laboratories, more than any other country (and ten times the number in France). In short, the sheer size and magnitude of the U.S. technological establishment is awesomely impressive. Further, the number of American Nobel Price winners and the 35 percent U.S. authorship of the world's leading scientific and technical journals are additional indicators of the significance of U.S. technological capabilities. These statistics, of course, should not blind us to the fact that other nations, most particularly Japan, are rapidly advancing, both absolutely and relatively, and that the U.S. dominance today is no guarantee of a similar position in 15 or 20 years. Yet the current and near-term situation can only be described as exceedingly rich in capabilities and potential.

This huge scale gives U.S. R&D efforts several advantages. Projects can draw from a much larger pool of personnel and can tap an excellent university research system. "Second, funding for mission-oriented programs . . . rarely falls short of the critical mass required to complete the development stage and usually has a higher continuity than program funding elsewhere."[48] It should be pointed out that the products directly born of mission-oriented research account for a rather small share of the economy, so diffusion is an important component of the overall impact. Fortunately, the relatively high levels of mobility of U.S. scientists and engineers serve to promote such diffusion.

U.S. capital markets, and particularly the availability of venture capital, do very well in providing financing for a broad range of innovative activities, while the generally competitive nature of the overall economic system (including relative ease of entry) promotes endeavors by new firms in arenas not exploited by established companies. Additionally, as Henry Ergas points out,

an active market for corporate control provides an effective means of liquidating new firms that do poorly and incorporating into large concerns the activities of those that do well. At the same time, the takeover market reduces the risks associated with entry by diversification. Large U.S. firms tend to enter new markets by buying smaller firms already operating in those markets, knowing that if the venture failed, it could be disposed of. . . .[49]

U.S. mission-oriented research tends to involve a relatively large number and diversity of agents as well as a willingness to disseminate program results. Such willingness not only promotes diffusion, but has been a key factor in securing political backing for research programs. Additionally, regarding government-financed R&D in the private sector, the 1980 Patent Law Amendments Act established a uniform policy allowing contractors . . . to own inventions resulting from federal R&D funding. The assurance this act provides . . . has greatly facilitated patent licensing . . . and has encouraged industrial participation in federally supported university research.[50]

The pattern of technological evolution is one of experimenting, selecting, and diffusing. Within this pattern, efficiency is obtained essentially through shifting or transferring resources out of old uses and into new ones, and deepening, which is enhancing productivity in current uses. The higher the degree of resource mobility, particularly labor, the greater the contribution of shifting. And the greater the degree to which assets are firm- or industry-specific, the more important deepening becomes. The United States has operated in a shifting mode, whereas Germany has emphasized deepening. Japan has managed a unique combination of the two.

Relatively high labor and capital mobility is a major factor behind the U.S. emphasis on shifting. People bring their ideas with them when they enter new fields or firms. Further, because of labor mobility, the incentives for a business to undertake investments in transferable labor are reduced. Accordingly, deepening efforts are somewhat muted.

This shifting pattern can be related to technological trajectory and profitability. Shifting behavior naturally corresponds to emphasizing the emergence or initial phase of technological trajectories. Yet in this phase, with high R&D costs, intense competition, and substantial uncertainties, rates of return are relatively low. It is in the consolidation phase that there is considerable cost reduction and scope for substantial profits. But a relative lack of craftspeople, a minimum of employer investment in labor, and relatively high wages have served to reduce the comparative advantage which the United States once had in mass production techniques. Accordingly, U.S. firms have been reaping the major advantages of innovation relatively early in the cycle, while others, such as the Japanese, have earned greater financial returns during the more profitable stabilization phase. However, because manufacturing wages in the 1980s have been relatively tame, while productivity has grown, U.S. manufacturing will enter the 1990s more competitive and better able to profit in the stabilization and maturity phases.

Interestingly, the shifting process in which the United States has concentrated explains the abandonment of mature fields that U.S. industry once pioneered. Yet it requires continuous innovation and new activities so that the United States can be there first and reap some return in the initial stage before stabilization and substantial foreign competition evolve. Importantly, a "system of mission-oriented research, which helps ensure that the frontiers of these activities are constantly being explored, may provide a useful source of ongoing stimulus to this process."[51]

INDUSTRIAL TECHNOLOGY AND MILITARY POWER

As pointed out earlier, the federal government has spent heavily on R&D related to national defense. In 1987, some 32 percent of the nation's total R&D outlays were related to military projects. Although the direct economic benefits of these projects are limited to a number of industries, their results have frequently been adapted to broader uses and the potential economic benefits to the entire society can be enormous. Thus, through defense R&D, society benefits both from improved U.S. defense capabilities and from the civilian adaptations of defense-generated technology. Expenditures on defense and space have resulted in important technological spillovers. For example, early advances in the electronics industry were mostly the result of defense R&D efforts that were adapted for civilian applications. According to F. M. Scherer, IBM's preeminence in electronic computers resulted from its experience under huge SAGE air defense system contracts.[52] Hughes Aircraft Company's leading position in communications satellite technology stemmed from a long series of missile and space system efforts. In the post-World War II period, military technology has been responsible for the creation of some new civilian industries: computer, jet aircraft, nuclear power, and space communications. Their development began with a perceived military need, and defense research funds brought these totally new and geopolitically important civilian industries into reality.

Defense contracts have thus led to many technological advances in industry. Examples of civilian products that are direct spin-offs from space and military R&D include teflon, Corning ware, and freeze-dried foods. Further, management tools for handling large, complex projects (such as critical path analysis) directly derive from military development. And as modern warfare has moved increasingly into an era of high technology, it is our industrial technological edge on which our security critically depends. With the original stimulus of military contracts, civilian applications of defense-related technology can further technological change within industry and in turn lead to military applications. A more recent example is DARPA, which stands for the little-known Defense Advanced Research Projects Agency. This agency has had such a profound impact on the U.S. economy that some call it "America's MITI," after Japan's famed Ministry of International Trade and Industry.[53] DARPA's basic research has a potentially high spin-off for military as well as civilian applications. For example, stealth, Star Wars, and smart weapons began as DARPA research initiatives, as did advanced integrated circuits, computer graphics, computer networks, and even the civilian space program. DARPA recently has moved into promising new areas of research, including robotics, manufacturing technology, and superconductivity. Based on DARPA's track record, such research activities will have substantial technological impact on the U.S. industrial economy.

DARPA, it should be stressed, does not conduct research on its own, but instead finances high-risk, high-payoff projects that have potential military application. This basic research, however, often also has broad civilian applications, as

DARPA's track record indicates. According to the research head of one of the nation's leading computer designers, "They are the sole driver of computer technology. That's it. Period."[54] With a fiscal 1989 budget exceeding $1 billion for the first time, some of the leading programs with industrial applications include Sematech ($100 million), a semiconductor industry consortium for which DARPA provides 50 percent funding; high-definition television ($30 million over 2–3 years); superconductivity ($25 million); neural networks ($33 million over 20 months); and microwave and millimeter-wave monolithic integrated circuits ($67 million) for the development of advanced chips made of gallium arsenide. Major current weapons projects include advanced aircraft, submarine warfare, lasers, nuclear monitoring, sensors, armor, and smart weapons.

Conversely, civilian technologies such as large-scale integrated circuitry, which did not originate from defense contracts, are now being employed in new weapon systems. The Department of Defense is currently subsidizing research into high-speed integrated circuits and there are likely to be many civilian applications. Importantly, defense research is usually closer to the frontiers of what is scientifically possible than civilian efforts. And with government funding, the economic constraints are less binding. Accordingly, it is professionally exciting and attracts highly qualified people. Such research can exert profound impacts on industrial technology.

This discussion extends the debate on a national industrial policy that was introduced in chapter 3. Those advocating such a policy maintain that the United States already practices such a program, but does so in an uncoordinated and illogical fashion. A defense agency, DARPA, sponsors and supports research as do a number of other agencies. Tariffs and other productive devices give further support, but these are all uncoordinated efforts. Further, it is argued that the defense orientation of DARPA makes it unsuitable for the demands and needs of the commercial market. The greater secrecy surrounding military research can also slow progress. Accordingly, advocates support an NIP. On the other hand, it is not clear that a civilian agency would have a better track record than DARPA. Finally, the prospect of diverse U.S. civilian agencies working in a coordinated fashion seems utopian and unrealistic to NIP opponents.

INTERNATIONAL TECHNOLOGY TRANSFER

The diffusion of technology occurs not only in domestic industries but also across national boundaries. A firm can transfer its new technology abroad by embodying it in the export of goods and services, by direct investment in foreign countries, by licensing the new technology to foreign firms, or by engaging in joint ventures and coproduction agreements. The growth and spread of multinational corporations has increased the international diffusion of technology. Some international organizations, such as NATO (North Atlantic Treaty Organization) and COMECON (the Soviet bloc's Council of Mutual Economic Assistance) also play a role in the transfer of technology. Both NATO and COMECON have coproduction agreements as to the distribution of production and basic benefits in the location of technologies and pattern of trade.[55]

International technology transfer in the form of exporting technology, either embodied in products or via establishing subsidiaries through foreign investment, will be discussed further in chapter 6. With respect to the transfer of "disembodied technology" through the sales of patent licenses and blueprints, the receipts and payments of licensing fees and royalties can be used as indicators of both the amounts of U.S. technical know-how transferred through this channel and the directions of technology flows. The data show that total U.S. earnings in royalties and fees have grown virtually continuously since 1960, while outpayments to foreigners have also grown steadily. Nonetheless, the small 1960 positive balance in royalties and fees, numbering only in the hundreds of millions of dollars, reached $11 billion by 1987. Clearly, the United States continues to be a substantial net exporter of technology, with sales of know-how exceeding payments by 2 to 1 in 1987. If this balance is further disaggregated, one can examine the net balance associated with unaffiliated foreign residents. These flows represent arms-length transactions following market criteria alone rather than including transfers between corporate affiliates. The latest data available, 1985, show that U.S. receipts exceeded payments by more than 4 to 1.[56] Japan was the largest foreign demander of U.S. technology, while U.S. demand was greatest for British know-how. These data attest to the substantial capabilities and preeminence of the U.S. technological base.

International technology transfer has attracted a great deal of attention in the United States in recent decades. There have been concerns as to the amount and kinds of technology transferred and what impacts such flows are likely to have on the U.S. economic and strategic posture. National security has clearly played an important role affecting such technology flows. During the 1950s and 1960s, the United States placed strategic controls on its exports to communist countries. The basic restrictive legislation has been the Export Control Act of 1949, as amended in subsequent years. Originally, export restrictions were embodied in a list of some 1,300 product categories (including their associated technologies) that could not be exported without validated licenses from government. The act was amended in 1969, 1979, and most recently in July 1985.

The national security aspects of technology transfer have remained a major consideration in the law. Under the new legislation, the 1985 Export Administration Act Extension, the U.S. Department of Commerce and U.S. Customs Service share responsibility for drafting and enforcing guidelines on the export of sensitive technology. The Defense Department retains its authority to review licensing decisions on such exports. The law did relax restrictions on the export of high technology to Japan and members of NATO. However, penalties are stiffened for U.S. citizens, companies, or foreign countries that divert sensitive U.S. technology to unfriendly nations. In the most drastic possible punishment, U.S. imports from an offending foreign country can be terminated.

The denial of critical technologies to the Soviet bloc or other potential adversaries is not something that one nation alone, even the United States, can effectively implement. A multilateral organization, COCOM (Coordinating Committee), presently consisting of the NATO countries (except Iceland and Spain) and Japan, was formed in 1949 to govern strategic exports to the Soviet bloc. The Berlin blockade gave impetus to this informal organization, which maintains a list of items not to be exported and a set of procedures for exceptions from this list. Not based on a treaty, COCOM operates according to unanimous decision. Its major functions are to agree upon and publish lists of prohibited items and to coordinate export control enforcement efforts. In today's highly competitive world, it has not been easy to gain agreement on export prohibitions. COCOM, located in Paris, actively functions, but amid a great deal of controversy.

Monitoring such flows is quite difficult, as is the assessment of what constitutes a strategic technology that should be denied to unfriendly states. If U.S. firms are not allowed to sell technology, other sellers are likely to transfer something similar. Further, in our open society, it is difficult to keep information from those truly determined to have it. Clearly, U.S. firms investing in technology have more incentive to do so if they can gain revenues by its worldwide transfer. So there are difficult economic and security trade-offs. Finally, it should be noted that it is in the arena of dual-use technologies that the greatest assessment and decision-making difficulties are to be found.

A recent example of the trade-offs in technology transfer is the Bush administration's plan to help Japan develop the new FSX jet fighter. Instead of selling U.S.-made F-16s to Tokyo, General Dynamics will provide technical secrets to Japan, which will allow it to develop a more advanced version. Critics argue that Japan could simply buy an off-the-shelf F-16 for $15 million, about half the per-plane cost of developing a new fighter. By producing it on its own with the help from the United States, Japan would get aircraft technology that cost $7 billion to develop. It may also, at some future date, enter export competition against us. On the other hand, proponents believe that Japan could develop a jet fighter on its own, even without U.S. assistance. The FSX pact can provide, they argue, mutual advantages. According to Defense Secretary Richard Cheney, this deal will give U.S. companies more than $2.5 billion in technology sales and some 22,000 man-years of employment. The Senate also moved to assure that Japan honor its commitment to reserve 40 percent of the development and production work for U.S. firms.[57] Clearly, this is a difficult area for decision makers.

To summarize, technology can unlock all doors, and the U.S. technological potential is truly immense. Yet our resources must be employed more effectively, with the time spanning invention and marketplace significantly reduced. We have been slow to employ robots and have tended to put too little emphasis on process innovation. Very importantly, the scientific and technical competence (and awareness) of the general population must be raised. Nonetheless, the system is appropriately moving in the right directions. But the mandate of the 1990s is that it must move faster.

NOTES

1. National Science Foundation, *Methodology of Statistics on Research and Development* (Washington, D.C.: U.S. Government Printing Office, 1959), p. 124. For a discussion of the phases of technological progress related to R&D, see also Committee for Economic Development, *Stimulating Technological Progress* (New York: Committee for Economic Development, 1980), Ch. 2.

2. Rachel McCulloch, *Research and Development as a Determinant of U.S. International Competitiveness* (Washington, D.C.: National Planning Association, October 1978), p. 19.

3. Kim B. Clark, and Zvi Griliches, "Productivity Growth and R&D at the Business Level: Results from PIMS Data Base," in Zvi Griliches, ed., *R&D, Patents, and Productivity* (Chicago: University of Chicago Press, 1984), p. 394.

4. Jora Minasian, "Research & Development, Production Functions, and Rate of Return," *American Economic Review*, May 1969.

5. Robert Evenson, "The Contribution of Agricultural Research and Extension to Agricultural Production" (Ph.D. dissertation, University of Chicago, 1968).

6. U.S. Department of Commerce, *Statistical Abstract of the United States, 1988* (Washington, D.C.: U.S. Government Printing Office, 1988), p. 561.

7. Ibid., pp. 556–61.

8. For a detailed discussion of impacts of government on technology in various industries, see Richard R. Nelson, ed., *Government and Technical Progress—A Cross-Industry Analysis* (New York: Pergamon Press, 1982).

9. National Science Foundation, *Science Indicators, 1985* (Washington, D.C.: U.S. Government Printing Office, 1986), p. xiii.

10. Joseph A. Schumpeter, *The Theory of Economic Development* (Cambridge, Mass: Harvard University Press, 1934), Ch. 2.

11. Gerhard Rosegger, *The Economics of Production and Innovation* (London: Pergamon Press, 1980), p. 210.

12. Ibid., p. 162.

13. Ibid., p. 211.

14. Harold J. Barnett et al., "Global Trends in Non-Fuel Minerals," in Julian L. Simon and Herman Kahn, eds., *The Resourceful Earth—A Response to Global 2000* (New York: Basil Blackwell, 1984).

15. Simon and Kahn, p. 14.

16. Council of Economic Advisors, *Economic Report of the President, 1986* (Washington, D.C.: U.S. Government Printing Office, 1986), p. 123.

17. The Clayton Antitrust Act (1914) restricted the use of tying contracts. They were not declared by the act to be absolutely illegal. However, they are unlawful when their effects "may be to substantially lessen competition or tend to create a monopoly."

18. Rosegger, p. 176.

19. Ibid.

20. For empirical evidence, see Nelson.

21. For more interesting examples, see Walter Backingham, *Automation—Its Impact on Business and People* (New York: Harper and Brothers, 1961), p. 21.

22. See Isabel V. Sawhill, "Human Resources," in G. William Miller, ed., *Regrowing the American Economy* (Englewood Cliffs, N.J.: Prentice-Hall, 1983), p.108.

23. Robot Institute of America, *RIA Worldwide Survey and Directory on Industrial Robots* (Dearborn, Mich.: Robot Institute of America, 1981), p. 1.

24. U.S. International Trade Commission, *Competitive Position of U.S. Producers of Robotics in Domestic and World Markets* (Washington, D.C.: U.S. Government Printing Office, December, 1983).

25. Japan Institute for Social and Economic Affairs, *Japan 1989: An International Comparison* (Tokyo: Keizai Koho Center, 1989), p. 27.

26. Reported by the Associated Press, see *The Times-Picayune/The States Item*, New Orleans, Sunday, June 8, 1986, p. B-9.

27. Ibid.

28. *Newsweek*, June 16, 1986, p. 53.

29. H. Allan Hunt and Timothy L. Hunt, *Human Resource Implications of Robotics* (Kalamazoo, Mich.: W. E. Upjohn Institute for Employment Research, 1983).

30. Reported by the Associated Press, see *The Times/Picayune/The States Item*, New Orleans, June 14, 1986, p. D-1.

31. James M. Utterback, "Innovation and Industrial Evolution in Manufacturing Industries," in Bruce R. Guile and Harvey Brooks, eds., *Technology and Global Industry* (Washington, D.C.: National Academy Press, 1987), p. 39.

32. Edwin Mansfield et al., *Technology Transfer, Productivity, and Economic Policy* (New York: W. W. Norton, 1982), p. 189.

33. Robert R. Nathan Associates, *Net Rates of Return on Innovations*, Report to the National Science Foundation (Washington, D.C., July 1978).

34. Manfield et al., p. 152.

35. Ibid., p. 153.

36. Ibid.

37. Edwin Mansfield, *Technological Change* (New York: W. W. Norton, 1971) p. 175.

38. Ibid., pp. 80–81.

39. Peter Drucker, "The 10 Rules of Effective Research," *Wall Street Journal*, May 30, 1989, p. A22.

40. Ralph Biggadike, "The Risky Business of Diversification," *Harvard Business Review*, May 1979.

41. See Edwin Mansfield, "Technology and Productivity in the United States," in Martin Feldstein, ed., *The American Economy in Transition* (Chicago: University of Chicago Press, 1980).

42. Mansfield, *Technological Change*, p. 93, for example, finds that larger firms introduce new techniques more quickly than smaller firms." However, the National Science Board, *Science Indicators* (Washington, D.C.: 1976), p. 118, found that over the 1953–73 period the very largest firms accounted for only one-third of the innovations, while the smallest firms "produced about 4 times as many major innovations per R&D dollar as the middle-size firms and 24 times as many as the largest firms."

43. Walter Adams and James W. Brock, *The Bigness Complex* (New York: Pantheon Books, 1986), p. 51.

44. Henry Ergas, "Does Technology Policy Matter?" in Guile and Brooks, p. 194.

45. Ibid., p. 192.

46. National Science Foundation, *International Science and Technology Data Update: 1988* (NSF 89-307) (Washington, D.C.: 1988), pp. 28–29.

47. Ibid., p. 48.

48. Ergas, p. 197.

49. Ibid., p. 202.

50. Ibid., p. 199.

51. Ibid., p. 205.

52. F. M. Sherer, *Industrial Market Structure and Economic Performance* (Chicago: Rand McNally, 1980), p. 143.

53. *U.S. News & World Report*, December 26, 1988/January 2, 1989, pp. 94–95.

54. Andrew Pollack, "America's Answer to Japan's MITI," *New York Times*, March 5, 1989, Section III, p. 8.

55. See Jack N. Behrman, *Industrial Policies: International Restructuring and Transnationals* (Lexington, Mass: D.C. Heath, 1984), Chs. 6,7.

56. National Science Foundation, *International Science and Technology Data Update: 1988*, pp. 84–87.

57. See *Wall Street Journal*, May 12, 1989, p. A4, and May 18, 1989, p. B2.

5

Productivity

Productivity trends and concepts are not only enigmatic and arcane to the general public, but in different ways just as nebulous and mysterious to professional economists. Yet vigorous productivity growth is literally the "key to the kingdom," the instrument that can open wide the gates of progress and material advance. A productive nation will more easily be able to address issues such as social services, aging, national defense, and infrastructure needs. It is chiefly productivity that has elevated U.S. living standards well beyond the wildest fantasies of people living 100 years ago. Solid productivity gains, by stimulating growth and reducing unemployment, will greatly assist with the federal deficit problem. The enhanced quality and performance characteristics associated with higher productivity will similarly assist in rectifying our contemporary trade deficits.

Conversely, if productivity is mediocre, economic performance is likely to be anemic, today's "twin-deficits" will probably worsen, and living standards will stagnate or retrogress. This latter possibility may seem bizarre or unreal, but such change would not be unique from a historical perspective. For example, after the fall of the Roman Empire, productivity levels dropped precipitously for several hundred years, rising only at a snail's pace sometime after the tenth century. "It is estimated that at the time of the American revolution, England had barely reattained the productivity level of Rome in the third century A.D."[1] Closer to home, U.S. productivity advance, which was so impressive during the 1960s, fell by more than half during the 1970s, with absolute declines recorded in 1979 and 1980. Accordingly, neither economic progress in general nor productivity in particular can be taken for granted. "Onward and upward" is a wonderfully positive expression, but hardly an economic law. Productivity advance must be understood and sought; otherwise, it will not happen.

Unfortunately, the exact measurement of productivity is fraught with difficulties, while the explanation of trends has baffled the best minds. This chapter, then,

117

is intended to explain productivity concepts, provide basic data, and to report the most informed and plausible explanations of the productivity situation.

CONCEPTS

Productivity is an efficiency measure. It is not output, but rather a relationship between inputs and outputs. It must be stressed that all production is a *joint* undertaking; virtually all activities involve the simultaneous and coordinated use of land, labor, materials, and capital. It is often not difficult to measure the output from a given combination of inputs, such as 100 bushels of corn or 50 tons of steel. If these same inputs begin to produce in the same time span twice the corn or steel, the productivity of this combination has obviously doubled. *Total factor productivity* (sometimes called multifactor productivity) recognizes the jointness of productive activities and attempts to relate output to all inputs in a weighted fashion. In the above example, total factor productivity has clearly increased.

Factor productivity, however, such as the productivity of labor or capital goods, is a partial productivity measure. It directs attention to the specific contribution of some particular factor or input. In practice, however, such contributions cannot be accurately captured since resources are used jointly. For example, assume that two identically productive workers employed for two hours and utilizing a given set of wood, hammers, and nails are able to produce two widgets. One can accurately say that this input "team" produced one widget per hour, but how much of that was due to human labor? How much was due to the wood, to the nails, or to the hammers? If any of those inputs were missing, there would be no widgets. So they were essential and we know exactly how much they can jointly produce, but we have no way of exactly attributing to each input its specific contribution. If one worker is released, presumably widget output will fall, perhaps to only one. This, however, does not prove that the released worker by himself contributed one widget, for if a complete widget were attributable to him alone, the other would be attributable to the other identical worker. This leads to the ridiculous conclusion that the two widgets could thus be accounted for by labor alone, leaving no contribution for materials or tools. Clearly this is preposterous. The best that can be accurately stated is that with two workers and materials, two widgets are produced; with one worker and materials, only one widget (and some leftover materials) is produced. The specific contribution of each factor, however, is moot. Accordingly, economists have attempted to calculate multifactor or total factor productivity numbers.

Despite the validity of the above logic, for a variety of reasons measures of specific factor productivity have been demanded. The resulting calculations, despite careful work, take considerable "license" and are essentially derived by dividing a total product by the quantity of some particular input, say labor hours. Thus a figure for average labor productivity is "divined." Such figures are calculated quarterly and annually, thereby permitting comparisons over time. While the basic method does not truly capture specific contributions, annual comparisons over a prolonged period do provide trend indications. A more appropriate measure would be a total factor productivity. Its calculation, however, also involves significant difficulties, particularly in assigning appropriate weights to the various inputs. And the numbers calculated, while more conceptually appropriate, are of little practical use. If, for example, the measured productivity of labor rises, workers can go to management with data to justify a wage boost. The figures constitute a bargaining weapon, despite conceptual weaknesses. On the other hand, if total factor productivity increases, it is difficult for any single resource to take the credit; it is less clear how this might have occurred. Was it due to better management, greater worker efforts, or what? For these reasons, there have been few nonacademic demands for total factor productivity statistics.

Productivity is affected by many influences. One important ingredient is the availability of similar inputs. Assume for a moment that a particular piece of land yields 1,000 bushels per acre. If the number of workers on that land is increased, total output will rise. The measured productivity of land, the fixed factor, will also increase. In effect, the land is more productive since it is now utilizing more labor. It is worked more intensively and is therefore more productive. On the other hand, the productivity of labor will eventually decline since each worker on average has less land to utilize. This declining extra output associated with additional inputs working in conjunction with a fixed factor (land of a specific size and quality in this case) is called the law of diminishing returns. Diminishing returns can have a powerful influence on production costs and productivity trends. In a point to be elaborated shortly, the rapid growth in the U.S. labor force during most of the past 15–20 years suggests that diminishing returns should be operational. And, indeed, the statistics bear this out.

As noted, productivity is usually measured per unit of some factor of production. Labor productivity, calculated as output per labor hour, is the most commonly found figure. This is the case because labor has historically been scarce and precious in the United States. Further, work force data are readily available, and wages in the marketplace are closely tied to labor productivity. Finally, the use of labor hours entails a minimum of conceptual problems. We could and often do calculate the productivity of capital; however, there are significant conceptual and technical difficulties. What is the unit of measurement—is it only plant and equipment, or are inventories, cash, and other investments to be included? How should capital be valued—purchase price, constant dollar value, or current market price? Given such inherent difficulties coupled with the fact that the owners of capital (who might care most about such statistics) are far less numerous than the owners of labor, capital productivity measures on a national scale are not readily available.

Of course, at the business enterprise level there are a number of techniques utilized in an attempt to estimate the productivity of the various factors of production employed. Indeed, such estimates, however derived, are necessary management data to efficiently allocate and deploy assets. This is the monitoring function described in chapter 2. Every input that is bought or hired is presumed to have productive capabilities. The relative productivities of each factor coupled with their prices are critical ingredients in the choice of input combinations. Further, in multiplant operations even within the same company, productivity may differ substantially among various factories, even though all produce essentially the same products in the same fashion. Productivity studies and analyses can thus be useful tools in improving efficiency throughout a corporation.[2]

DATA GATHERING AND PRODUCTIVITY MEASURES

Most data for national productivity measures are provided by the Bureau of Labor Statistics (BLS) which utilizes supporting output data from the Department of Commerce and the Federal Reserve. Hundreds of dedicated scholars, data gatherers, and statisticians attempt to compile, classify, and analyze the relevant information. Sophisticated statistical techniques are applied to our best output and input estimates. Official statistics are available for most SIC producing sectors. Unofficial estimates for many remaining industries are also available. The following quotation from a 1982 study of the foundry industry gives some indication as to the considerable detail and information provided:

Productivity has increased in the major sectors of the foundry industry for which BLS publishes measures. Output per employee hour in gray iron foundries (SIC 3321) rose at an annual rate of 2.3 percent during the longer term 1960–79, while output per employee hour in steel foundries (SIC 3324, 3325) increased at a lower annual rate of 1.0 percent over the same period.

Productivity gains varied within the period. Output per employee hour in gray iron foundries rose at an annual rate of 2.8 percent during 1960–67, and increased at a 2.4 percent rate during 1967–79. In steel foundries, output per employee hour increased at an annual rate of 2.5 percent during 1960–67, and 0.8 percent between 1967 and 1979.[3]

Some caveats are warranted concerning the quality of published productivity figures. Complete accuracy demands unequivocal measures of both outputs and inputs, to include quality differences and changes over time. This is a very demanding standard. Even when outputs are perfectly homogeneous and measurable, we still may not get completely correct figures due to normal error factors in counting and estimation. If quality differs, either in types of outputs or among differing producing units, aggregation will also introduce inaccuracies. Finally, when quality of output changes over time, intertemporal comparisons are less meaningful. For example, if we are only sustaining past levels of automobile output, but the current models are much more efficient and safe, has productivity really been at a standstill?

For the service sector, measurement of units of output is generally far more difficult. Accordingly, there are far fewer productivity estimates available, although in some service areas measurement is quite possible. We can, for example, monitor how many hamburgers a fast-food establishment produces each day or week. In transportation, a unit of service such as ton miles can be readily identified and measured.

There are a wide, sometimes bewildering, variety of productivity figures available. Almost all subsequent references in this chapter (as well as in virtually all public sources) will describe factor productivity measures, most specifically labor productivity, as opposed to the more esoteric total (multifactor) calculation. The most common classifications are national and sectoral, and absolute levels versus growth rates. International comparisons, perhaps the weakest link in the productivity measurement chain, are nonetheless quite common. Official data come from the Bureau of Labor Statistics, while private estimates cover areas that the BLS does not formally tackle or issue.

Absolute productivity values depict a specific level of performance. Estimates in Table 5.1, for example, indicate that for the business sector as a whole, output per hour of work in 1987, measured at constant 1982 prices, had an average value of $19.26. This was about $23.03 in 1987 dollars. It should be stressed that both absolute values and growth rates by sector are quite suspect in the eyes of many analysts, both for methological and empirical reasons. Accordingly, they are being utilized here more for heuristic purposes than for their exactness. The highest output per hour for any sector was communications, at more than double the national average, followed closely by finance, insurance, and real estate, which was 36 percent above average. Contrast these hourly values with the lower sector areas—farming, construction, and other services—all of which were about 25 percent below average. Retail trade and government enterprises stood at the very bottom, both only 60+ percent of the business sector average. Clearly, the U.S. economy shows wide productivity differences by industrial sector. For example, looking at the period 1947-73, the National Commission on Productivity and Work Quality found five product fields with average annual productivity growth exceeding 5 percent: petroleum refining (5.8%), man-made fibers (5.7%), hosiery (5.4%), household appliances (5.3%), and malt liquor (5.1%). Those over 4 percent included drugs (4.9%), cement (4.5%), aluminum (4.5%), and flour (4.1%). On the other hand, at the lower end of their rankings were footwear (1.3%), glass containers (1.7%), steel (1.8%), copper, lead, and zinc (2.3%), bakery products (2.4%), and paints (2.5%).[4] Figure 5.1 clearly depicts an important cleavage that began in the mid-1960s. Productivity growth in the nonmanufacturing sectors has been very stunted, whereas in the manufacturing sectors it has maintained a solid and historically consistent pace.

When productivity figures are quoted in the press, they most frequently refer to growth rates rather than absolute levels. Growth rates depict percentage changes in real output per unit of input, most commonly labor hours. Public discussions of the "productivity decline" invariably refer to decreases in the rate of growth, not to absolute decreases. Although there is often significant annual variation, official BLS data show a substantial decline in business sector growth rates. Two years in the 1960s recorded productivity increases of 4 percent or higher, while the decade compounded annual average was a robust 2.9 percent. The average

Table 5.1
Industrial Productivity by Sector, 1987

Industry	Value ($ 1982)
Farming	13.69
Construction	14.36
Nondurable manufacturing	20.54
Durable manufacturing	23.58
Transportation	22.81
Communications	39.66
Wholesale trade	25.29
Retail trade	12.05
Finance, insurance, real estate	26.22
Government enterprises	11.71
Other services	14.35
Business sector	19.26

Source: Unpublished measures, Bureau of Labor Statistics.

for the 1970s was only 1.3, and for the first nine years of the 1980s, the figure (1.6 percent) was still below historic trends. For some years (1974, 1979, and 1980) the annual rate was negative, indicating that measured productivity levels had actually fallen.[5] These labor productivity growth rate declines are mirrored in the multifactor productivity estimates. For example, in the nonfarm business sector the rate of increase from 1948 to 1965 was 2.02 percent, slowing to 1.04 percent for 1965–73, and falling to a very meager crawl of 0.21 percent per year over the 1973–87 period.[6] By any and all measures, then, the average pace of productivity advance has markedly slowed.

International comparisons depict either comparative growth rates among nations or comparative absolute levels of output per unit of input. Such comparisons are even more difficult than strictly domestic measures. They are subject to the usual measurement caveats in terms of their exactness as well as some further complicating influences. Different nations have differing degrees of accuracy in collecting and classifying data. Currency translations involve problems both in concept and in concrete terms (and particularly so in the world of fluctuating exchange rates). The safest comparisons are for manufacturing. Worldwide definitions are most similar, measurement problems are smallest, and accuracy is greatest. Nonetheless, it is of interest to note that the BLS deems the difficulties in making international comparisons (and particularly on a sector-by-sector basis) too great to arrive at meaningful numbers. Accordingly, it does so only at the highest levels of aggregation.

Although it does not provide data on foreign absolute productivity levels, the BLS does publish international comparisons of manufacturing productivity growth *rates*. Two points are obvious in its array (see Table 5.2). First, the United States ranks last in the 1960–73 years and next to last during 1973–79. Second, the productivity slowdown has been a global phenomenon and not one unique to the United States. Japan's increase in the 1980s was only 56 percent of the rate for the 1960–73 period. None of the countries listed showed immunity to the decline. Interestingly, the 1970s were an utter disaster for manufacturing productivity in both the United States and the United Kingdom. Each bounded back well in the 1980s, with the U.S. performance actually a little above the 1960–73 average.

A few additional comments are warranted to put U.S. productivity trends and statistics into a better perspective. First, business sector output per hour grew by roughly 2 percent annually from 1900 through 1950. Accordingly, the performance of the 1960s (2.9 percent compounded annual growth) was clearly above trend, while the 1970s and 1980s were well below trend. Second, the relationship between absolute levels and growth rates merits illustration. Although farm productivity levels have traditionally been lower than nonfarm activities, the rates of increase, particularly in the 1948–65 period, were higher than the corresponding rate for the whole economy. Hence, the agricultural sector contributed positively to national productivity growth rates even though its level was below average. Nonetheless, the transfer of labor from agriculture to more highly valued manufacturing or other jobs still raised overall national productivity levels.

Quarterly productivity data often excite media attention, but are too erratic and short term to give much useful information. Further, they are generally revised, sometimes significantly. The discrepancy between any particular quarter and the annual average, even after revision, is frequently substantial. For example,

Figure 5.1
Growth of Output per Hour and Capital Stock per Worker, Manufacturing and Nonmanufacturing, 1948–88

Index, 1948 = 100

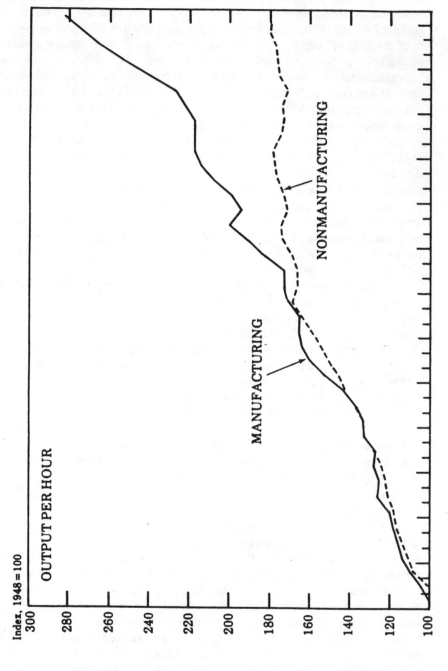

OUTPUT PER HOUR

NONMANUFACTURING

MANUFACTURING

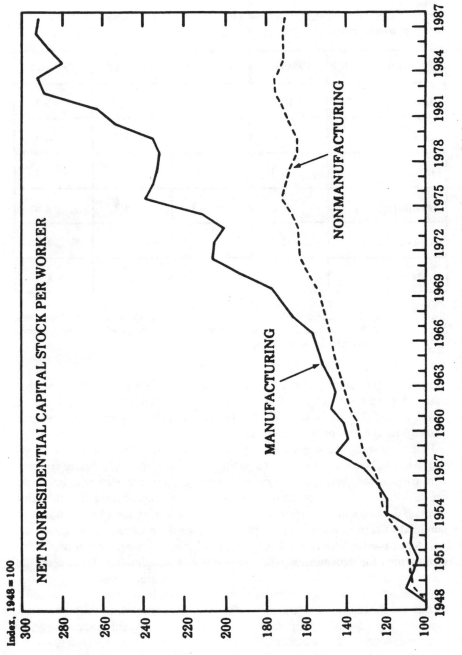

Index, 1948 = 100

NET NONRESIDENTIAL CAPITAL STOCK PER WORKER

NONMANUFACTURING

MANUFACTURING

Source: Council of Economic Advisors, *Economic Report of the President* (Washington, D.C.: U.S. Government Printing Office, January 1989), p. 50.

Table 5.2
Growth of Manufacturing Output per Hour, Six Countries, 1960–88
(average annual rates)

Country	1960-73	1973-79	1973-88	1979-88
Japan	10.3	5.5	5.7	5.8
Italy	6.4	5.7	4.7	4.1
France	6.4	4.6	3.7	3.1
Germany	5.8	4.3	3.3	2.6
Great Britain	4.2	1.2	3.3	4.7
United States	3.3	1.6	2.7	3.4

Source: Bureau of Labor Statistics, *News: International Comparisons of Manufacturing Productivity and Labor Cost Trends, 1988*, June 30, 1989, p. 8, and Bureau of Labor Statistics revisions of data released on August 3, 1989.

business sector output per hour for the first quarter of 1980 came in at a respectable 2.8 percent annual rate. The year, however, ended with a negative rate of −0.3 percent. The first quarter of 1984 posted a terrific 4.6 percent, but the final annual average was only 2.5 percent.

Finally, it should be stressed that measured productivity rates are strongly affected by the business cycle. The reasoning is straightforward. As sales contract during recessions, there are fewer factory orders. Output falls. However, managers are reluctant to dismiss production workers immediately, hoping that the sales (orders) decline will be temporary and short, and fearing the permanent loss of qualified workers. Accordingly, employment does not decrease as rapidly as output. Since productivity is a ratio of output to input, a numerator that falls more rapidly than the denominator will produce declining quotients. Of course, the mathematics are reversed after the recession trough. Output climbs rapidly without big increases in labor inputs (because much underutilized labor was "carried" during the downturn). For example, after the 1960 recession, 1961 showed a healthy 3.5 productivity gain; the 1971 figure was 3.2 percent. Interestingly, in more recent years, the "snapbacks" from recession have been less robust—only 2.8 percent in 1976, 1.5 percent in 1981, and 2.6 percent in 1983.

It merits note that 15 years ago or less there were a number of observers who believed that there was no secular decline in real productivity growth. While measured productivity increases were declining, it was argued that there were "uncaptured" outputs that, if appropriately included, would bring rates back to trend. Specifically, this argument suggested that improved air quality, a safer work place, less fatigued workers, and higher quality outputs would account for the measured decline. Today, however, we continue to witness an anemic performance. Further, we have estimates of some "uncounted" factors. It is true, of course, that productivity gains taken in the form of reduced worker fatigue or fewer pollution emissions will not appear in the calculated statistics because such by-products are not included in the output numerator. Unfortunately, while such effects are real and not inconsiderable, they are very far from the complete story. Edward Denison reports that changes in pollution abatement costs did not affect the growth rate until the 1964-69 period. They subtracted 0.02 percentage points in 1964-69, 0.10 points in 1969-73, and 0.23 points in 1973-75.[7]

Clearly, the added resources involved in improving air quality progressively lower measured productivity, particularly in the 1974-75 time frame, a period that represented a peak in pollution abatement costs with respect to productivity impacts. "The deduction fell back to 0.08 points in 1975-78."[8] When pollution costs are added to safety and health regulations and to the costs of dishonesty and crime, the three "contributed importantly to the decline in output growth observed in the 1973-76 period."[9] Over longer periods, however, the contribution is much less, and even at the peak cannot account for the bulk of the slowdown. Additionally, both Gallup and Roper polls in the 1970s, as well as other indicators, suggest that the quality of U.S. output is far more likely to have declined than improved in that decade, a factor that would tend to give the published figures an offsetting upward bias. Accordingly, the universal consensus today is that the productivity problem is real, not a statistical illusion, and a secular, not temporary, phenomenon. Indeed, the anemic 1.3 percent average business sector output growth of the 1970s has been only modestly improved during the first nine years of the 1980s.

ECONOMIC GROWTH AND SOURCES OF PRODUCTIVITY CHANGE

Economic growth essentially consists of applying either more inputs to production, better inputs (higher productivity), or some combination. A 10 percent increase in resources, for example, should yield a 10 percent increase in output. If productivity improves 10 percent, potential output will also increase by that amount. Hence, with all resources 10 percent more productive and with 10 percent more inputs, output potential will grow by 20 percent. Potential output serves as a limiting case as well as a guide to economic policy makers. Of course, due to business cycle fluctuations or other disturbances, an economy's actual performance may not reach its potential.

For example, if the economy slips into recession, output will decrease; however, if the labor force is growing or there is an excess of investment over depreciation (so that the capital stock increases), the economy's potential output will grow despite actual output declining. When economists estimate the full employment GNP, they are calculating potential output. If actual output is proceeding at a slower pace, policy makers may choose to undertake stimulative actions that will raise real production closer to its potential.

It is of interest to survey past U.S. growth patterns to see the relative contributions of factor increases versus productivity change. An early 1970s study compares two 60-year periods, revealing almost 4 percent annual growth from 1840 to 1900, followed by 3.12 percent during the next 60 years.[10] The bulk of the earlier period's advance derived from added inputs, with additional labor accounting for almost half and additions to the capital stock adding one-quarter. Only 17 percent was attributed to improved productivity during this period. From 1900 to 1960, however, added capital was responsible for about 19 percent, added labor for 35 percent, and productivity growth for 44 percent, more than doubling its role in the previous 60-year period.

Denison's study of the 1948–81 period attributes to additional inputs collectively only 34 percent of annual growth, with the remainder resulting from increased productivity.[11] Thus we see a secular trend spanning over 100 years for growth to be increasingly driven by productivity rather than added inputs. Second, this substantial productivity thrust is divided into two parts, one attributable to education and the other labeled advances in knowledge and other factors, a category whose influence was more than twice that of education. Clearly, change in technology has been a major element in this category.

Data from more recent periods, however, indicate a reversal of the secular trend favoring rising productivity as the growth locomotive. Since 1961, U.S. GNP growth has increasingly resulted from the application of more labor rather than from increased productivity. During the 1960s, employment gains accounted for 43 percent of real GNP growth. From 1970 to 1973 it was 61 percent and in the 1974–82 period, employment growth accounted for 95 percent of the GNP advance. This anomalous reversal of previous trends in large part coincided with demographic factors—the surge of young people and married women into the labor force.

Looking at a longer twentieth-century period, Denison has estimated that potential output in the United States grew by a 3.4 percent annual average over the 1929–69 years.[12] Although the number of workers increased, this growth-promoting factor was significantly negated by a reduction in working hours. However, improved productivity (quality of labor) more than offset the loss due to fewer hours. Additional capital goods created about 15 percent of the growth, while a better allocation of resources (such as the movement of workers from low-productivity farm jobs to higher productivity urban employment) and economies of scale (see chapter 7) also made meaningful contributions. The former accounted for 9 percent of growth, while scale economies contributed 12 percent. A large residual—labeled advances in knowledge and not elsewhere classified—added almost one point per year, or 29 percent. Clearly, then, growth derives from a combination of causes and no single "fix" will bring vast changes. Further, the large size of what has become known as "Denison's residual" suggests that there is still much that we do not fully understand.

As has been demonstrated, until recently productivity had become increasingly important in the U.S. growth picture. During the next decade it will become even more important—net additions to the labor force will be small and the demand for reduced working hours will continue. However, previous analysis has indicated that the pace of U.S. productivity advance since the late 1960s has significantly fallen, with very poor overall performances over the past 20 years. What accounts for this productivity malaise? Such an important question merits careful examination. Unfortunately, even the closest scrutiny fails to fully explain this enigma. Lester Thurow has aptly labeled the productivity problem "a wound of a thousand cuts." Its causes are numerous and it needs to be examined from many angles.

One such angle is a view of factor proportions. From the early 1800s until the early 1960s the rate of increase in labor hours continuously declined. Coinciding with that decline is a long upward trend in labor productivity growth. But during the last 20 years, when labor hours sharply increased, labor productivity growth began a precipitous fall. These relationships are not fortuitous. They reflect the law of diminishing returns.

When factor proportions vary, with labor increasing more rapidly than the capital stock, labor productivity can be expected to suffer since the average amount of capital per worker falls. Diminishing returns thus set in, even with the assumption that additional labor is of equal quality. In the recent U.S. case, however, the surge of young people and married women entering the labor force for the first time (or after prolonged absence) brought less-experienced workers. Accordingly, diminishing returns were reinforced by seemingly lower quality inputs.

For any given increase in the capital stock, labor productivity will be lower the greater the increase in the number of workers associated with that capital stock. Unless the economy is able to make capital formation soar in response to a soaring labor force, the available capital per worker—and hence productivity—must be adversely affected. During the 1970s and early 1980s, two factors—maturation of the baby boom population and the increasing participation of women in the labor force—accounted for an upsurge in labor hours. Over the 1948-73 period the capital labor ratio (net nonresidential capital stock divided by total hours worked in the private nonfarm sector) grew by almost 3 percent a year. However, from mid-1972 to mid-1979, capital per worker grew at only 0.6 percent, "leaving the level of capital per worker by mid-1979 about 17 percent lower" than if the previous trend had continued.[13] "Alternatively, the net capital stock was about $200 billion (1972 prices) lower."[14] Figure 5.1 vividly illustrated the correlation between growth in capital stock per worker (substantial in manufacturing, far less so in nonmanufacturing) and output per hour. Clearly this impact is substantial, although variously estimated. John Tatom concluded that insufficient capital formation reduced annual productivity growth by a very significant 0.7 percentage point, and Norsworthy, Harper, and Kunze found the 1973–78 slowdown to be "dominated by the effects of reduced capital formation."[15] Thurow, Denison, and Kendrick, on the other hand, estimate the role of capital to be less significant, but still substantial.

Several points merit note. First, rates of capital formation can be influenced by government policy, particularly via tax laws, interest rate policy, price stability, and the maintenance of high levels of aggregate demand. Second, inasmuch as fewer new workers are now entering the labor force, productivity performance should be positively affected as long as net capital formation maintains or improves upon previous trends. As yet, however, a rebound is not in sight, which also casts some doubt on the inexperienced worker hypothesis. Finally, it has been the history of the human race that diminishing returns have been offset by new technologies and new modes of working and organizing man's activities, In the long and constant struggle against diminishing returns, mankind has clearly been winning. But in recent rounds—the past 20 years—diminishing returns seem to be winning. So again comes the question, what has happened? Certainly insufficient capital formation is one explanation.

One way of viewing the productivity slowdown is to look at sectoral contributions. For years, the shift of resources out of agriculture and into higher productivity areas was a strong source of national gain. "From 1948 to 1965, 9.1 billion manhours . . . (or 8 percent of the total number of hours worked in the entire private economy) left agriculture. . . . By the early 1970s . . . this process was nearing an end, and from 1977 to 1983 less than 0.2 billion manhours of work were released. . . ."[16] According to Thurow, "the shrinkage of agriculture employment explains 12 percent . . . of the observed drop in the national productivity growth rate between the 1948–65 and 1977–82 periods."[17] Resource reallocations—out of low return arenas and into higher return sectors—will clearly make a positive contribution. Currently, however, the relatively small number left in agriculture no longer permits this kind of reallocation to be capable of substantially raising national productivity levels. Far more promising are shifts out of sectors in which the United States has lost comparative advantage and into sectors that are more suitable. The shift from "metal-bashing" to high technology is clearly the right kind of reallocation and is taking place, albeit not without some pain and friction.

In the construction sector, efficiency has for seemingly unexplained reasons faltered seriously. Once higher than the national average, construction productivity today is not only far below that average, but also below its 1965 peak level. Indeed, official data place its 1987 level at only 62 percent of its average in the 1960s and some 22 percent below the 1977 level. Thurow suggests that 13 percent of the national productivity decline is attributable to problems in this industry.

This mystery of absolute decline in measured construction productivity can be at least partially solved. Some would say that the numbers are simply wrong, the result of poor concepts, poor measurement, and the difficulty of quantifying outputs correctly. Certainly it may be the case that the quality of output has improved, but is not captured in the calculations, in which case the decline is not really as steep as the numbers suggest. Nonetheless, this would hardly explain all or even most of this rather shocking phenomenon. Second, the basic production function is unchanged. While there have been many incremental improvements in tools and materials, there have been few major breakthroughs in construction technology or mode of operation. A man can only hammer so fast. Accordingly, major productivity advances should not be expected, although incremental growth surely could have been forthcoming. Several other factors have been at work. First, the deteriorating system of national, state, and local roads and highways plus increased congestion has meant delays in receiving construction materials. Workers do more standing around and waiting. Since labor hours are there, but materials are not, measured productivity (output per hour) must fall even if construction workers themselves are not less skilled or hardworking. Second, to the degree that public morals and policing have deteriorated, there may be greater theft and/or damage of building materials. Here again the labor denominator remains the same, but less output would appear in the numerator. Third, if union work rules have reduced flexibility or if worker attitudes have soured, such occurrences would also contribute to declining performance. Finally, according to 1988 research, drug and alcohol abuse "is a problem for 10 percent to 15 percent of the nation's construction workers, costing the economy more than $10 billion a year. . . ."[18]

The deterioration in public infrastructure is not limited to harming the construction sector alone. Indeed, a recent study by David Aschauer, senior economist with the Chicago Federal Reserve Bank, attributes as "much as one-quarter of the productivity decline in the private sector in the 1970s and 1980s . . . to the dramatic decline of public infrastructure spending."[19]

In the mining sector, areas of easiest access are always addressed first, which means that unless there are major technical breakthroughs, over time productivity must decline substantially. This performance, according to Thurow, accounts for 6 percent of the total decline. Problems in electrical utilities account for an additional 13 percent.

The accelerated trend toward employment in service industries is another drag on national productivity. Between 1977 and 1982, service jobs absorbed some 65 percent of all employment growth in the private sector. However, by 1983 service productivity had fallen to only 61 percent of the national average. Such resource deployments have the opposite effect of the move out of agriculture and, according to one authority, probably account for an additional 12 percent of the national productivity decrease.[20] But in large part this explanation begs the question. Why have the services, at least as a group, not advanced their performance?

Thurow makes a convincing case when arguing that much of the productivity data in at least one major sector of services, health care, understate true contributions.[21] Since this is a growing field, such understatement looms larger over time. Even more important, however, is the sociology of large organizations that dominates U.S. office work, for it has effectively militated against productivity improvement. Indeed, it often works in the opposite direction. Thurow points out that U.S. banks, which computerized their accounting systems and added automatic tellers, discovered that by 1982 "it took more hours of work to produce a unit of output with computers and automated tellers than it used to take in 1977 without them."[22] Several factors are at work here and the discussion is hardly limited to banks, but is applicable to office and white-collar work throughout our nation.

New technologies have been introduced and additional information generated, both of which should be productivity enhancing if used properly. But we have not generally done so. Copying machines, which so greatly facilitate information flows, have instead created information clogs and consumed enormous volumes of paper and millions of unnecessary labor hours. Office memos between two or three parties end up getting sent everywhere (in the interest of "keeping everyone informed"). Accordingly, more paper is utilized initially, there is greater waiting time at the duplicating machine, someone must consume more time in delivering to 30 in-boxes instead of two, wastepaper baskets fill up sooner, and the garbage disposal bill rises. Further, decision making may be delayed or postponed as suggestions come from uninformed, disinterested, or "spoiler" third parties. Of course, this need not be the case. Two or three heads are better than one when they are informed, concerned, affected by the outcome, and interested in furthering the goals of the organization rather than those of some subunit of which they are a part. Nor is this process always a drag. But too often this rich and useful technology, whose purpose is to facilitate information flows and speed decision making, instead becomes a source of additional costs and delays.

Fax machines are another example of possible technology misuse. Clearly they have tremendous potential, if properly utilized. Effective utilization, however, requires sagacious application and proper procedures. Improperly employed, they will be productivity retarding. For example, a brokerage house with several offices in the Washington, D.C. area traditionally allowed each branch to open new accounts. After all its offices were equipped with fax capabilities, however, it was decided that the new technology could allow a centralized location to quickly approve all such accounts. Accordingly, local offices had to fax applications to the center, but they lost many new accounts. With each office regularly calling the central approving line, the number was invariably busy, the customer had much longer to wait, and the system deteriorated rather than improved the service. As a another example, the *Wall Street Journal* in the spring of 1989 reported on problems of junk mail in the fax era.[23] Once such anomalies are recognized, of course, there are ways to deal with them. As yet, however, there is accumulating evidence that white-collar America is failing to effectively generate productivity from substantial information technology investments undertaken since 1978.[24] Indeed, there is disconcerting evidence that the opposite may be the case. The important point is this: unless appropriate and successful adjustments are made, innovations will not necessarily improve effectiveness. If executives use computers only for word processing, they are doing secretarial jobs at executive pay.

Here then is a major challenge. Organizations and procedures must adapt to new technologies and innovations, or their benefits will be dissipated and perhaps become negative. Thorstein Veblen once stated that history more frequently records the triumph of imbecile institutions over technology than is the reverse case. Office "productivity will only flow out of office automation if American white-collar workers are willing to change what the office does and how it operates."[25] In short, new and terrific technologies neither automatically nor easily graft to an on-going organization. If productivity is to be enhanced by innovations, it will happen only through concerted effort.

This is also a reminder that capital investment per se may not raise productivity. It must be used and it must be utilized properly and effectively. For example, during the first decade of nationalized coal in Great Britain, output per man-shift rose almost imperceptibly despite the closing of marginal mines and extensive capital investments that should have substantially raised productivity. However, it appears that miner attitudes and labor-management difficulties served to negate the advances that should have taken place. Abram Bergson has pointed out that despite Soviet capital stock per worker being comparable to several European countries in the 1950s and 1960s (and above Italy's), productivity was well below all of them, Italy included.[26]

Another major contributing area is that of education. There are a wide variety of indicators, including a steep and unprecedented 17-year decline in Scholastic Aptitude Test scores, suggesting that the educational system is failing to properly prepare American children for the rigors of the twenty-first century. And not only are American students failing to meet our past standards, they do poorly in international comparisons as well. For example, U.S. high school pupils have been scoring in the bottom quartile in mathematics ability, while the average Japanese student has equivalency to the 95th percentile among American students. Recent research finds that if the academic achievement gains of the 1948–73 period had been maintained, workers today would have 2.9 percent greater productivity. This translates into a 1987 GNP that would have been $86 billion larger, with the annual cost "projected to double within 15 years."[27] This research reveals and quantifies what many have long believed—that a deficient educational system has enormous costs that permeate every aspect of society. Indeed, the "cumulative total social costs through 2010 of the test score decline have a present value . . . in 1987 of $3.2 trillion,"[28] equivalent of the entire GNP in 1981.

Clearly these costs are staggering and the values foregone could have very adequately funded many pressing national needs. Further, since there is generally a lag between high school education and significant economic contributions to society, even if we could tomorrow instantaneously transform the effectiveness of the U.S. educational establishment,[29] the results would not be reaped for many years. Indeed, "when the academic achievement of students completing their schooling declines substantially, the economic costs are large and last for generations."[30] Education, then, has an important role to play and undoubtedly accounts for a large portion of Denison's unexplained residual.

Other factors contributing to the productivity slowdown merit a brief listing. If appropriately addressed, they could substantially assist in a rebound. They may be broadly categorized into two groupings, those generally internal to an organization and therefore subject to managerial influence, and those external to the firm and likely to be best addressed via public policy. In the first category one must certainly list attention to worker problems, needs, and appropriate risk/reward relationships. Profit sharing and incentive schemes, quality circles, and similar activities are the kinds of programs that might address these challenges. Further, innovative management techniques seem essential. Has the U.S. corporation grown too large? Is it old and decrepit? Perhaps we need leaner organizational structures with reduced bureaucracy.[31] In recent years, for example, General Motors has acquired companies to which it feeds capital, but allows them to be autonomous, self-contained units. Also, what has happened to U.S. management's focus —is it upon production, quality control, or service or is it upon financing schemes or acquisitions? Peter Drucker maintains that fear of unfriendly corporate takeovers has biased managerial perceptions and diverted management attention from productivity-related concerns.[32] U.S. managements may also have higher turnover rates than are economically optimal. Finally, greater flexibility at all levels is warranted.

Factors external to the firm would include the already discussed deteriorating national infrastructure and regulatory burdens and interferences. Regarding public investment, whereas during "the period 1953 to 1969 public non-military capital accumulation averaged 1.5 percent of gross national product . . . during . . . subsequent years . . . the percentage . . . has fallen to a mere 0.4."[33] The tandem relationship between U.S. productivity trends and government investment is quite remarkable. Further, international correlations between productivity growth and public investment as a percent of gross domestic product find the United States at the bottom, with the stronger productivity performers showing much higher public investment efforts. Concerning infrastructure's likely boost to productivity performance, the summary statement of David Aschauer, economist at the Federal Reserve Bank of Chicago, is impressive:

Raising the level of public investment spending from its current abysmal level of less than one half a percent of GNP to a modest two percent—some 80 to 90 billion dollars per year—would work wonders, quite likely wonders comparable to those of modern medicine in dealing with human disease.[34]

Regulatory burdens in terms of compliance paperwork alone probably also play a role. For example, during the 1970s the Eli Lilly Company spent about $15 million annually to gather information and file forms for various government agencies. In September 1975, Standard Oil (Indiana) had to store the information necessary to comply with just one agency, the Federal Energy Administration, on 636 miles of computer tape! Clearly, these requirements involve manpower, but no increase in output, hence they are productivity retarding.

Oil is also often mentioned, the price shocks of the 1970s and their lasting disruptions alleged to be important retarding factors. Further, since the entire world was hit by the same substantial boosts in energy costs, this would help to explain the global nature of the slowdown. Alas, while it is undoubtedly true that for certain periods following the price shocks measured productivity was obviously impacted, perhaps substantially, the role of oil in the long-term decline does not appear to be significant.[35] And today, despite almost a decade of falling prices (real 1989 oil prices were at about the same level as the preembargo 1973 rates) the world has not witnessed a positive rebound in productivity, thus casting further doubt on the significance of the relationship.

Another popular explanation holds that weak R&D spending has had a prime role to play. Here again, however, there are scant data to support an effective argument. Zvi Griliches maintains that the "decline in productivity growth cannot be attributed to a decline in R&D expenditures. They did not decline that much."[36] His conclusion is supported by most productivity scholars. Of course, it may not be outlays, but instead the effectiveness of those outlays and the efficiency and speed of diffusion. Accordingly, those seeking to raise productivity should be concerned if our R&D efforts wane.

The degree of market competition and international trade also have a role to play. A study of British industry revealed that those sectors most exposed to international competition had the highest rates of productivity growth, while those least exposed had the lowest rates.[37] Finally, the nature of a rich society—its changing values and attitudes—may militate against continuing productivity progress. After all, despite continuing and improving excellence in education, Japan's productivity growth rates have also slowed. Indeed, this explanation, although difficult to prove, would account for the uniform productivity slowdown in all economically advanced countries.

IMPACT OF DEFENSE EXPENDITURES ON NATIONAL PRODUCTIVITY

Although most productivity scholars have not considered it as a meaningful contributor, one school of thought maintains that the productivity malaise derives primarily from the economic costs associated with military spending. Most popular during and shortly after the Vietnam War, this hypothesis asserts that there is a significant military drag on national productivity and that the size and nature of the defense budget are the basic causes of U.S. efficiency declines. More specifically, the hypothesis claims that (1) the defense budget absorbs funds that would otherwise be invested; that (2) defense production attracts the best and brightest of engineering and technical talent, thus robbing the private sector of critical human capital; that (3) efficiency is of low order importance in defense industries and a cost push mentality develops and spreads throughout the economy; and finally that (4) defense disproportionately absorbs R&D funds, thereby depriving the country of basic and applied industrial research. This line of reasoning is generally supported by selected simple correlations showing higher productivity countries spending smaller proportions on defense.

There are a number of serious problems with this argument. Of course it is true that if defense funds were channeled into investment, the resulting greater capital formation should lift productivity levels. However, there is no particular reason to believe that cuts in the military budget would indeed go to investment. Instead, they are likely to be directed into consumption, either public or private. What happened to the so-called Vietnam peace dividend? Virtually throughout the 1970s real defense outlays were falling, yet productivity also declined. Indeed, in the 1980s reviving productivity occurred simultaneously with increased, not reduced, defense outlays. While defense does attract highly qualified and motivated individuals, its demand tends to raise relative wages and thereby increase the numbers of Americans choosing these technical/scientific occupations.

With regard to the use of R&D funds, U.S. productivity rates were highest in the 1960s, when defense and space programs dominated R&D activities. Although some correlations have been drawn between percentage of GNP devoted to civilian R&D and economic growth, it is not percentages, but actual dollars, that drive such efforts. Despite a lower percentage, actual dollars spent on civilian R&D have consistently been much greater in the United States than elsewhere. One must also consider that defense R&D does have civilian applications, as chapter 4 noted. Further, as mentioned, the R&D contribution is only one of many and most investigators believe the bulk of the problem lies elsewhere. Finally, the argument that efficiency and costs are of low priority in defense procurement is a weak one with only very limited validity. Former Secretary of Defense Harold Brown has aptly addressed this hypothesis:

Deficiencies of U.S. industry in productivity and in competition with other countries, notably Japan, are very much less a consequence of the diversion of technical talent to military R&D than they are of a variety of business organization and labor union practices, and of government regulatory, employment, tax, and antitrust policies.[38]

Clearly, the productivity malaise stems from a variety of sources. Further, despite a multitude of careful and detailed analyses, there is still substantial room for further explanation. As Denison has concluded: "What has happened is, to be blunt, a mystery."[39]

Mystery or not, it is agreed by all that productivity growth is crucial. The data also clearly indicate that the bulk of the problem is not in the manufacturing sector, whose performance has been relatively strong, but elsewhere.[40] In a world of rapid information dissemination and ease of capital movements, it is to be expected that the gap between foreign productivity levels and our own will decrease. "But none of the others, not even Japan, has so far surpassed us in overall productivity level, and there is no evidence indicating, except in some particular industries, that they are about to."[41]

NOTES

1. William J. Baumol, "Is There a Productivity Crisis?" *Science* 243 (February 3, 1989), p. 611.

2. See Robert H. Hayes and Kim B. Clark, "Explaining Observed Productivity Differentials Between Plants: Implications for Operations Research," *Interfaces*, November/December 1985, p. 314.

3. U.S. Department of Labor, *Technology and Labor in Four Industries* (Washington, D.C.: Bureau of Labor Statistics), January, 1982, p. 15.

4. National Commission on Productivity and Work Quality, *Fourth Annual Report*, March 1975.

5. Bureau of Labor Statistics, Office of Productivity and Technology, June 1, 1989, press release.

6. John H. Bishop, "Is the Test Score Decline Responsible for the Productivity Growth Decline?" *American Economic Review* (March 1989), p. 178.

7. Edward F. Denison, *Accounting for Slower Economic Growth* (Washington, D.C.: Brookings Institution, 1979), p. 71.

8. Ibid., p. 72.

9. Ibid., p. 74.

10. Lance E. Davis and others, *American Economic Growth* (New York: Harper & Row, 1972), p. 39.

11. Edward F. Denison, "The Interruption of Productivity Growth in the United States," *Economic Journal*, March 1983.

12. Edward F. Denison, *Accounting for United States Economic Growth, 1929–1969* (Washington, D.C.: Brookings Institution, 1974.)

13. John A. Tatom, "The Productivity Problem," *Review*, Federal Reserve Bank of St. Louis, September 1979, p. 7.

14. Ibid.

15. J. R. Norsworthy, Michael J. Harper, and Kent Kunze, "The Slowdown in Productivity Growth," *Brookings Papers on Economic Activity*, No. 2 (1979), p. 421.

16. Lester C. Thurow, *The Zero-Sum Solution* (New York: Simon and Schuster, 1985), p. 73.

17. Ibid.

18. See "Labor Letter," *Wall Street Journal*, December 6, 1988, p. 1.

19. David Aschauer, quoted in Bob Rast, "Infrastructure Crisis Grips U.S.," *Times-Picayune*, April 9, 1989, p. A3.

20. Thurow, p. 83.

21. Ibid, pp. 78–79.

22. Ibid, p. 81.

23. Michelle Manges, "Junk Mail in the Age of Fax," *Wall Street Journal*, May 3, 1989, p. B1.

24. *Productivity*, March 1989, pp. 1–3.

25. Thurow, p. 82.

26. Jan Tinbergen, Abram Bergson, and others, *Optimum Social Welfare and Productivity* (New York: New York University Press, 1972), pp. 72–75.

27. Bishop, p. 193.

28. Ibid., p. 179.

29. It should be recognized that "blame" for this failure lies not solely at the feet of the U.S. educational establishment. Changing folkways, family patterns, and sociological trends all play important roles.

30. Bishop, p. 194.

31. See John A. Byrne, "Is Your Company Too Big?" *Business Week,* March 27, 1989, pp. 84–94.

32. Peter F. Drucker, "Taming the Corporate Takeover," *Wall Street Journal,* October 30, 1984, p. 30.

33. David Aschauer, "Does Public Capital Crowd Out Private Capital?" Occasional Paper, SM-88-10, Federal Reserve Bank of Chicago, undated, p. 13.

34. David Aschauer, "Rx for Productivity," *Chicago Fed Letter,* Federal Reserve Bank of Chicago, September, 1988, p. 3.

35. Among productivity scholars, Jorgenson is the exception on this question. See Dale W. Jorgenson, "The Answer is Energy," *Challenge,* November–December 1980.

36. Zvi Griliches, "R&D and Productivity," *Science,* July 3, 1987, p. 237.

37. Andrew Fox, "Productivity Growth in U.K. Manufacturing Industry," *Barclay's Review,* February 1984, pp. 14–16

38. Harold Brown, "Technology, Military Equipment, and National Security," *Parameters,* March, 1983, p. 16.

39. Denison, *Accounting for Slower Economic Growth,* p. 4.

40. See Edward Denison, *Estimates of Productivity Change by Industry* (Washington, D.C.: Brookings Institution, 1989) for further elaboration on the measured differences between manufacturing and nonmanufacturing productivity. His analysis suggests that the differences are not as great as they appear.

41. Baumol, pp. 613–14. See also Susan Hickok, Linda A. Bell, and Janet Ceglowski, "The Competitiveness of U.S. Manufactured Goods," *Quarterly Review,* Federal Reserve Bank of New York, Spring 1988, p. 10.

6

International Influences

The United States has an open economy, one that is linked to other nations through a complex network of international trade and financial relationships. Though it has a rich, highly diversified resource base and a vast domestic market, the United States can and does gain by these exchanges with other countries. Because the endowments of land, labor skills, and capital differ among nations, the opportunity costs of producing goods and services will vary. Accordingly, international trade yields mutual (although not necessarily equal) gains to all trade participants as they exchange each others' specialties.

However, because nations use different currencies, such trade poses foreign exchange complications. In addition, foreign trade is subject to numerous political interferences and controls. Such disturbances can be very disruptive, as the OPEC oil embargo and limitations on grain sales to the Soviets amply demonstrated. Nevertheless, due to modern communications and transportation, the world is getting smaller and all countries are in fact tied together through trade and a more integrated world market. This globalization trend is clearly illustrated by the secularly rising proportion of world income over the past 40 years, which is generated in the foreign trade sector. Indeed, no nation today can enjoy isolated prosperity. On the other hand, increased interdependence brings a host of economic problems and vulnerabilities, which in turn generate considerable political, foreign policy, and national security challenges.

COMPARATIVE ADVANTAGE AND TRADE PATTERNS

The basic reason for a nation to engage in trade (either internal or international) derives from the benefits of specialization. Since those benefits are maximized when this relative concentration of effort is based upon the principle of comparative advantage, this tends to be the trend, albeit with important exceptions. The principle suggests that all countries can obtain a larger quantity and greater variety of goods if each item is produced by the nation with the lowest relative costs. A country gains by specializing in the production of goods that it can produce relatively cheaply and exchanging them for other desired goods for which it is a relatively higher cost producer. Accordingly, it makes sense for Japan, which has few material resources but a highly efficient labor force, to import many raw materials and export VCRs, cameras, and other manufactured goods. By the same line of reasoning, it is advantageous for the United States to import bananas and export computers. It is important to note that today's comparative advantage can be tomorrow's comparative disadvantage. Relative to the U.S. factor proportions, Japan's resource endowment during one past period yielded a comparative advantage in textiles, which were exported to the United States. With changing factor proportions and technologies, however, Japanese textiles have tended to be displaced by those of Taiwan, Hong Kong, and elsewhere. But a lost comparative advantage in textiles was replaced by a new comparative advantage in motor vehicles, also exported to the United States (in huge and growing quantities until quotas, the "voluntary" auto restraints, were imposed in 1982). Interestingly, even if a nation were to be held in limbo for a period, so that nothing within it changed, its comparative advantages would probably still shift due to changing conditions elsewhere. Comparative advantage, then, is clearly a fast-moving train, one becoming more rapid all the time. Nations and businesses that do not get on and off quickly and nimbly will be left behind watching the smoke and wondering what went wrong.

The difference between absolute advantage and comparative advantage must be understood. Absolute advantage means getting more output from a given set of inputs. A professor may be able to both type and do research better than the department secretary. These are absolute advantages, but should the professor attempt both or specialize? If the latter, on what basis? Clearly, his or her comparative advantage is in research and it is there that the professor's efforts should be concentrated. This also applies to nations. The United States may be able to produce a given product better than some foreign country, but it may still choose to import that item so that it can concentrate its efforts in an area in which it has an even greater absolute advantage. This is the true meaning of comparative advantage. Advanced nations do tend to concentrate where they are most ahead; poor countries' comparative advantages lie in areas where they are least behind in an absolute sense. Accordingly, nations often import products they themselves can produce, but they choose to import anyway. Alternately, they simply may not have the capability to produce some items.

For the United States, many basic resources fit this latter category. For example, we depend almost entirely upon other countries for diamonds, coffee, and natural rubber. Further, a number of minerals that are critical inputs to essential civilian outputs as well as military goods, such as manganese, cobalt, bauxite, tantalum, and columbium, virtually all come from abroad. And well over half of the country's supplies of tin, asbestos, nickel, cadmium, and zinc are from foreign sources. Some of these minerals are necessary ingredients for many of the new specialty steel alloys and other new materials that are used extensively in the production of high technology and military equipment.

Traditionally, except in wartime, the United States has relied upon market forces to develop new mineral resources. The market, biased by some questionable government interventions, has led to the current dependency condition, which is not irrational from a strictly economic perspective. However, given the unstable condition of the world, such imports are subject to potential supply disruptions. The United States is vulnerable in several mineral resources of strategic importance: bauxite, chromium, cobalt, columbium, manganese, the platinum group, tantalum, and titanium.[1] These are among the 31 minerals that are considered sufficiently strategic and critical to be included in the goals for the National Defense Stockpile. According to the Strategic Material Stockpiling Revision Act 1979, the stockpile should be sufficient to sustain the United States for a period not less than three years in the event of national emergency. But this objective has never been achieved. Interestingly, Japan and our European allies are far more dependent upon strategic minerals imports than is the United States. By contrast, the Soviet Union is largely self-sufficient in minerals.

Another critical import is oil. When originally conceived, the Strategic Petroleum Reserve was envisaged to contain 1 billion barrels. The reserve is currently authorized to 750 million barrels, and a congressionally mandated study is now under way in the Department of Energy concerning the 250-million-barrel increment. The reserve is currently being filled at the rate of 62,000 barrels per day and at the end of fiscal 1989 the stockpile had reached 571 million barrels. The United States is party to an oil sharing arrangement with its allies (who are much more vulnerable to disruption) in the event of another energy crisis. By the end of 1989 the United States was satisfying over 50 percent of its oil demand with imports, up from a low of 30 percent in 1983 and close to the 1977 peak year of almost 55 percent.

The United States trades with virtually every nation of the world, with many of its industries depending on foreign countries either for markets or for raw materials. During the 1950s and 1960s, imported products averaged a little more than 4 percent of the GNP. Today they account for 12 percent. Exports, on the other hand, which were in the 5 percent range in the 1950s and the 6 percent range in the 1960s, now account for almost 10 percent of our GNP. In the mid-nineteenth century, the United States exported primarily raw materials and foodstuffs—about 70 percent of the total. Exports today are dominated by finished manufactured products. Reflecting the industrial shifts described in chapter 2, high technology items presently account for over 40 percent of this total. On the import side, automobiles and capital goods were each roughly $85 billion in 1987, with industrial supplies and materials at $71 billion. Due to energy conservation and weak world oil prices, petroleum, which in 1980 was close to 30 percent of our import bill, was only 9 percent in 1987 and 1988, with 1987 outlays some $36 billion below the 1980 peak.

Because ongoing global trade patterns are greatly influenced by a multitude of governmental distortions throughout the world, such patterns do not perfectly reflect global comparative advantages. Nonetheless, the composition of its trade provides a rough guide to the comparative advantages of the United States. Rich agricultural resources together with advanced farm technology enable American farmers to be highly competitive, the agricultural industry relying heavily on foreign markets to sell rice, wheat, soybeans, cotton, and tobacco. Exports of these products have varied from one-fourth to more than one-half of total U.S. agricultural output. Farm exports, it should be noted, peaked in 1981 at $44 billion and declined to just under $30 billion in 1987, reflecting the green revolution overseas and Third World debt problems. Additionally, the U.S. skilled labor force, combined with high rates of technological advance through education and R&D efforts, yields a U.S. comparative advantage in the production of highly sophisticated machinery and equipment. Conversely, the United States clearly does not have a comparative advantage in most minerals or fuels. In recent years some important trading partners, especially Japan, have developed comparative advantages and distinctive, quality products in automobiles, electronics, and other items. Accordingly, the U.S. competitive edge in these areas has declined. On the other hand, Japan has a comparative advantage equivalent to that of the United States in office machinery (including computers), and a weaker position than either the United States or the European nations in general industrial machinery and professional, scientific, and control instruments. Finally, Japan has a decided comparative disadvantage in the trading of chemicals, wood products, and tobacco.

For the first two post-World War II decades, the United States enjoyed a far disproportionate international trade status because its industrial plant and equipment remained intact during the war, whereas Europe and Japan lost substantial portions of their industrial capacities. The United States realized merchandise trade balance surpluses ranging between $1 billion and $7 billion annually in the 1950s and 1960s. However, as other countries, especially Japan and the industrial nations of Europe, restored their economies, the U.S. surplus fell to less than $1 billion by 1969. This declining net export trend continued, with the United States experiencing merchandise trade deficits in every year from 1974 to the present. The deficit reached a record of $160 billion in 1987.

Reflecting these developments, the U.S. share of exports in the world market has shown a general downward trend since the 1950s. At the end of World War II, the United States was the world's dominant industrial producer, capturing approximately 60 percent of global export of manufactured goods in the late 1940s. That trade pattern, however, was distorted. During the 1950s and 1960s the European and Japanese economies reentered the world market with rising productivity and enhanced capacity. Accordingly, they competed vigorously and effectively. The U.S. share of world exports naturally fell. Other factors contributing to this decline include both the relatively recent growth of productive capacity in the newly industrializing countries (NICs) and the liquidity and financial problems of most of the world in the early 1980s. Another significant ingredient was the strong dollar (a point to be elaborated shortly). Nonetheless, despite substantial changes in global trade patterns over the past 30 years, according to GATT (General Agreement on Tariffs and Trade) data, the United States is today the world's second largest exporter (11.3 percent of world exports), a shade behind West Germany (11.4 percent) and still ahead of Japan (9.3 percent).

Foreign production capabilities are also manifested by the pervasiveness of imports, which have increased in value tenfold since 1960. This import presence is visible everywhere one looks, yet despite today's record levels, imports remain relatively low. Indeed, it is a tribute to the vastness of the U.S. economy that imports, so pervasive in final goods (automobiles, VCRs, etc.), in intermediate items (integrated circuits), and as raw materials (petroleum), comprise only 12 percent of the GNP.

It remains to be noted that global import or export shares can be deceptive and misleading, as can trade balance figures, particularly when invoked as indicators of U.S. competitiveness. Being of vast size both physically and economically, the United States can produce goods on the East Coast and ship them 3,000 miles to California, but these never enter as exports in the trade figures. Anything that Japan or Germany ships such a distance will always be an export, contribute to their balance of payments, and increase their share of world trade. Further, if a country, say the United States, were to produce 10,000 computers, exporting none but selling them throughout the country, yet import 20 computers (because 10,000 were insufficient for domestic needs), such imports would contribute to a trade deficit, a high tech deficit at that! But would either a general deficit so created or a specific product category deficit mean that U.S. computer producers were not competitive? Surely nothing of the sort can be inferred from trade data alone. Competitiveness is quite a nebulous concept and there is far more than meets the eye in trade figures as well as far less than meets the eye in most trade discussions. Further, the term "competitiveness" itself is in point of fact more a rallying cry than a term with concrete economic meaning.

PRODUCT LIFE CYCLE

Sophisticated manufactured products represent an important category in U.S. exports. While trading of such products in the world market may substantially assist the initial domestic producers to grow, it also induces foreign producers to imitate these new and profitable products. A theory of trade, known as the product life cycle model,[2] a more popularly known elaboration of the technological trajectory described in chapter 4, can be used to explain the behavior pattern of U.S. manufactured goods exports. The model basically suggests that the introduction of new products is a mode of technological innovation that affects the pattern of international trade, especially the pattern of trade between developed and less mature countries. New products are first likely to be developed and produced in a technically advanced economy because demand for such products first appears where incomes are high and tastes are sophisticated. In addition, the high level of labor skills in the advanced country gives it a comparative advantage in development and initial production of such products. In this stage of the product cycle, the pioneering producers have a monopoly in export markets.

However, as both exports and foreign demand increase and the production process becomes increasingly standardized, overseas production becomes more attractive. U.S. firms then establish branches abroad, resulting in reduced U.S. exports of their products. As the state of maturity is approached, the good and its standardized production process are easily copied and more economically produced elsewhere in the developed world and in lower wage, developing countries. These latter nations, which have a comparative advantage in labor-intensive goods, will eventually achieve sufficient competitive strength to produce the products not only for their own markets, but for export to the advanced countries where the items originated. The United States then tends to become a net importer. Examples can be found in textiles, consumer electronics, and other high-value-to-weight items. Thus, the export effects of product innovation will be heavily influenced by international technological diffusion and lower labor costs abroad. Indeed, the period in which innovators "may expect to enjoy their lead over the encroaching competition is often quite short, meaning that flexibility and the capacity to adjust are crucial."[3] Unfortunately, the gigantic modern U.S. corporation too frequently fails to display this very flexibility and adaptability.

THE DOLLAR AND INTERNATIONAL FINANCIAL FACTORS

An international financial network is necessary to support and facilitate international trade. From the late 1940s until 1972 the system operated on a gold exchange (or gold/dollar) standard, which established and maintained relatively fixed exchange rates. The dollar was the critical key currency. Chronic U.S. balance-of-payments deficits, however, resulted in net dollar outflows and a surfeit of U.S. exchange on world markets.

By the 1970s the fixed exchange rate system had become unsustainable and a system of flexible (fluctuating) rates ultimately took form. In theory, rates are completely free (clean float) to reflect movements of supply and demand; they can fluctuate as often and widely as stock, bond, or commodity prices. In practice, however, these rates are often "managed" (dirty float) by interventions of central banks that seek either to support or drive down the conversion rates of particular currencies.

Fluctuating rates have added great complexity to the system and have engendered many sophisticated financial techniques and manipulations. Presumably, floating rates were to more accurately reflect changes in the relative purchasing power of currencies and give national monetary authorities greater leeway to address domestic problems. However, movements of capital that are not primarily designed to finance trade have increasingly come to dominate foreign exchange markets. This, coupled with conflicting national policy directions, has tended to cause great volatility in exchange markets. These capital flows reflect differential inflation rates, investment opportunities, and interest rates. Higher interest rates and/or superior prospective investments in one country attract foreign capital, raising demand for the recipient currency. Greater safety (from expropriation, usage restrictions, and other limitations) is another attracting influence. Clearly, the U.S. value as a safe haven is an important attracting factor. Interestingly, foreign capital inflows from 1981 to 1984 hovered over a fairly constant range. During 1983 and 1984 much of our net foreign capital inflow was really the result of less U.S. capital seeking foreign opportunities. U.S. private capital outflows declined by over 50 percent during 1983, and during the first three quarters of 1984 were actually negative (more capital was repatriated from overseas than was sent). Contrary to the conventional view, then, these data suggest that the dollar's strength was as likely to have come from a reduced U.S. demand for foreign currencies as it was from expanding foreign dollar demands.

Changes in the total value of a country's exports and imports also affect its exchange rate, as do changes in relative real incomes and financial condition. Whereas the large excess of imports over exports should have depressed the dollar, over the period spanning 1980 through February 1985, the dollar's value rose over 80 percent relative to the currencies of ten industrial countries in the Federal Reserve Board's trade-weighted index.[4] This is best explained by the vigorous U.S. expansion plus tax cuts, both of which attracted foreign funds, as did the safe haven, low inflation rate, and relatively high U.S. interest rates. Accordingly, with U.S. investors staying home, which lowers the supply of dollars, while foreigners raised demand by attempting to invest here, the rise of the dollar becomes much more understandable.

Some further clarifying points concerning dollar strength and weakness merit note. During the 1970s the dollar depreciated substantially against the yen and deutsche mark (DM). Comparisons to 1980, then, date from the dollar's low point rather than some average value in the 1970s. Second, during the period of dollar strength, the dollar rose substantially against most world currencies, but not all. For example, from 1979 through the first half of 1986, the dollar was relatively stable compared to the currencies of Singapore and Taiwan. While the dollar rose over 80 percent against an index of currencies, its rise against the yen was actually quite modest—less than 15 percent.

The link between exchange rates and trade flows is critical and must be understood. Markets give indications of comparative advantage via price and cost signals. With fixed (equilibrium) exchange rates, prices more clearly depict information concerning factor endowments and opportunity costs. Under a fluctuating system, however, prices and costs may vary due to exchange rate movements rather than basic alterations in comparative advantage. Indeed, such currency swings tend to obfuscate and confuse, and are clearly a contributing factor to shifting international competitiveness, with the subsequent dislocation of workers and facilities throughout the world. When real factors, such as changing relative productivities, alter comparative advantage, then such painful adjustments are necessary and socially useful. On the other hand, because a sustained currency appreciation will eventually affect resource allocations, if it is later reversed by depreciation, then such costs are unnecessary and dysfunctional. This is one of the major potential problems with such an exchange rate regime.

In an economy without foreign trade, unit labor costs could be determined by changes in wages relative to changes in productivity. A 10 percent increase in hourly pay accompanied by a 10 percent increase in productivity leaves unit labor costs unchanged. If compensation outstrips productivity, those costs rise; if it is less, unit labor costs fall. In a world of flexible exchange rates, however, the international value of a national currency can play havoc with the above relationships.

This can be illustrated by a simple numerical example. Assume the following: (1) $1 = 2 DM, (2) the same item is produced in two countries, with labor costs in both Germany and the United States comprising 50 percent of total product cost, (3) the goods have equivalent production costs—$10 in the U.S. and 20 DM in Germany, (4) the dollar suddenly appreciates 50 percent relative to the DM, making it $1 = 3 DM. It follows from the first three assumptions that labor costs per unit in each country were equal initially at $5 and 10 DM, respectively. While the exchange rate change (assumption 4) does nothing directly to the U.S. unit labor cost, the dollar value of the German costs falls. At the new exchange rate, labor's 10 DM are valued at only $3.33, while they are still $5 in the United States. Thus, while expenses in national currencies are unchanged, when valued in terms of the stronger dollar, German labor costs are now lower. Previously, the 20 DM item sold for $10 to the United States, meeting the U.S. price in our market. After dollar depreciation, however, 20 DM cost only $6.67, so the import will undercut and replace U.S. products right here.[5]

Note that just as rising productivity can reduce labor costs, an appreciating currency can overwhelm the positive productivity impacts. Indeed, this is exactly what occurred. "U.S. productivity growth since 1981 has equaled the trade-weighted average of 11 overseas competitors,"[6] reflecting its substantial manufacturing gains in 1983 and 1984. Since wage boosts were relatively modest, unit labor costs fell by 3.8 percent in 1983 and 0.4 percent in 1984. However, the substantial appreciation of the dollar over the 1980–84 period translated the 1 percent average annual decrease in relative unit labor costs into "7 percent per year increase after adjustment for the relative change in the foreign exchange value of the dollar."[7] More recently, while Japanese unit labor costs measured in yen fell 2 percent between 1987 and 1988, they rose 10–12 percent when measured in U.S. dollars"[8] due to yen appreciation. Currency appreciation, however, does have benefits. Imports decline in price, lowering the cost of living and producing. Cheaper imported raw materials and intermediate products that are embodied in exports tend to facilitate those sales. Clearly, then, exchange rates—by impacting on unit labor costs, raw material expenses, and energy costs—will affect the international competitiveness of a nation's products. Yet causality in trade and financial relationships is far from clear. The issue reeks with complexity, despite the cocksure statements of many contemporary observers. In the nineteenth century one international financial scholar is alleged to have remarked, "Not one in one hundred really understands the currency question, yet you meet him everyday." This statement rings true over 100 years later.

DIRECT INVESTMENT AND NET ASSET POSITION

Investment trends clearly manifest the globalization process. The Department of Commerce defines direct foreign investments to include all foreign business organizations in which a U.S. person, organization, or affiliated group owns an interest of 10 percent or more.[9] Foreign direct investment here is similarly defined. Such investment is not simply an international transfer of capital, but involves ownership and control of foreign assets as well. As opposed to portfolio investment—the transfer of funds only seeking rates of return rather than control—direct investment requires managerial decision making. It also involves flows of technology and entrepreneurial skill to the host country where they are combined with local inputs for production for local and/or export markets. According to the product life cycle model, U.S. manufacturers initially gain a monopolistic export advantage from product innovations developed in our market; later they invest abroad to exploit lower costs of manufacture and to prevent loss of the export markets to local producers. U.S. direct foreign investors are most typically large firms from oligopolistic industries.

Since 1950 U.S. direct investment abroad has mainly flowed to the advanced industrial nations—Western Europe and Canada accounting for 88 percent of this total by 1987. Investment in Japan was only 6 percent. In the developing countries, about three-fourths of direct U.S. investment was traditionally centered in Latin America, although by 1987 the proportion had fallen to 61 percent.[10] But the newly industrializing lands in Asia, such as Korea and Hong Kong, have gained substantially since 1980. Nonetheless, because of high political risks and limited market opportunities, U.S. companies are more prone to invest in economically advanced nations.

The manufacturing industry has been the most attractive arena for U.S. firms, absorbing 41 percent of U.S. investment abroad in 1987. Manufacturing investors go overseas primarily to facilitate foreign market penetration and to obtain low-cost sourcing of manufactured products for use in the United States or elsewhere. U.S. direct investment efforts in petroleum and other extractive industries in developing countries evidenced a significant upturn by 1984, accounting for more than one-third of total U.S. direct investment in these countries. Our corporations in this field tend to seek raw materials that are not available at home or that are available at a higher cost. Examples can be found in petroleum companies such as Exxon, mineral companies such as Anaconda and Kennecott, and many upstream integrated metals companies such as United States Steel and Alcoa.

There have been many concerns about U.S. direct investment abroad—to wit, they export jobs, technology, and tax revenues; they could also hurt the balance of payments and aggravate antitrust problems. Many of these concerns today seem less compelling than previously, except for the issue of the export of U.S. jobs. However, according to empirical evidence, direct U.S. investment abroad does not export jobs.[11] Such investment has usually been made by multinational corporations, which generally follow the product cycle by moving production to an area with a comparative advantage, such as low-cost labor. Many of the multinationals also go abroad to avoid tariffs, discriminatory foreign government procurement policies, and similar impediments. Accordingly, their foreign production probably replaces few U.S. exports since the latter were bound to diminish anyway. Furthermore, when they engage in natural resource ventures (e.g., bauxite), servicing, or distribution activities in foreign countries, no export displacement takes place at all. Last, but certainly not least, such investments do "bring home the bacon." For 1984, the latest year of available statistics, "foreign subsidiaries paid $11.8 billion in dividends to their U.S. parents on profits . . . for a payout rate of 39 percent. In some years, this payout rate has been as high as 60 percent."[12]

While Americans traditionally championed the cause of foreign direct investment when we were the investors, generally lecturing to the recipients on the manifold benefits to them, now that there is substantial foreign investment here, those arguments seem lost. Indeed, now that the shoe is on the other foot, we are finding that it pinches. Fortunately, these are phantom pains born of imagination, ignorance, and xenophobia. An awakening to the facts should clear both the air and the grumbling.

Foreign direct investment here has made an important contribution to U.S. capital formation. Expenditures on plant and equipment made by foreign investors accounted for 11 percent of total investment in plant and equipment from 1980 to 1982;[13] in 1986 foreigners financed 50 percent of U.S. investment. These investments in the United States began to surge in the late 1970s. A major contributing factor was the depreciation of the U.S. dollar. While such depreciation made it harder for foreigners to export to the U.S., it did reduce the foreign cost of investing in this country. Additionally, growing overseas economic strength, social and political tensions abroad, the depressed state of the U.S. stock market, and disquieting U.S. protectionist sentiments further contributed to the rapid increases of foreign investment in that decade. Many of these forces were still at work in the 1980s, with some changes. With Latin America and other developing nations in serious economic and social turmoil, and with Europe in a prolonged recession, the only viable investment outlets were the United States and Japan. Yet investing in Japan was difficult and foreign to Europeans, so the expanding U.S. economy became even more attractive. Further, encouraging changes in U.S. tax laws raised rates of return here and thereby attracted foreign investors. Although the dollar was strong, its baffling and seemingly relentless rise meant that foreign assets would be denominated in an appreciating currency.

In 1987 foreign direct investment in the United States amounted to $262 billion. Great Britain, with $75 billion, was the largest foreign source, almost doubling its total of three years earlier. The Dutch, not the Japanese, were the second largest, with a $47 billion stake. Japan was third with only 13 percent of the foreign total.[14] In 1988 Britain invested an additional $21.5 billion and Japan $14.2 billion. Accordingly, as 1988 ended, Japan held the second position, its direct investments about half the value of Britain's. In 1981 the OPEC countries held 3 percent of foreign direct investment here. Despite a major jump in 1988, their share has fallen to only 1.9 percent. Finally, in terms of global holdings, the United States is still the largest direct foreign investor in the world, with the United Kingdom second and Japan a close third.

Our much maligned manufacturing sector has been the most attractive industry to foreign investors. Between 1980 and 1984, one in every four dollars of foreign capital flowing to the United States was channeled to manufacturing. In 1987, $91 billion (35 percent of the total) was in this sector. In 1988 foreigners invested $31 billion in U.S. facilities, a 50 percent increase over 1987. Clearly, this is a major vote of confidence. Yet the media continue to describe such infusions with expressions like "Foreign investors continued to feast on U.S. businesses in 1988 . . . "[15] Other industries, such as petroleum, wholesaling, real estate, and finance, have also absorbed a considerable amount of foreign investment.

Just under 4 percent of the U.S. labor force was employed by foreign subsidiaries in 1983; for manufacturing the figure was 7 percent.[16] In 1988 newly established foreign firms employed 33,871 people, while acquired businesses, many strapped for funds, employed almost 650,000.[17] Over the 1977–85 years, while overall employment in U.S. manufacturing declined nationally, "employment for affiliates increased in virtually all manufacturing industries. . . ."[18] Further, foreign investment is highest in those sectors that produce "traded" goods as opposed to those catering strictly to the domestic market. Accordingly, they assist U.S. export efforts as well as domestic employment.

Despite staggering numbers, the foreign presence in the U.S. economy is really quite small, although growing. Direct foreign investment as a share of total tangible wealth more than quadrupled from 1972 to today. While this sounds impressive, the original share was 1 percent. Accordingly, current ownership is still under 5 percent. In manufacturing, where foreign investments are concentrated, the 1985 share was 10 percent.[19] Recall the Department of Commerce's definition: if foreigners own as much as 10 percent, it is deemed foreign-owned (10 percent may be sufficient for control), although the perhaps silent, overwhelming majority is American. Surely Roosevelt's admonition, "We have nothing to fear but fear itself," is applicable in this matter, one that has been blown grossly out of proportion.

Some people fear that foreign investors might use U.S. resources in opposition to our national interests. Such fears are largely groundless because foreign firms in the United States are subject to the same tax, securities, antitrust, and labor legislation as any U.S. firm. Our nation, like most others, limits or controls foreign direct investment in areas related to the national interest, such as broadcasting, nuclear and hydroelectric power, and military production. Furthermore, in an emergency, the federal government has the power to impose export controls or to seize foreign assets.

DEBTOR NATION?

In 1985 the United States, for the first time since systematic official record compilation began in 1919, became a net international debtor. Its international creditor status peaked in 1981 at $141 billion; by 1986 it was the world's largest debtor, a condition shocking to the great majority of Americans, most of whom do not know exactly what this means, although they do believe wholeheartedly that it must be bad. At the end of 1988 foreign-owned U.S. assets exceeded the official value of U.S.-owned foreign assets by $532.5 billion. About 89 percent of U.S.-owned international assets are in private hands, with the government holding the remainder. In 1987, 26 percent of our assets were direct investment. Foreign governments, on the other hand, held 18.4 percent of foreign-owned assets, while direct investments were 17 percent of the foreign asset total. Foreign corporate stockholdings were 11 percent, while 5 percent was holdings of the federal debt. Over 60 percent of 1987 foreign investment was new equity capital.[20] Interestingly, it was not until 1988 that foreign direct investment ($328.9 billion) here exceeded our overseas direct investments ($326.9 billion).

While the trend in net asset position is indisputable, the official numbers are quite misleading. Government holdings of gold, a U.S. international asset, are valued at only $42.20 per troy ounce. Revaluing this asset closer to its market worth, $400, "reduces the apparent net debt position of the United States by one-fourth."[21] Further, because U.S. direct investments are valued at book (historical) cost, their rising value over time is not recognized. Accordingly, the official bookkeeping entries are just not very realistic.[22] Further, "in 1987 the service on the gross U.S. debt abroad amounted to less than 2 percent of GNP and was less than U.S. earnings on assets abroad."[23] In 1988 we also earned more. Ordinarily it is net creditors who receive net earnings, so the official annual flow figures are at variance with official balance sheet figures. "One recent estimate correcting for some of these measurement deficiencies suggested that the United States continued to be a net creditor in 1987 by about $50 billion."[24]

One can legitimately ask how this seeming reversal from net creditor to net debtor came about, and why so quickly. It has basically been the substantial net inflows of foreign funds in recent years that have led to the reported changed international investment position of the United States. But these inflows must be properly understood. The net inflows have resulted from a greatly reduced U.S. willingness to extend credit to foreigners, while foreigners have shown a continuing interest in investing and extending credit to the United States. Such net capital inflows, by definition, correspond to current account deficits. Net financial inflows cannot take place without trade deficits. The lines of causality, however, are less clear. Is it net inflows that forced a trade deficit? Or has it been the current account deficit that has required foreign financing? The latter view is the conventional wisdom, that inflows were necessary to finance the trade deficit, implying that trade called the tune and capital inflows danced. The second and highly touted implication is that U.S. industry—workers and management—are simply not competitive. However, global capital flows now swamp the amounts necessary to finance trade. Perhaps it is capital movements calling the tune while trade is doing the dancing. If so, we are competitive. U.S. industry is okay. The only necessary adjustment is a lower exchange value to the dollar (or limitations on capital inflows).

It should be noted that large and growing capital inflows predate our debtor status. Some interesting data shed further light on this issue. Americans are regularly investing in foreign assets and also divesting themselves of those assets, with the net position traditionally positive—that is, we invest more overseas each year than we divest (net capital outflow). Foreigners invest and divest as well. Such endeavors are another manifestation of globalization. U.S. net outflows in 1980 were almost $83 billion, rising to almost $110 billion in 1981 and to $127.8 billion in 1982. These capital outflows exceeded growing foreign net inflows, meaning that the United States was a net provider of credit. In 1983, however, even though foreign inflows fell by $11 billion, the United States became a net capital importer. How? Net outflows of U.S. funds dropped to only $43.3 billion, and fell again in 1984. American investors were bringing their money home, either because they were liquidating bad investments or finding better ones here. But this is not surprising—a vigorous economy and appealing tax law changes inspired foreigners to invest here, why not Americans too?

In 1987 net U.S. outflows were a negative $11.4 billion, meaning that more funds were repatriated than invested. Had U.S. outflows of the first three years of the 1980s continued their pace (instead of reversing), the United States would still be a net creditor (on the books) and by an even larger amount than ever, even allowing for the continuing foreign inflows. But why keep foreign assets when American ones look better? Yet if it is capital flows that call the tune, then a trade deficit must result.

This, of course, is just one piece of a very complex picture, but it is a perspective rarely aired, probably "crowded out" by federal budget deficit discussions. Whatever the causal relationships, it is clear that the net U.S. asset position has been deteriorating, even if we do not know the exact numbers. Further, in future years net investment income on the U.S. balance of payments may be zero or negative.

However, being a debtor is not necessarily bad. Most Americans are debtors, but still pay their bills on time and are glad to have the credit. Being a debtor nation means foreigners want to extend us more credit than we are willing to grant to them (which of course means that we must buy more from them than they buy from us). "While the United States was growing from a nation of three million people spread along the Atlantic Coast into one of the world's great powers, we were consistently a net debtor nation."[25] The key question is, how has this credit been utilized? The answer is not perfectly clear. If it all went to investment and was wisely invested, it would pay for itself many times. To the degree that it instead goes for consumption or ineffective investments, it will not pay for itself, so future interest payments will be a net burden. Then again, since our debts (and not all foreign holdings are debt—some are equity) are denominated in dollars, even a continuance of our moderate 4 percent inflation will cut their value by half in only 18 years. Herbert Stein, former chairman of the President's Council of Economic Advisors, estimates that as "a result of the capital inflow—and accompanying trade deficit—over the past eight years, the stock of productive capital in the U.S. is now about $700 billion higher than it would otherwise have been."[26] For a nation that does not have enough of its own savings, we are in fact quite fortunate that foreigners have made theirs so available to us.

Finally, the expression "debtor nation" is completely misleading. In accounting terms, if foreigners have more assets here than we have there, we are deemed a debtor nation, even if we have no debts at all. In point of fact, foreigners hold both debt and nondebt assets (essentially equity positions) in our country. By the end of 1988, although our alleged net debtor position was $532.5 billion, foreign nondebt holdings were about $535 billion, some 30 percent of their total investments. Equity, of course, is a residual ownership position that is not paid off and requires no mandatory interest or dividend payments, although the latter frequently do occur.

MERCHANDISE TRADE AND THE TRADE DEFICIT

As indicated earlier, the pattern of U.S. trade is essentially guided by comparative advantage. In recent decades, the United States has been a net importer of consumer goods, fuels, lubricants, and other industrial supplies and materials. Since 1968 we have also experienced a trade deficit for automotive products. U.S. industries have either lost or possess a diminished comparative advantage in such items. Some areas where U.S. industries do enjoy a comparative advantage are agricultural goods, chemicals, capital goods, and military items. Prior to 1971 this country realized an overall trade surplus. With only one exception, we have had trade deficits ever since, although in the 1970s they were relatively small, averaging about 0.5 percent of GNP. In 1987 the deficit was 3.0 percent.

One caveat concerning trade and balance-of-payments statistics is in order. Since the late 1960s the quality of these numbers has been increasingly questioned, particularly as the statistical discrepancy account (formerly called errors and omissions) began to become relatively large and exhibit erratic behavior. There are no adequate explanations. While the trends that the trade and payments statistics indicate are probably correct, the precise magnitudes are very questionable. The trade deficit could actually be substantially lower than the reported numbers or substantially higher.[27] However, with such deficits now exceeding $100 billion annually, there is no question that the account balance is significantly negative. What, then, is the source of these very large deficits?

Financial flows have already been mentioned as a possible explanation. A related explanation cites macroeconomic policy imbalances within the United States, specifically large federal deficits. It is suggested that such budget deficits, coupled with a relatively antiinflationary monetary policy, differentially raise U.S. interest rates. In turn, foreign money pours in, demanding dollars and thereby raising the dollar's value. The strong dollar then expands U.S. imports and reduces exports. Although a careful examination of this hypothesis is less than fully convincing, the important thing for this discussion is that here again neither labor nor industry appear deficient. Rather, the policy prescription is to fix the budget deficit and, with macroeconomic policy balance restored, the trade balance will not be far behind.

Trade analysis is yet another source of deficit explanation, although trade and finance are really inextricably linked. U.S. trade patterns in the 1970s witnessed surpluses with Latin America and Europe, but deficits with Japan. When Europe experienced prolonged recession in the first half of the 1980s and Latin America and Third World countries fell under the weight of the debt crisis, our trade surplus markets withered. So trade with these areas moved into deficit as they tightened their belts. Importantly, it was our having deficits that served as the locomotive for their economic growth, leading Europe out of recession and allowing the Third World to earn foreign exchange for debt servicing. If we were unwilling to allow Latin America to have trade surpluses (by implementing quotas or similar protective measures), in all likelihood the debt crisis would have exploded, and defaults and their reverberations would be felt throughout the world. In all probability, dictatorships would mushroom as a means of maintaining order. Our deficits with the Third World, then, have been instrumental in keeping it politically as well as economically viable.

The United States was once the dominant world exporter of manufactured goods. The sources of its comparative advantage mainly consisted of the large amounts of human capital embodied in their labor force—that is, high labor skills stemming from education and training, technological superiority based on R&D expenditures, and economies of scale resulting from the large domestic market. But the structure of comparative advantage is neither stable nor enduring. The factors causing such shifting include the increasing international mobility of capital, the faster dissemination of technology, and the narrowing differential between the economic capability of the United States and its trading partners. In addition, the strong dollar of the first portion of the 1980s placed a net burden on all U.S. exports. Similarly, the rising dollar significantly contributed to the dollar cost of imports remaining flat for four years, thus greatly stimulating import demand.

As important as the strong dollar was, it would be prudent to heed the statement of Willard C. Butcher, chairman and CEO (chief executive officer) of Chase Manhattan Bank, N.A.: "Significant trade imbalances do not result from only one culprit . . . the tendency to try to find one scapegoat and blame all our ills on it is counterproductive."[28] The largest bilateral trade deficit is with Japan, yet the dollar did not appreciate tremendously relative to the yen, and indeed in 1986 was below the 1977 yen rate. Further, "the fall in the dollar's value from 1985 to 1987 was not accompanied by a decline in the trade deficit, the deficit in manufacturing, or the deficit for the five deficit-related industries."[29] Accordingly, other factors clearly play a role and must be considered. The listing below includes some other possible influences aside from the strong dollar:

1. Management focus
2. Relative economic strength
3. Productivity and wage trends
4. Cost of capital
5. Quality differences
6. Dependence on foreign oil
7. Reliability as a supplier
8. Policy imposed limitations
9. Falling world agricultural prices

Clearly, management focus is important. The large U.S. market tends to receive the vast bulk of U.S. corporate attention, particularly when the complexities of export markets are encountered. Globalization has not sunk in fully as yet. Trade and exports are often an afterthought, and accumulating evidence suggests that U.S. pricing in the face of exchange rate changes has been inappropriate,[30] whereas foreign tactics have been far more judicious. The dearth of Americans trained in foreign languages is another impediment. And other demands on management may crowd out export efforts and efficiency. Peter Drucker, for example, has suggested that many top business leaders believe takeover fear is the "main cause of the decline in America's competitive strength in the world economy and a far more potent cause than the high dollar."[31]

The Council of Economic Advisors to the president has estimated that the reduction of Third World imports in response to debt service problems probably accounts for 25 percent of the U.S. deficit, while the more rapid expansion of income in the United States than most of the world accounts for still another 25 percent.[32] Exuberant U.S. demand, stemming from strong and sustained economic growth after 1982, is very important, perhaps more than the 25 percent estimate suggests. Rapid economic growth generates substantial demands and frequently the domestic economy is unable to satisfy them all. In the attempt to do so, goods that might have been exported are diverted to American buyers. Conversely, rising U.S. demand is catered to by both domestic and foreign producers. Often, particularly in growth periods, U.S. suppliers are already producing the maximum and imported items, particularly capital goods and components, are necessary not only to satisfy domestic demand (instead of replacing domestic producers), but to enable rapid growth to continue. John Tatom finds that this exactly describes the U.S. economy over the 1980–85 period. "Declining net exports reflected increased domestic purchases that outstripped the relatively rapid growth of domestic production."[33]

The differential productivity trends described in chapter 5 are also very important. With wage levels higher than the rest of the world, lagging productivity made many U.S. products noncompetitive. To blame noncompetitiveness on the price increasing effect of a strong dollar, but ignore the same pressures emanating from high wage levels or lagging productivity, is a half-done, half-baked explanation. This same line of reasoning can be applied to capital costs, which also appear to have been differentially high in the United States.

Quality, technical capabilities, and service differences may also be very important, particularly with differentiated products. In very price sensitive items, usually homogeneous products like agricultural outputs, any cause of higher prices can be critical. On the other hand, where products are differentiated, price sensitivities (elasticities) are lower and costs or the exchange rate are less important. For example, in a Conference Board survey of 500 U.S. companies, almost one-third reported that "in some areas of their companies' principal lines . . . certain private foreign companies and industrial sectors have technology superior to their own."[34] For the larger companies, the percentage was even higher. Many foreigners believe that American after-sale service is very poor, thus putting our exports at a competitive disadvantage. In the area of consumer goods, if buyers (American and foreign) perceive that U.S. products are shoddy or that foreign-made items are of higher quality, imports will certainly increase and exports will be damaged.

In many parts of the world the United States has been deemed an unreliable supplier. For example, in June 1973 the Nixon administration, in an attempt to minimize the price increasing impact of domestic crop shortages, abruptly embargoed U.S. soybean exports to Japan. The shocked Japanese were caught completely by surprise and, being highly dependent upon U.S. supplies, decided to diversify import sources. Contacts with Brazil, relatively new to the soybean business, were established, and a thriving trade emerged. That year also saw a brief embargo on iron and steel exports. Dockworkers' strikes and other work stoppages have also caused lateness or nondelivery. One executive of a U.S. multinational company has noted that "more and more, people are asking us, 'How do I know that a year from now I'll be able to get parts?' "[35] Moreover, foreign policy decisions have increasingly invoked economic sanctions, further reenforcing fears concerning U.S. unreliability.

In a related vein, U.S. exports have been limited by policy-imposed constraints not directly related to foreign policy. "For example, the Trans Alaskan Pipeline Authorization Act prohibits the export of oil from the North Slope Fields."[36] The logical customer would be Japan. Similarly, the export of timber from federal lands is prohibited. Again, Japan is the most obvious customer. "Removing these two restrictions could reduce the U.S. trade deficit by as much as $20 billion."[37] It should also be recognized that during the first six years of the 1980s the United States averaged more than $60 billion of petroleum imports annually. Falling oil prices have eased this burden substantially, but oil imports were 90 percent of the trade deficit in 1983 and close to 50 percent in 1984 and 1985.[38] Greater domestic progress toward nuclear power would have reduced such outlays, as would the opening of vast "wilderness" areas to oil and gas exploration. Total decontrol of natural gas would also assist.

A number of legislative enactments, such as the Foreign Corrupt Practice Act and the Export Administration Act, may meaningfully complicate export sales and discourage such efforts. Also, the collapse of world agricultural prices cannot be ignored. The United States has a strong comparative advantage in agriculture and exported a record $44 billion in 1981. By 1987 such exports netted just under $30 billion. In 1980 these revenues accounted for 20 percent of total U.S. exports; by 1987 they were only 12 percent. This is not an issue of failing competitiveness. This decline does not reflect bad management, low productivity, or ignorance of foreign markets. Yet it had a significant impact. Of course, sooner or later food prices will rise. It would be convenient for the U.S. trade picture if this occurred prior to or simultaneous with the eventual rise in oil prices.

It is believed by many that imports—driven by cheap foreign labor, borrowed technologies, and unfair trade practices—have been the cause of ferment and disruption in U.S. manufacturing. Yet two recent, carefully done studies effectively dispute this. J. Hayden Boyd concludes that "the trade deficit did not 'cause' a change in manufacturing output."[39] He isolates six problem industries, finding that "the timing of their decline does not correspond to the emergence of large trade deficits beginning in 1982 and 1983."[40] Real output in both motor vehicles and leather/footwear began declining in 1978. Apparel began in 1979. Boyd maintains that the trade deficit was caused by macroeconomic forces. Tatom uses a similar methodology—a disaggregation analysis of industrial production.[41] He finds that the largest changes in industry trade deficits were in transportation equipment, nonelectric machinery and electrical machinery, then apparel and primary metals. These accounted for two-thirds of the swing in the manufactured goods balance, which had a 1980 surplus of $20.7 billion, but fell to a deficit in 1985 of $132.5 billion. Yet these industries as a group experienced almost 5 percent annual growth rates from 1980 to 1985, whereas manufacturing as a whole enjoyed only 3.4 percent (while the real GNP grew by only 2.6 percent). The computer industry (non-electrical machinery) led the way, sufficiently strong to bring up the overall rate despite some sluggish performances elsewhere. Interestingly, from 1985 to 1987, even with a fall in the dollar, the deficit increased further, a condition Tatom attributes to slower domestic production growth.

The across-the-board decline in the U.S. trade balance, embracing almost all industries and all trade partners, provides meaningful prima facie evidence that the problem does not derive from a sloppiness of industry or lethargy of labor, unless one believes that this too occurred uniformly throughout U.S. industry. Accordingly, the capital inflow theory or budget deficit hypothesis look much better than the noncompetitiveness hypothesis. As has already been suggested, trade data reflect a multitude of conditions combined in a very complex, intricate network. Lines of causality are unclear and every reverberation has multiple feedback effects. Using the trade deficit to justify a lack of a competitiveness allegation, with the implication that U.S. workers are not trying hard enough or are sloppy, that managements are inept or misguided, is simply not credible when all facts are examined. This does not mean that U.S. industry is without flaws or that substantial improvements cannot be obtained. Certainly in chapter 5 and elsewhere throughout this book numerous failings have been noted. But trade deficits by themselves in no way demonstrate that a nation's industry or labor are doing poorly.

Indeed, it is difficult to decide exactly what the trade data are telling us, even if we knew the data were accurate. Our standard indicators, for example, take no account of the rise in U.S.-controlled production abroad. Much of the loss of U.S. manufactured goods exports has not gone to foreign competitors, but to overseas subsidiaries of U.S. companies. The game is clearly getting more confusing, thanks to globalization. It now appears that the players wear several uniforms and it is hard today to really tell what the teams are. Is IBM-Japan really a U.S. firm producing overseas or is it a Japanese company? Indeed, "as economic institutions become more global in scope . . . the concept of a competitive national economy becomes uncertain and obscure."[42] "Because of the ambiguity of the term 'competitiveness,' the picture with regard to U.S. competitiveness is not clear,"[43] and when one works to sort out the relevant data, the "evidence suggests that much of the current discussion of declining U.S. competitiveness does not fit the facts."[44] Concerning this issue one is hard pressed not to agree with Mark Twain's comments about the music of Wagner—"it's not as bad as it sounds."

Finally, some mention of current U.S. trade policy is warranted. Since policy in a democracy ultimately reflects the hopes, fears, and feelings of the population, it is to be expected that U.S. foreign economic policy would react to public perceptions, correct or incorrect. In 1988 the Omnibus Trade and Competitiveness Act was passed. While many congressional proposals sprang from local economic self-interest or unfounded fears, the interplay of the administration and Congress produced a bill very similar to the trade act of 14 years earlier. Both provided authorization for trade agreements in the hopes that the president might be able to expand trade by arriving at mutually satisfying, liberalizing arrangements with foreign nations. The 1974 act included a section 201 escape clause providing temporary relief to industries harmed by trade. In 1988 minor modifications were made to section 201. A new trade remedy, section 301, was introduced in 1974 in an attempt to enforce trade agreements and respond to unfair foreign practices. In 1988, reflecting the fears and concerns this chapter has discussed, section 301 was strengthened. Some now label it "super-301." Lastly, some minor amendments to other trade remedies were included in the 1988 law.[45]

The new 301 provisions are the most controversial part of the recent legislation.[46] The basic thrust is to make it more difficult for the president and his representatives to ignore overseas trade practices that some would deem objectionable. The new law mandates that the U.S. Trade Representative designate whether a foreign country is "unfair" and, if so, to act in response. In the spring of 1989 Japan, Brazil, and India were designated as unfair traders; negotiations are now under way to deal with the problem. It is too early to assess the utility of super-301; the debate has strong adherents on both sides.

A positive development for U.S. exports was a July 1989 Commerce Department decision removing licensing requirements on a broad range of high technology exports to 18 countries that have agreed to cooperate with U.S. export controls. Some $20–$30 billion of potential exports are covered and this should enhance our export efforts and performance.

LABOR MARKET IMPACTS

The most widely publicized impact of foreign trade, more specifically of imports, is "jobs lost due to foreign competition." While there is some truth in this observation, as a generalization it misses the point and is unsubstantiated, if not totally contravened, by the facts. An examination of aggregative data reveals no relationship whatsoever between U.S. import volumes and levels of employment or rates of unemployment.

During the period from 1946 through 1984, imports rose in every year, with only eight exceptions. Yet the unemployment rate, rather than continuously rising, instead fluctuated. Contrary to the popular belief, in those eight years of declining imports the unemployment rate rose in seven and was down in only one. This result is easily explained. Each of these years was a period of recession. The low level of aggregate economic activities was the true cause of both reduced imports and higher unemployment rates. Examining this claim on a slightly different basis—employment levels—also fails to produce supportive data. Coinciding with almost continuous increases in imports have been virtually continuous increases in employment. Again, contrary to the "imports cost jobs" assertion, in six of those eight years of declining imports, employment levels declined as well.

Some might perceive the above analysis to be too simplistic. Perhaps the correlation appears when imports surge rather than change incrementally. This refinement, however, also fails to produce any supporting evidence. In 1984 imports increased by the largest jump in history, yet the unemployment rate that year experienced the biggest decline in the entire postwar period. Indeed, in the eight years of largest import increases, the unemployment rate fell in five, was unchanged in one, and increased in only two (1980 and 1982, both recession years). This popular hypothesis also fails if cross-national data are examined. Nations with higher percentages of imports do not display any tendency toward consistently higher unemployment rates.

Popularizers of this claim fail to recognize that imports also generate employment. It was estimated, for example, that in 1983 the imported car industry created close to 200,000 jobs, several times the number of employees at Chrysler Corporation.[47] Further, if Americans save money by purchasing imports, the funds are redirected into other spending outlets, thereby creating other jobs. Finally, raw materials imports, like the $40+ billion currently spent annually for petroleum, are critical to keep the U.S. economic machinery and employment moving forward.

Clearly some jobs are lost when U.S. products fail to compete adequately against imports, but even here the causal relationships are unclear. Is it imports that caused the closing of plants or excessively high wages, low productivity, managerial inefficiency? Mordechai Kreinin, for example, finds that to be competitive with German and Japanese counterparts, average labor compensation in the U.S. iron and steel industry must fall 31–40 percent, while in automobiles the corresponding figure is 18–24 percent.[48] In the absence of imports, of course, such domestic encumbrances would undoubtedly sustain jobs longer, but the cost increases passed on to consumer would then reduce spending (and jobs) in other sectors of the domestic economy. Further, while industry executives often blame their woes on foreign competition, other changes are often far more significant. In the steel industry, for example, the greatest challenge has come from plastics, not imports. In short, a careful examination of the data produces only one conclusion: neither import levels nor changes in those levels are significant determinants of aggregate U.S. employment. Some recent, highly sophisticated economic modeling reaches this same basic conclusion, finding that import barriers have not increased American jobs, but rather have changed the composition of employment by shifting jobs around, usually in the wrong direction—from areas of comparative advantage to areas of relative disadvantage.[49]

If aggregate data reveal no relationships, what about sectoral evidence? It is clearly the case that some industries have been hit harder than others. High-cost producers are obviously more apt to fold in the face of added competition (domestic or foreign) than more efficient performers. Yet even here import penetration is not necessarily sufficient to cause employment reductions. Other factors may be far more important. Indeed, this exactly describes the first half of the 1980s. Employment changes even at the industry level do not correlate with changes in the degree of net import competition, despite several well-publicized cases of apparel, footware, and steel to the contrary. As an example, "the electronics components industry enjoyed the greatest percentage growth in employment of all 73 industries . . . even though the industry's exports less competing imports . . . declined by nearly nine percentage points."[50] Conversely, the railroad equipment industry suffered the most severe employment decline, some 49 percent, despite increasing preexisting surplus of exports over competing imports, by the largest margin of any of the industries studied. To sum up, even at the industry level, those "with the sharper rises in net import competition have not experienced slower than average employment growth."[51]

In the last two decades, the effects of product life cycle have induced the manufacture of labor-intensive products to move away from the United States. The broad picture of U.S. trade patterns seems to indicate that the United States will export the services of human capital (i.e., skilled or educated labor) and import the services of unskilled labor. On the export side, for example, aircraft production is extremely human-capital-intensive, while on the import side, consumer textiles are unskilled-labor-intensive in production. Accordingly, those industries that had major job gains due to foreign trade include computer, aerospace, construction, mining, and oil field equipment. Such trade patterns reflect comparative advantage in a world of increasing specialization and interdependence.

Finally, it has been alleged that protection will save high-wage jobs and that without such protection, even if new jobs are found, they will be low-pay occupations, the so-called McDonalds effect. Here again, however, a popular claim lacks empirical justification. David Tarr's analysis, for example, finds that "there is no evidence for the McDonalds effect."[52] Concerning the nearly 19 million nonagricultural jobs created during the current economic expansion, "over 90 percent are full-time, and over 85 percent of these full-time jobs are in occupations in which average annual salaries exceed $20,000."[53] All of this has occurred simultaneously with record trade deficits.

Mention should be made of trade interventions and global protectionist undertakings. Although tariffs have generally come down worldwide, nontariff trade barriers (NTBs) have increased significantly. At one time it was clear that the rest of the world employed NTBs far more than did the United States. Our trade patterns and balances undoubtedly reflected this asymmetry. However, there has been some substantial foreign liberalization, while at the same time the United States has in recent years imposed significant limitations on auto imports, steel, apparel, footwear, and many other items. The growing trade deficits of the 1980s, then, are hardly attributable to "unfair trade practices" against U.S. goods since those practices have diminished while our own have increased.

NATO DEFENSE BASE AND MARKETS

The United States plays a preeminent role in NATO because the security of Western Europe has long been regarded as vital to the security of the United States. Since its inception, NATO has largely relied on U.S. strategic nuclear forces to deter the Warsaw Pact. In addition, the United States maintains ground forces in Europe and has pledged a large share of required military support necessary in a full-scale mobilization. One important issue is defense burden-sharing.

In terms of relative NATO defense efforts, the United States, Portugal, Greece, and Great Britain contributed 5 percent or more of their Gross Domestic Product (GDP) to defense in the 1970–75 period. In 1980, the U.S. share fell slightly (to 5.6 percent), but was still significantly higher than the NATO Europe average of 3.7 percent. By 1982 the U.S. percentage stood at 6.5 percent, while the European partners maintained their previous proportions. Equipment outlays represent a long-term defense contribution, as compared with manpower, which can be mobilized or demobilized fairly quickly. Production of modern sophisticated military equipment, as pointed out in chapter 2, requires a considerable amount of lead time and is intimately involved with the industrial base. In 1980 Great Britain was first in this category, allocating 25 percent of defense outlays to equipment. The United States ranked second, with 20.3 percent. In the same year, the

United States contributed almost 40 percent of the total active NATO force (the share of the labor force allocated to active duty is about the same in the United States as in Europe). Generally, since mid-1970, in terms of burden-sharing within NATO, the percentage of total NATO defense outlays contributed by the United States has remained at about 60 percent.[54]

In the aftermath of World War II, West European countries were given surplus weapons under the Mutual Defense Assistance Act of 1949 and the Mutual Security Acts of the early 1950s. It was estimated that by 1958 over half of the heavy equipment used by NATO members in Europe came from the United States or Canada.[55] While the United States continued to dominate the free world's military arms production, in the 1970s European defense industries grew significantly, in part due to heavy governmental subsidies. They became serious U.S. competitors in the European arms markets as well as in Third World countries. The clamor arose in Europe for a "two way street"—that is, greater balance in defense trade and exchange between the United States and Western Europe. Reflecting and contributing to this growth, transnational consortia, such as Euromissile, Concorde, and the Anglo-German-Italian swingwing fighter, emerged to challenge U.S. military exports. This economic competition has subsequently sharpened national political differences among NATO members.

The goal of strengthening NATO and appropriately pooling and allocating its industrial and technological resources requires greater cooperation and, perhaps, the creation of a cooperative defense industrial system. For example, one study found that in 1978 NATO employed "31 different types of anti-tank weapons where five would suffice, and 11 different types of aircraft for five combat missions," thus resulting in wastes "estimated from $10–$15 billion" annually.[56] NATO's best efforts to date have been directed toward what is known as RSI (rationalization, standardization, and interoperability). Rationalization has led to mergers of some European aircraft industries, project collaboration, codesign, and coproduction.[57] Weapons standardization and interoperability, on the other hand, can improve military effectiveness in the Alliance and save R&D costs and system redundancy. One achievement with respect to RSI was the ROLAND II mobile all-weather air defense system. ROLAND II was developed by the French-German consortium, Euromissile, and licensed for coproduction in the United States by Hughes Aircraft Company and Boeing Aerospace. According to one estimate, ROLAND II saved the government more than $500 million in development costs and reduced development time by 50 percent.[58] Unfortunately, NATO's RSI efforts are adversely affected by economic competition in arms production and export sales among the member countries, thereby decreasing the likelihood of significant further success.[59] Additionally, differing threat perceptions and a reluctance to depend upon foreign suppliers serves to greatly minimize the various national military establishments' enthusiasm for greater RSI undertakings. Politically, it is difficult to rationalize production when unemployment levels are high. Finally, since the United States has a strong comparative advantage in a wide range of military products, the drive toward production efficiencies is likely to run counter to the European desire for a two-way street.

This is not to suggest that globalization has completely bypassed the market for military equipment. It has not. McDonnell Douglas's KC-10 airframe, for example, has upper fuselage panels and a tail fin supplied from Italy, with Mitsubishi (Japan), and Casa (Spain), and Menasco (Canada) also supplying critical portions. And the MD-80, also built in the United States, is sourced in Switzerland, Italy, Sweden, Canada, Australia, and the People's Republic of China. Yet too often such international sourcing is driven not by economic capabilities and comparative advantage, but by political negotiation and diplomatic maneuvering. The outcome is more expensive equipment and lower capabilities for all participating nations.

Accordingly, current military production and trade within the Western Alliance have come under significant criticism. The constituent nations tend to practice various degrees of autarky (self-sufficiency), for both domestic political/economic and military reasons. Further, the current stage of RSI represents piecemeal and ad hoc approaches rather than a coordinated and rational plan. The present mix of coproduction agreements, memoranda of understanding, licensing, and similar efforts evoked a wry comment from Sir George Edwards, former chairman of British Aircraft Corporation, who jested that the "beauty of two countries cooperating on a weapons project and sharing everything 50/50 is that it only costs each two-thirds."[60] This, according to critics, is one important reason for the contrast between high technology commercial products, which have consistently fallen in price, and high technology military items, which consistently rise. The civilian outputs are far more standardized and produced in large volumes for a market that is global in scope. Military markets, on the other hand, are relatively fragmented and separate. Advanced nations find it difficult to depend on external sources, even allies, for military items. So they import very reluctantly and as minimally as they can. The consequence is low volume and relatively high unit costs. Further, competition (which is almost always cost reducing by its nature) becomes minimal since monopolistic national production facilities produce essentially for their own defense establishments.[61] It has been cogently argued that a continuation of present trends and efforts will witness a further escalation in weapons costs to the point where it will be politically impossible for Western states to fiscally fund an adequate defense.[62] Order quantities will be continuously reduced, thus eroding military production capacity. Mobilization and surge potential will, it is argued, be empty phrases, with conventional defense capabilities becoming increasingly anemic compared to those of the Warsaw Pact. While others may hold this fear to be exaggerated, it is unquestionably true that despite longstanding friendship and security ties, protectionism is deeply entrenched within NATO military markets and the resulting economic costs are substantial.

To summarize, globalization is an increasing and pervasive trend. U.S. trade patterns *are* showing appropriate shifts, responding to changing world conditions and capabilities. Further, U.S. trade deficits reflect many factors besides the capabilities and performance of labor and management. Our trade deficits have been the critical factor in the world's avoiding global economic chaos. At the same time, the United States enjoyed low-priced consumer and producer goods and greatly benefited from capital transfusions that have played a critical role in assisting the transition of U.S. industry as it prepares for the twenty-first century.

Finally, the chapter demonstrated the complexity of international economic and financial issues and stressed that just as the concept of national frontiers is losing economic significance, so too are concepts of trade and payments deficits, particularly as indicators of that nebulous and abused expression, international competitiveness.

NOTES

1. See James E. Mielke, "Strategic and Critical Minerals and Materials," in Harold L. Bullis, *A Congressional Handbook on Mineral Import Dependency/Vulnerability.* A report to the House Finance and Urban Affairs Subcommittee on Economics Stabilization, 97th Congress, 1st Sess., September 1981.

2. Raymond Vernon, "International Investment and International Trade in the Product Cycle," *Quarterly Journal of Economics*, May 1966; Louis T. Wells, Jr., "A Product Life Cycle for International Trade?" *Journal of Marketing*, July 1968; and David Dollar, "Technological Innovation, Capital Mobility, and Product Cycle in North-South Trade," *American Economic Review*, March 1986.

3. Sven W. Arndt and Lawrence Bouton, "Trade and Financial Interdependence in the World Economy," *AEI Foreign Policy and Defense Review* 5, no. 4 (1985), p. 24.

4. Stanley W. Black III, "Integrating Forces in the World Economy," *Economic Review*, Federal Reserve Bank of Atlanta, December 1985, p. 9.

5. This calculation assumes that German nonlabor costs also remain constant. If, however, the product contained imported components from countries whose currencies also appreciated relative to the DM, nonlabor costs would rise, thus raising the DM price and providing offsetting pressures that reduce the advantage of lower unit labor costs.

6. Edwin Dean and others, "Productivity and Labor Cost Trends in Manufacturing, 12 Countries," *Monthly Labor Review*, March 1986, p. 6.

7. Ibid., p. 9.

8. Bureau of Labor Statistics, *News: International Comparisons of Manufacturing Productivity and Labor Cost Trends, 1988*, June 30, 1989, p. 5.

9. Department of Commerce, *U.S. Direct Investment Abroad, 1977* (Washington, D.C.: U.S. Government Printing Office, 1981), p. 2.

10. U.S. Department of Commerce, *Survey of Current Business*, August 1988.

11. See Jane Sneddon Little, "Multinational Corporations and Foreign Investment: Current Trends and Issues," in John Adams, ed., *The Contemporary International Economy—A Reader*, 2nd ed. (New York: St. Martin's Press, 1985), pp. 401–2.

12. *NBER Digest*, July 1989, p. 2. For elaboration, see James Hines and Glenn Hubbard, *Coming Home to America: Dividend Repatriations by U.S. Multinationals*, National Bureau of Economic Research Working Paper No. 2931.

13. Black, p. 7.

14. *Survey of Current Business*, August 1988, pp. 74–75.

15. John Hillkirk, "Foreigners Stake in USA Surging," *USA Today*, May 3, 1989, p. B1.

16. Bank of Japan, Research and Statistics Department, "U.S. Competitiveness in Manufacturing," Special Paper No. 153, September 1987, p. 24.

17. Hillkirk.

18. William J. Kahley, "Direct Investment Activity of Foreign Firms," *Economic Review*, Federal Reserve Bank of Atlanta, Summer 1987, p. 43.

19. Jerry J. Shipley, "Foreign Ownership of the U.S. Economy: Myth or Menace," speech to the National Economists Club, Washington, D.C., July 21, 1988. See also Mac Ott, "Is America Being Sold Out?" *Review*, Federal Reserve Bank of St. Louis March/April 1989, pp. 47–64. Ott estimates the foreign claim in 1987 on the net U.S. reproducible nonconsumer capital stock to be 3.5 percent (p. 60).

20. Data from *Survey of Current Business*, June 1988, p. 77.

21. Council of Economic Advisors, *Economic Report of the President 1989* (Washington, D.C.: U.S. Government Printing Office, 1989), p. 132.

22. Just as unrealistic is valuing U.S. bank claims on Third World countries at book value when their economic worth merits substantial discounting. Such adjustment, of course, would increase, not reduce, our net debtor status.

23. *Economic Report of the President 1989*, p. 130.

24. Ibid., p. 132–33.

25. Milton Friedman, "In Defense of Dumping," *Journal of Economic & Monetary Affairs*, Winter 1986, p. 98.

26. Herbert Stein, "Don't Worry about the Trade Deficit," *Wall Street Journal*, May 16, 1989, p. A14.

27. See Donald L. Losman, "If We Only Knew How Trade Figures Are Balanced," *Wall Street Journal*, August 27, 1985, p. 30.

28. Willard C. Butcher, "Four Principles Governing our Monetary and Trade Challenges," *AEI Foreign Policy and Defense Review* 5, no. 4 (1985), p. 43.

29. John A. Tatom, "The Link Between the Value of the Dollar, U.S. Trade and Manufacturing," *Review*, Federal Reserve Bank of St. Louis, November/December 1988, pp. 32–33. Of course, foreign producers absorbed varying portions of their markups in order to maintain newly gained U.S. market share in the face of dollar depreciation.

30. See Jack L. Hervey, "Dollar Drop Helps Those Who Help Themselves," *Chicago Fed Letter*, Federal Reserve Bank of Chicago, March 1988.

31. Peter F. Drucker, "Taming the Corporate Takeover," *Wall Street Journal*, October 30, 1984, p. 30.

32. Council of Economic Advisors, *Economic Report of the President 1984* (Washington, D.C.: U.S. Government Printing Office, February, 1984), pp. 42–50.

33. Tatom, p. 34.

34. James R. Basche, Jr., *Technology Imports into the United States* (New York: The Conference Board, 1983), p. 3.

35. Art Pine, "U.S. Trade Restrictions . . .," *Wall Street Journal*, May 26, 1982. p. 56.

36. Murray L. Weidenbaum, "U.S. Export Curbs Contribute to the Trade Deficit," *Wall Street Journal*, April 2, 1985, p. 28.

37. Ibid.

38. From 1978 through 1985 U.S. oil consumption fell 17 percent while production rose 3 percent, but that trend has been reversed. From 1985 to 1987 production fell

8 percent while consumption rose 6 percent. Imports now represent 50 percent of our supplies and low world oil prices will not continue forever. Accordingly, this threat looms and the balance of trade will ultimately reflect it.

39. J. Hayden Boyd, "Manufacturing Growth and the Trade Deficit: Does Trade Cause the Decline of Industries?" U.S. Department of State Working Paper Series, PAS WP/88/9, November 1988, p. 3.

40. Ibid., p. 8.

41. See Tatom.

42. Harvey Brooks and Bruce R. Guile, "Overview," in Bruce R. Guile and Harvey K. Brooks, eds. *Technology and Global Industry* (Washington, D.C.: National Academy Press, 1987), p. 8.

43. Ibid., p. 9.

44. Rachel McCulloch, "U.S. International Competitiveness in a Changing Global Economy," in Carl-Ludwig Holtfuerich, ed., *Economic and Strategic Issues in U.S. Foreign Policy* (New York: Walter De Gruyter, 1989), p. 5.

45. See Alan F. Holmer and Judith H. Bello, "The 1988 Trade Bill," U.S. Department of State Special Report No. 180, December 1988.

46. See Jim Powell, "Super-301: The Economic Equivalent of Civilian Bombing," *Wall Street Journal*, May 30, 1989, p. A22.

47. John Andrew, John Helyar, and Bill Johnson, "Imports Often Blamed . . ." *Wall Street Journal*, February 29, 1984, p. 1.

48. See Mordechai E. Kreinin, "Wage Competitiveness in the U.S. Auto and Steel Industries," *Contemporary Policy Issues*, January 1984.

49. See David G. Tarr, *A General Equilibrium Analysis of the Welfare and Employment Effects of U.S. Quotas in Textiles, Autos and Steel* (Washington, D.C.: Federal Trade Commission, February 1989).

50. Norman S. Fieleke, "The Foreign Trade Deficit and American Industry," *New England Economic Review*, July/August 1985, p. 50.

51. Ibid.

52. Tarr, p. 7-7.

53. *Economic Report of the President 1989*, p. 7.

54. James R. Golden, *NATO Burden Sharing Risk and Opportunities* (New York: Praeger, 1983), pp. 30-31.

55. Phillip Taylor, "Weapons Standardization in NATO: Collaborative Security or Economic Competition," *International Organization*, Winter 1982, p. 99.

56. Herman Gilster, *Economics and NATO Standardization*, Directorate for International Economic Affairs, Office of the Assistant Secretary of Defense for International Security Affairs, August 1978, p. 1.

57. Bernard Udis, "Lessons from Aerospace: The Prospects for Rationalization in NATO," *Orbis*, Spring 1981.

58. Robert Roderick, "ROLAND: Exchange of Expertise," *National Defense*, May/June 1978, p. 579.

59. See Taylor, p. 110.

60. Quoted in Thomas A. Callaghan, Jr., "The Structural Disarmament of NATO," *NATO Review*, June 1984.

61. As one example, a major U.S. prime contractor, having found only two domestic suppliers of a particular electronic component, priced at $120, obtained a license for a

Japanese firm. As a result of this added competition, the price eventually fell to $40. See Hal Bratt, Jr. et al. "The Potential Effect of Domestic Content Legislation on DOD Procurement," Industrial College of the Armed Forces, Research Report, May 1986, p. 64.

62. See Callaghan, and his 1986 report prepared for the Department of Defense, "Pooling Allied and American Resources to Produce a Credible Collective Conventional Defense."

7

Performance

How well does U.S. industry perform? This is the universal "bottom line" question. Unfortunately, it is not amenable to a simple answer because, like international issues, it too is a multidimensional question. One basic measure is profit, but there are many other indicators such as technological progress, quality, and international receptiveness, just to name a few. This chapter examines various important aspects of performance in U.S. industry. It also deals with the deindustrialization hypothesis.

COSTS

Any time an economic resource is utilized, a cost is involved. If the resource is not owned by the employing organization, an out-payment remuneration must be made. Examples include wages, electricity, rent, material costs, bond interest, and so on. Economists describe these as explicit costs and they generally revolve around contractual agreements. If an economic resource owned by the firm is utilized, a cost is still involved, but no cash payment is necessary. These are implicit costs and include the use of business-owned money or property. They should be valued by their opportunity cost—that is, their worth in their next highest use. Theoretically, in long-run equilibrium the opportunity costs of using a specific resource in alternate undertakings would be equal. Such equilibrium positions, however, are never achieved in practice. While opportunity costs do not involve cash outlays, they are very important for managerial purposes. The commitment of funds or personnel to project A must be compared to the alternatives available, such as project B or C. Opportunity costs, then, are meaningful for managerial decision making, although they have no place in budgeting or taxation considerations.

Business costs may be divided into two other components, fixed and variable. Variable expenses change as output changes, whereas fixed costs are unrelated to production volumes. Electricity, wages, and raw materials would fall in the first category; general overhead and property taxes would fall in the latter. Average costs of production (ATC or average total cost) are the per unit cost of producing any particular volume of output. Marginal costs (MC) are variable expenses; they reflect variable input prices and the law of diminishing returns. Technically, MC is the cost of producing only one additional unit of output; in practice, it is the cost per unit of each additional batch (extra costs divided by the extra quantity). On the other hand, fixed costs, like factory mortgage payments or the company president's salary, are unresponsive to output changes. Since fixed costs do not vary with output, dividing the same amount by increased production lowers the average fixed cost (AFC) per unit. This is the "spreading of overhead" effect. At any output level, the combination of AFC plus AVC (average variable cost) yields ATC for that output. Finally, by mathematical necessity, MC always intersects the low points on both AVC and ATC.

As the top panel of Figure 7.1 shows, at eight units of output ATC is lowest. Any production levels larger or smaller than eight will entail greater unit costs. Clearly, then, costs depend at least in part on the rate of production. This suggests that both business cycle fluctuations and erratic procurements (such as often occur with Department of Defense purchases) are likely to be cost increasing because it becomes difficult to maintain optimal production runs when sales are subject to wide swings. The level of the ATC curve also depends on input prices. If rents increase, both AFC and ATC move upward. If energy and labor increase in price, MC and AVC will shift upward, again forcing ATC to rise. Conversely, input price declines, such as lower oil prices, will lower ATC. The general shape of the ATC reflects physical production relationships. In some fields diminishing returns begin early and are very steep, making the curve rise rapidly; in others they are delayed and gradual. Finally, if there are innovations or technical breakthroughs, these act to shift the cost curves downward and perhaps modify their shapes.

Two other influences merit mention. First, the size or scale of operation often has a bearing on costs. Large-scale operations frequently lower the ATC curve. This is known as economies of scale. Figure 7.2 depicts scale economies characterizing the first three business sizes, but with firm number 4, diseconomies of scale occur. Size then becomes disadvantageous. Notice too that the optimal size plant is lowest cost only when its rate of operation is appropriate. If it is operating significantly under or above the minimum ATC quantity, its unit costs will be higher than some other firms. For example, in Figure 7.2 if normal operating output were at point L, plant 2 would have lower average costs than plant 3. Accordingly, firm size can be an important determinant of unit costs, although advantages accruing to large size can be undone by inefficient rates of operation.

Scale economies primarily derive from *indivisibilities*, either in inputs themselves or in production processes. The existence of indivisibilities suggests that neither inputs nor production processes can be continuously adjusted and still have output always yielding proportional responses. As a crude example, one can conceive

Figure 7.1
Economic Profits and Losses

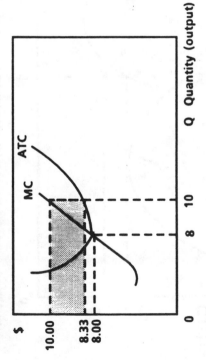

NOTE: Economic profits exist when selling price exceeds average total cost. For example, at a price of $10, ten units are produced and sold. Total revenue is $100. At 10 units of production, ATC = $8.33. Therefore, total cost is $83.30. Hence economic profit is $16.70 (shaded area). At a price of $8, eight units become the best production level. Total revenue is $64. ATC is also $8, so total costs are $64. Economic profit at this price is zero--only normal profit is earned.

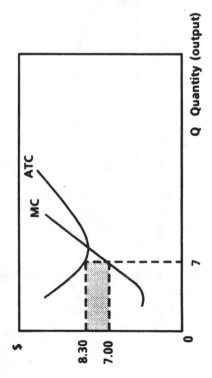

NOTE: Economic losses exist when price falls so low that it is below average total costs. For example, at a price of $7, the best operating output is seven units, yielding a total revenue of $49. At seven units, however, ATC is $8.30, yielding total costs of $58.10. This exceeds revenues by $9.10. The shaded area depicts the ecomomic losses (negative profits).

Figure 7.2
Scale Economies: Average Total Costs for Different Firm Sizes

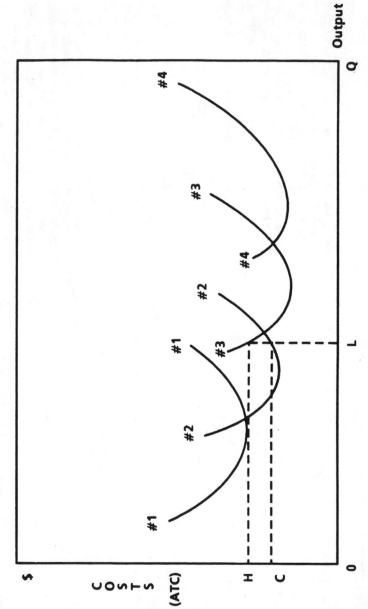

Note: Although plant #3 can produce at the lowest average total costs possible, if it were to operate only at output L, its costs per unit would be OH, which is higher than the average cost of that same output (OC) if plant size #2 were producing it.

of a worker employing a shovel to dig a ditch, removing a certain amount of material per hour. If the shovel were reduced to half its size, the worker might only be able to produce half the excavating, a proportionate response. But at some point reducing the shovel size will evoke a more than proportionate loss. When the shovel becomes small relative to the loads and hardness of materials it is digging, it will bend or break. Indeed, continuous reduction in size is not even possible since at some point it will cease being a shovel and become a spoon! This is the meaning of the term indivisibility. Economies of scale take advantage of indivisibilities—the scale of production allows the use of shovels instead of spoons, the use of computers instead of calculators.

Alternately, a shovel's size can be increased only so much before it becomes unmanageable. Many production processes evidence similar indivisibilities. As larger sized equipment or higher volume processes are employed, unit costs may decline due to more than proportionate output increases. If carried too far, however, size can become cumbersome, as in the super large shovel example, with output rising less than proportionately or not at all.

Scale economies may also derive from financial factors, such as the ability to buy inputs or materials in such large quantities that the supplying firm can afford to lower its selling price (either because it is a monopolistic-type seller currently operating with low volumes and high fixed costs per unit or because the seller also enjoys scale economies). Finally, there may be cost advantages unrelated to scale economies per se, but definitely related to the size of the purchaser. A sole (monopsonistic) buyer may be able to take advantage of product-specific investments made by the supplier to demand price reductions. This is what was called holdup in chapter 2. Alternately, by virtue of its own size and economic power a very large and influential buyer may be able to force price concessions from suppliers. John D. Rockefeller's Standard Oil was rather notorious for this practice toward the end of the nineteenth century.

Scale economies may be realized in terms of three categories of production organization: (1) product-specific advantages, (2) plant-specific advantages, and (3) multiplant economies. Product-specific economies are associated with high-volume production of a particular item, whereas plant-specific economies are associated with the total output of a single production facility, which generally encompasses several different products. Plant-specific economies derive either from indivisibilities or from *economies of scope*. These occur when the simultaneous production of several items can be done at lower cost than their production in isolation by other firms. Such advantages tend to be associated with mutually advantageous interdependencies in production—that is, economies resulting from the scope of the firm's operations.

Often scale economies are limited to plant-specific advantages. However, there may also be managerial and organizational benefits associated with the operation of many production facilities (although this is by no means always the case). These too, it should be noted, can be dissipated if the total organization becomes too large. Probably the most common source of diseconomies of scale derives from managerial and informational problems associated with very large organizations. By the time information is received at the higher decision-making echelons, either too much time has elapsed to address the problem appropriately or the information has become so distorted that effective policy decisions cannot be rendered.

Another cost influence, one that might be deemed a dynamic economy of scale, is most popularly called *learning curve advantages*. Learning curves relate unit costs to cumulative output and are so named because they represent increases in productivity gained through experience. Learning-by-doing on the part of workers is one source of such economies, although most are generated by improvements in production processes obtained over time and with the deliberate efforts of the whole production "team." Interestingly, although learning advantages often become common knowledge, a significant proportion of the benefits accrue only to the firms doing the learning.

Learning curve cost reductions can be quite important. They are particularly relevant in labor-intensive efforts and where organizational learning can make substantial differences. In the machine tool industry, for example, the unit cost of additional production tends to fall by 20 percent for each doubling of cumulated output.[1] The learning curve phenomenon is also commonly found in the aircraft and electronic industries. In effect, as output grows cumulatively, the entire ATC curve moves lower. Learning curve advantages are relevant for defense procurement since longer production runs add experience and thus cut costs. They also support the contention that for economic reasons the Western Alliance should pursue the rationalization, standardization, and interoperability (RSI) efforts discussed in chapter 6.

The learning curve is also a significant planning tool that enables managers to estimate production costs at predicted output levels. With a constant reduction of $x\%$, improvements are deemed on a $100\% - x\%$ learning curve. For example, if the constant reduction is 20 percent, the improvement is designated as being on an 80 percent learning curve. The average cost per unit of output at lower volumes, say 10,000, would be higher than at 20,000, the cost at 10,000 being calculated as $1/.80$ times the average cost per unit at 20,000 units. Learning curves are typically plotted against unit costs as a function of cumulative output.

As important as scale economies can be, they should not be oversold, something that many believe has happened in corporate America. Whereas in the past only large firms could afford a mainframe computer or other sophisticated technological innovations, the trends of past years have been for prices to come down and access to increase. Accordingly, smaller size is less a barrier to advantageous procurements. This has the effect of making smaller organizations cheaper. In Figure 7.2 the average total cost curves of firms 1, 2, and 3 would fall, thereby assisting smaller firms to be competitive with larger ones. Further, "new methods of work organization, and a new importance of local market responsiveness all can decrease the significance of scale economies. . . ."[2]

Yet, while "economies of scale appear to be diminishing in factory production they have been on the increase in marketing, finance and risk management."[3] It appears that uncertainty promotes growth in financial functions as a damage-limiting mechanism. With the continued shortening in the half-life of knowledge, erratic national economic policies, and progressive globalization trends, uncertainty appears to be an inherent characteristic of the modern age. Accordingly, opposing forces are at work, with production and some marketing trends favoring smaller and more flexible organizations, while risk and financial demands favor larger entities.

A few caveats regarding costs are worth mentioning. It is important to recognize that organizational structures can either facilitate or impede information flows, thus impacting on costs. Accordingly, since efficiency is in part related to organization, organizational form affects costs and profitability. Depending upon the kind of business, some structures are more suitable for monitoring and coordinating than others. Difficulties in controlling shirking and assessing/rewarding input productivities can significantly raise costs and lower performance. For example, in "U.S. manufacturing, the ratio of central-office to plant employees rose from 4.5 in 1963 to 7.2 in 1982."[4] Was this appropriate or did it tend to build a relatively unproductive layer of bureaucracy? Today's slightly more than 50 percent of central-office workers are involved in clerical, administrative, or managerial pursuits. Data from several sources imply that the bureaucratic layer suggestion has substantial elements of truth.

There are two sources of unproductive activity related to any employment. One is vacations, holidays, and sickness. "In larger manufacturing firms, this type of payment for not working increased from 5.4 percent of total payroll cost in 1953 to 10.2 percent in 1986."[5] Second is shirking—time on the job but spent in unproductive endeavors from the perspective of the organization. "This source of paid on-the-job leisure increased from 2.1 percent to 3.3 percent of payroll costs. . . ."[6] To the degree that the work ethic may have declined or American drive for business success has abated, the need for monitoring becomes greater so as to minimize such moral hazard (shirking) costs. Probably a significant difference between the contemporary U.S. work force and the Japanese or Korean is that in the latter the work ethic is strong, as is the fear of "losing face." Accordingly, the need for and costs of monitoring are much lower.[7] American managements, on the other hand, would do well to devote more resources to assessing the quality of employee time on the job. This brings us back to organizational form, for some are clearly more suitable than others in accomplishing this task. Interestingly, recent research finds that "takeovers do reduce corporate overhead. In companies changing owners, the ratio of central-office employees to plant employees declined about 11 percent."[8] Further, while overall central office employment in newly acquired firms grew some 16 percent less than in those not changing ownership, the growth of R&D staffs in each was about the same. It appears, then, that "fat" has been discovered and is being trimmed, while the "meat" is being preserved.

To the degree that U.S. corporations have this fat, and to the degree that they must devote resources to cope with moral hazard, this puts them at a competitive disadvantage in global markets when they face the products of societies that do not confront such problems. Of course, "an incentive scheme that *prevents* shirking is superior to a monitoring scheme that *detects* and then *punishes* shirking."[9] Clearly, the U.S. corporation could undertake substantial improvements in this area. Nonetheless, some monitoring activities would still be necessary.

Finally, in addition to payroll costs for not working one must add the significant costs of generous fringe benefits. Since wages are taxed, but most fringe benefits are not, the latter have grown disproportionately over the years. For example, a National Association of Manufacturers poll indicates that in 1988 health-care costs of its membership rose nearly 30 percent and "represented an average of 37% of profit."[10] Such benefits extend not only to current employees, but generally to retirees as well, and it is estimated that health care costs in the future will grow at least tenfold as the number of retirees increases (the ratio of workers to retirees, presently about 3:1, will fall to 2:1 by the year 2000).[11] In addition to these expenses, the litigious nature of American society costs corporate America billions. For example, in 1987 General Motors spent roughly $120 billion on outside legal fees alone as well as paying its own lawyers and associated expenses. These expenses constitute a large and growing overhead.[12] Further, since they are independent of output, they constitute a quasi-fixed cost that raises production break-even points, thereby posing a threat during economic downturns. Finally, since these overheads tend to be higher than those of our overseas competitors, they too constitute a drag on international competitiveness.

On the positive side, such overheads can be dealt with via cost containment, cost sharing, and greater flexibility. Further, with substantial manufacturing producitivity gains and modest wage demands in the 1980s, unit labor costs for most of that decade were more than tame. Indeed, they fell 1 percent in 1987 and half that amount in 1986. Accordingly, wage moderation and productivity gains offset such overhead growth.

PROFITS

As pointed out in chapter 1, the profit motive is the driving force that leads market participants to take risks and try new business undertakings. It is a key ingredient in our economic system, playing a critical role in allocating scarce productive resources. It is because of profits that the competitive price system works to allocate resources to their most highly valued uses. Unless a normal rate of return or better can be earned, a firm is unlikely to survive for long. If the market functions properly, an absence of normal profits suggests that something is wrong. Consumers either are not willing to pay for the full cost of resources used in providing the goods or services or those items are being inefficiently produced. Profits thus transmit signals on how well an industry performs. Through their impacts on resource allocation, profits also influence the distribution of income.

For the economist, profit levels are determined by what is left over from revenues after payments have been made (or returns earned) to all inputs, including rates of return for equity capital and owner time inputs (implicit costs). An entrepreneur utilizes these resources in a business venture, as do other firms. If a wrong estimate is made about the costs of using inputs and the potential revenue from the sales of products, costs may run ahead of revenues. The entrepreneur then earns a negative rate of return (negative profits or losses). On the other hand, if highly productive uses are found for the company's resources, revenues exceed costs and thereby earn a positive rate of profit (see Figure 7.1).

Corporate profit statistics are derived from accountants' calculations. Accordingly, they are larger than the economist's concept, since implicit costs have not been deducted. Inasmuch as such costs are very difficult to measure, business statistics on profits do not consider them. It should nonetheless be recognized that accounting profits may well be economic losses. For example, a corporation showing $1 million in accounting profits perhaps should have earned $10 million for implicit interest on equity funds. In that case, the economic profit is a negative $9 million. If it pays taxes on the $1 million, the real economic loss is even greater. Despite this limitation in the data, the corporate profits statistics are one indicator of success and financial health. Nominal corporate profits have generally risen over the past 45 years. As a percentage of GNP they have been relatively stable, ranging from 3 to 6+ percent since 1951, tending to be lower in recession years. Adjusting for inflation, however, real after-tax corporate profits as a percentage of the real GNP show a declining trend. The highest annual shares were in the immediate post-World War II period, exceeding 8 percent from 1947 to 1950. On the other hand, no year since 1980 has reached 5 percent, and no year since 1981 has achieved 4 percent. Indeed, as a share of GNP the annual average for the 1980s is lower than any individual years since 1947. Clearly, neither nominal nor inflation-adjusted data support the widely held perception that corporate profits have been commanding an increasing share of the nation's income.

Looking at actual levels of real after-tax corporate profits, on the other hand, finds corporate health generally showing progress until 1981. Indeed, no years since 1981 have even approximated the average of 1975-79, which was $186.7 billion. In fact, the average for the years 1982-88 is only $126.5 billion, well below any year since 1971.[13] This mirrors a secular decline in rates of return to capital, at least in part reflecting increased competition resulting from globalization. Nonetheless, it is troubling data, for corporations are the U.S. vehicle of industrial expansion and progress. If they do not prosper, it does not bode well for the general society. A further refinement of the statistics, however, demonstrates a somewhat more robust situation as well as the important influence of taxes.

The dramatic slowdown in inflation has virtually eliminated the illusory inventory profits of the 1970s, while depreciation adjustments deriving from the 1981 tax changes have substantially surged this noncash expense. Thus sheltered from taxation, the resulting huge cash flows were an important factor in the investment boom of the 1980s. Such improved quality of corporate profits over the first half of the decade reflects the significant influence of tax and price stability policies discussed in chapter 2. The inflation slowdown and new tax laws very clearly benefited corporate America as a whole. However, subsequent tax legislation and new proposals are likely to have the effect of lowering general after-tax profit levels.

A brief review of more disaggregated profit trends is illuminating. In the durable goods sector, primary metals have done very poorly almost throughout the 1980s, with very severe losses in 1982 and 1983, but conditions improved in 1987 and 1988. In fabricated metals the profit trend has been fairly flat, except for a two-year dip (again in 1982 and 1983), and a rise during the past few years. Reflecting import competition, profits in electrical and electronic equipment as a group have declined in the 1980s, while motor vehicles had major losses in two of the first three years of this decade, then greatly improved during the period of restricted Japanese imports. Other durable goods industries, although hit hard in 1982 and 1983, have generally advanced. In the nondurables arena, there were substantial profit declines in petroleum and coal, while food and kindred products have been relatively steady performers. Chemicals and allied products have shown consistent profits in the 1980s, the annual totals fluctuating. Nondurables had five years in a row of declining profits, then a strong upturn in 1987. Finally, general profit trends in manufacturing in the 1980s compare favorably to the financial industry, but evidence far less growth than in transportation, public utilities, or wholesale and retail trades. It is important to recognize that differential performance will over time bring about reallocations of resources as capital and talent leave lagging fields to gain higher returns in the more successful ones. For example, reflecting generally continuous poor performance in metal production, the United States Steel Corporation (USX) has been reducing its steel efforts and acquiring companies in other sectors of the economy.

It is interesting to note the dichotomy between actual profit levels and the public's perceptions of profits. A poll that asked Americans what they believed the rate of profit to be (based on sales) and what they thought a reasonable profit should be for the typical manufacturing concern exposed abysmal ignorance. The average estimate was 37 percent, while the same respondents deemed 26 percent to be reasonable. In point of fact, the actual profit rate was only 3.8 percent.[14] Accordingly, the public's perceptions magnified actual profits by a factor of ten!

Investment in plant and equipment is another performance indicator. Such outlays add to the capital stock and thus affect the economy's capacity to produce. Investment fluctuates with considerable volatility. It has been a major factor in business cycle turns. Investment spending played an important role in the strong U.S. economic expansion dating from 1982.[15] In 1984, which was the second year of growth, total purchases of producers' durable equipment was $148 billion (in 1972 dollars), as compared with an average of $55.6 billion (in 1972 dollars) for the five previous second years of recovery.[16] Reflecting the industrial evolution discussed in chapter 23, high technology industries, such as office computing, accounting machinery, and electronic communications equipment, have become increasingly important as sources of capital formation in the industrial sector. Not surprisingly, private purchases of high tech producers' durable equipment rose at an annual rate of 15.8 percent for 1977 to 1984, double the rate of growth on all other producers' durable equipment.[17] Such developments reflect both vigor in the industrial sector and structural adjustments evolving along the lines of comparative advantage. Substantial investment in producer durables also reflected favorable tax legislation. In the first portion of the 1980s the effective rate of tax on such investments—defined as the percentage increase in user cost resulting from taxation—was −4 percent. Tax legislation implemented in late 1986, however, eliminated this subsidy and replaced it with a positive rate of 13 percent. Accordingly, changed tax laws will have a depressing effect upon equipment investment, although they should contribute to more efficient investment by eliminating tax-induced asset shuffling and similar socially unproductive undertakings. To fund future investments, of course, corporations must have profits in addition to favorable legislation.

MARKET POWER, ADVERTISING, AND PROFIT

Profits may derive from efficiency or market power. Because price and profit are closely related, firms in monopolistic or oligopolistic markets may earn high rates of return simply due to the effects of market power on pricing capabilities. For example, in the 1971–77 period, Bausch and Lomb, a monopoly in the optical market, charged over $60 for soft contact lenses that cost less than $1 to produce.[18] Empirical evidence indicates that market share is an important source of high profitability. One estimate maintains that a 10 percent increase in market share adds about 2.5 percent to the profit rate.[19]

The positive association between market concentration and price levels follows predictable patterns. Prices in oligopolistic industries tend to rise at fairly steady rates, whereas in the more competitive industries prices fluctuate widely, falling sharply during recessionary periods. Large oligopolistic firms, by controlling substantial shares of market supplies, find it easier to maintain prices and profits during cyclical downturns as well as in the long turn. The basis of this market power is barriers to entry, for without them new firms would increase supply and thus erode the exaggerated returns. It should be stressed that barriers to entry in no way guarantee profits (since demand may not be sufficient). However, if there are economic profits, the sellers can retain them far longer than under more competitive conditions.

An important caveat is relevant at this point. Earlier it was suggested that the "efficiency of internal exchange is a function of organizational form."[20] Business structure counts, yet virtually all studies of U.S. industrial profitability have ignored this important variable. This suggests that "past conclusions concerning the relationship between firm size and profitability may not be valid. . . ."[21] For U.S. industry, this commends some serious self-examination. For economists, it is a fertile field for research.

In an industry where producers possess meaningful market power, the same output may be differentially priced to various buyers. This can occur either when costs are uniform or when there is some variation in both prices and costs. Firms pursuing such a pricing policy are said to practice price discrimination. In this case, the sellers try to isolate buyers and charge them different prices according to variations in demand elasticities in the several segments of the market. For example, electric companies have long had five to ten different rate schedules for different customer groups. Pharmaceutical companies sell drugs to large, bulk-volume buyers, such as the Veterans Administration, at a substantially lower price than to other buyers. Price discrimination can be very profitable and sellers will naturally do as much of it as they are able. It reflects market power and can be a major factor for higher profits in monopoly and oligopoly markets.

Advertising intensity may also meaningfully affect profits. Evidence indicates that advertising tends to be high when demand is inelastic and marginal cost of production is well below price.[22] The ratio of advertising expenditures to sales has been found to strongly correlate with firm and industry profit rates.[23] Since large segments of the industrial sector are still occupied by oligopolistic firms, their product differentiation efforts have led to intensive advertising undertakings. In 1983, advertising expenditures in the United States were estimated to be over $75 billion. This exceeded the amount all state and local governments spent on public welfare. By 1987 they were almost $110 billion, about the amount it took to pay all Department of Defense employees that year, military and civilian. In that year 26.8 percent of advertising dollars went for newspaper and magazine advertising, almost 22 percent for television and radio, and 17.4 percent for direct mail.[24] As a result, in recent years the sale of advertising space has been the chief source of revenues of newspapers. Radio and television broadcasters (excluding educational stations) also derive virtually all their revenues from the sale of advertising time.

From the standpoint of many sellers, advertising is an important means to create and reinforce image differentiation. The purpose of such image differentiation is to shift demand toward the product advertised and lower its elasticity. Seen from the perspective of each seller, advertising is primarily intended to capture sales from rivals and, secondarily, to enlarge the total market. Such competitive advertising, however, also raises costs. Nonetheless, because the advertised brand usually represents a goodwill asset, the image-conscious producer will try hard to maintain adequate standards. Consumers may benefit by gaining knowledge of a firm's products, how they are priced, or how they might be used. Oral hygiene, for example, is undoubtedly better because of toothpaste and mouthwash commercials. An advertising-induced market expansion may also achieve economies of scale in production that would otherwise have been unattainable. By providing relevant information, advertising also reduces consumer search costs.

However, the advertising of many products is almost exclusively image creating. For example, Clorox, the leading nationally advertised bleach, enjoys the largest share of the market of liquid household laundry bleach, though this product is offered in a highly standardized form—a 5.25 percent sodium hypochlorite solution. Other examples include soaps, cosmetic and toilet goods, aspirin, and beverages.

To the degree that advertising creates an image of differentiation when in fact there are no physical differences in the products or their attributes, consumers end up paying a higher price without additional benefits (although "thinking" they have a better product is in fact some benefit). This also gives the seller market power. Not surprisingly, as a percentage of sales, advertising tends to be higher for consumer goods than for capital goods. The latter have professional buyers who are very knowledgeable and more influenced by performance than by slogans or commercials.

While a strong and successful product image, perhaps created via advertising, can be a barrier to new entry, it should also be recognized that advertising is also a principal means whereby new products or firms can grab consumer attention. As such, advertising can facilitate entry and reduce market concentration. In a cogently argued analysis, Robert Ekelund and David Saurman maintain that on net balance advertising, by reducing barriers to entry and providing information, clearly benefits consumers.[25] They point out, for example, that the prices of eyeglasses, legal services, and a host of other items are lower where advertising is permitted.

To summarize, while empirical studies confirm a correlation between profits and advertising intensity, the causal relationships are unclear. Undoubtedly in some cases advertising has succeeded in creating so strong an image that demand becomes quite inelastic, so prices can rise sufficiently to allow economic profits that may not be whittled away by new entrants due to a strong advertising-induced consumer attachment. On the other hand, it may simply be a case of large firms in monopolistic and oligopolistic situations having sufficient funds to engage in this form of nonprice product promotion. If so, any economic profits derive from nonadvertising sources and are more reflective of imperfect competition than a cause of it. Finally, it should be recognized that advertising does provide consumers with information and is thus a vehicle whereby new entrants can enter established markets. In such instances it is clearly competition promoting. While false and misleading advertising should clearly be unlawful, other attempts to limit advertising will most likely inhibit competition and thereby reduce consumer welfare.

EFFICIENCY

An important aspect of performance is economic efficiency. It is concerned with how productive resources are allocated among various types of goods and services and with the effectiveness with which these resources are employed. In economic theory, efficiency is divided into two major categories: allocative and X-efficiency. Allocative efficiency concerns input distributions and is related to the market structure. A competitive market tends to move toward equilibrium at an optimal level of resource allocation, one reflecting both consumers' preferences and the costs of utilizing the factors of production. On the other hand, in a monopoly market resource misallocations result. By restricting output, the monopoly or oligopoly firm may be able to charge a price higher than marginal costs of production. For example, sales at $10, when the marginal cost is only $6, indicate a strong consumer preference for that item. If that is the profit-maximizing price, the monopolist has no incentive to further cater to this strong consumer desire. However, under competitive conditions, increased supplies would be forthcoming, ultimately lowering price and raising marginal costs (until at equilibrium, if achieved, marginal cost and price would be identical). Under noncompetitive conditions, then, consumer welfare is reduced because preferences for more output are ignored.

By restricting output, monopolistic industries employ fewer inputs than would otherwise be employed. These resources, in turn, will either be unemployed or crowd into another field, which then tends to overproduce. In short, the allocation of inputs and relative quantities of outputs do not appropriately reflect consumer preferences and real costs. Some economists estimate that the burden of misallocations of resources is probably about 1 percent of GNP.[26] This percentage may seem small, but with a $5 trillion GNP, it comes to $50 billion per year, hardly an inconsequential sum. However, as indicated earlier in this book, the U.S. economy has become far more competitive during the 1980s, with many of our entrenched oligopolists now scrambling for the consumer dollar. Deregulation and foreign competition have intensified and institutionalized more competitive conditions. Accordingly, the generation of profits through market power rather than catering to customer wants is very much on the decrease. Indeed, recent research suggests that the deadweight loss due to oligopoly power in U.S. manufacturing is only 0.10 percent.[27] For society, then, competition clearly pays.

X-efficiency is internal efficiency; it refers to keeping costs down to the "minimum" possible level.[28] X-inefficiency results when certain inputs are not combined in a fashion leading to maximum output at a minimum possible cost. If this happens, it is most likely due to inertia, disorder, or slothfulness in the internal operation of a dominant firm, conditions that derive from a lack of competitive pressures forcing costs to the minimum. Economic theory suggests that competitive firms must minimize costs of production to survive in the long run; however, the monopolist or strong oligopolist may be able to live a quiet life and will not be driven out even if it fails to minimize costs.

X-inefficiency can grow large and persist even over fairly long periods. The higher production or overhead costs caused by such inefficiency represent another social cost of noncompetitive conditions or nonvalue-maximizing behavior. Common forms in which such inefficiency is guised are management "perks," wages and salaries higher than warranted, and an organization and its employees "enjoying the good life" (hardly working instead of working hard).

Economists have not discovered a sound technique for measuring aggregate X-inefficiency. However, it has been found to be a common problem in the industrial sector, where X-inefficiency may raise costs by more than 10 percent above their efficient level.[29] The total cost of X-inefficiency for the whole economy could perhaps be 2–4 percent of GNP, although in today's more competitive economy the figure is probably closer to 1 or 2 percent. This small portion is still a lot of money. Applying 2 percent to a $5 trillion economy yields $100 billion, an amount sufficient to pay for Star Wars (Strategic Defense Initiative) or rebuild the U.S. infrastructure.

INNOVATION AND TECHNOLOGICAL CHANGE

Technological change is yet another performance dimension. Dynamic efficiency in an organization results in technological changes that raise the ratio of total outputs relative to inputs. Technological change includes innovation, which spurs growth, boosts productivity, and lifts profits (at least initially). Industries producing aircraft, missiles, computers, electronics, and machinery represent the most dynamic segments of the industrial sector, and there has been great technological opportunity and advance in those segments in recent years. Their R&D expenditures have been substantial, accounting for about 60 percent of all industrial R&D. The R&D in aircraft, missiles, electronics, and communications, it should be noted, are heavily funded by the federal government.

How do individual firms within a single industry perform in achieving dynamic efficiency? They all presumably face the same opportunities for technological changes. According to J. K. Galbraith, among others, big firms tend to be more progressive than small. In his words, "a benign Providence . . . has made the modern industry of a few large firms an excellent instrument for inducing technical change."[30] In other words, the big diversified firms can better afford R&D outlays, take risks, achieve economies of scale, and wait longer for a payoff from R&D than smaller firms. The empirical evidence, however, does not substantiate this argument.[31] Though R&D is concentrated in large businesses, successful, inventive outputs do not closely correlate with size. Indeed, R&D intensity does not seem to increase beyond medium-sized firms. According to F. M. Scherer, "a little bit of bigness—up to sales levels of $250 to $400 million at 1978 prices levels—is good for invention and innovation. But beyond the threshold further bigness adds little or nothing, and it carries the danger of diminishing the effectiveness of inventive and innovative performance."[32]

Despite empirical evidence that R&D incentive and ability best blend in the middle ranges of market structures (leaning toward the competitive side), the multinational operations of big firms do enhance R&D profitability. This is true because licensing the use of innovations abroad can be a substitute for on-site production and marketing. One estimate suggests that for multinational corporations, on the average, 29 to 34 percent of the profits from R&D projects come for overseas explorations.[33]

There seems to be a general presumption that the rate of innovation has waned in U.S. industry. This conclusion is based on inferences and indirect evidence. In terms of R&D spending, for example, a declining proportion of the GNP has been devoted to these efforts, while endeavors by our main overseas competitors have been increasing faster than our own. Similarly, since innovation can be a key source of productivity growth, a slowdown in innovation could be inferred from the pallid overall U.S. productivity performance of the past 15 years. Additionally, inasmuch as one of the most expensive (perhaps as much as 40 percent) aspects of the innovation process is investment in plant and equipment, since this indicator had also been lagging, there was still another reason to believe that innovation has necessarily suffered. Finally, there has been a reduced number of patents granted to Americans and an increasing number granted to foreigners.

Such evidence, however, is not conclusive. For example, as chapter 4 suggested, "gross patent statistics do not tell us much about the economic significance of patents."[34] Further, exports of R&D-intensive manufactured products progressed substantially in the 1960s and 1970s. And in the 1980s, despite a nonrobust export performance in general, R&D-intensive products have done relatively better than most other U.S. exports. Rather than being totally bleak, then, "the picture is one of both significant problems and substantial strengths."[35] As Martin Bailey and Alok Chakrabarti have written:

The United States has an unparalleled education and scientific base, and it puts about as many resources into R&D as Japan, Germany, and France combined. . . . Seventy percent of all European computer equipment is U.S.-built or supplied by American companies. The much-feared Japanese effort to build a super computer aided by a government grant of $500 million over 10 years, has to be weighed against the $3 billion that IBM spent on R&D in 1984 alone.[36]

Other positive signs include the relative robustness of industrial R&D despite severe recessions in the early 1980s and the fact that U.S. universities, after a major dip in the 1970s, are now turning out more engineers.

It merits note that productivity advance can be greatly assisted by process innovation, but as mentioned earlier, the United States has emphasized product innovation. However, this latter form of innovation is generally more readily subject to duplication and copying. Further, useful innovative activities will not achieve their ultimate fruition unless they can be transformed into successful production. "When the United States has had superior technologies to offer, it has frequently been unable to get them into quantity production with good quality control and reliability ahead of its competitors."[37]

Accordingly, it is unclear as to whether innovation itself has been failing or other factors are at work. Whatever the case, it is clear that the United States has a comparative advantage in technology and innovation and that the potential for great performance exists. However, fulfilling this potential requires greater managerial emphasis and an improved transition to production. External to the firm, government incentives in terms of tax credits and deductions may well be appropriate, particularly if, as seems to be the case, the social returns to innovation are higher than the earnings the innovating companies can appropriate to themselves (due to the rapid flow and diffusion of technical information to competitors both at home and overseas). Additionally, exemptions from antitrust laws may be warranted to allow several firms to work jointly in the early stages of a new development.

Two final points relate to the influence of government. First, there has been a consistent consensus among business respondents over a prolonged period indicating that the increase in governmental regulations has discouraged innovative efforts. This has occurred both because of the costs associated with regulatory compliance and because of the uncertainty and instability of many regulatory standards. Second, while specific targeting of R&D via tax and other measures is a positive step, it must be recognized that the "rate of innovation is heavily dependent on the general economic climate in the United States."[38] Accordingly, maintenance of high levels of aggregate demand and robust growth are critical ingredients for innovative vibrance.

QUALITY

Product quality is also a dimension of industrial performance. It is hard to measure, and particularly so when aggregating. Perceptions of quality and qualitative change, however, have been monitored and tabulated. It is clear that the U.S. public believes that the general quality of American-made goods began to deteriorate seriously in the 1970s.[39] There existed numerous sources of quality degradation, particularly in the context of the inflationary environment of that decade. Nonetheless, while the perception is quite real, its accuracy as a generalization is difficult to prove or disprove. Comparisons would have to be done on a case-by-case basis. In fact, only scant empirical work has been undertaken to assess changes in the quality of U.S. goods over time.

Mirroring U.S. opinions, the quality image of U.S. products has seriously eroded overseas. A 1987 poll, for example, found that "only 6 percent of West Germans and 9 percent of Britons associated the words 'Made in the USA' with high quality."[40] And there have been innumerable studies comparing the quality of Japanese products to their American counterparts. Garvin, for example, studied manufacturers of room air conditioners.[41] The average quality of performance of Japanese-produced units was far superior to American outputs. Similarly, Peter G. Peterson, former secretary of Commerce, found several other examples.[42] In automobile production, he noted, some 96 percent of Japanese vehicles left the production line ready for delivery, while only 75 percent of U.S. cars were so fit. In 1973, only 3 percent of Japanese television sets required service calls during their warranty periods. The corresponding U.S. figure was 20 percent. Another example cited is integrated circuit chips. Hewlett-Packard found that 0.16 percent of U.S. chips failed the acceptance test, while none of the Japanese chips did. After use in the field for 1,000 hours, the Japanese failure rate was only one-tenth of the U.S. figure. Hajime Karatsu reports that with just a few exceptions, "American manufacturers had yields so low that they could not meet orders, and the failure rates of their products could not begin to compete with that of Japanese RAMS. . . ."[43] Additional evidence abounds. Clearly, then, on an international competitive basis, the quality of U.S. products has shown a need for substantial improvement. As mentioned in chapter 4, increased automation and use of robotics would not only address the quality dimension, but would raise productivity as well. The attractiveness of American goods, to both U.S. residents and foreigners, would thereby be enhanced, thus reducing U.S. trade and payments deficits.

The good news in this regard is that a quality revolution is—and has been—under way. "The efforts on quality are being reflected in all aspects: design, development, manufacturing, features, terms of delivery, and follow-up service."[44] Cross-country quality appraisals for the 1980s "show very generally how well the United States competed in quality terms over the past few years."[45] In 11 broad industry groupings that account for 15 percent of U.S. manufactured goods production, quality problems were found in five, but "two of these five industries had eliminated their quality deficiencies by the end of the appraisal period."[46] American quality was deemed superior to foreign quality in four industries, with the remaining two having product mixtures with some superior and some inferior items. "Anecdotal evidence also suggests a significant improvement in the quality performance of U.S. manufactured goods in recent years."[47] Further, there is every indication that U.S. manufacturers now consider quality to be of the highest importance.

MANAGEMENT FOCUS

With the increasing absence of direct accountability allowed by the separation of management and ownership, corporate executives have been relatively free to pursue their own ends. Economic theories describing corporate behavior have thus tended to discard profit maximization as a realistic goal and instead concentrate on nonvalue-maximizing goals (such as maximizing total sales, size of organization, etc.), provided there is sufficient (not maximum) profit to keep stockholders reasonably satisfied. Whereas an unflinching search for maximum profit allowed economists to more easily describe and predict corporate behavior, the introduction of other goals has made traditional descriptions less appropriate. Additonally, in the absence of profit maximization, a number of business practices and styles have developed that have since proved inimical to U.S. industrial development. Indeed, nonvalue-maximizing behavior has at times been nothing short of outrageous.[48] Further, these patterns have been reinforced by stresses and pressures operational in the general economic environment. Changes in the external environment, particularly in the 1970s, coupled with new internal orientations and practices, introduced significant burdens (X-inefficiencies), thus negatively impacting upon costs, quality, and export initiatives.

One characteristic accompanying the rise of giant corporations has been a new system of personnel rotation and advancement. Traditionally, upper echelon managers were also owners or operating close to the owners. They staffed particular positions for relatively long periods and tended to stay with the same company for the bulk of their careers. This created substantial management expertise, company-specific productivity enhancement, and an institutional memory. Personnel tended to be assessed on the basis of long-term performance. Technical expertise, as in engineering, design, and quality control, were critical factors in career advancement and managerial decision-making power. Today, however, executive tenure at specific positions has tended to shorten, and far greater mobility of personnel, both within and among companies, exists.

Indeed, job-hopping has become an integral part of the corporate culture, at least in part due to what seems to have become a standard compensation practice—newly recruited outsiders tend to earn more than equivalent insiders, a practice that is undoubtedly not only discouraging to long-time employees, but probably a factor increasing shirking as well. For example, research into CEO compensation indicates not only that externally recruited CEOs are paid more than internal promotees, but that the margin is very substantial, approximately $100,000 and unrelated to differences in business performance.[49] Concomitantly, "fast-track" advance has become much more common. This increasing mobility prompted the following Japanese observation: "high-level American executives . . . seem to come and go and switch around as if playing a game of musical chairs at an Alice in Wonderland tea party."[50] Employment longevity still characterizes many of our top corporations, such as IBM and Procter & Gamble, but it is greatly reduced in recent decades in the business community as a whole.

Over time, the management skill mix has changed as well. Marketing, legal, financial, and personnel functions gained in relative importance at the expense of technical expertise. Corporate executive ranks have come to be increasingly populated by lawyers, while the "distance," professionally as well as physically, between top management and the factory floor has greatly lengthened. Not surprisingly, much of the executive "management is out of touch with advanced manufacturing technology and is unaware it is being used far less than assumed. . . ."[51] Further, a recent survey shows that less than 50 percent of male managers and only 20 percent of female managers believe their companies have their best interests in mind.[52] While the management of numbers and dollars is important, any organization that mismanages its people is sure to encounter difficulties.

The decade of the 1970s ushered in a period of rampant inflation. Increasingly, profits could be earned by inventory investment and financial manipulations. Legal and financial personnel gained ascendancy in the corporate hierarchy, while production and quality control individuals tended to lose influence. It would hardly seem to be sheer coincidence that during this decade productivity waned, quality declined, and the international position of U.S. goods fell. As Robert Hayes and William Abernathy have noted, "When executive suites are dominated by people with financial and legal skills, it is not surprising that top management should increasingly allocate time and energy to such concerns as cash management and the whole process of corporate acquisitions and mergers."[53]

The new skill mix characterizing the "men at the top" also in part explains another phenomenon for which U.S. management has been roundly criticized.

While the product life cycle goes far in explaining the move to overseas production and assembly, many maintain that this movement became an easy way around cost increases, a path of least resistance chosen by individuals who did not possess the expertise to cope with rising wages via effective production management. Karatsu, for example, claims:

No sooner do valuable new technologies start to create jobs within the United States than the work is snatched away and shipped abroad. . . . During this same period Japanese semi-conductor makers decided to counter rising wages by automating their assembly lines, at the same time that Japan's car makers were also bringing large numbers of robots into their plants.[54]

The shift in emphasis in U.S. corporations from quality control and production is also vividly demonstrated by repeated cases of foreign companies taking over U.S. production facilities that had been plagued by absenteeism, high reject rates, and related maladies. Under foreign managements, these same workers and factories have often done complete turnabouts.

In addition, a decidedly short-term orientation took hold. The unprecedented and unpredictable inflation of the 1970s made long-term planning far more difficult and risky, at the same time increasing the payoff from short-term and financial investments. Accordingly, long-term and strategic planning moved lower on the corporate priority pole, as did the status and power of those engaged in that function. Most R&D, for example, is long-term undertaking, but it did not capture sufficient top management attention. There has been insufficient "push" to quickly bring R&D endeavors to the marketplace in the form of quality products. The quickened pace of corporate personnel turnover, both within companies and among them, also had the effect of magnifying short-term orientations at the expense of longer term perspectives. In the automobile industry, for example, as the dollar depreciated in the 1970s, U.S. companies had an opportunity to regain lost market share from imports by holding their own prices constant (as the dollar cost of imports rose). Consistently, however, domestic prices were raised when the dollar fell, a self-defeating pattern that was renewed in the second half of the 1980s. In the short term, this may have increased corporate revenues, thus enhancing the status of the personnel currently involved in that area. The long-term effect, however, has been a continuous decline in market share. Yet, with relatively rapid personnel rotations, a market share over time is difficult to associate with particular individuals, whereas the short-term increased revenues are more easily associated, a fact readily known to the personnel involved.

Giant corporate size can also bring political influence, and a growing proportion of lawyers and public relations capabilities suggests that political clout will increasingly be utilized. It is not beyond the pale of reason or experience to suggest that some large corporations may find it easier to make profits by efficiently working the Washington political scene rather than their own production and marketing capabilities. If such corporate political clout is reinforced by organized labor's legislative efforts, inefficient and socially costly outcomes result. The restrictions on Japanese automobile imports and limitation of foreign steel are clear cases in point.

In addition to inflation, another change in the external environment has affected internal management decision making and further eroded long-term orientations. This relates to the stock market and the rise of the "institutional" investor. "With $1.5 trillion—and soon to reach $2 trillion—in assets, pension funds now own one-third of the equity of all publicly traded companies in the U.S., and 50 percent or more of the equity of the big ones."[55] Pension fund managers concentrate on immediate gains. Consequently, "any business that needs money—every business sooner or later—has to be managed to live up to the expectations of the pension-fund managers."[56] Accordingly, another important change in the environment external to firms is serving to reinforce the short-term orientation that current personnel rotation policies have promoted. The implications for appropriate R&D, innovation, and successful strategic decision making are all decidedly negative. The same is true for international performance. As one foreign observer has noted, "Success in trade is the result of patient and meticulous preparations, with a long period of market preparation before the rewards are available. . . . To undertake such commitments is hardly in the interest of a manager who is concerned with his or her next quarterly earning reports."[57]

This issue of management focus, capabilities, and resulting performance is far from settled, however, despite the negative factors just discussed. American management does have success stories and there are firms that have not succumbed to the new trends. Robert Lipsey and Irving Kravis, for example, have pointed out that it is important to distinguish between the competitiveness of U.S. firms per se versus competitiveness of firms operating in the geographic confines of the United States. A declining share of world exports emanating from the United States suggests decreasing country competitiveness. However, the proportion of world exports attributable to U.S. companies (including foreign affiliates) reflects corporate competitiveness, which in turn derives from their specific managerial and technological capabilities and performance. U.S. multinationals have performed quite well. While U.S. comparative advantages have clearly shifted, "the comparative advantage of U.S. multinational firms hardly changed at all between 1966 and 1977."[58] This suggests that

the decline in U.S. shares in world manufactures in the late 1960s and 1970s was not, as sometimes alleged, to be found in deficiencies in American management or declines in American technological leadership. The share of exports produced under U.S. management—that is, by U.S. multinational firms operating at home and abroad—actually increased. The decline in the U.S. share, it may be inferred, reflects a relative diminution in the advantages of the U.S. as a production location.[59]

In summary, while there are some glaring weaknesses and inefficiencies in U.S. corporate managerial structures, there have been some solid performances as well.

INTERNATIONAL COMPETITIVENESS

Yet another parameter of industrial results is international performance. As explained earlier, U.S. industries dominated world production and export in the first decades following World War II. However, as the major industrial nations recovered and reentered world markets, U.S. shares declined. The growth of the newly industrialized countries, with their associated export efforts, has served to accelerate this reduction.

Inasmuch as trade tends to be based on comparative advantage, shifting trade patterns—particularly over prolonged time periods—reflect dynamic movements in relative national advantages. Transportation and communications advances have stepped up the globalization process. Since major foreign competitors have generally grown more rapidly and had higher ratios of investment to GNP, the U.S. portion of global capital stock has fallen substantially. However, "the U.S. share of skilled labor has decreased relatively little, and its share of global arable land has actually increased."[60] Accordingly, capital-based exporting should be increasingly difficult, while a growing specialization in products with a highly skilled labor content should become more dominant in the U.S. export picture. Indeed, this has exactly been the case. The range of U.S. exports has increasingly narrowed and become more specialized over the past 15 years, with concentrations in capital goods, military items, chemicals, agricultural products, and services. Further, an increased emphasis on high technology outputs—to include computers, aerospace, office equipment, communication equipment, engines, and turbines—is evident in U.S. export performance.

As noted in chapter 6, there are many factors (productivity, relative price level changes, quality, exchange rates, GNP growth rates, trade policies, and agreements) that affect import and export volumes. Due to dollar depreciation, compared to 1970 the "relative export prices for American manufactured items were 13.5 percent lower in 1980,"[61] with the associated volumes of U.S. manufactured exports increasing almost 30 percent more rapidly than the corresponding volume of imports. Relative prices and economic conditions changed, however, and beginning in 1982 imports began to soar while export volumes remained relatively flat, thus creating a negative trade balance in manufactured items. This deterioration was distributed widely. The "balance worsened between 1980 and 1984 in every major commodity category except military-type and other goods,"[62] with the most significant deteriorations occurring in capital goods, consumer items, and automotive vehicles, parts, and engines. Yet, as chapter 6 indicated, negative trade-balances do not necessarily imply poor operating performance or the need for major changes. There may well be a need, but trade balance figures will not demonstrate it either way.

In recent years, however, our strong high technology performers have also experienced deteriorating trade balance positions, giving cause for concern even to the optimists. When the high technology trade balance, which enjoyed a $26.6 billion surplus in 1980, fell to a $2.6 billion deficit in 1986, concern switched to alarm, an alarm not assuaged by a 1987 return to surplus of a meager $591 million. Yet other, less publicized, indicators cast a different perspective.

The U.S. share of world high technology exports has been remarkably stable, with 1984 only marginally below the corresponding 1965 figure. Looking specifically at product categories, the 1980 share fell some 10 points in aircraft and parts, but still held 50 percent of the world market, exactly equal to the 1965 figure. Office computing equipment, engines and turbines, plastics, and synthetics all had about the same 1980 share as in 1970. Agricultural chemicals were the one exception to stability, evidencing continuous and sizable growth in market share.[63] In terms of trade balances, however, the surplus in high technology has all but disappeared. Although exports have evidenced steady growth, a continuing surge of imports—reflecting U.S. economic growth and industrial restructuring—brought negative net numbers to this balance by 1986. But was this really true? Are we really "unfavorable" even in our strength?

In January 1989 four Department of Commerce economists completed a study of the high technology trade balance, with some interesting conclusions. They found that the official data, "although technically correct, do not provide an accurate picture of international trade in high or advanced technology products because of the level of aggregation used in their construction."[64] Because the Department of Commerce classifies each product in a high technology category as high tech, it includes "many products which would not individually be considered high tech. . . ."[65] As the product life cycle predicts, new products eventually become standardized. They become "old hat" and other nations develop comparative advantages in their production. Yet these items are still included in official high technology balance calculations. Developing a much more realistic basket of advanced technology products, the authors found that the high technology trade balance did indeed decline over the 1982–87 period, but by far less than the official figures. Whereas published Department of Commerce data recorded a deficit for 1986, more refined calculations produce a positive balance of $15.6 billion (in 1982 it was $24.5 billion); and in 1987 it rose to $19.4 billion. The Bureau of the Census also tracks high technology trade, and these findings are even more positive. In 1986 the advanced technology balance exceeded $16 billion; in 1987 it increased to just over $20 billion, and in 1988 it rose to $28 billion.[66] These studies indicate that the United States continues to be a vigorous international competitor, that our high technology sectors are indeed healthy and competitive. For example, in the still globally small, but growing, supercomputer market, the United States has an 80 percent world share.

Here again, then, the picture is not bleak, but positive. Yet conscious efforts, both on the part of U.S. policy makers and the corporate sector, will have to be undertaken to insure our continued international competitiveness. In particular, flexibility and a willingness to stay on the technological frontier, even as the half-life of knowledge declines, is required. A willingness to seriously tackle export markets and stay for the long-term is yet another pressing mandate.

For example, it appears that recently short-run business considerations have again contributed to lost market share. Foreigners have been more responsive to exchange rates than their U.S. counterparts. "Most U.S. exporters appear to have made relatively small adjustments to profit margins . . . . evidence indicates that some U.S. exporters in fact increased profit margins even as the dollar appreciated."[67] Accordingly, at a time when a rising dollar was already making U.S. products more expensive, U.S. exporters attempted to raise profit margins, virtually assuring a loss in market share. Foreigners, on the other hand, have evidenced a much greater willingness to be flexible in order to maintain their foothold in the U.S. market.

CHANGING STRUCTURE—DEINDUSTRIALIZATION?

It is generally believed that the United States has shifted gradually from a manufacturing economy to a service one. Today the service sector accounts for better than 70 percent of GNP and 7 of every ten nonfarm jobs. This sector covers a wide range of activities: accounting, advertising, architecture, engineering design, consulting, communications, education, finance, government, health care, information handling, insurance, legal, shipping, tourism, transportation, utilities, and so on. In 1982 manufacturing employed under 20 percent of all civilian workers, while the entire goods-producing sector employed only 29 percent. On this basis—share of employment—the United States is clearly and increasingly a service economy. However, it has been such an economy since shortly after World War II.

It is also widely perceived that manufacturing is in a state of decline, that a deindustrialization is taking place. Further, the argument holds that this decline is in large measure driven by international competition, a point already addressed in chapter 6. Such generalizations, however, are erroneous and misleading. Further, they are likely to engender ill-advised public policies.

To understand the role of trade in the structure of contemporary U.S. industry, is it necessary to view basic factors and trends. First, it must be recognized that manufactured products as a share of consumer spending have been undergoing a secular decline, mainly as a result of rising income—a pattern not unlike the position of agriculture. Second, the declining portion of employment in manufacturing in part reflects the considerably more rapid productivity growth of the manufacturing sector since the mid-1970s. Third, because the demand for manufactured products is very sensitive to the growth rate of overall GNP, manufacturing output was disproportionately affected by the relatively slow real economic growth since the first oil shock. Fourth, changes in U.S. comparative advantage have brought new patterns of manufacturing employment and product emphasis. Finally, cyclical factors and exchange rates, both short-run in nature, have meaningfully affected this sector.

High technology orientations have already been mentioned in the previous discussion of international competition. The data clearly show this new emphasis in the changing structure of the manufacturing sector. Whereas in 1960 high technology accounted for only 27 percent of manufacturing value-added, the figure steadily increased, reaching 38 percent in 1980. On the other hand, the share of capital-intensive value-added fell from 32 to 27 percent. The resource-intensive share declined from 23 to 20 percent, while the labor-intensive share was constant. From 1970 to 1980 total manufactured goods value-added rose by 33.1 percent, but high technology value-added grew a very significant 61.0 percent. Reflecting this increasing emphasis, high technology employment rose 16 percent.

Domestic demand was weak in old-line industries like tobacco, wood containers, iron and steel, leather goods, but rose substantially in the high tech area. For example, during the 1970s demand increased over 200 percent for electronic components and for office, computing, and accounting machines. For optical equipment, the figure was 123 percent; for plastics, it was 90 percent.[68] Clearly a significant restructuring within the manufacturing sector has been in progress, one described by the Bank of Japan as "progressing in an unprecedentedly wide scale,"[69] with favorable accomplishments. It should be stressed that this metamorphosis derives overwhelmingly from economic and technological forces operating within the domestic U.S. economy rather than external to it. Where foreign trade has had an influence, it rather consistently reinforced trends that were domestically driven. Norman Fieleke, for example, found trade deterioration widespread throughout U.S. industry from 1980 to 1984. Nevertheless, he concluded that "neither the detailed industry data nor the aggregative data indicate that U.S. producers have suffered greatly from the increased trade deficit."[70] A few, of course, were seriously harmed, but most were only marginally affected. He concludes that the "deindustrialization of American industry by foreign competition is more nearly a matter of myth than of substance."[71] Robert Lawrence reaches a similar conclusion:

The United States did not experience absolute deindustrialization in the 1970s. U.S. employment in manufacturing expanded, and given the growth rate of output, investment growth in manufacturing was remarkably rapid. In contrast to its decline from 1960 to 1973, the share of manufacturing in total U.S. fixed business capital actually increased from 1973–1980.[72]

Trade, however, has become of greater importance than ever before, and this too represents another change. "About one of every five dollars of U.S. manufacturing output is shipped abroad."[73] Accordingly, while trade is hardly dominant, it is an increasingly significant influence. Further, the degree of integration of the U.S. industrial sector with overseas economies is clearly indicated by the fact that in 1984 "one-third of the total manufactures export growth consisted of increases in exports of parts for assembly abroad, much of which subsequently returns to the United States in the form of imports of assembled goods."[74] Globalization is clearly upon us.

Interestingly, another structural change is the evolution of the manufacturing sector in a more competitive direction. Whereas in 1958 the share of manufacturing output originating in the competitive arena was 56 percent, by 1980 this figure had increased to 69 percent.[75] The influence of antitrust, imports, and, later, deregulation have been important factors in this shift. Within the manufacturing sector, almost 50 four-digit industries moved to a more competitive status, while few made a reverse shift. Accordingly, even in 1980 William Shepherd could write that the "United States economy now appears to be far more competitive than at any time during the modern industrial period."[76] In the past decade, the U.S. economy became even more competitive, thanks to deregulation, globalization, and other domestic changes. Included in the latter is the significant growth of small manufacturers. For example, over the 1976–84 period, "measured by changes in the number of jobs, firms, establishments, and sales, small businesses expanded relative to large manufacturing firms."[77] To what can this be attributed? "New information-based technologies . . . are especially beneficial to small manufacturers because they lower entry costs, reduce the minimum efficient size of production runs, and lower setup costs."[78] The changing relative prices of labor and capital have also promoted small business growth, as has the proliferation of independent business services companies. In an age in which there are increasing demands for flexibility, speed of reaction, and market-niche development and specialization, the growth of small business in general, and small manufacturing in particular, is most welcome and positive.

While the share of total employment in manufacturing has clearly and steadily declined, the absolute numbers have varied. Employment rose in the 1970s, reaching a peak in 1980 and then declining as a result of serious recession. But the decline has reversed. Net employment growth over 1976–84 was due to small manufacturers, who added 1.2 million new jobs while the big manufacturing firms lost 300,000.[79] Given the brisk pace of productivity gains in manufacturing and the industrial restructuring that has occurred, substantial employment growth is not to be expected. Nonetheless, 1988 ended with 19.4 million people employed in manufacturing, the highest number since 1981, and by mid-1989 the figure was up to 19.7 million.

How does our manufacturing performance compare internationally? Surely our national security partners and economic competitors have experienced some of the same employment and income trends. The answer is affirmative—services are increasingly being demanded in both Europe and Japan, while manufacturing employment as a share of total jobs has decreased. However, if one compares U.S. manufacturing output as a share of the major industrialized countries' manufacturing total, the results are clear and perhaps surprising. U.S. manufacturing held a 31.7 percent share in 1980. By 1985, despite the strong dollar, it had risen to roughly 33.5 percent, and in 1986 and 1987 it reached 34 percent.[80] It would seem that Patrick Henry's famous statement should be paraphrased: If this be deindustrialization, let us make the most of it!

Another measure of trends in the manufacturing sector is the size of the real net capital stock. Except for a leveling in 1982–83, the real net capital stock has been growing continuously. The 1987 data show U.S. real fixed private capital at $11.9 trillion (1982 dollars). The manufacturing capital stock was at its highest ($1.43 trillion), with both durables and nondurables showing steady growth in the 1980s.[81] "Indeed, the level of U.S. real manufacturing investment to real manufacturing sales increased substantially . . . from its average level during the 1970s."[82] Perhaps even more impressive is the increase in the U.S. real manufacturing investment relative to manufacturing employees, which since 1982 has been well above both Japan and Germany. "Although the U.S. ratio reflects to some extent the greater need to replace an older capital stock than is the case in Japan and Germany, replacing equipment still leads to an increasing spread of new technology."[83]

Finally, manufacturing's share of the real GNP evidences no secular decline. Indeed, "real manufactures has been remarkably, stable at roughly 21 percent of GNP over the past thirty years. . . ."[84] Clearly, in its economic evolution the U.S. economy earlier shifted from the agricultural era to the age of manufacturing (smokestack industries). It is now witnessing a transformation within its manufacturing sector and a further tilting toward services. Except in terms of employment proportions, however, the service sector has not expanded at the expense of manufacturing. It is probable that U.S. manufacturing may take a path similar to that of agriculture. Utilizing relatively fewer inputs, it may nonetheless increase productivity substantially and maintain international competitiveness. Indeed, "U.S. goods-producing industries have borne up well under the onslaught of foreign competition."[85] However, manufacturing's continued viability will require substantial creativity in managerial and organization arrangements. These are already under way but remain an ongoing challenge.

Accordingly, the "deindustrialization" image has scant empirical support and seems to result from generalizations based on one or two highly visible, yet atypical industries. It is the frictions associated with change rather than the new realities that seem to have grabbed center stage. Further, while foreign competition has made its presence felt, domestic factors have been the overwhelmingly dominant influence on the progress and nature of the industrial system. In short, the U.S. industrial sector retains continuing and substantial importance as well as enormous potential. It is dynamic, becoming more competitive, and undergoing an appropriate metamorphosis. To achieve its potential, however, it must be properly managed. It also needs to operate in an economic environment and under economic policies that are supportive of growth, efficiency, and dynamism.

DEFENSE PRODUCTION CAPABILITIES

While the economic health of U.S. manufacturing is strong, from a national security perspective the picture is less sanguine. There are major vulnerabilities and disconcerting problem areas. Some 215 industrial sectors, primarily in manufacturing, account for 95 percent of DOD purchases. But the base has been shrinking as suppliers either close or opt to leave defense business for more desirable civilian activities. The thaw in U.S.-Soviet relations begun in late 1989 will only accelerate this trend. Yet defense industrial capabilities are important. The potential to mobilize defense production is itself a meaningful deterrent to foreign aggression. If deterrence fails, wartime production is critical to saving lives and bringing a conflict to an expeditious and acceptable conclusion. Defense production capabilities are also essential for assisting allies, a point made famous by the Lend-Lease program (almost $20 billion from 1941 to 1945), but certainly important in more recent supplies to Israel, Korea, and the United Kingdom. It is appropriate to begin a brief assessment by asking what the United States wants from its defense industrial base. Essentially, the major tasks are quality production at reasonable cost, technological sophistication, assuredness of production, and the ability to surge needed outputs and mobilize the economy.

Because the defense industrial base is an integral part of the entire industrial structure of the United States and indeed cannot be separated because it is so interwoven, it reflects the same trends and forces that have been described throughout this book. Quality standards have been a problem and it is clear that real levels of Defense Department procurement have been reduced due to quality degradation. Putting a dollar figure on the costs of quality failure is very difficult and any such estimates must be recognized for having a wide margin of error. Nonetheless, some ballpark figures can at least demonstrate the seriousness of potential problems in this arena. In May 1982 Senator John Warner stated that roughly $13.5 billion was being spent to correct defects or retool poorly manufactured defense inventories.[86] In June 1983 a DOD deputy-secretary suggested that quality failures were costing perhaps as much as $28 billion annually, while later that month a rear admiral noted that the cost of some weapon systems could be cut by 50 percent if contractors produced the end item properly the first time.[87] Quality problems have caused enormous paperwork commitments as well, with several hundred thousand material review actions each year. Finally, but hardly of minor importance, these peacetime costs may pale in significance compared to the possible or actual loss of lives that occur either in combat or during exercises if the appropriate systems do not function as expected.

On the more positive side, the Department of Defense has undertaken significant actions in conjunction with defense contractors to minimize quality problems. Further, the general recognition of the importance of quality and how to address it—in large measure forced upon us by foreign, particularly Japanese, competition—has indeed permeated the U.S. industrial base as well.

Defense equipment is extremely expensive. For such high-cost items, it is very important to have cost-effective production. To the degree that productivity problems have affected the base, this has tended to raise costs. Government procurement in uneconomical production runs has also led to output levels far lower than optimum, again raising unit costs. Monitoring activities have also proved quite expensive; both the government and contractors have committed very significant quantities of resources to monitoring functions, in part reflecting what has been called the adversarial relationship between defense contractors and the Department of Defense. Accordingly, there are numerous production inspections and mandated approvals, which cause delays and require industry to commit a commensurate volume of resources to respond and deal with government monitoring. While some monitoring is undoubtedly necessary, it appears clear that current costs are too high and much efficiency is lost. The layers of "fat" discussed earlier are clearly to be found on both sides of the defense acquisition process. Finally, the uncertain nature of defense orders also imposes costs on contractors. While many endeavors have been undertaken and are ongoing to minimize such costs (such as multiyear procurement[88]), there is still much to be done.

Technological sophistication is also critical. Inasmuch as the United States has not chosen to match the Warsaw Pact tank-for-tank or soldier-for-soldier, it has opted for superior weapons and more qualified personnel to offset numerical inferiority and geographic distance. Accordingly, the economy in general and the defense base in particular must have both the technical and the production capability to be at the technological edge. As mentioned in chapter 4, U.S. technical capabilities are unrivaled; however, our ability to get new technologies into the field, as in the civilian sector, has been far less than desired. Indeed, it generally takes more than a decade from concept development to initial fielding for most sophisticated defense systems. Since quantitative inferiority requires qualitative superiority, it is critical that we not only stay on the leading technological edge, but that we be able to field the appropriate systems before they become dated.

Assuredness of production is also important. This means that we must be able to rely upon the U.S. base to deliver the required systems, munitions, and spares on time and for a sustainable period, if necessary. To the extent that weapon systems today depend on offshore procurements—mineral resources, components, and such, there is always the possibility that the sea lines of communications could be cut or that supplying nations may decide to maintain a judicious neutrality until the war is over. Offshore dependencies are numerous and growing. Submarine manufacturing, for example, requires bearings made in Sweden. Vast quantities of imported semiconductors permeate many military systems, and a very substantial proportion of the 40 minerals most essential in U.S. production processes come from overseas sources. Indeed, the true magnitude of this offshore dependence is not fully known, and it is only recently that attempts have been undertaken to assess its extent and the vulnerabilities involved.

Additionally, many individual foundries, forgings, and other relatively small, but critical, production facilities have closed their doors, thus creating dependencies on small sole-source suppliers who have little or no capability to increase production rapidly in a crisis. This point was made all too vividly after the October 1973 Israeli war when the United States attempted to surge tank production in order to replace gaps caused by shipments to the Israelis. It was a full five years before such shortfalls could be filled. Reliance upon many sole-source procurements is likely to produce major bottlenecks in the event of a significant mobilization. Further, sole-source procurement is always questionable, not only because it puts the government in an unfavorable price/cost bargaining posture, but because strikes, accidents, or sabotage can halt production of items critically needed elsewhere. Interestingly, offshore procurements have on several occasions allowed prime contractors to continue production when a sole-source domestic supplier experienced a strike or other output disruption. In wartime, however, such overseas procurements may not be possible. Increasingly, lead times both reflect degradation of critical areas of the defense base and give indications of potential mobilization problems. In 1988, for example, there was a 27-month lead time for aircraft auxiliary power units and radars, a 24-month lead time for engine fuel controls and avionics, and a 28-month waiting period for landing gear.[89]

Finally, the economy must be able to mobilize; defense industries need the capability to surge production. This in turn suggests a need for excess capacity in order to be able to increase defense output rapidly. Yet maintenance of such capacity would raise peacetime procurement costs, thus reducing the real volume of defense acquisitions. If the nation wants this capability, it must be willing to pay for it.

Further, having sufficient inventories is another ingredient necessary for surge and mobilization, yet just-in-time and related inventory management schemes, while appropriate in peacetime, are serving as "destockpiling" endeavors. It is generally accepted today that it would take about 18 months to launch a major and effective mobilization. Will ambiguous warning provide the correct signals? Will it allow sufficient time for us to act? Will we be willing to undertake the difficult political choices?

Further complicating the defense situation is the dichotomy of optimality conditions between peacetime and wartime production. Peacetime procurement is least expensive when inventories are kept low, production is high enough to allow operations on the low point of the average total cost curve, and supplies come from the cheapest possible sources, domestic or foreign. To surge for wartime production, however, low inventories and overseas supplies become obstacles to be surmounted. High rates of peacetime production that leave only small portions of unused plant capacity do not allow meaningful expansibility for wartime surge. Clearly, then, there are some important and difficult trade-offs. Such challenges can of course be addressed, but they require a financial commitment. Defense producers will maintain and stockpile adequate inventories if they are paid to do so, but they cannot undertake such costs without remuneration.

Economic progress and strength, then, are clearly important elements of national power. However, such gains neither guarantee industrial mobilization capabilities nor necessarily reduce the difficulties of surge and mobilization demands. Defense industrial planning, coupled with adequate industrial capabilities assessments, are absolutely vital.

This chapter has demonstrated that far from being anemic, the U.S. manufacturing sector is doing quite well, both compared to its own past record and compared to its international competitors. Investment and productivity have been healthy and organizational and industrial restructuring are appropriately proceeding. The move is definitely in a high technology direction and contrary to popular belief, U.S. high technology products are indeed very internationally competitive. Finally, just as the Soviet Union can have an inefficient and antiquated economy, yet be capable of impressive defense production, so too a first class and vigorous "butter" goods economy can have serious problems in its defense output capabilities. What is required for success in the latter is appropriate planning and a sufficient commitment of funds to insure that the plans can be implemented.

NOTES

1. Edwin Mansfield, *Economics*, 4th ed. (New York: W. W. Norton, 1983), p. 788.

2. Harvey Brooks and Bruce R. Guile, "Overview," in Bruce R. Guile and Harvey Brooks, ed., *Technology and Global Industry* (Washington, D.C.: National Academy Press, 1987), p. 7.

3. Gunnar Eliasson, "International Competition, Productivity Change and the Organization of Production," in H. W. de Jong and W. G. Shepherd, ed., *Mainstreams in Industrial Organization—Book I* (Boston: Kluwer Academic Publishers, 1986) p. 140.

4. *NBER Digest*, June 1989, p. 1. See Frank Lichtenberg and Donald Siegel, "The Effect of Takeovers on the Employment and Wages of Central-Office and Other Personnel," National Bureau of Economic Research Working Paper No. 2895.

5. Daniel S. Hamermesh, quoted in the *Wall Street Journal*, June 13, 1989, p. A20. See Daniel S. Hamermesh, National Bureau of Economic Research Working Paper No. 3800, December 1988.

6. Hamermesh, *Wall Street Journal*.

7. See Beth V. Yarbrough and Robert M. Yarbrough, "The Transactional Structure of the Firm: A Comparative Survey," *Journal of Economic Behavior and Organization*, July 1988, particularly pp. 23–24.

8. *NBER Digest*, p. 1.

9. Yarbrough and Yarbrough, p. 24.

10. Robert J. Esther, "Health-Care Costs for Businesses Soared," *Wall Street Journal*, May 24, 1989, p. A2.

11. Amanda Bennett, "Firms Stunned by Retiree Health Costs," *Wall Street Journal*, May 29, 1988, p. 41.

12. See Amy Dockser, "Companies Rein in Outside Legal Bills," *Wall Street Journal*, November 9, 1988, p. B1.

13. Data obtained taken from U.S. Department of Commerce, Bureau of Economic Analysis Statistical Indicators Division, July 15, 1989.

14. Opinion Research Corporation, "Public Attitude Toward Corporate Profits," *Public Opinion Index* (Princeton, N.J.: Opinion Research Corporation, August 1983).

15. George A. Kahn, "Investment in Recession and Recovery: Lessons from the 1980's," *Economic Review*, Federal Reserve Bank of Kansas City, November 1985.

16. Ibid., p. 30.

17. Robert T. Clair, "The Labor Intensive Nature of Manufacturing High-Technology Capital Goods," *Economic Review*, Federal Reserve Bank of Dallas, March 1986.

18. William G. Shepherd, *The Economics of Industrial Organization* (Englewood Cliffs, N.J.: Prentice-Hall, 1979), p. 262.

19. Ibid., p. 270.

20. Henry Ogden Armour and David J. Teece, "Organizational Structure and Economic Performance," in Jay B. Barney and William G. Ouchi, ed., *Organizational Economics* (San Francisco: Jossey-Bass, 1986), p. 200.

21. Ibid.

22. See Robert Dorfman and Peter O. Steiner, "Optimal Advertising and Optimal Quality," *American Economic Review*, December 1954.

23. See William S. Comenor and Thomas A. Wilson, "Advertising, Market Structure and Performance," *Review of Economics and Statistics*, November 1967; and Leonard W. Weis, "Advertising, Profits and Corporate Taxes," *Review of Economics and Statistics*, November 1969. For more recent discussion, see Douglas F. Greer, *Industrial Organization and Public Policy* (New York: Macmillan, 1980), p. 456.

24. U.S. Department of Commerce, *Statistical Abstract of the United States, 1989* (Washington, D.C.: U.S. Government Printing Office, 1989), p. 551.

25. Robert B. Ekelund, Jr. and David S. Saurman, *Advertising and the Market Process: A Modern Economic View* (San Francisco: Pacific Research Institute for Public Policy, 1988).

26. Shepherd, p. 383.

27. See Micha Gisser, "Price Leadership and Welfare Losses in U.S. Manufacturing," *American Economic Review*, September 1986, pp. 756–67, and his "Price Leadership Reply," *American Economic Review*, June 1989, pp. 610–13.

28. See Harvey Leibenstein, "Allocative Efficiency vs. X-Efficiency," *American Economic Review*, June 1966; and his *Beyond Economic Man: A New Foundation for Microeconomics* (Cambridge, Mass.: Harvard University Press, 1976).

29. Shepherd, pp. 379–80.

30. John Kenneth Galbraith, *American Capitalism* (Boston: Houghton Mifflin, 1956), p. 86.

31. See Greer, chapter 23.

32. F. M. Scherer, *Industrial Market Structure and Economic Performance*, 2nd ed., (Chicago: Rand McNally, 1980), p. 422.

33. See Edwin Mansfield and others, "Foreign Trade and U.S. Research and Development," *Review of Economics and Statistics*, February 1979.

34. Harvey Brooks, "Technology and Competitiveness," in Bruce R. Scott and George C. Lodge, eds., *U.S. Competitiveness in the World Economy* (Boston: Harvard Business School Press, 1985), p. 345.

35. Martin Neil Bailey and Alok K. Chakrabarti, "Innovation and U.S. Competitiveness," *The Brookings Review*, Fall 1985, p. 14.

36. Ibid.

37. Brooks, "Technology and Competitiveness," p. 355.

38. Edwin Mansfield, "Innovation, Investment, and Productivity," *The Wharton Magazine*, Summer 1981, p. 41.

39. See Donald L. Losman, "A Deflation in Quality," *Across the Board*, July 1980.

40. John Hillkirk, "Tug-of-awards over Top Quality," *USA Today*, March 24, 1988, p. 8B.

41. David A. Garvin, "Quality on the Line," *Harvard Business Review*, September–October 1983, pp. 65–75.

42. Peter G. Peterson, "The U.S. Competitive Position in the 1980s—and Some Things We Might Do About It," speech to the Center for International Business, March 1981.

43. Hajime Karatsu, "The Deindustrialization of America," *KKC Brief*, Keizai Koho Center, No. 31, October 1985.

44. James E. Olson, "The United States and Japan," *Speaking of Japan*, Keizai Koho Center, September 1988, p. 23.

45. Susan Hickok, Linda Bell, and Janet Ceglowski, "The Competitiveness of U.S. Manufactured Goods: Recent Changes and Prospects," *Quarterly Review*, Federal Reserve Bank of New York, Spring 1988, p. 12.

46. Ibid.

47. Ibid.

48. See Michael Totty, "Questionable Deals . . . ," *Wall Street Journal*, January 17, 1989, p. 1.

49. John R. Deckop, "Determinants of Chief Executive Officer Compensation," *Industrial and Labor Relations Review*, January 1988. See also Amanda Bennett, "A Great Leap Forward for Executive Pay," *Wall Street Journal*, April 24, 1989, p. B1 for data on the substantial CEO pay raises of 1988.

50. Quoted in Robert H. Hayes and William J. Abernathy, "Managing Our Way to Economic Decline," *Harvard Business Review*, July–August 1980, p. 74.

51. "Private Study Finds Executive Management Out of Touch with Advanced Technology," *Aviation Week and Space Technology*, April 11, 1989, p. 147.

52. Selwyn Feinstein, "Labor Notes," *Wall Street Journal*, June 6, 1989, p. 1.

53. Hayes and Abernathy, p. 75.

54. Karatsu, p. 3.

55. Peter F. Drucker, "A Crisis of Capitalism," *Wall Street Journal*, September 30, 1986, p. 32.

56. Ibid.

57. Ryohei Suzuki, "Worldwide Expansion of U.S. Exports—A Japanese View," *Sloan Management Review*, Spring 1979, p. 1.

58. Robert E. Lipsey and Irving B. Kravis, "The Competitive Position of U.S. Manufacturing Firms," *Banca Nazionale del Lavoro Quarterly*, June 1985, p. 144.

59. Ibid.

60. Robert Lawrence, "Is Trade De-industrializing America?" *Brookings Papers on Economic Activity*, Vol. 1, 1983, p. 145.

61. Ibid., p. 131.

62. Norman S. Fieleke, "The Foreign Trade Deficit and American Industry," *New England Economic Review*, July/August 1985, p. 45.

63. Department of Commerce, International Trade Administration, *United States Trade Performance in 1984 and Outlook* (Washington, D.C.: U.S. Government Printing Office, June 1985), p. 4–5.

64. Thomas Abbott et al., "Measuring the Trade Balance in Advanced Technology Products," Department of Commerce, Center for Economic Studies Discussion Paper, CES 89-1, January 1989, p. 1.

65. Ibid., p. 2.

66. Data given in July 18, 1989, letter from Foreign Trade Division, Bureau of the Census.

67. Catherine L. Mann, "Prices, Profit Margins, and Exchange Rates," *Federal Reserve Bulletin*, June 1986; and Jack L. Henry, "Dollar Helps Those Who Help Themselves," *Chicago Fed Letter*, Federal Reserve Bank of Chicago, March 1988.

68. Data taken from Lawrence, pp. 140–145.

69. Bank of Japan, Research and Statistics Department, *U.S. Competitiveness in Manufacturing*, special paper no. 153, September 1987, p. 20.

70. Fieleke, p. 52.

71. Ibid.

72. Lawrence, p. 156.

73. Department of Commerce, *United States Trade Performance*, p. 3.

74. Ibid.

75. William G. Shepherd, "Causes of Increased Competition in the U.S. Economy, 1939–80," *Review of Economics of Statistics*, September 1982, pp. 613–27.

76. Ibid., p. 613.

77. Edward Starr, "The Growth of Small Manufacturers: 1976–1984," *Business Economics*, April 1988, p. 41.

78. Ibid., pp. 42–43.

79. Ibid., p. 41.

80. John A. Tatom, "The Link Between the Value of the Dollar, U.S. Trade and Manufacturing Output: Some Recent Evidence," *Review*, Federal Reserve Bank of St. Louis, November/December 1988, p. 31.

81. John C. Musgrave, "Fixed Reproducible Tangible Wealth, 1984–1987," *Survey of Current Business*, August 1987, p. 85.

82. Hickok, Bell, and Ceglowski, p. 14.

83. Ibid.

84. Reuven Glick and Michael Hutchison, "The Dollar and Manufacturing Output," *Weekly Letter*, Federal Reserve Bank of San Francisco, August 26, 1988, p. 2.

85. Fieleke, p. 52.

86. John Warner, Bottom Line Conference, Ft. L. J. McNair, May 1982.

87. "Less Bang for the Buck," *Hartford Courant*, June 28, 1983.

88. Currently, only about 7 percent of the defense budget is legally commited longer than one year, although operationally the figure is much higher.

89. Air Force Association and USNI Military Database, *Lifeline in Danger* (Arlington, Va.: Aerospace Education Foundation, September 1988), p. 3.

PART II

8

Steel: International Position and Mobilization Capabilities

David G. Tarr

In the past 30 years there has been a dramatic shift in the pattern of steel production, exports, and imports around the world. The basic trends are summarized in Table 8.1. In 1950 the United States produced almost half of the world's steel; by 1984, it produced less than 12 percent of it. The United States became a net importer of steel in 1959, and has imported over 20 percent of its steel throughout most of the 1980s. The European Community tripled its steel production between 1950 and 1970. Its output now has been reduced from the peak of the early 1970s, but the European Community remains a net exporter of steel products. Japan, however, emerged as a major player in the international steel market during the 1960s and early 1970s with an increase in production of over 100 million tons between 1960 and 1973 (the peak year for Japanese production). In fact, Japan's increased production capability is underestimated by the production figures, because Japan is estimated to be operating at only about 65 percent of capacity in the last decade.[1] As will be shown, in the last 10 to 15 years some developing nations, especially Brazil and Korea, have also emerged to become important players in the international steel market.

The years since 1974 have been especially difficult ones for the steel industry in the United States. Production has dropped by more than one-third and employment has fallen by even more. Except for the most recent years there have been either large losses or small profits in the 1980s. Crude steel production fell from 145 million tons in 1974 to 74.6 million tons in 1982. By 1988 it had rebounded to almost 100 million tons, but still only 69 percent of 15 years earlier. Imports as a share of U.S. consumption doubled over this same period, reaching a high of 26.4 percent in 1984. Over the 1979–86 period shipments of steel mill products dropped 30 percent. Table 8.1 summarizes these data and other key indicators of industry health.

Table 8.1
U.S. Steel Industry Statistical Highlights, 1974-88: Production, Capacity, Imports, Employment, and Profits

Year	Crude steel production*	Capacity* (crude steel)	Shipments of Steel Mill Products*	Imports*	Imports as a % of apparent consumption	Employment (thousands of workers)	Net income** Amount (millions of U.S. dollars)	Percentage of sales
1988	99,924	112,000	83,840	20,891	20.3	169	-559***	-1.7***
1987	89,151	112,200	76,654	20,414	21.3	163	1,017	3.8
1986	81,606	127,000	70,263	20,692	23.0	175	-4,150	-16.7
1985	88,259	133,600	73,043	24,256	25.2	208	-1,834	-6.5
1984	92,528	135,300	73,739	26,163	26.4	236	-31	-0.1
1983	84,615	150,600	67,584	17,070	20.5	243	-2,231	-9.1
1982	74,577	154,000	61,567	16,663	21.8	289	-3,384	-12.0
1981	120,828	154,300	88,450	19,898	18.9	391	1,653	3.8
1980	111,835	153,700	82,853	15,495	16.3	399	681	1.8
1979	136,341	155,300	100,262	17,518	15.2	453	806	2.0
1978	137,031	157,900	97,935	21,153	18.1	449	1,277	2.6
1977	125,333	160,000	91,147	19,307	17.8	452	22	0.1
1976	128,000	158,300	89,447	14,285	14.1	454	1,377	3.7
1975	116,642	153,100	79,957	12,012	13.5	457	1,595	4.8
1974	145,720	----	109,472	15,970	13.4	512	2,475	6.6

* In thousands of net tons.

** Total corporation, 1974-78; steel segment only from 1979 forward.

*** 1988 sales increased 30 percent, but special charges of 2.9 billion were taken. Without such charges profits would have been the highest since 1974.

Source: American Iron and Steel Institute, *Annual Statistical Report*, 1980, 1984, and 1987.

The U.S. government has reacted by applying restraints on imports. How well are these policy measures suited to meet the problems with which the industry must deal and how might these policies be best modified? This chapter addresses such questions and examines the fundamental causes of the decline in the U.S. steel industry. Finally, the adequacy of steel supplies for national defense is addressed and evaluated.

THE CAUSES OF THE CRISIS

Decline in Demand

In the past 15 years, growth in overall demand for steel has been extremely sluggish; it can essentially be characterized as a period of zero growth. In 1973–74 steel production peaked in the noncentrally planned economies at about 519 million metric tons. After a recession in 1975, steel demand began to recover, until in 1979–80 it approximated its 1973 level. Since 1980, however, steel production has remained at or below 500 million metric tons in the noncentrally planned economies; 1982 and 1983 were especially disastrous.

The years 1973–74 were very optimistic ones for the future of the world steel industry. Most forecasters of steel demand predicted significant growth in demand over the 1975–85 period.[2] As a result, a number of nations undertook major greenfield expansion projects for their steel industries.[3] The optimism of 1974 turned to pessimism by the early 1980s, as many companies, especially those in the United States and European Community (EC) experienced significant losses.

The overall trends mask an even more ominous trend as far as the United States, European Community, and other industrialized countries are concerned. From 1973 to 1984, there was a significant decline in steel consumption in the industrialized countries, from 416 to 322 million metric tons, while consumption in the developing countries increased by a total of 81 percent, from 100 to 181 million metric tons. Over this period demand fell by 36 million tons in the United States to 113 million tons and by 33 million tons in the European Community to 95 million tons. Thus while steel demand in the developing world has been increasing, the opposite trend is apparent for the industrialized world.

Most forecasts of demand through 1995 predict continued slow growth, in the aggregate, of about 1 percent for the noncentrally planned economies. Again, however, there is a sharp contrast in the expected growth patterns of the industrialized countries and the developing world. For the next decade, the forecast of the International Iron and Steel Institute (IISI) is for no growth in the industrialized countries, but growth of 3 percent in the developing countries.[4]

The reason steel demand is growing in the developing world and not in the industrialized countries is explained by IISI's intensity of steel demand curve; the curve is based on data it has collected showing that per capita consumption of steel increases (at a decreasing rate) with national per capita income up to a maximum and then starts to decline.[5] There are a number of reasons the steel intensity curve has the observed shape, including: (1) infrastructure expenditures tend to be significantly reduced after a given level of development; (2) since 1974 the share of service industries has been rising in most OECD countries. As economies shift into banking, financial services, and insurance and away from traditional smokestack industries, there is a clear decline in the demand for steel; (3) there is a saturation level with respect to some consumer durables, such as refrigerators, which once reached results in slower growth; (4) manufacturers of products such as automobiles and cans have substituted alternate materials; and (5) technological advance has reduced the demand for steel. For example, it is estimated by IISI that continuous casting reduces the demand for raw steel by 15 percent. In the decade from 1974 to 1984, the industrialized countries went from 15 percent of their steel produced by continuous casting to 64 percent, whereas the developing nations went from 15 percent to 36 percent. Also, the development of stronger, thinner gauge steel has reduced the demand for final steel products.[6]

Change in Relative Costs

Emergence of Japan. In a study that has come to be known as the Federal Trade Commission Staff Steel Report, the causes of new patterns of steel trade flows over 1956–76 were examined.[7] The report concluded that the changing production pattern was primarily explained by changes in relative costs. Chapter 3 of that report, especially Table 3.1, provides details of the change in variable steel costs between the United States and Japan. The United States went from having slightly lower costs at the beginning of the period to costs over $100 per ton greater than Japan at the end of the period.

Emergence of Developing Countries. Whereas Japan was considered to be the low-cost producer of steel in the world in the mid-1970s, the Republic of Korea is now considered to enjoy that position. The data of Table 8.2 reveal that as of 1984, Korea enjoyed a cost advantage of about $166 per ton over the United States and $77 per ton over the European Community. Although the table exaggerates the cost advantage enjoyed by Brazil and Korea by about $20 per ton (because these countries produce a product mix that is somewhat less finished), the data suggest that steel is a product where the technology is no longer progressing rapidly. In a world of free trade, production might well shift, gradually and in the long run, toward the developing world.[8] This is a clear example of the dynamic nature of comparative advantage, as described in chapter 6.

Raw Materials and Transportation Costs. When one examines the data in Table 8.2, it is apparent that labor cost differences are the dominant explanation of the cost differences. Raw materials costs are not much of a factor in the overall comparison, but they can make a difference in the case of particular plants. Steel and the raw materials used in making steel are relatively heavy products for their value. Transportation costs can loom large in the totals, if it is necessary to ship large distances by rail or truck. For this reason, location on deepwater ports,

Table 8.2
International Comparison of Steel Input Costs, 1984 (in dollars per net ton shipped)

	Labor	Coal & Ore	Energy	Capital	Total	Difference from U.S. cost
U.S.	170	102	76	55	403	zero
EC	97	102	48	67	314	89
Japan	82	97	46	77	302	101
Brazil	44	86	50	114	296	126
South Korea	24	97	48	85	256	166

Note: Product mix of steel output—that is, the proportion of high- and low-value steel products—is similar for the steel industries of the United States, the European Community, and Japan. The steel industries of Brazil and South Korea produce a higher proportion of less sophisticated products, which causes the differential between their cost and that of the U.S. industry to be overstated by $15 to $25 per net ton shipped.

Source: Walter Adams and Hans Mueller, "The Steel Industry," in Walter Adams, ed., *The Structure of American Industry* (New York: Macmillan, 1986), p. 107.

with the resulting access to raw materials and the ability to ship the output at relatively low transportation charges, provides advantages. Thus, countries with poor access to raw materials from domestic sources, such as Japan and Korea, do not have a raw materials cost disadvantage and have an advantage in shipping their output to many destinations.

This fact should be borne in mind regarding the pattern of closure observed among the U.S. steel plants and likely in a market-oriented closure pattern in the European Community. Plants located on the Great Lakes, with access to Mesabi range iron ore via water transportation (and the high quality Appalachian coking coal) and proximity to markets such as Cleveland, Detroit, and Chicago, are in relatively good position. Inland plants in places like Pennsylvania and Ohio, however, are finding it very difficult to survive.[9]

Labor Costs. The increase in the relative labor costs of the United States is the result of the combination of two factors: improved relative productivity of our competitors and an increase in our own labor compensation costs. To a lesser extent, these considerations have also been important for the European Community. In the mid-1960s, the U.S. steel worker produced roughly twice as much steel per hour as his Japanese, German, French, or British counterpart (with the German worker producing slightly more than the other three). By 1982, if the output of the U.S. worker is placed at 100, the Japanese worker is at 141, the German worker 108, the French worker 100, and the British worker 71.[10] Data underlying Table 8.2 suggest that the Korean industry has labor productivity comparable to the British.[11] Thus the United States no longer has a significant productivity advantage and the Japanese have surpassed both the United States and the European Community.

Steelworkers around the world typically earn wages above those earned by the average manufacturing worker in their country. During the 1960s and early 1970s hourly labor costs had been less than 50 percent above the average for U.S. manufacturing workers. During the late 1970s, however, they soared to the point that by 1982, U.S. steelworkers were earning 93 percent more than the U.S. average.[12] In Europe, however, steelworkers earn a much lower premium over their respective manufacturing workers—between 7 and 32 percent. Only in Japan do steelworkers earn a premium comparable to the United States (a premium that, in the Japanese case, appears to be productivity-based).

The combined productivity and wage trends explain the significant shift in relative costs against U.S. integrated producers. The trends are not as dramatic for the European producers, but they have also been surpassed in the productivity area by the Japanese; and they are faced with the emergence of steel producers in the developing world who have hourly labor costs of less than one-quarter of theirs. These changes are significant and reflect major shifts in global comparative advantage.

Exchange Rates. Clearly, as chapter 6 indicated, the shifts in exchange rates over the last decade may be very important in explaining relative competitiveness at any point in time. The trade weighted value of the U.S. dollar rose over 80 percent from 1980 through February 1985, and then began to decline. Yet, while dollar depreciation has significantly helped, the relative improvement of the United States is less than the percentage decrease in the value of the U.S. dollar. For example, because raw materials and energy are usually priced in dollars on world markets, Japanese costs for such items are lower after the appreciation of the yen against the dollar. Nonetheless, although the gap in relative costs between the United States and its competitors has not been eliminated, it has been considerably narrowed.[13]

Mini-Mills. The pessimistic comparison of the U.S. steel industry's cost position does not extend to the "mini-mills." These are small nonintegrated plants that recycle scrap into certain rolled steel products, such as bars and rods. Mini-mills often reap high profits from a combination of modern technology, good location (in growing Southern and Western markets overlooked by the majors), and a work force unencumbered by restrictive work rules. Since 1960 these operations have increased their share of U.S. steel production from about 3 percent to 20 percent. Interestingly, most of this ground was recaptured market share from imports.

The mini-mills are likely to make further inroads into the sales of the major domestic producers. If they succeed in developing continuous casters that allow them to produce flat-rolled products at a lower minimum efficient size, the inroads could be dramatic.[14] This development may also be dependent on whether producers can turn direct reduction (a process that renders iron ore usable as a raw material in mini-mill furnaces, thereby dramatically reducing scrap requirements) into an economically viable option. Otherwise, scrap prices may be bid up, cutting into the mini-mill's profitability.

The large integrated producers, unfortunately, appear incapable of emulating the mini-mills. Armco has closed its mini-mill in Houston, and Bethlehem sold its two mini-mills in Los Angeles and Seattle. These companies are encumbered by their contracts with the United Steelworkers; thus they have higher wages and, possibly even more important, restrictive work rules.

OTHER EXPLANATIONS OF THE CRISIS

A number of other explanations have been offered for the steel crisis, both by supporters and critics of the U.S. steel industry. Although none of them is judged to be a very important explanation of the changed steel industry, some of the more widely known theories will be reviewed.

Oligopolistic Pricing

It has been alleged that the oligopolistic pricing patterns of the U.S. integrated steel producers contributed significantly to the erosion of their market share by imports.[15] By attempting to maintain high domestic prices, they offered a "price umbrella" to foreign producers who could then price lower than domestic producers and capture the market.

There appears to be considerable support for this view of steel pricing prior to 1960. Donald Parsons and Edward Ray argued in 1975 that, in the first half of the twentieth century, U.S. steel pricing was characterized by dominant firm and dominant cartel pricing, respectively.[16] The econometric estimates of both Richard Rippe[17] and Richard Mancke[18] also imply that steel pricing was not competitive prior to 1960. They find, however, that unlike pre-1960, after 1960 prices rose and fell with demand. Moreover, the Federal Trade Commission Staff Steel Report documented that steel pricing became much more competitive after 1960.[19] The Rippe and Mancke studies also come to this conclusion, as well as Scherer[20] and Adams and Mueller.[21]

There were a number of factors that contributed to more competitive steel pricing after 1960. Most important among these are:

1. The United States became a net importer of steel in 1959. Imports rose from 1.2 percent of apparent steel consumption in 1955, to 17.1 percent in 1971, to over 25 percent in 1984.

2. The share of the United States Steel Corporation fell from 65.4 percent of the market in 1902, to 25.7 percent in 1961, and 22.1 percent in 1976; U.S. Steel could no longer act like a dominant firm after 1960 and instead began joining the "chiselers" in offering discounts off list price.

3. The mini-mill emerged as a significant competitive force in the steel industry. Mini-mills increased their share of domestic production from about 3 percent in 1960 to about 20 percent in 1984. While these producers generally regard their pricing decisions as too small to affect industry-wide prices, collectively they are important.

Thus it is reasonable to conclude that steel prices in the United States closely approximate marginal costs. They may exceed marginal costs, but only for short periods of time. Therefore, oligopolistic pricing does not appear to be a reasonable explanation of the changes in steel trade flows that have occurred since 1960, because the pricing approximates that of a competitive industry.

Dumping and Subsidies

It is claimed by representatives of the U.S. steel industry that dumping and subsidies are the cause of their problems, and that if they could only compete on a "level playing field" imports would not be a problem. Yet there are anti-dumping and countervailing duty laws available to firms if they believe that dumped or subsidized goods are entering the United States to their harm. In fact, the U.S. steel industry has extensively availed itself of these laws by initiating well over 100 cases against imported steel since 1982.

Interestingly, the dumping side of the unfair trade practices laws tilts the playing field in favor of domestic firms. Economic efficiency generally calls for marginal cost pricing;[22] this means that prices should exceed average total costs during an economic boom, but fall below average total costs during a recession.

Despite these economic efficiency considerations, if a foreign firm prices below average total costs during a recession, in both its home market and the United States, it will be determined to be dumping under the new definition of dumping. None would seriously accuse the U.S. steel firms of dumping, yet the huge losses they incurred in 1982 and 1983 would have resulted in significant dumping margins being found against them for these years if they had been judged by the Department of Commerce antidumping rules. Since domestic steel firms are not subject to the U.S. antidumping laws, foreign firms are thus judged under a harsher standard regarding what is a legally acceptable minimum price.[23]

Regarding subsidized imports of steel, there are a number of foreign firms that do indeed receive significant subsidies of steel. The Federal Trade Commission Staff Report established that subsidies were too small to explain steel trade flows prior to 1977. Since then subsidies have risen for a number of foreign producers. The problem for the domestic firms, however, is that the firms that are receiving the subsidies are not the ones that are the most significant threat to the domestic market.

The cases launched in 1982 are most instructive in this regard. A massive antidumping and countervailing duty investigation was launched by the U.S. Department of Commerce and the U.S. International Trade Commission, after complaints were filed by the major U.S. integrated steel producers. Initially 132 complaints, charging very substantial receipt of subsidies and dumping, were filed against producers from Belgium, France, West Germany, Italy, Luxembourg, the Netherlands, and the United Kingdom, as well as from Brazil, Romania, South Africa, and Spain. The Department of Commerce is charged with the determination of the subsidy or dumping margin, and the International Trade Commission is charged with the question of whether the industry is injured by virtue of the subsidized or dumped imports.

With respect to the European Community, the Department of Commerce found a very diverse pattern of subsidies. A number of the European Community producers were found to be subsidized by substantial margins, but a large portion of the European Community capacity was determined to be unsubsidized or subsidized by only a small amount. The large French producers Usinor and Sacilor were found to be subsidized at between 11 and 21 percent; the Italian firm Italsider was subsidized at 26 percent; the Belgian firm Cockerill-Sambre was subsidized at a rate of 13 percent; and the British Steel Corporation was subsidized at a rate of 20 percent. On the other hand, seven of the eight large German firms were found to be unsubsidized and the eighth was found to be subsidized at only 1 percent;[24] the large Dutch firm of Estel Hoogovens, 14 small British firms, and the Belgian firm of Clabecq were also found to be unsubsidized; in addition, the Luxembourg firms of Arbed and MMR-A were found to be subsidized at the low rates of 0.5 percent and 1.5 percent, respectively.[25]

This diverse pattern of subsidy determinations by the Department of Commerce proved very troublesome on both sides of the Atlantic, and it set the stage for a negotiated settlement. From the perspective of the producers in the United States, countervailing duties in an amount equal to the subsidy margins and limited to those producers who were found to be subsidized would simply not accomplish very much in the way of protection. The four nations from which the United States imports the most steel are Japan, Canada, West Germany, and South Korea (55.6 percent of imported steel mill products in 1984 came from these four countries). There were no cases brought against Japan or Canada; West Germany was exonerated by the Department of Commerce proceedings, and the Republic of Korea would, in subsequent proceedings, have only very negligible duties assessed against it. Even if the duties were implemented against the European Community producers found to be subsidized, other unsubsidized producers in the European Community or elsewhere could take their place. If all unsubsidized foreign producers, especially Japan with its huge amount of excess capacity, were allowed to sell in the United States without fear of trade restrictions, imports would certainly maintain if not increase their share of domestic apparent consumption. Thus it is not unfair trade practices (dumping and subsidies) by foreign producers that have caused the U.S. steel industry its difficulties.

Technological Lethargy

Critics of the U.S. steel industry have alleged that its problems derive from the fact that its managers have made a series of bad decisions regarding the adoption of appropriate technology. Much has been written on both sides of this subject starting with the article by Walter Adams and Joel Dirlam.[26] The criticism has focused on the two most important technological innovations in the steel industry in the past 40 years: the basic oxygen furnace and continuous casting. In particular, it is alleged that the important competitors of the United States adopted these technologies faster.

The key point in evaluating these arguments is to understand that it is not always the profitable decision to invest in a new technology. This will depend very much on the circumstances of the particular firm and plant. In particular, if one has just made a capital investment in the old technology and a new technology becomes available, the optimal choice may be to wait until the old technology has depreciated enough before one invests in the new technology, a point made in chapter 4 when technological diffusion was discussed.[27] This, in fact, was the case for the basic oxygen furnace and for continuous casting.

Moreover, the United States for some time now has not been a profitable place to invest in new steel capacity.[28] Thus some of its major competitors, who were adding to capacity much faster than the United States, were found to have higher levels of basic oxygen furnace or continuous casting capacity; but the United States did not make a disproportionate number of bad or unprofitable decisions.[29] In fact, if one develops an appropriate measure of *efficient* decisions (that is, the percentage of investment in the new technology, given that an investment is made), the United States is seen to have adopted the new technology at least as fast as its major competitors. The countries that adopted these technologies slowly are the centrally planned economies and countries with a high percentage of their steel firms owned by their government.[30] Thus the declining competitiveness of the U.S. steel industry does not appear to be attributable to bad management decisions regarding technology adoption.

POLICY REACTION IN THE UNITED STATES

Recent Protection History

The U.S. steel industry has obtained significant amounts of trade protection since 1969. To the extent that it has perceived a crisis, the U.S. government has responded with intermittent periods of trade protection.

The first major action was the "voluntary restraint agreements" (VRAs) with the European Community and Japan that were in effect from 1969 to 1974. These agreements limited the amount of steel that the European Community and Japan were allowed to sell in the United States. Due to the worldwide boom in steel demand during 1973 and 1974, however, these restraints were not binding in these last two years.[31]

The next major episode of protection was the initiation of the "trigger price mechanism" (TPM) in 1978. The TPM was, in principle, to have established a minimum price for imports below which imports could not enter without being subjected to an expedited antidumping investigation. By requiring imports to be priced at a higher level, the effect of the TPM was to establish a "price umbrella" on imports under which domestic producers could more effectively compete at higher prices.[32] It has been estimated that the TPM induced an increase in import prices of approximately 9 percent.[33]

In 1982 a major effort was undertaken by the majority of the integrated U.S. steel producers to obtain antidumping and countervailing duties on imports from producers in the European Community and a number of other countries. This process led to the signing of another VRA with the European Community.

In early 1984 the United Steelworkers of America and Bethlehem Steel Corporation petitioned the U.S. International Trade Commission (ITC) for relief from imports under section 201 of the Trade Act of 1974; this section allows exclusion of fairly traded imports if they are assessed to cause substantial injury. The ITC recommended that quotas be imposed, but the president rejected formal quotas through the 201 process. Instead, he directed his trade representative to negotiate VRAs with virtually all major foreign suppliers of steel to the United States, so as to reduce imports from about 25–26 percent to 18.5 percent of domestic consumption, excluding semifinished.

Cost of the Existing Quotas

David Tarr and Morris Morkre have estimated the annual costs to U.S. consumers of the 18.5 percent quota to be $1.1 billion in 1983 U.S. dollars.[34] Of this, $779 million consists of inefficiency costs to the U.S. economy, while the remainder constitutes a transfer from U.S. consumers to U.S. producers. The estimates also reveal that non-U.S. producers are expected to earn $557 million in quota rents, compared with $428 million in additional profits for U.S. producers. Over the five-year scheduled life of the VRAs, they are estimated to cost U.S. consumers $4.8 billion and the economy $3.4 billion in present value terms.

In order to obtain some perspective on the costs of the quotas, Tarr and Morkre also estimated the costs in terms of the number of jobs protected and earning losses saved. The quota was likely to temporarily protect 9,951 jobs. This means that the costs to consumers are $114,000 per job per year and the costs to the economy are $81,000 per job per year (far more than the average steel worker earned). For every dollar of earnings losses saved by otherwise displaced steelworkers, consumers lose $35 and the economy loses $25.

Impact of the Quotas on Adjustment

Each of the three episodes of protection described above has been announced by the respective administration with the hope that the industry will use the breathing room offered by the protection to modernize and become competitive with its foreign rivals. Indeed, the current protection was authorized by Congress through the Trade and Tariff Act of 1984, which included the requirements that continuation of the trade relief in any year is contingent on the major steel producers reinvesting "substantially all of their net cash flow from steel operations to reinvestment and modernization of their steel operations."[35] As the trends in labor productivity would suggest, previous efforts in this regard have been unsuccessful. For example, there has not been a "greenfield" integrated steel plant built in the United States since Bethlehem's Burns Harbor facility was constructed in 1962. Indeed, given international cost comparisons and trends in demand, it is not surprising to learn that calculations of the profitability of such investments indicate that they are very unprofitable at current prices.[36]

A more serious problem than the quota program not being likely to achieve the goal of a modern efficient steel industry in the United States is the fact that it may hurt the integrated steel producers in the long run. The major problems of the U.S. integrated producers are its labor costs, the decline in demand, and the rise of the mini-mills. How will protection affect each of these areas?

Regarding labor costs, protection often makes it more difficult to obtain the further wage concessions and work rule modifications that are required to make the integrated producers more competitive. This would exacerbate the integrated producers' problems with not only international competition once the quotas are removed but also with the mini-mills.

Regarding the decline in demand, the industry has suffered in part because of a switch to alternate materials and in part because more steel is being brought into the country in the form of manufactured products. The amount of steel imported indirectly through manufactured products rose from 1.2 million tons in

1962 to 5.2 million tons in 1973.[37] By causing U.S. prices to rise, the quotas will promote the use of alternate materials and encourage research and development into new ones. Moreover, manufacturers of products that use steel will have a greater incentive to locate their plants out of the United States, where they can benefit from the lower world prices. Once investments are made in alternate technologies or production sites, it will be difficult for the U.S. steel industry to win back these markets. Thus, rather than helping the industry in the long run, protection can be expected to result in a less competitive integrated steel sector when it is lifted.

NATIONAL DEFENSE USES OF STEEL AND THE POLICY IMPLICATIONS

Are market forces adequate to provide for sufficient steel in the event of a national emergency or is it necessary for the U.S. government to intervene in some fashion? At first glance it would appear that the market is adequate because ordnance and other military uses of steel have only accounted for 0.5 percent, or less, of the steel shipments of U.S. steel firms in the last decade. Of course, the economy has essentially been on a peacetime footing since the early 1970s. The prior decade, however, was the period of the Vietnam war. However, ordnance and other military uses of steel rose only to a maximum of 2.2 percent of steel shipments in 1968.

In Table 8.3, data are presented that show the particular lines of steel products that were demanded for ordnance and military uses in 1975 and 1984. Other than semifinished products, plates, sheets, strip, and pipe are the ones most in demand. Even for these, however, ordnance and other military uses account for a rather small proportion of the total domestic shipments (1.3 percent for plate, 0.1 percent for hot rolled sheets, and 2.7 percent for cold rolled strip).

Since a war of the size and type of Vietnam appears to present little difficulty in terms of the nation's steel supplies, one must hypothesize a national emergency exceeding Vietnam proportions for there to be a potential problem regarding the adequacy of steel supplies. The greatest mobilization in American history was World War II. A war of this type would be a worst case scenario. In terms of the realities of modern warfare, however, it is not clear that this eventuality has a very significant probability of occurrence. Nonetheless, concern has been expressed regarding the adequacy of steel supplies in a maximal scenario. This concern has focused on the supplies of steel plate.[38] Since plate has been identified as the likeliest weak link in the chain of steel supplies for defense, its adequacy will be analyzed in detail.

Reflecting the concern over steel plate supplies, two detailed studies have been done assessing the peak ordnance and other military demand for steel plate under various emergency scenarios. One study was done at the Industrial College of the Armed Forces (ICAF);[39] it determined, in detail, the specific applications of armor and alloy steel plate for military uses, such as in tanks and ships. The general

Table 8.3
**Types of Shipments of Steel Mill Products: Total and Shipments
for Ordnance and Military Use, 1984 and 1975**

Products	1984		1975	
	Ordnance and military use	Total shipments	Ordnance and military use	Total shipments
Ingots, blooms, billets, slab	75.9	1.306	122	2,578
Skelp	-	11	-	34
Wire rods	-	3,090	.6	1,298
Structural shapes (3" & over)	.5	3,868	1.7	4,697
Steel piling	-	288	-	429
Plates	55.1	4,339	47.8	8,761
Rails	-	965	-	1,248
Rail accessories	-	182	.002	*339
Wheels (rolled and forged)	-	59	.007	*216
Axles	-	33	-	69
Bars-hot rolled (including light shapes)	35.1	7,255	92.3	8,146
-reinforcing	7.0	4,432	-	3,666
-cold finished	10.0	1,406	-	1,486
Tool steel	-	61	.003	69
Pipe and tubing-standard	2.2	743	13.7	2,096
-oil country goods	-	1,406	-	2,577
-line	-	775	.04	1,721
-mechanical	1.7	940	4.2	1,202
-pressure	-	89	.06	332
-structural	-	270	-	258
-stainless	.003	52	-	42

Table 8.3 (continued)

| | 1984 | | 1975 | |
Products	Ordnance and military use	Total shipments	Ordnance and military use	Total shipments
Wire-drawn	.7	963	1.9	1,625
-nails and staples	-	147	-	265
-other merchant wire products	-	112	.01	264
Black plate	-	286	.2	486
Tin plate	-	2,765	.03	4,151
Tin free steel	-	945	-	1,000
Tin mill products-all other	.2	66	.06	50
Sheets-hot rolled	16.3	13,133	42.9	11,222
-cold rolled	14.0	13,664	36.6	12,841
Sheets and strip-galvanized	.5	6,758	3.9	3,720
-all other metallic coated	-	1,109	.2	555
-electrical	-	490	-	563
Strip-hot rolled	1.8	650	4.7	961
-cold rolled	27.5	1,002	9.7	901
Total-All Grades	242.0	73,740	404.7	79,957
Percentage	0.3		0.5	

* A concordance between the 1975 and 1984 classification was defined for these entries.
Source: American Iron and Steel Institute, *Annual Statistical Report*, 1975 and 1984.

mobilization scenario presumed a mobilization proportional to the World War II buildup. It was estimated that 40 percent of the steel produced during World War II was for military purposes.[40] The authors of the ICAF study then assume that 40 percent of our increased production *capacity* would be required for military purposes in a modern mobilization. They conclude that 455,000 tons per year of alloy and armor steel plate would be required for military purposes in the event of a mobilization of this great magnitude.

Another study, which appeared in the Federal Emergency Management Agency-Department of Defense (FEMA-DOD) report, was done by the Office of Industrial Base Assessment of the Office of the Secretary of Defense.[41] Until recently, the Department of Defense received data on, and recorded on a quarterly basis, all peacetime purchases of "controlled materials" for ordnance and other military purposes. These materials are so designated because they would be allocated to activities considered essential to the national defense in time of national emergency. From these reports, the DOD calculated maximum ordnance and other military peacetime uses of carbon, alloy, and armor steel plate, by taking the maximum use of any of the subcategories of use in the 1980–84 period and summing over these maxima. The DOD mobilization definition is: "A declared national emergency in which national resources will be allocated on a priority basis. A two-year expansion from surge to nonsurge levels (sic) to significantly increased defense production is assumed in mobilization. Nondefense requirements are assumed to decline by about 50 percent under mobilization conditions."[42] On this basis the DOD scenario assumed that surge demand and mobilization demand are 2.5 times and 5 times peak peacetime demand, respectively. Under mobilization conditions, the DOD study comes to conclusions very similar to the ICAF study for the products that they both estimate. The DOD study concluded that the total demand for plate for military purposes (for both carbon, which was not estimated by the ICAF study, and for armor and alloy steel) under general mobilization conditions is 1,433,000 tons.

In order to assess the adequacy of steel plate supplies, it is necessary to add "essential civilian requirements" for steel plate to the above estimates of military demand for steel plate and compare this total to potential steel plate supplies. To obtain an estimate of essential civilian requirements, the amount of steel plate consumed in the United States for all purposes must be estimated. From 1982 to 1984, U.S. apparent steel consumption ranged from 4.8 to 5.8 million tons per year;[43] like the long-term trend in steel consumption overall, plate consumption has shown a long-term decline. Assume then that 5.8 million tons per year is normal peacetime demand for plate, and adopt the DOD mobilization scenario assumption of a reduction of supply to nonmilitary users of 50 percent.[44] Then 2.9 million tons per year of steel plate are required for essential civilian needs. Utilizing the DOD estimate for ordnance and military demand for steel plate, a total of 4,333,000 tons per year of steel plate are required for defense and essential civilian needs in a general mobilization.[45] These numbers need to be compared with potential supplies.

Domestic shipments of steel plate in 1984 were 4,339,000 tons. According to the American Iron and Steel Institute, the industry was operating at 68.4 percent of capacity in 1984; this is up from 48.4 percent and 56.2 percent in 1982 and 1983, respectively, but down from capacity utilization rates of the previous seven years.[46] Similarly, there was underutilization of plate rolling capacity. Specifically, the FEMA-DOD study estimated domestic plate capacity, during 1983–85, at 9.2 million tons per year.[47] These estimates clearly imply that supplies from domestic capacity alone are more than adequate to meet military requirements of steel plate, even in a general mobilization.[48] That is, 9.2 million tons per year of domestic steel plate capacity exceeds the 4.33 million tons per year of military and essential civilian demand in a general mobilization.

Moreover, the above figures regarding available supplies in a national emergency refer only to domestic capacity. The U.S. imports steel from a great variety of countries (including Brazil, Mexico, South Korea, and most West European nations), and the countries from whom it imports the most steel (Japan, West Germany, and Canada) are considered to be among its most reliable allies. In fact, since World War II supplies from our allies have not been impaired. The FEMA-DOD study regards the imports from Mexico and Canada as readily available during emergencies. Incorporating these supplies into the estimates of available supplies, the FEMA-DOD study also concluded that adequate supplies are available to meet general mobilization requirements.[49]

Thus the consensus of the studies through the mid-1980s is that steel plate supplies are adequate to meet even general mobilization needs.[50] The concern raised by some of the studies is that plate capacity may decline in the future; if it does it may fail to meet general mobilization requirements. The policy implications of these concerns, however, are not obvious. For one thing, there are some technological developments that may facilitate a realignment of plate capacity in the United States, away from the integrated producers and toward smaller, more efficient operations, analogous to the shift toward mini-mills.[51] Second, and more fundamentally, the arguments of the earlier sections of this chapter suggest that protection of the domestic market from foreign competition is not the answer. Protection may well be counterproductive to the goal of having a viable steel industry in the long run and it has been shown to be very costly to the economy. Moreover, general economic theory has shown that national defense objectives are met most efficiently when a policy instrument that most directly affects the desired outcome is chosen.[52] A direct subsidy for a specific purpose, such as modernizing or maintaining excess capacity, is an example. Since protection raises prices to consumers, it is a very indirect and costly way of achieving the desired outcome of a given level of steel capacity. Further, it in no way guarantees that extra business revenues will be employed to address defense needs. In fact, for the reasons mentioned above, it is not only likely to be counterproductive to this objective, but to national defense objectives as well.

An instrument that would appear to affect the desired outcome of adequate plate capacity very directly would be government acquisition and mothballing of

U.S. plate mills after they go out of business. Since steel mills appear to have virtually no alternate uses, and they take a great many years to depreciate to where they can not produce steel, this policy would appear to be feasible and come at relatively little cost of resources to the economy. The policy would result in a transfer of income from taxpayers to owners of unprofitable steel mills, but it would offer a return of greater capacity in reserve and would not require the economy to use resources that could be productively employed in alternate uses— that is, no real cost.[53] Thus, if in the future plate capacity should become a problem for the nation's defense, it would be wise for the secretary of Defense to consider this option.

CONCLUSIONS

This chapter has explained that in the last 15 years there has been a fundamental shift in the international steel industry. The industrialized countries have seen their demand decrease, while the developing countries have witnessed theirs increase. The estimates are that this pattern should continue through the year 2000. Also during the past 15 years, some key developing countries have become the low-cost producers in the world and have been capturing market share from traditional exporters in third markets. Finally, the established integrated producers in the United States have been losing market share to mini-mills within their own country.

In response to the significant dislocations of labor and reduced profits (or losses of capital), the United States has acted to protect its market through nontariff barriers. The estimates provided in this chapter document the expected result— the resource misallocation and rent transfer effects of these nontariff barriers considerably exceed the saved adjustment costs. Possibly less expected, however, it also has been argued that protection may aggravate the causes of the injury to the industry in the long run. Protection simply cannot solve the problem of declining domestic demand and loss of competitiveness in third markets. But by increasing the cost of steel to domestic consumers of steel, protection will accelerate the shift to alternate materials and to sites outside the protected regions by manufacturers of products that use steel as an important input. Moreover, it is likely to slow the cost-reducing effort of those firms who have the potential for surviving in the long run.

Recognition of these implications seems to be spreading. In February 1989, 21 senators sent a letter to President Bush regarding the important September decision concerning possible extension of the steel import restraint agreements (VRAs). The letter pointed out the costs of the steel VRA extension on the large (relative to basic steel) number of employees in steel-using industries. The past three years have been a period of resurgence for a U.S. steel industry that has gone through a painful restructuring and shrinkage. In 1987 profits were recorded for the first time since 1981. The scaled down, more profitable industry of today faces the 1990s much better positioned than it was when the 1980s began. Yet the future for the integrated producers in particular is still fraught with uncertainty.

Finally, this chapter analyzed the adequacy of steel supplies for national defense. It concluded that steel supplies were fully adequate for national defense needs under a maximal scenario. Although total capacity in late 1989 is down about 15 percent from the mid-1980s, the current situation is still adequate. Of course, if the industry continues to shrink, at some point in the future national security vulnerabilities may appear. If a problem should arise, protection would be a relatively costly and counterproductive method of meeting national defense needs.

NOTES

1. See Charles Bradford, *Steel Industry: Quarterly Industry Review* (New York: Merrill Lynch, April 1986), p. 82.

2. A very influential document in this regard was *Projection 85* by the International Iron and Steel Institute (Brussels, 1973).

3. A greenfield expansion is an entirely new facility; a brownfield expansion is the refurbishing or enlargement of an existing facility.

4. International Iron and Steel Institute, *Annual Report of the Secretary General* (Brussels, October 1985), p. 11.

5. Prior to the experience of the last decade, the curve was thought merely to increase at a decreasing rate throughout, without actually achieving a maximum and then declining. That is, if y equals per capita income, and $f(y)$ equals per capita consumption of steel, then it was previously believed that $f'(y) > O$ and $f''(y) < O$ for all y. The data of the last decade, however, appear to contradict the hypothesis that per capita consumption of steel is monotonically increasing in per capita income. Thus, while it is still believed that per capita consumption of steel increases at a decreasing rate with per capita income throughout most income levels (i.e., $f''(y) < O$, except for y quite large in relation to most countries' income levels), there appears to be an empirically relevant level of income, yo that varies across nations after which f decreases—that is, $f'(y) < O$ for $y > yo$.

6. Slow rates of growth in the economies as a whole clearly contributed to the decline in demand for steel in the industrialized countries. If lower energy prices are here to stay, this may stimulate economy-wide growth, which will give an impetus to steel demand.

7. Federal Trade Commission (FTC) Staff Report (R. Duke et al.), *The United States Steel Industry and Its International Rivals: Trends and Factors Determining International Competitiveness* (Washington, D.C.: U.S. Government Printing Office, 1977).

8. This should not be construed as an argument for subsidies for steel development. Rather, it is the suggestion that, in the long run, market opportunities may present themselves.

9. For a similar view see Robert Crandall, "The EC-US Steel Trade Crisis," in L. Tsoukalis, ed., *Europe, America and the World Economy* (Oxford: Blackwell, 1986).

10. Unpublished data obtained from the Office of Productivity and Technology, Bureau of Labor Statistics, U.S. Department of Labor.

11. Walter Adams and Hans Mueller, "The Steel Industry," in Walter Adams, *Structure of American Industry* (New York: Macmillan, 1986), p. 107.

12. See David Tarr, "Does Protection Really Protect?" *Regulation*, November–December 1985, pp. 29–34, for an explanation of why this phenomenon occurred. This premium has since fallen significantly.

13. See Bradford.

14. The minimum efficient size for producing flat-rolled products is currently over 3 million tons per year, whereas mini-mills typically produce about 0.5 million tons per year. See David Tarr, "The Minimal Efficient Size Steel Plant," *Atlantic Economic Journal* (1984), for a discussion of the minimum efficient size steel plant.

15. Walter Adams and Joel Dirlam, "Steel Imports and Vertical Oligopoly Power," *American Economic Review*, September 1964, pp. 626–55.

16. Donald Parsons and Edward Ray, "The United States Steel Consolidation: The Creation of Market Control," *Journal of Law and Economics*, April 1975, pp. 181–218.

17. Richard Rippe, "Wages, Prices and Imports in the American Steel Industry," *Review of Economics and Statistics*, February 1970, pp. 34–46.

18. Richard Mancke, "The Determinants of Steel Prices in the U.S. 1947–65," *Journal of Industrial Economics*, April 1968, pp. 147–60.

19. See Federal Trade Commission Report, Chapter 4.

20. Scherer concludes: "what once was [pre-1960] a clear example of collusive price leadership had evolved into something more closely matching the barometric model." By the barometic model he means that prices can not exceed marginal costs for extended periods of time. See F. M. Scherer, *Industrial Market Structure and Economic Performance*, 2nd ed. (Chicago: Rand McNally, 1980), pp. 178–80.

21. Adams and Mueller.

22. See chapter 2 for elaboration.

23. See Robert Crandall, "Steel Imports—Dumping or Competition?" *Regulation* 4 (July–August 1980), pp. 17–24; and Adams and Mueller for similar views. Another way of seeing this is that if a firm from Ohio and a firm from Ontario are both selling steel in Michigan, the firm from Ontario can be subjected to an antidumping action that is not possible against the firm from Ohio. Permanently low priced imports benefit the domestic economy, since they allow the economy to specialize in the production of those goods that it can produce with comparative advantage. Recognizing this fact, an alternate theory of dumped imports has been advanced by researchers for the American Iron and Steel Institute (See Putnam, Hayes and Bartlett, *Economics of International Steel Trade: Policy Implications for the United States* [Newton, Mass.: Putnam, Hayes, Bartlett, 1978]). It is that imports are dumped on a cyclical basis; that is, during recessions imports are dumped, but during booms imports can be obtained only at a premium over the prices charged by exporters in their home markets or over domestic prices. Empirical investigation of this phenomenon for the European Community, Japan and the United States, however, results in the rejection of this hypothesis for all three regions. See David Tarr, "Cyclical Dumping: The Case of Steel Imports," *Journal of International Economics*, February 1979.

24. We characterize the situation as unsubsidized when the Department of Commerce finding is that the rate of subsidy is too small to assess a duty. In fact, the subsidy rates for these German producers ranged from .015 percent to .15 percent, a situation characterized by the Department of Commerce as *de minimus*.

25. A complete list of the Department of Commerce determinations in these cases is available from the U.S. Department of Commerce press release of August 25, 1982. For comments on the appropriate methodology that the Department of Commerce should have employed in these cases see David Tarr et al., *Comment by the Federal Trade Commission's Bureaus before the U.S. Department of Commerce on Countervailing Duty Investigations*, Federal Trade Commission, mimeo, 1982. For an evaluation of whether the

Department of Commerce did in fact follow these principles, see Hans Mueller and Hans Van der Ven, "Perils of the Brussels-Washington Pact," *World Economy* 5 (1982), pp. 259–78, and Gary Horlick, "American Trade Law and the Steel Pact between Brussels and Washington," *World Economy* 6 (1983), pp. 357–62. Prior to the Department of Commerce estimate of subsidies, the only systematic effort to estimate subsidies in the steel industry was the FTC Staff Report (1977). Subsidies were found to be too small to affect trade flows with the possible exception of the British Steel Corporation (which was found to be subsidized at a rate of about 3 percent). Since the publication of that report, however, a number of European governments have made large infusions of capital into some of their steel firms. These infusions have often taken the form of equity acquisitions by the government, at a price for the equity that exceeded the market value. It is generally true that the Department of Commerce found little or no subsidies unless such a capital infusion was present. John Mutti, "Subsidized Production, World Steel Trade and Countervailing Duties," *Southern Economic Journal* 50 (1984), pp. 871–80 has also estimated the rate of subsidies to the European Community producers and has come to similar conclusions regarding the importance of these large capital infusions in the subsidy calculations.

26. Adams and Dirlam.

27. See Bela Gold, "Technological Diffusion in Industry," *Journal of Industrial Economics*, March 1981, pp. 247–69, and Gerhard Rosegger, "Diffusion of Technological Specificity: The Use of Continuous Casting," *Journal of Industrial Economics*, September 1979, pp. 57–63, for similar views. This is analogous to a consumer's decision on when to buy a new car, if a new car becomes available that gets better gas mileage, with all other things equal. The consumer who has an old fully depreciated car and is about to buy a new one, obviously buys the new technology (the one with better gas mileage). The consumer who purchased a car with the old technology just prior to the appearance of the new technology will probably want to keep that car until it has depreciated somewhat before acquiring a car with the new technology.

28. See Robert Crandall, *The U.S. Steel Industry in Recurrent Crisis* (Washington, D.C.: Brookings Institution, 1981).

29. There are examples of bad decisions by U.S. firms; but there are also examples of bad decisions by its major competitors, including the vaunted Japanese.

30. See David Tarr, "The Efficient Diffusion of Technology Across Nations," *Journal of Public Policy* 5, no. 2 (1986), pp. 541–60.

31. For an analysis of the effects of the VRAs, see James Jondrow, "Effects of Trade Restrictions on Imports of Steel," in W. DeWald, ed., *The Impact of International Trade and Investment on Employment* (Washington, D.C.: U.S. Government Printing Office, 1978). See also Crandall, *The U.S. Steel Industry in Recurrent Crisis*.

32. This also assisted the higher cost European producers who found Asian suppliers taking their share of the U.S. market.

33. See Donald Barnett and Louis Schorsch, *Steel: Upheaval in a Basic Industry* (Cambridge, Mass.: Ballinger 1983), pp. 239–42, for an evaluation of the TPMs role in the public policy debate on steel. Also see Crandall, *The Steel Industry in Recurrent Crisis*, and the Federal Trade Commission Staff Report, which deals with the distributional and efficiency consequences of the TPM.

34. David Tarr and Morris Morkre, *Aggregate Costs to the United States of Tariffs and Quotas on Imports* (Washington, D.C.: Federal Trade Commission, 1984).

35. Since most firms are already exceeding this requirement, it was not considered an onerous restraint. See *New York Times*, October 15, 1984, pp. D1, D6.

36. See Crandall, *The U.S. Steel Industry in Recurrent Crisis*.

37. Indirect imports of steel into the U.S.-Canada combined were (in million tons per year): 1.379 in 1962, 5.881 in 1973, 7.071 in 1979, and 6.795 in 1982. See International Iron and Steel Institute, *Indirect Trade in Steel—1962 to 1979* and *Indirect Trade in Steel—1982* (Brussels: 1982, 1985).

38. See the February 7, 1985, letter of the U.S. Trade Representative, William Brock, to the Federal Emergency Management Agency.

39. Industrial College of the Armed Forces, *The U.S. Steel Industry—Implications for National Defense*, A Mobilization Studies Research Paper (Washington, D.C.: National Defense University, mimeo, 1984).

40. Crandall, *The U.S. Steel Industry in Recurrent Crisis*, p. 99.

41. Federal Emergency Management Agency, *An Analysis of Domestic Steel Plate Rolling Capacity*, A Report Prepared for the U.S. Trade Representative (Washington, D.C.: FEMA, September 1985).

42. Ibid., p. III-5.

43. American Iron and Steel Institute, *Annual Statistical Report 1980* and *1984* (Washington, D.C.: 1981, 1985).

44. Consider the example of the use of steel for personal automobiles. Between 1966 and 1984, shipments of steel for automotive purposes ranged from a low of 14.5 percent of all domestic steel shipments in 1980 to a high of 23.9 percent in 1976. Yet in 1942, 1943, and 1944, virtually no automobiles for personal consumption were produced. In general, one can expect that the production of many durable goods for personal consumption would be drastically curtailed in a sufficiently significant general mobilization.

45. We are counting military use of steel plate during peacetime twice in this process. Adjusting for this double counting would reduce the estimate to closer to 4.30 million tons per year.

46. American Iron and Steel Institute, *Annual Statistical Report 1985* (Washington, D.C.: 1986).

47. FEMA, p. IV.3. The ICAF study, through the use of a questionnaire, also obtained estimates of domestic plate rolling mill capacity, by thickness of the plate. If one sums over the ICAF capacity estimates of the different plate rolling mills, one obtains an estimate of domestic aggregate plate capacity of 11.4 million tons per year.

48. FEMA, p. IV.4. The ICAF study (p. 47) comes to similar conclusions. That study also identifies a potential bottleneck in heat treating of plates one-half-inch thick and under. It believes this problem can be remedied with an investment of $4 to $6 million in a new facility on a lead time of 6 to 8 months.

49. FEMA's part of this study (as opposed to DOD) was to estimate military and civilian demand for steel plate in a general mobilization through an input-output model. Depending on the year of the mobilization, FEMA estimates that between 10.4 and 11.2 million tons per year of steel plate would be required. Given (from their Table V.4) that recent total U.S. consumption of steel plate was about half of these estimates and that nonessential civilian demand for steel plate would be significantly curtailed, the estimates are somewhat counterintuitive and one might wish to question the various assumptions that underlie the model. For example, the input-output coefficients were taken from 1977 data. Given the secular decline in steel demand, this will bias the estimates upward. Comparing apparent consumption of steel plate in 1984 with 1977 suggests a bias of about 40 percent due to this factor. Moreover, it was necessary for the authors to make assumptions regarding

how much steel plate each sector would consume per dollar of output. These coefficients, called "materials consumption ratios" (MCRs), were also based on pre-1982 levels of steel plate consumption and would thus analogously be biased upward. Moreover, in estimating these coefficients, due allowance would have to be given to the reduction in demand for plate for nonessential civilian uses. The authors of the FEMA study believe, however, that unlike other steel products, nonessential civilian demand for steel plate products is negligible. They argue that we should not expect military and essential civilian demand for steel plate to be less than during peacetime. Therefore, the materials consumption ratios they assume and their estimates reflect their assumption that there is no nonessential civilian demand for steel plate. It would be useful to obtain data relating to this assumption. Nontheless, FEMA's conclusions are similar to ours. Namely, available supplies are adequate to meet general mobilization needs. With FEMA's estimates, a potential problem in the future can arise sooner.

50. See David Tarr, "Free Trade in Steel: In the American Interest?" in John Q. Adams, ed., *The International Economy: A Reader* (New York: St. Martin's Press, 1979), and Crandall, *The U.S. Steel Industry in Recurrent Crisis*, for similar views regarding the adequacy of steel supplies in general.

51. One development is the "steckel mill process," developed by George Tippens and in operation in his Tuscaloosa, Alabama, plate plant. The mill purchases slabs and uses this apparently efficient process to produce carbon steel plate at a relatively low minimum efficient size operation.

52. See Jagdish Bhagwati, "The Generalized Theory of Distortions and Welfare," in J. Bhagwati, ed., *Trade, Balance of Payments and Growth: Paper in Honor of Charles Kindleberger* (Amsterdam: North Holland, 1971).

53. It would require the use of some resources in activities such as maintenance.

9

The Machine Tool Industry under Fire

William J. Corcoran

The machine tool industry is not highly visible. Changes in its fortunes do not readily make the front page or TV broadcast news. There are two reasons. First, its products are durable investment goods not seen by the ordinary consumer. Second, it is a small industry, producing only 0.10 percent of the gross national product.[1] However, if examined more closely, this industry is seen to be vital. It is said that machine tools are the master tools, the tools that make tools. Virtually every product is built on a machine tool or on a machine made by a machine tool.

Accordingly, technological change within the machine tool industry translates into technological change in manufacturing processes themselves, yielding lower costs, higher quality, and new products. The machine tool industry is also associated with national security since Department of Defense purchases (direct or indirect) account for some 20 percent of the industry's output.[2]

This sector, considered a mature one, is beset by two major challenges: technological change and the globalization of trade. Technological change has primarily taken place in the control function. Numerical controls and computer numerical controls allow machines to produce unattended by labor. Technological change has also occurred in coordinating the machine tool with other important inputs such as computer and automatic material handling systems. As a result, fully automated factories become a realistic possibility. The second challenge, globalization, is clearly indicated by the increasing ratio of total machine tool exports to total world production. Once a net exporter, the United States is now a net importer and the industry is clearly under fire. The U.S. machine tool industry is currently failing to meet both these challenges.

This chapter addresses three areas. First, the structure of the industry is described, both its physical characteristics—what does the industry produce?

227

how does it produce it? what are the new developments?—and its economic characteristics—what is the size distribution of the industry? what are the barriers to entry? who are the main users of machine tools? The second major objective is to describe the industry's recent decline and the possible causes of that decline. The third is to assess the implications of the decline, including a national defense point of view, and to consider some possible policy prescriptions.

DESCRIPTION OF THE U.S. MACHINE TOOL INDUSTRY

Physical Characteristics

Machine tools are power-driven devices that are used mainly by durable goods manufacturers to produce metal parts and equipment. This industry is divided into two sectors: the metal-cutting sector (SIC 3541), which produces over 70 percent of the value of machine tool output, and the metal-forming sector (SIC 3542). Machine tools that are produced by the metal-cutting sector remove or cut metal material from a metal workpiece—a steel bar or casting. The primary metal cutting machine tools are lathes (the father of machine tools), planing machines, drilling and boring machines, grinding machines, and milling machines. Each of these carries out a specific relative motion between a workpiece and a tool that cuts away the metal; both are rigidly mounted on the machine tool. On a lathe, the tool is fed into and along a rotating workpiece. On a planing machine the tool is fed into a workpiece that reciprocates beneath it. On drilling and boring machines the tool is rotated and fed into the workpiece producing a round hole. And on a grinding machine, used for polishing, and a milling machine, used for making cuts of various depths, the tool is rotated, moved along and fed into a workpiece.

Machine tools produced by the metal-forming sector are presses, forges, punching, shearing, and bending mechanisms. Metal-forming operations involve two opposing tools moving together to strike, squeeze, or shear the workpiece.

Grinding and polishing machine tools accounted for the largest value of output shipped in 1986 ($422.0 million), followed by lathes ($261.7 million), presses and forging machines ($290.2 million), machining centers, which are numerically controlled and combine several cutting operations ($204.1 million), bending and forming machines ($175.3 million), and milling machines ($162.2 million).[3] The SIC sectors that are the main users of machine tools are nonelectrical machines (36.7%), fabricated metal products (22.7%), transportation equipment (13.8%), and electrical machinery (11.2%).[4] The direct and indirect impacts of the automobile industry and the aerospace industry account for approximately 40 percent of the purchases from the machine tool sector.[5] Other industries that are large users of machine tools are construction equipment, farm machinery, mining equipment, oil field equipment, and consumer durables.

Computer Numerical Controls

The use of computer numerically controlled (CNC) machine tools has revolutionized this industry. Machine tools become both more adaptable and flexible
because one can easily edit and store programs in a computer, and little skill or
training is needed to operate CNC units because the programming has been greatly
simplified. Further, the computer has greatly enhanced the scope of control: in
addition to directing the movement of the tool and the operational speed, the tool
can be selected, inserted, removed, and changed; the workpiece can be fed into,
fastened, or taken out; and several cutting operations such as drilling, boring,
and milling can be combined in one machine—a machining center.

Machine tools are often used as part of a transfer line. The number of different
parts produced on a transfer line is usually low, from one to ten, while the size
of the production run is large, 20,000 to 50,000, or more. The machines used
on a transfer line have little flexibility since they are built for a single or narrower set of purposes, such as cutting, forming, welding, and so on. The initial
setup expenses for transfer line production are very large. However, these outlays,
if spread over a large volume, result in low average total costs.

There is also a need for metalwork in small batches. One estimate is that 75
percent of all worldwide metalworking operations is by batch production and that
85 percent of all batches have fewer than 50 parts.[6] Because many changes must
be made to work on the parts of different batches, flexibility is important. The
numerically controlled machine tool is ideal in this situation. Numerical control
of machine tools consists of numerically coded commands that direct the various
motors, switches, and drive units that control the motion of the machine tool.
The first ones were developed in the early 1950s for the U.S. Air Force at the
Massachusetts Institute of Technology. Information to make a part was read by
a control unit from paper tape. A different part could be produced by changing
the tape. The outcome was flexibility, speed, and reliability for parts produced
in small batches.

Two more developments made numerically controlled machine tools a practical reality. One was the replacement in the early 1970s of inflexible hard-wired
circuitry in control units by soft-wired minicomputers. The second, around 1975,
was the use of microcomputers for numerical control units. These provided the
basis for the CNC machine tool.

Flexible Manufacturing

When a machining center is combined with some kind of automatic pallet
changer and a materials handling system, it is called a flexible manufacturing
cell. The materials handling system transports the workpieces from storage to
a machine, between machines, and then back to storage. A cell can be composed
of several machining centers between which the materials pass sequentially. Control of the operations occurs at each of the machining centers.

Another step up from the flexible manufacturing cell is the flexible manufacturing system (FMS). An FMS is characterized by a larger number of machining centers, and a larger number of additional devices of increased complexity, such as automatic guided vehicles that transport the workpieces, washing devices, and measuring devices. But most importantly, in an FMS the whole operation is controlled by a central computer. This allows the workpieces to be taken from storage, brought to a particular machine, and worked. Then the workpiece is transported back to storage, to another machine, or remains at the same machine for further metal-cutting operations. The workpiece may then be replaced by a different workpiece subjected to an entirely different metal-cutting operation.

As a result, an FMS system has the following advantages: increased flexibility, volume, and machine utilization; reduced work in process inventory; fewer machines; reduced labor costs and lead times; more consistent product quality; less floor space; and reduced set up costs and tool inventory. By 1987 there were 101 FMSs, both large and small, with a total value of $349 million, shipped to U.S.-owned manufacturing facilities. This number is expected to grow by 815 systems valued at over $2.0 billion by 1990.[7]

Other New Developments

Machine tools are also being applied to new materials. The traditional materials cut by machine tools have predominantly been steel and iron. Machine tools are now being used on composites, graphite, pressed powdered metals, plastics, and, more recently, ceramics.

Developments are also occurring in the use of the computer to extend control over the manufacturing process. Computers used in this way are called CAD/CAM systems (computer aided design and computer aided manufacturing). With such systems, a part can be designed in three dimensions on a computer screen, and with the appropriate software the computer can translate this design into instructions for cutting the part on a CNC machining center. In some cases the part can be designed directly by the customer. The advantage of CAD/CAM is that manufacturers can offer superior quality—higher precision and closer tolerances—which may offset the lower wage advantage of foreign producers.

Cyclicality

The machine tool industry is noted for the extreme cyclicality of the new orders it receives. These cycles may be as long as ten years from peak to peak, with swings in new orders averaging between 25 and 35 percent. On a year-to-year basis, variations from $+90$ to -75 percent have occurred, as shown in Figure 9.1.

This cyclicality has been a continuing characteristic of the machine tool industry both in the United States and abroad. The fluctuations in new orders have caused serious adjustment problems—firms have allowed backlogs to build during

Figure 9.1
Year-to-Year Change in Net New Orders of Machine Tools, 1957–88

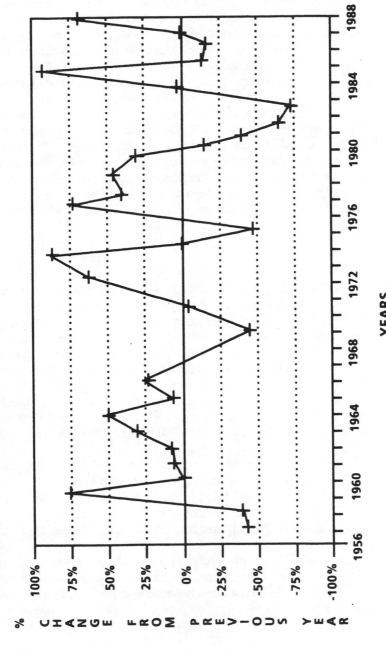

Source: NMTBA—The Association for Manufacturing Technology.

periods of expansion and have difficulty carrying workers during periods of contraction.

The cause emanates from machine tools being a durable investment good. Relatively small cycles in the demand for final goods become multiplied into larger cycles in the durable or investment goods industries. This is known as the "accelerator effect." When there is a perceived increase in the demand for final products, firms producing these products will try to meet this demand by enlarging their own plant and equipment. Such increase in investment demand is normally a much larger proportion than the original instigating change. That is, a 10 percent increase in final product demand may lead to a 20 or 40 percent increase (or more) in producer demands for investment goods, the exact amount depending upon the life of capital equipment and capital/output ratios. Since machine tools are also an investment for the investment goods industries, they are subject to an enhanced accelerator effect. Furthermore, since machine tools are quite durable, the level of replacement demand is low. Accordingly, swings in new orders dominate the total demand for machine tools and the accelerator effect is again magnified.

Size and Concentration

Producing less than 0.10 percent of the U.S. GNP, machine tool industry employment is only 0.06 percent of the total U.S. employment, an estimated 64,600 employees in 1986.[8] The largest machine tool firm in the United States, Cincinnati Milacron, was 357th on the Fortune 500 in 1987. It had 9,275 employees and its sales of $828 million were less than 1 percent of the sales of the largest firm, General Motors.[9] Indeed, if the whole industry were combined into one firm, it would only be 139th in size on the Fortune 500. The average size of firms in the industry is also small. In 1982 there were 1,392 firms, with an average of approximately 56 employees.[10] Some 600 of these were actually machine tool builders, while approximately 40 percent of the firms produced parts and accessories.[11]

The industry is becoming more concentrated. The four-firm concentration ratio, measured by the proportion of shipments or output from the top four firms, was estimated to be 22 percent in 1977, 34.2 percent in 1980, and 46.9 percent in 1983.[12] Additionally, in 1982 the 12 top producers made 85 percent of the machine tools produced in the United States.[13] However, it is not likely that the rising level of concentration should be of concern because foreign machine tools are excluded from the tally. Imports comprise a significant proportion of machine tool products sold in the United States. This makes the threat of overconcentration rather irrelevant. In fact, a primary concern of this chapter focuses on the question of whether U.S. machine tool producers will even be able to survive.

Barriers to Entry

Another important structural consideration is barriers to new business entry. When barriers exist, firms already in the industry are protected from new competition; there will be less pressure to minimize cost or advance technology. But the increase in the number of new establishments suggests that entry is indeed feasible. In 1963 there were 1,167 establishments and in 1982 there were 1,392, an increase of 19 percent.[14] This is impressive, given that the industry was experiencing declining growth during this period.

Economies of scale may constitute a barrier to entry. Unless entering firms can achieve economical production volumes, their costs will be too high to successfully compete. The "survivor test" is one method to determine whether scale economies exist. This method assesses the sizes of firms that are increasing in number and those that are decreasing, the presumption being that the size favored by cost conditions would grow in frequency.

In the machine tool industry two sizes of firms appear to be favored. One is very small, five to nine employees. The number of firms in this category increased by 46 percent, while firms in all categories increased by only 19 percent.[15] This indicates few, if any, economies of scale. However, small size may be favored for the production of machine tool accessories, dies, tools, jigs, and fixtures, but not machine tools themselves. As mentioned earlier, some 40 percent of the establishments produce accessories rather than machine tools.

The second level at which size is favored, occuring mainly in the metal-cutting sector, is from 500 to 999 employees. The number of firms at this level grew from 15 to 24, an increase of 60 percent. This sharply contrasts with the meager 3 percent increase for all machine tool firms greater than 100 employees.[16]

There is yet further evidence of the existence of economies of scale at this size. A study conducted by Staffar Jacobsson in 1987 found that for CNC lathes, production scale economies may be exhausted at volumes of production between 500 and 700 units per year.[17] These numbers translate into approximately 420 and 590 employees, respectively, as estimates for the minimum size to capture all scale economies.[18] These numbers are consistent with the increase in the number of firms in the size range 500 to 999 employees. Accordingly, scale economies do seem to exist in the production of metal-cutting machine tools. Nonetheless, the financial requirements to reach the minimum economical scale do not appear so stringent as to be a prohibitive barrier to entry.

The supply of human resources could also be a barrier to entry. Of particular importance in the machine tool industry is the availability of managers, engineers and designers, and skilled operators. Managing a machine tool firm requires technical and engineering skills that are not often possessed by today's new graduates. Formerly, these managers rose from the ranks of the engineering profession, but the industry is not attracting them today.

There is also a shortage of engineers who can design modern CNC machine tools. To a large extent these skills involve an accumulation of expertise within a group context and are not easily obtained by new engineer graduates. As employment declines in the industry, the accumulated expertise dissipates and is almost impossible to reassemble.

The skills to operate the machines and the familiarity in working with the materials are also in short supply. The declining fortunes of the industry and its extreme cyclicality are a deterrent to those who might seriously consider a career in this sector. These human capital shortages may pose serious barriers to entry for new firms and are a constraint limiting the expansion of domestic production capacity.

Product Differentiation

The machine tool industry has typically had clear lines of product differentiation. One is between the metal-cutting and the metal-forming sectors. A second occurs within each of these sectors when firms have specialized in developing and producing one type of machine with a few models—for example, lathes, milling machines. Specialization is carried even further to the extent that customization or special engineering is required. In effect, such specialization, with its accumulated expertise, can be a barrier to entry even to existing firms. Accordingly, at least up to the recent past, product segmentation somewhat protected firms from competition.

Two factors indicate that product differentiations within the industry may be declining in importance. One is the existence of machining centers made possible by the use of computer numerical controls. Since these combine several metal-cutting operations, machining centers overlap several specializations and undermine specialized product niches.

The second factor is also due to technological change and the evolving nature of the production process. As FMS develops, the machine tool becomes more integrated with other inputs. Its design must be carried out with this integration in mind. Thus, instead of specializing, machine tool producers must interact with the producers of other inputs and coordinate and adapt their designs.

Of the 47 FMS systems in the United States in 1985, all but five had been built by machine tool producers, which supports the proposition that machine tool producers do hold a key position as integrators of these inputs.[19] However, these five exceptions (which were built in-house) indicate that alternatives to using machine tool builders for integrating FMS do exist.

Overall, the conclusion must be that the machine tool industry is very competitive. Even though there may be some limitations on the supply of human inputs that might deter entry, opportunities do exist. Nonetheless, in the face of foreign competition and changing technology, the U.S. machine tool industry is not faring well.

DECLINE OF THE U.S. MACHINE TOOL INDUSTRY

Evidence

All current data indicate that the industry is in a drastic decline. From 1967 to 1985 the U.S. GNP increased by 390 percent, and shipments from all U.S. manufacturing industries grew by 308 percent, but the shipments from the U.S. machine tool producers grew by only 69 percent.[20] When this is adjusted for inflation, real output actually declined. From peak year to peak year (1986 dollars), shipments were at $8.27 billion in 1956, $7.38 billion in 1967, $5.55 billion in 1975, $6.01 billion in 1980, and $2.58 billion in 1986.[21] Not surprisingly, total industry employment fell from 116,400 employees in 1967 to an estimated 64,600 in 1986. Even more pronounced is the 65.7 percent decrease in production workers, from 81,400 in 1967 to an estimated 27,900 in 1986.[22] The overall decline was by far the most severe in the 1980s, although there has been some recovery since late 1987.

Nor are the international trade statistics comforting. For example, the United States was the world's largest producer of machine tools from 1945 to 1971. Then it dropped to second. In 1982 it fell to fourth place behind Japan, West Germany, and the USSR.[23] From 1970 to 1986 world production of machine tools increased from $8.27 billion to $28.5 billion, a 7.7 percent growth per year.[24] This was accompanied by an increase in globalization. In 1969 total world exports of machine tools were 29 percent of world production; in 1986 this figure exceeded 47 percent.[25] Yet the share of world production exported by the United States fell from over 6 percent in 1964 to less than 2 percent in 1986.[26] Within the U.S. market itself the proportion of domestic consumption supplied by imports climbed from 3.8 percent in 1964 to 49.8 percent in 1986. Machine tool imports have exceeded exports since 1978 and the trade balance has sharply worsened since 1982. The U.S. share of world machine tool imports increased from about 7 percent in 1976 to 22 percent in 1985. Interestingly, the Japanese share of world exports rose by exactly equivalent proportions, 7 percent to 22 percent.[27]

U.S. labor productivity adds to this somber picture; it increased by only 1 percent per year from 1959 to 1973 and decreased by 0.7 percent per year from 1973 to 1981.[28] This compares very unfavorably to the 2.8 percent increase in productivity for all durable goods during the same period; yet it is not surprising. A growing industry expands its capital equipment, embodying the latest technological change and providing opportunities to gain experience, both of which translate into increased productivity. These are absent in a declining industry.

Causes of the Decline

Weakening Demand. Various levels of demand impact on the demand for machine tools. At the most aggregate level is the national economy, and at the least aggregate is the demand from industries that purchase directly from the machine tool sector. At each level real demand has been generally characterized by moderate increases. Real growth in the U.S. GNP from 1969 to 1986 has been about 2.5 percent per year,[29] with some significant interruptions in the form of severe recessions. Japan by contrast experienced more than twice the U.S. rate (6 percent), its machine tool sector experiencing a very positive accelerator effect while ours had rather subdued growth from domestic activities.

A second factor has been the long-term, secular decline in the demand for metal products, in particular the declining demand for steel discussed in chapter 8. In the United States between 1977 and 1986, crude steel production declined by 3.0 percent per year.[30] It is therefore not surprising to find that shipments of machine tools, which cut and shape metal, predominantly steel, were adversely affected.

The decline in machine tool demand is also due to the low growth of particular industries that are the main users. Between 1979 and 1986 motor vehicles, aerospace, transportation equipment, and nonelectrical machinery all had growth rates of only about 2 percent.[31] Fabricated metal actually declined by 0.2 percent, while electrical machinery grew at about 4 percent. All these industries suffered absolute declines in 1982. Fabricated metals and transportation equipment also had declines in 1980 and 1981, aerospace in 1981, and motor vehicles in 1979 and 1980.

Being a derived demand, it is clear that the slow growth in the use of machine tools is clearly responsible for a large part of the decline in the machine tool industry. However, there are other factors as well. For while real American consumption of machine tools declined by 0.6 percent per year from 1977 through 1986, the production of machine tools declined by ten times that rate, or 6 percent per year.[32] The difference is accounted for by the increase in imports, mostly from Japan.

Relative Price and Import Penetration. The price of Japanese machine tools sold in the United States is between 20 and 40 percent below comparable U.S.-made machines.[33] Product prices are clearly affected by costs of production. Overall, costs in Japan are some 23 percent beneath costs in the United States for comparable machine tools. Part of the reason is that hourly earnings are some 36 percent lower.[34]

A second reason is the existence of economies of scale. The Japanese concentrated on producing standardized basic machine tools of low performance and low power. By doing so they were able to tap a high-volume market of medium- and small-sized firms that are prime users of machine tools. This market appears to have been entirely neglected by U.S. firms as they sought profits elsewhere.

The exchange rate is a third reason for lower foreign prices of foreign machine tools. Imports in the United States had increased steadily between 1964 and 1980, despite the low dollar in the 1970s. In 1964 imports were less than 4 percent of the total U.S. machine tool consumption; they rose to slightly less than 24 percent in 1980.[35] But in the 1980s foreign incursions turned into a rout. Between 1980 and early 1985 the effective exchange rate of the U.S. dollar rose by almost 60 percent. The period of the "superdollar" caused U.S. goods to become more expensive to foreigners while goods produced abroad became cheaper in the United States. During this period U.S. imports of machine tools rose to such a degree that by 1987 over one out of every two dollars spent was for the purchase of foreign machine tools.[36] For machining centers and numerically controlled lathes the evidence is even more sobering. By 1987 over two dollars out of every three were spent on imports.[37] It is evident that the demand for machine tools is rather elastic, and the strong dollar of the first half of the 1980s had a significant negative effect on domestic production.

More recently, the reverse phenomenon is occurring. In 1988 the effective exchange rate fell below the level that existed in 1980. The U.S. capital goods industry experienced a 36 percent surge in exports through most of 1988 and a reduction in imports. Orders for machine tools grew by 79 percent from September 1987 to September 1988.[38] Thus, both accelerator and exchange rate effects have improved the fortunes of this industry.

As chapter 6 suggests, the inroads made by imports are not entirely due to cost and exchange rate differences. The exchange rate has returned to the level that existed in 1978, yet the negative trade balance does not appear to be on a correction track. Nor does the machine tool industry appear to be returning to the level of shipments that existed in 1980.

It is interesting to note that exporting countries have not shared equally in the rise in U.S. imports. In fact, every major country exporting to the United States had a declining share except Japan. From 1980 to 1986, U.S. imports of machine tools increased by $957 million.[39] Of that increase, the Japanese have supplied $680 million or close to 72 percent.[40] In 1977 Japan surpassed West Germany as our largest supplier of machine tools; in 1986 it surpassed all other countries combined, supplying 52 percent of all imports.[41] Japan clearly appears to have developed a strong comparative advantage in this area.

Japanese success is mainly concentrated in numerically controlled lathes and machining centers that together comprise over sixty percent of all of the different types of machine tools that are imported from Japan.[42] In fact, virtually all U.S. imports of numerically controlled lathes and machining centers are Japanese.[43] It appears that different government policies account for some of the differences between the performance of the U.S. and Japanese machine tool sectors.

Government Policy Impacts

U.S. Policy. In the United States, government policy toward business generally encourages competition. Within this framework, entrepreneurship that reallocates resources toward successful new products is rewarded. Free international trade is generally supported to encourage competition and to realize comparative advantage benefits. Further, U.S. policies are generally generic, with no specific industry targeted for success.[44] In March 1983, however, the National Machine Tool Builders Association petitioned the secretary of Commerce to impose import quotas, contending that imports threatened to impair national security. In

May 1986 the president decided to seek voluntary restraint agreements with four major suppliers (West Germany, Taiwan, Japan, and Switzerland) and by the end of 1986 agreements with Japan and Taiwan were concluded. Germany and Switzerland declined to participate.

Further government involvements derive from the influence or bias imparted by the expenditure pattern of its agencies. U.S. producers concentrated their efforts on large buyers, particularly the aerospace industry and the concomitant military demand. Their contracts stressed large units, high levels of performance, and a systems approach where cost and price were not the primary considerations. These involved a high degree of customization and often very demanding specifications. This was a narrower segment of the market with unique demands as well as uncertain orders.[45] The Japanese do not have an aerospace industry and their defense industry is much smaller.

It was the contracts for these low-volume, large systems that captured the industry's attention. The broader segment of the market was missed—the small/medium-sized customers with a demand for a basic low-cost, low-powered, low-performance machine tool. As one industry spokesman is reported to have said, "The segment wasn't apparent to us as it was to them (Japanese)."[46]

At present the U.S. machine tool builders hold a competitive advantage in large, sophisticated machine tools that are characterized by high power, high precision, high tolerance, and extensive customization.[47] Here software and integrating the constituent parts are the main challenge. The overseas market, however, is quite limited for this type of machine tool.[48] The Japanese hold the lead in small- to medium-size systems that are standardized and cost efficient.

Japanese Policy. The Japanese international trade policy regarding machine tools substantially differs from U.S. policy. Its main objective is to expand exports. Their specific policy orientation can be understood within the context of the "theory of the firm," as described in chapter 2, while the U.S. orientation has been to better foster the workings of the market.

The firm is an alternative to the market for allocating resources. Where search costs, contracting costs, and other transaction costs of using the market are high, the firm may be preferred. Markets tend to be characterized by short-term relationships and transactions that involve relative certainty. Firm-like transactions are characterized by long-term relationships and can better confront the problems of uncertainty and asymmetric information. The firm has been described as a "nexus of relationships" modeled within a principal-agent perspective and in which the principal indirectly coordinates the agent through an appropriate incentive structure.

The actors involved include the firms in the machine tool industry, their customers, the suppliers of capital, and the suppliers of technology. The coordinating mechanism and the primary relationship is that between the Japanese government and the machine tool industry. The government, mainly through the Ministry of International Trade and Industry, has organized the machine tool industry as a "firm." MITI is the principal and the machine tool establishments are agents. The term "Japan Inc." is perfectly appropriate. An initial effective move was the passage of legislation that allowed relevant government agencies to be involved in many aspects of the firms' relationships.[49] These laws authorized the government to coordinate the industry and rationalize production, to form and subsidize industry associations, to promote interfirm activities with immunity from antitrust, to stimulate production by banning specific foreign machinery, to provide government-sponsored R&D, low-interest loans, tax incentives, and to create favorable depreciation schedules.

One particularly noteworthy and unique industry-wide agreement required that all firms concentrate their production activities in those machines that already held more than a 5 percent market share and were more than 20 percent of their firm's total production. This legal agreement provided an avenue for the industry to provide cost-effective machines, developed by already established firms. It limited competition within the industry, cemented industry niches, and enabled a high volume of sales.

It is not clear whether the Japanese government actually had the foresight to pick the successful machine tools. But these policies appear to have increased the probability that the successful machine would emerge. In this sense one can say that a comparative advantage in producing CNC machine tools was "acquired."

It appears that Japanese government policies can be interpreted as pushing the machine tool industry into the "growth phase" of the product cycle.[50] Typically in the emerging or initial phase the sales are low and increase slowly, the technology is imperfectly known and risky, and the cost is relatively high. It is larger firms that are generally the early buyers. They are able to spread the expense of the new product and are better able than smaller firms to handle the risks. In this early phase sellers emphasize the customization and performance of the new product. In the stabilization and growth phase the sales increase rapidly and the technology becomes better known. Small- and medium-sized firms now become the primary purchasers and the emphasis shifts to standardization. This results in high volumes and lower prices, the higher volumes enabling scale economies and learning curve advances.

In Japan between 1970 and 1974 small- to medium-size firms made up from one-third to one-half the market for numerically controlled machine tools.[51] Between 1976 and 1981 the share of these firms increased to two-thirds; the market grew by 40 percent per year. The price of CNC lathes in Japan fell by 32 percent, as opposed to that of conventional lathes, which increased by almost 60 percent. The advantages of standardized products and high volumes are clearly demonstrated.

In the relationship between the firms and their customers the Japanese concentrated on reducing risk. The risk of investing in any particular technology by machine tool builders was reduced because the Japanese machine tool market, comparable in size to the American, was protected from imports. The market was also shielded from foreign investments. U.S. firms at the technological frontier were deemed a significant threat.

In addition to the natural stimulus of rapid economic growth, medium and small businesses were given special depreciation schedules or special tax exemptions when they purchased numerically controlled machine tools, and in the relationship between capital investors and the machine tool firms the Japanese government provided direct financial assistance through subsidies and loans. These actions effectively reduced the financing costs in Japan to roughly half the corresponding U.S. figures.[52]

The Japanese government carefully fostered the relationship between the suppliers of technology and the machine tool firms. Two national laboratories conducted machine tool R&D under government auspices. Grants were given for further developments. And any information of new technology was widely disseminated. In general the Japanese organized the machine tool industry like a "firm," providing incentives for the channeling of resources in directions of high success probability.

The United States, on the other hand, has relied on the market to allocate resources. However, where the transaction costs of using the market become too great, firm-like relationships may be the preferred means of allocating resources. It is difficult to say whether transaction costs were indeed too high in the case of U.S. machine tools. Perhaps U.S.-style entrepreneurial capitalism is inferior to Japanese-style indirect coordination. Or perhaps it is simply a case of differential financial incentives and subsidies. Further, if U.S. economic growth had averaged 6 percent, perhaps our machine tool sector would also be booming. Even without these caveats, our producers were clearly too biased in their activities by government procurement. Further, the high exchange rate particularly battered the industry. Third, Japanese competition has been lethal.

Finally, it should be noted that the market mechanisms may be appropriately working, even if the results are not palatable. Comparative advantage may have shifted and is perhaps gone forever. Or is it? The bottom line may not yet have been reached. It may still be appropriate for U.S. firms to have focused on software and the integration challenges of FMS.[53]

Implications for National Defense

Technical and Industrial Criticality. Since machine tools are the machines that produce machines, they are at least once removed upstream from the production of a final product. Of course, production usually involves many stages, so machine tools may be involved at several stages. Note also that machine tools are an essential component in producing metal products, which make up 44 percent of total U.S. manufacturing output. These linkages make machine tools a critical supplying sector and validate concern over the possible extinction of the domestic industry.

Because it is a critical supplying sector, the industry has had a key part in the transfer of technology; and this may ultimately be its most important role. Technological advance results in cost reductions, increased productivity, and in new products. Productivity increases in machine tools serve the entire economy because they are upstream in the production of practically all final goods and services.

Machine tool technological advance also increases U.S. competitiveness by enhancing productivity and modernizing capacity. In this regard, some major U.S. industries, such as aerospace and automobiles, are absolutely dependent on appropriate machine tools. Finally, technological advance within the machine tool industry has been important in developing new technologies in other industries, such as electronics, precision instruments, and optics; and it is crucial to the automation of manufacturing processes.

In production matters generally the Department of Defense's concerns are to maintain reliable, effective, and up-to-date equipment and materials so that the defense industrial base will be effective, expandable to meet surge requirements, and sustainable for defense needs over the long haul. National security concerns about the decline of the machine tool sector can be understood within these parameters. If machine tools come predominantly from a foreign nation, the potential for an interruption of supplies would exist. This would be intolerable. The second concern stresses the role of machine tools in the transfer of technology. Specifically, there is more likely to be a lag in the introduction of new technology here if its development occurs on foreign soil. A nation without a competitive machine tool industry is less likely to quickly share in the latest advances. Further, it is difficult to see foreign machine tool suppliers being appropriately responsive to the specialized industrial or military needs of the United States. As a result, the latest machine tool technology may not be available for defense industries.

Policy Arena. On the international level, the market mechanism allocates production activities to those countries that have a comparative advantage—those that produce goods at a lower relative cost. By this scheme each country benefits and total world output is increased. Such expansion of international trade would result in a decline of some industries and expansion of others. The industries that are declining move to countries that can produce at the lowest cost. Overall, resources will be more productively employed. In considering policy changes, it is important to maintain an awareness of the advantages of these market mechanisms.

It is recognized in the economic literature that there are exceptions to an unfettered market whereby the desired allocation of resources is not brought about by market processes alone. This section of the chapter will focus on policy recommendations that consider the possible exceptions as they apply to the machine tool industry. Before going into this, however, a digression into nonprice competition is warranted.

Rivalry in the marketplace usually focuses on price competition, the firm offering the same product at the lowest price being deemed the most competitive. However, in actual markets nonprice rivalry has a role. Many buyers of foreign machine tools maintain that overseas suppliers have quicker delivery times, meet their users' requirements better, have more extensive after-sales service, and offer more reliable products. The question, then, is: Should U.S. policy be directed at these nonprice aspects specifically? For example, should a minimum level of reliability be mandated? The answer is no. That is neither easy nor costless. In the United States it would create an additional bureaucracy and probably serve to slow and burden the firms it is designed to assist. The companies that are competitive will meet the challenges—lower price, better quality, greater after-sales service, and so forth. Those that do not will exit from the market. This is the competitive process at work and it is unlikely that the Japanese-type intervention will succeed in such matters here.

Policy Justification. The necessity of a domestic industry for national defense is one exception to letting the market mechanism and international trade proceed unfettered. The production of machine tools as they are traditionally defined is clearly moving abroad and the competitive process is already resulting in very substantial offshore dependencies. The question is: Is the machine tool industry necessary for national defense? In the broadest sense, everything that can conceivably be used in war is necessary for national defense—even, for example, shoes. However, that does not mean the entire domestic demand for shoes should be produced within the United States.

The question of which products to produce at home and which to import, yet still maintain an adequate national defense, has many dimensions. What is the additional cost of producing at home rather than importing? Is the source of the imports likely to become enemy territory? Are there multiple sources of foreign supply? Can adequate and up-to-date stockpiles be maintained?

A comprehensive discussion of such national defense issues is well beyond the scope of this book, much less one chapter. However, some history and a review of current defense initiatives concerning machine tools provides perspective. Both in World War II (including Lend-Lease) and Korea the scarcity of machine tools was a major impediment to rapid industrial mobilization and the equipping of U.S. military forces. The industrial demand of World War II on the machine tool sector were not resolved until late 1942. Wartime production of machine tools reached over 800,000 by 1945, of which 100,000 went to our allies. At the conclusion of the war, governmental decisions resulted in the crippling of the industry. Over 300,000 machine tools were dumped on the domestic market at a price of 15 cents on the dollar. Over 30 companies went out of business. At the beginning of the Korean War the industry was ostensibly one-third the size that existed at the start of World War II, and new orders for machine tools jumped sixfold. War clearly imposes significant demands on this sector. Vietnam, however, did not pose an immediate crisis within the industry because of the duration of the war, the nature of the combat, and the policy of gradualism, which generally allowed industry to satisfy expanding military requirements.

Mobilization planners had serious difficulties in identifying machine tool requirements for these three wars. The problem has become even more complicated with the debate between proponents of short war preparedness and advocates of long war preparedness. Budgeting constraints result in competition for resources to improve readiness, to be able to surge military strength when needed, to modernize military forces, and to improve sustainability. Hence, defense outlays to provide machine tool capabilities beyond those required under present peacetime conditions meet competition from these other demands for defense budget dollars. The Department of Defense, aware of the critical role of machine tools, attempted to make provisions for meeting emergency needs following World War II, but these measures appear to fall short of currently estimated emergency needs. Under one of these programs there are three Defense Industrial Plant Equipment Centers to stockpile machine tools for mobilization, located in Ohio, Michigan, and California. The DOD maintains about 14,500 machine tools in the general reserve category. Of this total, about 6,000 are excess to current needs and the DOD has been trying to dispose of them without harming sales of domestic producers.

However, DOD officials believe that about 80 percent of the machines in general reserve are not readily available for use in a surge or mobilization situation because most of them are unsuited for current use. Further, the Department of Defense does not have the correct mix of machine tools necessary to respond to an emergency.

In addition to the general reserve category of machine tools, the government maintains Production Equipment Packages (PEP). These are essentially complete production lines that are either in use at contractor or government facilities or maintained in a layaway status. Currently, the Army has 167 and the Navy 19 PEPs. Yet according to various reports, the PEPs are in a condition similar to the machine tools in the general reserve. DOD officials have indicated that it would take 18 to 24 months to activate many of the PEPs, not the four months stated in DOD policy.

The government has long had a program whereby it has standby contracts with machine tool manufacturers that could be implemented in emergencies. Called the Machine Tool Trigger Order Program, it is intended to reduce the administrative lead time that would otherwise be required to initiate and negotiate contracts for machine tools. This program was allowed to lapse after the Korean War, but was reinstituted in the 1980s. There are currently almost 100 standby contracts in effect for 8,500 general-purpose machine tools valued at $1.25 billion. It is expected that these standby contracts would save an average of six months' administrative lead time.

Mobilization and surge requirements for machine tools have not been adequately defined. Further, DOD programs to provide machine tools for mobilization are currently of limited value because they are obsolete or unsuited to supplement present production capabilities. The situation suggests that the DOD should take action to more clearly establish its requirements and priorities under mobilization conditions and work with industry in developing capabilities to meet emergency needs.

It should be stressed that defense industrial capabilities must always be judged relative to potential threats and likely scenarios. Where the technology has matured we need only maintain production and keep quantities stockpiled to adequately defend against the enemy's production and stockpile.[54] But, with an expanding technology, uncertainty is great. One advance can wipe out an existing production technique or render a stockpile differentially deficient compared to the enemy's, thus putting warfighting sustainability in question. To the degree that the improved technology is offshore, the United States is more vulnerable to unknown developments. From a national security viewpoint the need to maintain domestic production capabilities is greater in areas of faster technological change.

What about machine tool technology in particular? Here it is thought that the basic techniques of machine tools will change very little.[55] Cutting and forming techniques are based on a mature technology. However, it is the technology surrounding the machine tool that is changing; specifically, in the controlling of the tool itself and in the integration of the machine tool with other functions—tool selection, automatic materials handling, and so on.

Manufacturing is moving toward an automated manufacturing process. In one sense this is the ideal solution from the defense perspective since automated manufacturing processes are more flexible. They allow an easier switch to defense production needs. However, in the automated manufacturing process, the machine tool is only one of a number of inputs that are necessary for the process to work. Along with the machine tool go robotics, automated handling equipment, computer control, sensors, automatic washing devices—all of which are areas of advancing technology. Further, all these separate inputs have to be integrated with a computer and the appropriate software. The main bottlenecks are likely "integration services" and software, and it is in the development of these that the United States still holds a lead.[56] It would appear, then, that maintaining the lead in the development of "integration services" and software would be a higher priority for national defense than maintaining a traditional machine tool industry that can meet all domestic needs. If these technical priorities are met, the remaining requirement is for a realistic, effective stockpiling scheme.

A second exception to letting the market process proceed without restraint is increasing returns to scale. Where these exist, average costs may fall to such an extent that the entire demand for a product could be produced economically by one or a few plants. As indicated, increasing returns do characterize much of the production of basic computer-controlled machine tools and machining centers. If demand were to be spread over too much production capacity the potential of low-cost, high-volume production would be lost. When increasing returns exist, the firms that are first to expand production may be able to dominate the industry by driving out rivals with lower prices. This is one possible result of the competitive process.

If increasing returns do exist, government can assist the industry with various protective measures that would raise demand and output higher than otherwise. Thus, in a sense a comparative advantage could be "acquired" that might not otherwise occur through the market process. It appears that this type of policy has been undertaken by Japan. Should it be done in the United States? Is further protection advisable?

The U.S. track record in this regard is not very promising. Trade protection has been enormously costly, has generally not preserved very many jobs, and has often allowed the industry to remain in comfortable, yet unproductive ways. Often under the umbrella of protection the conditions making for loss of comparative advantage worsen—that is, wages increase, management is sloppy, investments are directed elsewhere (such as U.S. Steel buying Marathon Oil). If support is warranted, other methods—such as direct subsidy, tax credits for investment—would seem far more appropriate.

It should also be noted that it is not clear as to how much in the way of cost reduction increasing returns will generate. This is an empirical question, one not only unique to each industry, but temporally unique as well. Today with a given technology, increasing returns may exist. Tomorrow with a new technology they may not. And certainly within a given technological context, they do not extend forever. At some point constant or decreasing returns to scale will be encountered.

Higher export volumes are one avenue toward higher production rates. Here government can work to establish greater access to foreign markets. The more open they are, the greater the likelihood of sales. Hence, a strong case can be made for constant diplomatic and negotiating pressure upon Japan and others to allow U.S. goods free entry. The extra sales volumes would certainly be welcome and helpful, with or without the benefits of increasing returns to scale.

Research and development is also not handled very well by the competitive market. The high up-front cost and easy imitation of new technology make investing in R&D extremely risky. Further, there are often few funds available for competitive firms to support an active R&D program. Prices are usually very close to cost and thus economic profits are small or nonexistent. Agriculture is a good example of a competitive industry that carries out little private R&D.

The machine tool industry is one that is hotly contested, both from domestic and foreign sources. The low level of R&D that is carried out is not in basic or applied research but mainly in development, which to some extent also includes customization paid for by the buyer. The Japanese government has extensively supported research and development in its machine tool sector. U.S. policy should do the same. In fact, some of this is already being done. For example, an automatic manufacturing research facility is located at the National Bureau of Standards. However, this is reported to be not very extensive and is concentrated in the area of standards and compatibility.[57] Also, a National Center for Manufacturing Sciences has been started at Ann Arbor, Michigan.[58] This is expected to be a privately funded organization; nonetheless, the State of Michigan and the Department of Defense have provided some seed monies.

Aside from policies dealing with market exceptions, there are other means to enhance the machine tool industry's ability to support a defense effort.[59] First, encourage development of FMS to the fullest extent. Flexible manufacturing is an ideal solution for switching from manufacturing consumer goods to weapon systems. Second, foreign-owned production facilities within the United States should not be discouraged. They would be available for wartime needs. Third, antitrust standards regarding cooperative ventures, joint bids, and the like should be clarified and relaxed since the flow of imports makes our machine tool market very competitive, even though domestic supplies may appear concentrated.[60]

CONCLUSIONS

The U.S. machine tool industry has been losing its competitive position in domestic and world markets. Although 1988 witnessed a 70 percent increase in orders, in constant dollars this peak year for the 1980s was still lower than some of the trough years of the previous two decades. Wracked by wide annual fluctuations in orders, the industry is suffering from a secular decline in the use of metal products and the onslaught of stiff foreign competition.

The process of decline has been hastened by (1) the strong dollar in the early to mid-1980s, (2) the industry's emphasis on DOD orders for large machine tool systems, which led to its neglect of the basic machine tool market, and (3) the Japanese government policies, which resulted in an "acquired" comparative advantage in the production of the basic numerically controlled machine tool.

As elsewhere in manufacturing, economic restructuring has been taking place within the machine tool industry. "Many firms reduced their size, increasingly acquired components from outside suppliers in the United States and abroad, or began to serve as distributors of imported machines."[61] The industry has downsized, total capacity declining by at least 25 percent from 1982 to 1986.[62] It is clearly a leaner industry, and both the VRA with Japan and the rising yen should make our market far more fertile for U.S. machine tool producers, although it is also likely to inhibit export sales (since Japanese output will be redirected). Another positive development is the increasing importance of manufacturing concerns in U.S. colleges and universities. At the same time, the manufacturing process is becoming more automated. The machine tool is becoming integrated with other inputs, such as robotics, computers, materials handling equipment, and it is the technology surrounding these other inputs that is most changing rather than the technology of the machine tool itself. The key factors appear to be the expertise and the appropriate software to integrate these different inputs. And it is here that the United States is maintaining a lead. All of this suggests that the machine tool industry's moving offshore may not be as alarming as it first appears, particularly if a substantial number of production facilities remain, stockpiles are appropriate, and there is a diversity in foreign suppliers. Finally, if the overall U.S. manufacturing sector can continue its economic vibrance, the machine tool industry will experience a beneficial and invigorating demand. A major recession, on the other hand, could be the final nail in the coffin.

NOTES

1. National Machine Tool Builders Association, *The Economic Handbook of the Machine Tool Industry, 1987–88* (McLean, Va., 1987), p. 4.

2. National Research Council, *The U.S. Machine Tool Industry and the Defense Industrial Base* (Washington, D.C.: National Academy Press), 1983, p. 53.

3. National Machine Tool Builders Association, p. 96.

4. Ibid., p. 268.

5. National Research Council, p. 53.

6. International Trade Administration, *A Competitive Assessment of the U.S. Flexible Manufacturing Systems Industry* (Washington, D.C.: U.S. Government Printing Office, 1985) p. 8.

7. Ross Associates Inc., *The FMS Industry: A Strategic Analysis* (Needham, MA: 1985).

8. National Machine Tool Builders Association, p. 250.

9. *The Fortune 500*, April 1988.

10. National Machine Tool Builders Association, p. 69.

11. International Trade Administration, p. 16; and National Research Council, *The Competitive Status of the U.S Machine Tool Industry* (Washington, D.C.: National Academy Press, 1983), p. 5.

12. International Trade Administration, *Competitive Assessment of the U.S. Manufacturing Automation Equipment Industries* (Washington, D.C.: U.S. Government Printing Office, 1984), pp. 10, 15; and National Research Council, *U.S. Machine Tool Industry*, p. 9.

13. Ibid., p. 11.

14. National Machine Tool Builders Association, p. 69.

15. Ibid.

16. Ibid.

17. Staffar Jacobsson, *Electronics and Industrial Policy: The Case of Computer Controlled Lathes* (London: Allen and Unwin, 1987), pp. 98–100.

18. From National Research Council, *Defense Industrial Base*, p. 30, in 1981 direct labor hours to produce a CNC lathe was 1,081. Assuming 2,000 hours per production worker per year, this implies 54 production workers per lathe. From National Machine Tool Builders Association, p. 253, production workers made up 64 percent of total employment in the metal cutting industry in 1983.

19. International Trade Administration, *Flexible Manufacturing*, p. 24.

20. National Machine Tool Builders Association, p. 5.

21. Ibid., p. 42.

22. Ibid., p. 250.

23. Ibid., p. 162.

24. Ibid., p. 163.

25. Ibid., pp. 163 and 167.

26. Ibid., p. 135.

27. Ibid., p. 162.

28. National Research Council, *U.S. Machine Tool Industry*, p. 17.

29. Ibid., chapter 6.

30. American Iron and Steel Institute, *Annual Statistical Report 1984* and *1980* (Washington, D.C.: 1985, 1981).

31. National Machine Tool Builders Association, p. 27.

32. Ibid., p. 126.

33. International Trade Administration, *Manufacturing Automation*, p. 23.

34. National Research Council, *Defense Industrial Base*, pp. 29 and 31.

35. National Machine Tool Builders Association, p. 126.

36. U.S. Department of Commerce, *U.S. Industrial Outlook 1988* (Washington, D.C.: U.S. Government Printing Office, 1989) pp. 23-3.

37. Ibid., pp. 23-7.

38. *Wall Street Journal*, October 31, 1988.

39. National Machine Tool Builders Association, p. 128.

40. Ibid.

41. Ibid.

42. Ibid., pp. 128 and 202.

43. Ibid., pp. 132 and 202.

44. Of course, actual U.S. trade policy is filled with exceptions to this, but most of these represent efforts to save or give adjustment time to ailing industries rather than attempting to propel certain sectors into world leadership roles.

45. Jacobsson, p. 55.

46. Ibid., p. 80.

47. International Trade Association, *Flexible Manufacturing*, p. 81.

48. In a 1986 survey of Korean industrial establishments, a consistent reply to the question, "Why are you not using more U.S. made machine tools?" was that while the U.S. quality was good, the range of offerings was too narrow and it was often the case that they (Koreans) did not need the very high quality (and expensive) machinery that American producers offered. (See Donald L. Losman, "Survey of Korean Industrial Establishments," unpublished manuscript, 1986)

49. International Trade Association, *Manufacturing Automation*, pp. 38-45.

50. Jacobsson, pp. 43-52.

51. Ibid., p. 45.

52. International Trade Association, *Manufacturing Automation*, p. 42.

53. A 1983 MITI survey concluded that Japan is behind—"there is a large gap"—the United States and West Germany are ahead in high performance machining center technology; and that Japan's package software is "substantially inferior." Referenced in National Research Council, *U.S. Machine Tool Industry*, p. 82.

54. The Committee on the Machine Tool Industry, National Research Council, reports that machine tool inventory levels are not sufficient, that sufficient appropriations will unlikely be available in the near future, and that current stockpiles are old and partly obsolescent. Ibid., p. 80.

55. International Trade Administration, *Manufacturing Automation*, p. 76.

56. Ibid., p. 83, and International Trade Administration, *Flexible Manufacturing*, pp. 31 and 81.

57. International Trade Administration, *Manufacturing Automation*, p. 37.

58. *U.S. Industrial Outlook 1988*, p. 233.

59. See National Research Council, *U.S. Machine Tool Industry*, pp. 57-73, and International Trade Administration, *Machine Automation*, pp. 82-89, for other possible policy options.

60. National Research Council, *The Competitive Status*, p. 67.

61. Anderson Ashburn, "The Machine Tool Industry: The Crumbling Foundation," in Donald A. Hicks, ed., *Is New Technology the Answer?* (Washington, D.C.: American Enterprise Institute, 1988), p. 77.

62. *U.S. Industrial Outlook 1986* (Washington, D.C.: U.S. Department of Commerce, 1987), pp. 21-22.

PART III

10

False Fears and Real Challenges

Ever since mankind was banished from the Garden of Eden it has faced continuous problems, a preponderance being of an economic nature. The problems of the United States as it marches toward the year 2000 are hardly unique. They abound in all societies—issues of health, aging, education, defense, and so on. Economic problems manifest themselves in a variety of forms—rapacious inflation, mass unemployment, budget deficits, trade deficits, stagnating or falling real levels of living, shortages of particular commodities. Some of these afflictions are more acute than others; some are part and parcel of an adjustment process and are one means of returning society to a more successful, more palatable path.

The federal budget deficit is certainly a problem. It reflects a credit card mentality, a "buy now, pay in some fuzzy future" perspective. Probably its most pernicious feature by far is the bias it imparts to both the aggregate level and the composition of federal spending. When government-provided goods appear relatively "cheap" to the 535 members of Congress and over 200 million constituents they represent, there is a natural inclination to provide an awful lot, to attempt to cure every problem and remedy every malady under the sun. Accordingly, the government tries to do too much, does not focus its efforts, and often runs at cross purposes with itself and other societal goals. But when $5.00 of "goodies" can be provided for only $2.50 of current taxes, the temptation has thus far proved irresistible.

There are many more technical, yet consequential, aspects of the federal deficit. Yet the deficit itself is simply a financing medium for the provision of public services. Perhaps taxes are not high enough. Perhaps the level of government services is too great. There is no golden rule written on tablets of stone commanding that there be no deficit spending or that deficits below some magic number are acceptable but those above that number spell disaster. We have chosen a particular means of financing (as opposed to higher taxes, inflation, or a lower

251

level of government services). There are problems with this choice, but the federal deficit itself is not the worst possible problem. Losing a major war would be much worse. Winning one, but with casualties and deaths in the hundreds of thousands, would be worse. Suffering the ravages of a terrible plague would be much worse. Nor is loss of human life the only scenario that can diminish the significance of the deficit. Most Americans would freely choose the current deficit with its associated problems over another nine- to ten-year Great Depression. Further, much of what has been attributed to the deficit is fairly nonsensical. Few Americans buy Japanese cars or Swiss machine tools because of the national budget deficit. There are many other factors involved and they generally tend to swamp any of the indirect influences the budget deficit might have.

In a welcome injection of sanity and sound judgment, Professor Robert Eisner's 1988 presidential address to the American Economic Association pointed out that even the economics profession has been on unsafe footing in some of its pronouncements and musings. He unambiguously demonstrated that the economic concept of deficits bears little relation to federal accounting figures used and the statistics so generated. Until we bring our concepts and numbers into better synchronization, much of the discussion will continue to replicate the Tower of Babel.

Yet the obsession that the deficit has become may well be far more damaging than any harm it might by itself generate. For concern with the deficit has clearly "crowded out" both other problems and a great deal of clear thinking. For example, during the early Reagan administration a president who would hardly be considered "soft" on national security issues found it necessary to eliminate new construction differential subsidies for American shippers who purchase vessels built in U.S. shipyards, and decided not to award any new operating differential subsidy contracts for U.S. shippers as they compete against foreign merchant marines, many of which not only have low wages and minimal benefits, but also reap a wide variety of substantial subsidies from their own governments. If the U.S. steel industry, holding 79 percent of the U.S. market, feels threatened, the U.S. merchant fleet (so vital for support and logistics in any major conventional war), which carries only 4 percent of our ocean-going international trade, is virtually extinct. Who would have believed that a president intent on restoring U.S. defense capabilities and military credibility would take such action? It is difficult to explain, except for fear of and obsession with the budget deficit. How else does one explain the crumbling U.S. infrastructure and government's reluctance to address so critical a national issue? How, when a restoration of productivity is so vital, does one explain a Republican administration's repealing the investment tax credit and reducing the benefits of depreciation, as it did in 1986? How else does one explain limitations on Individual Retirement Accounts in a nation sorely short of national savings? And why has the government cut back on funding for data gathering and assessment when the complexities of our age demand more, not less, information?

If the budget deficit were the only national problem, such measures might make sense. In a complex age, however, this tunnel vision comes at great cost. The budget deficit is not our only problem, nor is it likely to be our greatest problem. Yet it commands a disproportionate amount of political and legislative attention, thereby crowding out both focus and funding from other vital areas of our society.

The trade deficit, as discussed in chapters 6 and 7, is yet another source of unnecessary hand-wringing. Although it too brings benefits as well as problems, the benefits have been ignored while the problems have been exaggerated and addressed with unhelpful or counterproductive strategies. Together, these twin deficits have captured the political and media center of gravity, thus upstaging more fundamental problems and leading to misguided policies that in fact exacerbate the fundamental challenges.

There is a clear perception in our nation that we are in dire economic straits, that we are losing our manufacturing capabilities, that we are becoming a nation of hamburger stands. Fanning the flames of despair are the media and a number of soothsayers who, despite a poor track record and abundant evidence to the contrary, continually predict days of reckoning, the decline and fall of our nation, or that the world will soon come to an untimely end.[1] And the public is certainly convinced. A 1988 public opinion poll showed that 50 percent of the respondents believed America was dangerously slipping, with an additional 14 percent holding the view that we are in long-term decline. Some 57 percent strongly believed that Japan and Europe are winning the economic competition and taking away American jobs, with an additional 27 percent "somewhat agreeing."[2]

Such views are surprising in the midst of the longest peacetime economic expansion since Civil War days and the lowest unemployment rates since 1970. Further, a careful 1987 analysis shows that our savings and investment statistics have been distorted and that after appropriate adjustment, the shortfall in U.S. investment rates compared to other countries largely disappears.[3] Such misinformed public opinion often leads to misinformed and inappropriate public policies. This book has attempted to document the actual condition of U.S. industry, particularly the manufacturing sector, in an effort to reduce, if not shatter, the substantial gap between popular beliefs and reality. The manufacturing sector is alive and well. It is in a state of appropriate change. Rather than deindustrialization, manufacturing is experiencing an industrial renaissance. For example, referring to what the media describe as the "rustbelt," in April 1989 the Chicago Federal Reserve Bank reported that the "Midwest is in a full-scale manufacturing boom."[4] The Bank of Japan maintains that "industrial restructuring in the United States has been progressing at a remarkable pace. . . ."[5] And Herbert Stein, former chairman of the President's Council of Economic Advisors, reminds us that the economy does not hang in the balance, that there is no imminent crisis unless we talk ourselves into one.[6]

The U.S. global performance is far from shabby. The latest data show that in 1988, of the 15 largest companies in the world in terms of sales, 6 were U.S. firms, including General Motors in the second position. In terms of profits, 11 of the world's top 15 were U.S., with IBM, Ford, and Exxon heading the list.[7] Such a global performance is truly impressive. Not surprisingly, a May 1989 econometric service ten-year projection maintains that U.S. areas with the most likely growth will be exports, high technology, and capital goods. More specifically, computers and office machinery head the list, followed by communications services, railroad equipment, feed grains, electronic components, and even machine tools (reflecting healthy domestic investment, productivity gains, and a lower dollar).[8]

Further, there is every indication that in addition to our enormous economic strengths, we have made substantial progress in areas of weakness. Recognition of the importance of quality and how it is achieved and maintained seems to be nearly universal in U.S. manufacturing today. Structural changes in manufacturing, work-rule reductions, profit-sharing arrangements, and considerable investments "suggest further strong productivity growth and ongoing quality improvement. . . ."[9] Further, the "search for new work organization and management techniques is also steadily progressing."[10]

Additionally, it will probably take a whole generation on computers to reap the full benefits. Currently, we now have many computers available (although certainly not enough for all useful employment), yet often the people and organizations that have them do not fully understand their capabilities and proper usage. Therefore, we do not employ or deploy them effectively. Today's users have adapted to PCs, but did not grow up with them. The next generation, if properly educated, will far more effectively utilize these powerful tools.

The U.S. industrial base, then, has demonstrated a very credible performance in addition to having enormous potential. But let us not be Panglossian. Fulfilling its potential requires concerted efforts throughout the entire society—business, government, labor, education, and civic and social arenas. Everyone and every institution must come to recognize that change is the order of the day. We must accept it as a challenge and embrace it as an opportunity rather than trying to oppose or retard what is inevitable. Some general suggestions, following from the analyses of this book, will embrace two specific areas: business and government.

Two of the foremost policy areas for government are the maintenance of a stable macroeconomic environment and a competitive economic system. Stop-go economies greatly discourage business investment, while inflationary conditions enourage expansion of organizational sizes even as production economies are allowing smaller units to be equally efficient, if not more so. Inflation is the enemy of long-term planning and considerations; it biases investment patterns and brings to ascendency in corporations individuals who are best at coping with financial uncertainties rather than production, design, and quality challenges.

Maintenance of a highly competitive environment is also of the first order, for it is competition that spurs efficiency, innovation, and productivity, while at the same time serving as a curb on the natural greed that propels individuals and organizations. This mandates that government too must accept globalization and minimize its trade interventions. Closely following these is tax policy. It has been shown that taxes critically affect investment and profitability. Government incentives in terms of tax credits and deductions are appropriate, particularly since the social returns to innovation are probably higher than the earnings the innovating companies can garner to themselves. And encouraging investment is critical since it raises productivity and embodies the latest technologies. Although in the past it has been somewhat unclear as to how responsive business investment actually was to tax incentives, recent research suggests that "if current corporate financial behavior persists, investment may respond more strongly to investment stimuli than previously."[11]

It is also important that tax policy not take more than business can give, particularly in terms of taxing implicit costs as if they were earnings. Recognition of implicit interest, perhaps by allowing dividend deductibility or some other means to more closely treat equity and debt funding, is certainly warranted.

Last, but certainly not least, a significant upgrading of U.S. education capabilities and performance as well as our physical infrastructure is long overdue. Probably the single most important undertaking to elevate our scientific and technical thrust is not direct subsidies or targeting of any particular project or field, but instead grass-roots human capital development in this arena. Indeed, the entire educational infrastructure must be improved, with particular emphasis on minority development, as it is minorities who will increasingly comprise America's future labor force. Finally, both logic and empirical evidence demonstrate that economic growth and progress move in tandem with supporting social overhead capital. Public infrastructure has been a long-neglected arena, needing not only money but also imaginative deployment of the funds.

The United States also needs relatively more investment for net growth of our aging capital stock. This suggests that we must encourage growth in the supply of savings, both domestic and the inflow of foreign savings. Clearly, reducing the appeal of Individual Retirement Accounts and Japan-bashing are hardly policies that serve to promote these important goals.

The business sector too has considerable challenges. It must also embrace change rather than oppose it. It must recognize globalization and tailor its strategies and tactics accordingly. Interestingly, globalization has not yet made a major dent in U.S. business schools,[12] a deficiency in need of remedy. Yet business organizations themselves must further educate their own personnel as to globalization imperatives. Here too, however, U.S. business is not yet up to speed. A recent survey of 1,500 U.S. managers shows surprising insularity and lack of preparedness.[13] Yet there are U.S. companies doing very well in this regard. It is a matter of emphasis and direction, and it is long overdue. Further, to assist in U.S. competitiveness, business and government together must work to remove impediments to globalization success. For example, the United States must join the metric system. Financing for international transactions must become available to smaller firms, perhaps via nationwide branching for banks. And the U.S. government's prime trade job should be to break down barriers overseas, not erect them here.

U.S. managements must also exercise more initiative and tailor their perspectives to their own industrial and business settings. Fads and fears of being left behind have too often dominated top decision-making. If one or two banks, for example, enter into Third World lending, suddenly almost all banks are racing head over heels to do the same. The preoccupation with bigness is another example—simply because some firms find significant scale economies in getting larger does not mean larger size is appropriate for all. Robert Hayes and Steven Wheelwright, for example, when studying vertical integration in U.S. companies, were "struck by their lemminglike behavior."[14] They appropriately conclude that the "variety of positions that a firm can occupy in its strategic environment is too large and seeded with opportunities to be left to the dictates of conventional industry wisdom."[15] Yet there are too many disquieting signs that corporate America has done just that.

Corporate cultures are very strong (and often quite homogeneous) and almost always become very status-quo oriented, exactly the opposite of what is needed in a world of constant change, a world in which flexibility and speed of adjustment are critical. A hardening of the arteries seems to occur as organizations mature and enlarge. Change becomes a threat and forces emerge from every aspect of the organization to meet the threat. "Change has traditionally prompted management to pull the wagons into a circle, and it's hard to be aggressive when your strategy is merely to protect yourself."[16] Accordingly, there must be significant corporate education efforts concerning the necessity for change and the accompanying opportunities. If change becomes a part of the corporate ethos, innovation and adaptations (critical ingredients of a globalized, high technology world) will be greatly enhanced. Today it is speed in the implementation of innovation and the adaptation to change that are now of the utmost importance. When the United States held a substantial technical lead over almost everyone, in almost everything, speed was not important. We could consume inordinate time in implementing innovations and still be at the head of the pack with a product everyone else wanted. U.S. corporate innovation and decision-making styles developed in an atmosphere of U.S. international dominance. That era is now gone and the luxury of lethargy can no longer be tolerated. Yet it is not easily exorcised from our corporate modus operandi. Old habits and patterns do indeed die hard.

For example, it is only recently that corporate America is recognizing the disadvantages of large size. "Flexible manufacturing and new technologies have driven down break-even points. Specialized vendors have sprung up as alternatives to in-house providers. . . ."[17] And the growth of business services has served to put smaller companies in a more advantageous competitive position than ever. Yet it is one thing to recognize changes, but quite another to adjust and implement. As another example, employee involvement is now recognized as essential and is being actively sought, yet there remain significant obstacles to overcome,[18] many deriving directly from the inertia of a given corporate culture. While foreign competition and corporate takeover attempts may well jolt and dislodge inappropriate aspects of many corporate cultures, these are costly means of learning new ways. It would be far better—easier, more timely, and less expensive—for appropriate change to come from within rather than by external onslaught.

In summary, U.S. business has many success stories and we are already witnessing some great comebacks,[19] organizations that fought for survival and won by amending corporate culture, cutting fat, and internally transforming. It must be stressed that the impact of management cannot be overemphasized. In fact, according to several recognized experts, "the impact that management has on manufacturing performance is . . . not on the order of 5 percent or 10 percent but rather on the order of 50 percent or 100 percent."[20]

Finally, some words about defense concerns are warranted. In peacetime we want our defense industrial base to be able to generate the latest, most advanced technologies and to provide an impressive deterrent through the production of effective, reasonably priced equipment and systems. During wartime we want the ability to surge production and efficiently mobilize for a war effort. Defense is expensive. If we want these capabilities, we must be willing to pay for them. Can we afford to do so? From 1979 to 1988 real defense outlays increased roughly $100 billion, real per capita consumption increasing 1.8 percent annually. If defense outlays had proceeded according to President Reagan's earlier program, "and if all the additional resources came out of consumption, real per-capita consumption would now be 13.4% higher than in 1979, and the annual increase would have been 1.6% a year."[21] This would seem to be a small price if indeed we truly wish to maintain a vigorous defense posture.

The purpose of this book has not been to recommend specific policy changes or actions. It has not sought to promote a remedy or set of remedies for the patient. Rather, its purpose has been to demonstrate that the patient, despite many problems, some of which are quite serious, is still sound and extremely healthy. Further, we have attempted to separate the real problems from the popular fantasies. We do have real problems and they are serious, but hardly insurmountable. Accordingly, there is no need for panic or despair, but a recognition that the U.S. industrial structure is undergoing important but appropriate change. Further, there are a number of policy options available to government to ease and facilitate such change. The economy is not flirting with disaster, although such a statement is hardly a prescription for inaction.

Finally, the future and our course are still in our hands. For example, although real net exports declined by over 5 percent of GNP over the 1982–86 period, the economy still grew rapidly. We are not a fragile reed buffeted by shifts in external winds. Nonetheless, we still need to go with the flow. Globalism is the order of the day and we must get on the train. Indeed, we have already started. We need to fully embrace this trend and stop trying to combat the inevitable (and desirable) with self-defeating policies that benefit a favored few. We have the resources and capabilities—we need only the will and political fortitude. "If America has an Achilles' heel," writes Karen Elliott House, "it is a dispirited political leadership more comfortable with predicting American decline than committed to preventing it. . . . In almost every view, there is a shortage of guts in Washington, where officials elected to solve problems instead toss the toughest ones . . . to specially appointed and publicly unaccountable bodies."[22] At corporate, organizational, and educational levels, we must recognize that productivity is the prime goal and it must permeate our working, thinking, and behaving. Archibald MacLeisch once wrote in "Speech to a Crowd," "the world was yours: you would not take it."[23] Let us hope that this is not the American epitaph. It certainly need not be.

NOTES

1. See Paul A. Gigot, "The Bad News Is the U.S. Economy Keeps Humming," *Wall Street Journal*, July 14, 1989, p. A 10, for elaboration and examples.

2. Daniel Yankelovich Group, *Americans Talk Security*, National Survey No. 3, March 1988, pp. 82 and 89.

3. See R. E. Lipsey and I. B. Kravis, *Saving and Economic Growth: Is the United States Really Falling Behind?* (New York: The Conference Board, 1987). One such adjustment is the correction for relatively lower prices of U.S. plant and equipment investment, which means that real investment here has been higher than dollar comparisons with other countries suggest.

4. Robert H. Schnorbus and Philip R. Israilevich, "Midwest Manufacturing," *Chicago Fed Letter*, Federal Reserve Bank of Chicago, April 1989, p. 1.

5. Bank of Japan, Research and Statistics Department, *U.S. Competitiveness in Manufacturing*, Special Paper No. 153, September 1987, p. 20.

6. See Herbert Stein, "World Economy Does Not Hang in the Balance," *Wall Street Journal*, December 30, 1987, p. 18.

7. Amy Borrus, Dinah Lee, Victoria English, and Blanca Riemer, "Who's the Biggest of Them All?" *Business Week*, July 17, 1989, p. 139.

8. Priscilla Luce Trumbull, "Comparative Industry Performance," in the WEFA Group, *Industrial Analysis Service 10-Year Outlook*, May 1989, p. 4.

9. Susan Hickok, Linda A. Bell, and Janet Ceglowski, "The Competitiveness of U.S. Manufactured Goods," *Quarterly Review*, Federal Reserve Bank of New York, Spring 1988, p. 19.

10. Ibid.

11. Jonathan A. Neuberger, "Corporate Investment," *Weekly Letter*, Federal Reserve Bank of San Francisco, June 30, 1989, p. 3.

12. See Christopher Winans, "Business Bulletin," *Wall Street Journal*, July 20, 1989, p. 1.

13. See Jolie Solomon, "Managing," *Wall Street Journal*, July 12, 1989, p. B 1.

14. Robert H. Hayes and Steven C. Wheelwright, *Restoring Our Competitive Edge: Competing Through Manufacturing* (New York: John Wiley, 1984), p. 305.

15. Ibid.

16. Alan Weiss, "Letters to the Editor," *Wall Street Journal*, May 23, 1988, p. 19.

17. Ennius E. Bergsma, "Wanted: A List of Value to Holders," *Wall Street Journal*, April 8, 1988, p. 16.

18. John Hoerr, "The Payoff from Teamwork," *Business Week*, July 10, 1989, pp. 56–62.

19. See Ronald Henkoff, "This Cat is Acting Like A Tiger," *Fortune*, December 19, 1988, pp. 71–76.

20. Robert H. Hayes, Steven C. Wheelwright, and Kim B. Clark, "The Power of Positive Manufacturing," *Across the Board*, October 1988, p. 26.

21. Herbert Stein, "Lack of Will Isn't Economy's Fault," *Wall Street Journal*, January 20, 1988, p. 28.

22. Karen Elliot House, "The 90s & Beyond," *Wall Street Journal*, February 21, 1989, p. A 2.

23. Archibald MacLeish, "Speech to a Crowd," in Oscar Wallace, ed., *American Verse* (New York: The Pocket Library, 1955), p. 294.

Suggested Readings

GENERAL READING

Cohen, Stephen S. and Zysman, John. *Manufacturing Matters*. New York: Basic Books, 1987.

Feldstein, Martin editor. *The American Economy in Transition*. Chicago: University of Chicago Press, 1980.

Heilbroner, Robert L. *The Economic Transformation of America*. New York: Harcourt, Brace, Jovanovich, 1977.

Kiplinger Washington Letter. *The New American Boom*. Washington, D.C.: Kiplinger Washington Editors Incorporated, 1986.

Krooss, Herman E. *American Economic Development*, 2nd ed. Englewood Cliffs, N.J.: Prentice-Hall, 1966.

McConnell, Campbell R. *Economics*, 9th ed. New York: McGraw-Hill, 1984.

Obey, David and Sarbanes, Paul editors. *The Changing American Economy*. New York: Basil Blackwell, 1986.

Sommers, Albert T. *The U.S. Economy Demystified*. Lexington, Mass.: D. C Heath, 1985.

Thurow, Lester C. *The Zero-Sum Solution*. New York: Simon and Schuster, 1985.

CHAPTER 2

Adams, Walter, editor. *The Structure of American Industry*, 7th ed. New York: Macmillan, 1986.

Adams, Walter and Brock, James W. *The Bigness Complex*. New York: Pantheon, 1986.

Averitt, Robert T. *The Dual Economy*. New York: W. W. Norton, 1968.

Berhrman, Jack N. *Industrial Policies: International Restructuring and Transnationals*. Lexington, Mass.: D. C. Heath, 1984.

Collins, Eileen L. and Tanner, Lucretia Dewey, editors. *American Jobs and the Changing Industrial Base*. Cambridge, Mass.: Ballinger, 1984.

de Jong, H. W. and Shepherd, W. G., editors. *Mainstreams in Industrial Organization—Book I*. Boston: Kluwer Academic Publishers, 1986.

Gansler, Jacques S. *The Defense Industry*. Cambridge, Mass.: The MIT Press, 1980.

Miller, Ronald E. and Blair, Peter D. *Input-Output Analysis*. Englewood Cliffs, N.J.: Prentice-Hall, 1985.

Ricketts, Martin. *The New Industrial Economics*. New York: St. Martin's Press, 1987.

Scherer, F. M. *Industrial Market Structure and Economic Performance*, 2nd ed. Chicago: Rand McNally, 1980.

CHAPTER 3

Adams, Walter and Brock, James W. *Dangerous Pursuits: Mergers and Acquisitions in the Age of Wall Street*. New York: Pantheon, 1989.

Asch, Peter and Seneca, Rosalind. *Government and the Marketplace*. Chicago: The Dryden Press, 1985.

Chinloy, Peter. *The Cost of Doing Business*. New York: Praeger, 1989.

Irwin, Manley Rutherford. *Competitive Freedom versus National Security Regulation*. Westport, Conn.: Quorum Books, 1989.

Johnson, Chalmers, editor. *The Industrial Policy Debate*. San Francisco: Institute for Contemporary Studies, 1984.

Larner, Robert J. and Meehan, James W., Jr., editors. *Economics and Antitrust Policy*. Westport, Conn.: Quorum Books, 1989.

Noll, Roger G. and Owen, Bruce M. *The Political Economy of Deregulation*. Washington, D.C.: American Enterprise Institute for Public Policy Research, 1983.

Reich, Robert. *The Next American Frontier*. New York: Times Books, 1983.

Weidenbaum, Murray L. *Business, Government and the Public*, 2nd ed. Englewood Cliffs, N.J.: Prentice-Hall, 1981.

CHAPTER 4

Backingham, Walter. *Automation—Its Impact on Business and People*. New York: Harper and Brothers, 1961.

Betz, Frederick. *Managing Technology*. Englewood Cliffs, N.J.: Prentice-Hall, 1987.

Brandin, D. H. and Harrison, M. A. *The Technology War*. New York: Wiley, 1987.

Boretsky, Michael. "The Role of Innovation." *Challenge*. November–December 1980.

Cantwell, John. *Technological Innovation and Multinational Corporations*. New York: Basil Blackwell, 1989.

Chacko, George. *Technology and Management: Applications to Corporate Markets and Military Missions*. New York: Praeger Publishers, 1988.

Committee for Economic Development, *Stimulating Technological Progress*. New York, 1980.

Congressional Budget Office. *Federal Support for R&D and Innovation*. Washington, D.C.: Congressional Budget Office, April 1984.

Griliches, Zvi, ed. *R&D, Patents, and Productivity*. Chicago: University of Chicago Press, 1984.

Guile, Bruce R. and Brooks, Harvey, eds. *Technology and Global Industry*. Washington, D.C.: National Academy Press, 1987.

Hunt, H. Allan, and Hunt, Timothy, L. *Human Resource Implications of Robotics*. Kalamazoo, Mich.: W. E. Upjohn Institute for Employment Research, 1983.

Malvery, Linda; Hebditch, David; and Anning, Nick. *Techno-Bandits: How the Soviets Are Stealing America's High Tech Future*. Boston: Houghton Mifflin, 1984.

Mansfield, Edwin. *Technological Change*. New York: W. W. Norton, 1971.

Mansfield, Edwin; Romeo, Anthony; Schwartz, Mark; Teece, David; Wagner, Samuel; and Brach, Peter. *Technology Transfer, Productivity and Economic Policy*. New York: W. W. Norton, 1982.

Margiotta, Franklin D. and Sanders, Ralph. *Technology, Strategy and National Security*. Washington, D.C.: National Defense University Press, 1985.

Nelson, Richard R., editor. *Government and Technical Progress—A Cross-Industry Analysis*. New York: Pergamon Press, 1982.

Sanders, Ralph. *International Dynamics of Technology*. Westport, Conn.: Greenwood Press, 1983.

Schnaars, Steven P. *Megamistakes: Forecasting and the Myth of Rapid Technological Change*. New York: Macmillan, 1989.

Smith, Merritt R. *Military Enterprise and Technological Change*. Cambridge, Mass.: The MIT Press, 1985.

Steele, Lowell W. *Innovation in Big Business*. New York: American Elsevier, 1975.

Tushman, Michael L. and Moore, William L., eds. *Readings in the Management of Innovation*. 2nd ed. Cambridge, Mass.: Ballinger, 1988.

Van Creveld, Martin. *Technology and War*. New York: The Free Press, 1989.

CHAPTER 5

Black, Stanley W., editor. *Productivity Growth and the Competiveness of the American Economy*. Boston: Kluwer Academic Publishers, 1989.

Denison, Edward F. *Accounting for Slower Economic Growth*. Washington, D.C.: Brookings Institution, 1979.

Denison, Edward F. *Accounting for United States Economic Growth, 1929–1969*. Washington, D.C.: Brookings Institution, 1974.

Denison, Edward F. *Estimates of Productivity Change by Industry*. Washington, D.C.: Brookings Institution, 1989.

Denison, Edward F. "The Interruption of Productivity Growth in the United States." *Economic Journal*, March 1983.

Jorgenson, Dale, and Zvi Griliches. "The Explanation of Productivity Change." *Review of Economic Studies*, May 1969.

Kalder, Mary; Sharp, Margaret; and Walker, William. "Industrial Competitiveness and Britain's Defense." *Lloyd's Bank Review*, October 1986.

Kendrick, John W. *Productivity Trends in the United States*. Washington, D.C.: National Bureau of Economic Research, 1975.

Norsworthy, J. R., and others. "Slowdown in Productivity Growth." *Brookings Papers on Economic Activity*, No. 2. 1979.

Organization for Economic Cooperation and Development. *Productivity in Industry*. Washington, D.C., 1986.

Tatom, John A. "The Productivity Problem." *Review*, Federal Reserve Bank of St. Louis. September 1979.

Thurow, Lester. *The Zero-Sum Solution*. New York: Simon and Schuster, 1985.

CHAPTER 6

Adams, John, editor. *The Contemporary International Economy—A Reader*. 2nd ed. New York: St. Martin's Press, 1985.

Bhagwati, Jagdish, editor. *Trade, Balance of Payments and Growth: Papers in Honor of Charles Kindleberger*. Amsterdam: North-Holland, 1971.

Dixit, A. and Norman, V. *Theory of International Trade*. London: Cambridge University Press, 1980.

Ethier, Wilfred. *Modern International Economics*. New York: W. W. Norton, 1983.

Fieleke, Norman S. *The International Economy under Stress*. Cambridge, Mass.: Ballinger, 1989.

Golden, James R. *NATO Burden-Sharing—Risks and Opportunities*. New York: Praeger, 1983.

Hartley, Keith. *NATO Arms Co-operation*. London: George Allen & Unwin, 1983.

Hilke, John C. and Nelson, Philip B. *U.S. International Competitiveness: Evolution or Revolution?* New York: Praeger, 1988.

Nevaer, Louis E. V. and Deck, Steven A. *The Protectionist Threat to Corporate America*. Westport, Conn.: Quorum Books, 1989.

Spence, A. Michael and Hazard, Heather A., editors. *International Competitiveness*. Cambridge, Mass.: Ballinger, 1988.

Stern, Robert M., editor. *U.S. Trade Policies in a Changing World Economy*. Cambridge, Mass.: MIT Press, 1989.

CHAPTER 7

Barney, Jay B. and Ouchi, William G., editors. *Organizational Economics*. San Francisco: Jossey-Bass, 1986.

Davis, Donald D. *Managing Technological Innovation*. San Francisco: Jossey-Bass, 1986.

Ekelund, Robert B., Jr. and Saurman, David S. *Advertising and the Market Process: A Modern Economic View*. San Francisco: Pacific Research Institute for Public Policy, 1988.

Fleischer, Arthur Jr.; Hazard, Geoffrey, C., Jr.; and Klipper, Miriam Z. *Board Games*. Boston: Little, Brown, 1988.

Hicks, Donald A., editor. *Is New Technology Enough?* Washington, D.C.: American Enterprise Institute, 1988.

Schonberger, Richard. *World Class Manufacturing: The Lessons of Simplicity Applied*. New York: Free Press; London: Collier Macmillan, 1986.

Suzaki, Kiyoshi. *The New Manufacturing Challenge: Techniques for Continuous Improvement*. New York: Free Press; London: Collier Macmillan, 1987.

CHAPTER 8

Adams, Walter and Mueller, Hans. "The Steel Industry." In Walter Adams, editor., *Structure of American Industry*. New York: Macmillan, 1986.

Barnett, Donald and Schorsch, Louis. *Steel: Upheaval in a Basic Industry*. Cambridge, Mass.: Ballinger, 1983.

Crandall, Robert. *The U.S. Steel Industry in Recurrent Crisis*. Washington, D.C.: Brookings Institution, 1981.

Ehrlich, Everett; Schwartz, Elliott; and others. *How Federal Policies Affect the Steel Industry*. Washington, D.C.: Congressional Budget Office, February 1987.

Erceg, Christopher; Israilevich, Philip; and Schnorbus, Robert. "Competition Pricing Behavior in Steel." *Economic Perspectives*, Federal Reserve Bank of Chicago, March/April 1989.

Federal Emergency Management Agency. *An Analysis of Domestic Steel Plate Rolling Capacity*. A Report Prepared for the U.S. Trade Representative. Washington, D.C.: FEMA, mimeo, September, 1985.

Federal Trade Commission Staff Report (R. Duke, R. Johnson, H. Mueller, D. Qualls, C. Rousch, and D. Tarr). *The United States Steel Industry and Its International Rivals: Trends and Factors Determining International Competitiveness*. Washington, D.C.: U.S. Government Printing Office, 1977.

Hogan, William. *Minimills and Integrated Mills*. Lexington, Mass.: Lexington Books, 1987.

Industrial College of the Armed Forces. *The U.S. Steel Industry—Implications for National Defense*. A Mobilization Studies Program Research Paper. Washington, D.C.: National Defense University, mimeo, 1984.

International Iron and Steel Institute. *Projection 85*. Brussels: 1973.

Marcus, Peter and Kirsis, Karlis. *World Steel Dynamics: The Steel Strategist*, No. 9. New York: Paine-Webber, 1984.

Rosegger, Gerhard. "Diffusion of Technological Specificity: The Case of Continuous Casting." *Journal of Industrial Economics*, September 1979.

Tarr, David, "Cyclical Dumping: The Case of Steel Imports." *Journal of International Economics* 9, February 1979.

Tarr, David. "Does Protection Really Protect?" *Regulation*, November–December 1985, pp. 29–34.

Tarr, David. "The Efficient Diffusion of Steel Technology Across Nations." *Journal of Public Policy* 5, no. 2 (1986), pp. 541–60.

Tarr, David and Morkre, Morris. *Aggregate Costs to the United States of Tariffs and Quotas on Imports*. Washington, D.C.: Federal Trade Commission, 1984.

CHAPTER 9

Ashburn, Anderson "The Machine Tool Industry: The Crumbling Foundation." In Donald A. Hicks, editor., *Is New Technology the Answer?* Washington, D.C.: American Enterprise Institute, 1988, p. 77.

International Trade Administration. *A Competitive Assessment of the U.S. Flexible Manufacturing Systems Industry*. Washington, D.C.: U.S. Government Printing Office, 1985.

International Trade Administration. *A Competitive Assessment of the U.S. Manufacturing Automation Equipment Industries*. Washington, D.C.: U.S. Government Printing Office, 1984.

Jacobsson, Staffar. *Electronics and Industrial Policy: The Case of Computer Controlled Lathes*. London: George Allen and Unwin, 1986.

National Machine Tool Builders Association. *The Economic Handbook of the Machine Tool Industry, 1987–88*. McLean, Va., 1987.

National Research Council. *The Competitive Status of the U.S. Machine Tool Industry.* Washington, D.C.: National Academy Press, 1983.
National Research Council. *The U.S. Machine Tool Industry and the Defense Industrial Base.* Washington, D.C.: National Academy Press, 1983.

CHAPTER 10

Baumol, William J. *Productivity and American Leadership: The Long View.* Cambridge, Mass.: MIT Press, 1989.
Kash, Don E. *Perpetual Innovation: The New World of Competition.* New York: Basic Books, 1989.
Rutledge, John. *Rust to Riches: The Coming of the Second Industrial Revolution.* New York: Harper, 1989.

Index

About the Authors

DONALD L. LOSMAN is Professor of Economics at the National Defense University.

SHU-JAN LIANG is an Associate Professor of Economics at Loyola University, New Orleans.